T0302064

HIGH-FREQUENCY TRADING

Founded in 1807, John Wiley & Sons is the oldest independent publishing company in the United States. With offices in North America, Europe, Australia, and Asia, Wiley is globally committed to developing and marketing print and electronic products and services for our customers' professional and personal knowledge and understanding.

The Wiley Trading series features books by traders who have survived the market's ever changing temperament and have prospered—some by reinventing systems, others by getting back to basics. Whether a novice trader, professional, or somewhere in-between, these books will provide the advice and strategies needed to prosper today and well into the future.

For a list of available titles, visit our web site at www.WileyFinance.com.

HIGH-FREQUENCY TRADING

SECOND EDITION

A Practical Guide to Algorithmic
Strategies and Trading Systems

Irene Aldridge

WILEY

Published by John Wiley & Sons, Inc., Hoboken, New Jersey.

The First Edition of High-Frequency Trading: A Practical Guide to Algorithmic Strategies and Trading Systems was published by John Wiley and Sons, Inc. in 2010.

Published simultaneously in Canada.

For general information on our other products and services or for technical support, please contact our Customer Care Department within the United States at (800) 762-2974, outside the United States at (317) 572-3993 or fax (317) 572-4002.

Wiley publishes in a variety of print and electronic formats and by print-on-demand. Some material included with standard print versions of this book may not be included in e-books or in print-on-demand. If this book refers to media such as a CD or DVD that is not included in the version you purchased, you may download this material at http://booksupport.wiley.com. For more information about Wiley products, visit www.wiley.com.

Library of Congress Cataloging-in-Publication Data:
Aldridge, Irene, 1975–
    High-frequency trading: a practical guide to algorithmic strategies and trading systems/Irene Aldridge.—2nd Edition.
        pages cm.—(Wiley trading series)
    Includes index.
    ISBN 978-1-118-34350-0 (Cloth)—ISBN 978-1-118-42011-9 (ebk)—ISBN 978-1-118-43401-7 (ebk)—ISBN 978-1-118-41682-2 (ebk)   1. Investment analysis.   2. Portfolio management.   3. Securities.   4. Electronic trading of securities.   I. Title.
    HG4529.A43 2013
    332.64—dc23
                                                                                                2012048967

Printed in the United States of America
10 9 8 7 6 5 4 3 2 1

To my family

CONTENTS

If hiring activity is highest in profitable and rapidly expanding industries, then high-frequency trading (HFT) is by far the most successful activity in the financial sector today. Take, for example, the Jobs classifieds in the Money and Investing section of the *Wall Street Journal* on November 27, 2012. All five advertisements placed there were for high-frequency trading and related roles. Morgan Stanley alone was hiring four candidates in its high-frequency trading operation. HFT candidates were sought at all levels: associate vice presidents were required in HFT technology development, executive directors were needed in HFT strategy development, and vice presidents were sought for in HFT operations. To warrant the investment into new employees at all levels, prospective employees with HFT skills were clearly expected to generate high returns for their employers for the foreseeable future.

Despite considerable hiring in the field, the high-frequency trading industry is still in its infancy. While some claim that high-frequency traders comprise 60 to 70 percent of all market participants, such numbers are seldom reached in reality. Scientific examinations find that HFTs still account for as little as 25 percent of all market activity in such frequently traded instruments as the S&P 500 E-mini futures (see Kirilenko et al., 2011). As Figure 1 shows, even in the very liquid S&P 500 ETF (NYSE: SPY), high-frequency traders on average account for just 20 percent of daily trades.

As shown in Figure 1, the average levels of HFT participation in SPY remain remarkably stable: on most days in 2009 through 2012, 15 to 17 percent of all trades in SPY can be attributed to HFTs. At the same time, evidence of resource allocation to HFT suggests that the industry is growing at a rapid pace. A natural explanation reconciling the two observations exists: HFT has low barriers to entry, yet it can be extremely complex, requiring years of toiling with data to proficiently develop and deploy trading models.

Indeed, as any successful HFT operator will tell you, development of consistently profitable ultra-short-term trading strategies takes at least three years. While the number may seem extreme, it is not really different from the time required to develop proficiency or "block" in any other industry or specialization.

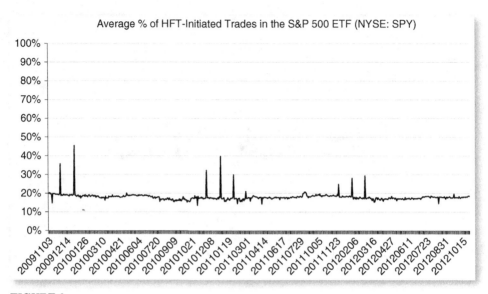

Average % of HFT-Initiated Trades in the S&P 500 ETF (NYSE: SPY)

FIGURE 1
Source: Aldridge (2012a)

HFT is particularly complex as the discipline rests at the confluence of two already complicated areas of study: high-frequency finance and computer science. Very few academic institutions offer programs that prepare students to be simultaneously competent in both areas. Most finance-trained people do not understand computer programming, and most computer scientists do not have a grasp on the required highly academic finance.

This book is written to fill that academic void: to supply true, accurate, and up-to-date graduate-level information on the subject of high-frequency trading, as well as to address the questions and opinions that many have about the subject. The book has a companion web site, www.hftradingbook.com, where you can find practical examples, updates, and teaching materials. I hope you find the book informative and helpful in your future endeavors.

ACKNOWLEDGMENTS

I am extremely grateful to my husband for tireless encouragement and insightful suggestions, to my son Henry for helping me keep a balanced perspective, to Gaia Rikhye for terrific front-line edits, and to my wise editor Bill Falloon, über-patient development editor Judy Howarth, diligent senior production editor Vincent Nordhaus, and terrific publisher Pamela Van Giessen for making it all happen.

xiii

CHAPTER 1

How Modern Markets Differ from Those Past

Structural change is not new to trading in financial instruments. If fact, it is the constancy of innovation that has helped drive the leadership of modern financial institutions. High-frequency trading (HFT) has stepped into the limelight over the past few years and delivered considerable operational improvements to the markets, most of which have resulted in lower volatility, higher market stability, better market transparency, and lower execution costs for traders and investors. This chapter of the book provides the overview of dramatic changes that precipitated in the securities markets over the past 50 years, and defines HFT and core strategies falling under the HFT umbrella.

Over the past two decades, the demand for computer technology in consumer markets has led to significant drops in hardware prices across the board, as discussed in detail in Chapter 2 of this book. As a result, technology-enabled trading has become cost effective, and the ensuing investment into software has made trading platforms more accessible and more powerful. Additionally, the savings from lower errors in message transmission and data input, higher reliability of order execution, and continuity of business through computer code, deliver a business case for deepening financial firms' reliance on their technology systems. The escalating complexity of regulations also requires more advanced reporting capabilities that are becoming prohibitively expensive without substantial platforms. The lower cost base squeezes margins further, and this puts pressure on the traditional full-service model. Figures 1.1 and 1.2 illustrate the financial services landscape circa 1970s and today.

In the 1970s and earlier, the market participants were organizations and individuals now considered "traditional" players. As Figure 1.1 shows, on the portfolio management or "buy" side, the markets engaged

- Discretionary asset managers, including pension funds, mutual funds, and hedge funds.

- Retail flow, including individual "mom-and-pop" investors, and others with comparatively smaller capitalization.

- Manual speculators, individuals involved in intraday proprietary trading for their own account or for the account of their bank.

  On the transaction facilitation, middle-men, or "sell" side, the markets supported

- Manual market makers (representatives of broker-dealers), taking short-term inventory risk, providing quotations to the buy side, and generally facilitating the buy-side trading for a fee.

FIGURE 1.1   Financial Markets in the 1970s, before Electronization

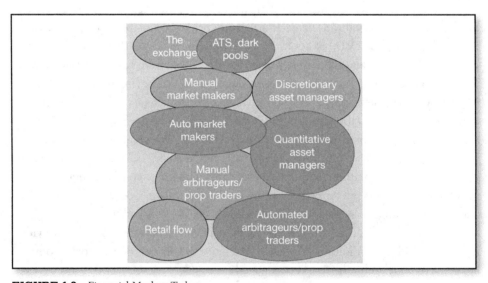

FIGURE 1.2   Financial Markets Today

- A single not-for-profit exchange in each asset class was established to curtail wild speculation by the exchange members and to lower transaction costs paid by the investors.[1]

The highly manual and therefore labor-intensive financial landscape of the 1970s was characterized by high transaction costs, leading to low turnover of securities; a high degree of error associated with manual processing of orders, and relatively high risk of trading, as traders predominantly relied on their experience and intuition as opposed to science in making their bets on the markets. Yet, the 1970s were also high margin businesses, with brokers receiving a large share of the spoils in the form of large commissions and, ultimately, the proverbial "fat-cat" bonuses to the tune of tens of millions of dollars.

Fast-forward to today's markets, illustrated in Figure 1.2: new entrants success-fully compete using lean technology and science to hash out precise investing mod-els, reshaping the markets in the process:

- Quantitative money managers, such as mutual funds and hedge funds, are using the precise science of economics, finance, and the latest mathematical tools to chisel increasingly close forecasts of securities prices, improving profitability of their investments.

- Automated market makers, for example, broker-dealers and hedge funds, harness the latest technology, studies of market microstructure, and HFT to deliver low transaction costs, taking over market share from traditional broker-dealers.

- Automated arbitrageurs, such as statistical arbitrage hedge funds and proprietary traders, use quantitative algorithms, including high-frequency trading techniques, to deliver short-term trading profits.

- Multiple alternative trading venues, like new exchanges and dark pools, have sprung up to address market demand for affordable quality financial matching services.

These innovations have changed the key characteristics of the markets, and largely for the better:

- The markets now enjoy vastly democratic access: due to proliferation of low-cost technology, anyone can trade in the markets and set quotes, a right formerly re-served to members of the exclusive connections-driven club of broker-dealers.

- Plummeting transaction costs keep money in investors' pockets; more on this later.

- Automated trading, order routing, and settlement deliver a new low degree of error.

---

[1] Most exchanges became not-for-profit only in the 1970s. From the time of their formation to the 1970s, however, the exchanges were very much for profit. In fact, the Buttonwood agreement of 1792 that laid foundation to the New York Stock Exchange, specified explicit profitability rules: no broker was allowed to charge less than 0.25 percent of the transaction volume, a staggering commis-sion by today's standards.

The extreme competition among the new entrants and old incumbent market participants, however, has also resulted in reduced margins for broker-dealers, squeezing out technology-inefficient players.

The way trading is done has changed over time and these newer approaches affected the relative power of consumers and institutions. In the 1970s' marketplace, the trading process would often proceed as follows:

1. Brokers would deliver one-off trading ideas to their buy-side clients. The ideas were often disseminated via countless phone calls, were based on brokers' then-unique ability to observe markets in real time, and were generally required compensation in "soft-dollar" arrangements—if the customer decided to trade on the idea, he was expected to do so through the broker who produced the idea, and the customer would pay for the idea in the form of potentially higher broker commissions.

2. If and when the customer decided to trade on the idea, the customer would phone in the order to the broker or the broker's assistant. Such verbal orders frequently resulted in errors: the noise on the brokers' trading floors often impeded correct understanding of customer instructions.

3. After receiving a customer's order, the broker's next steps would depend on the size of the placed order: while large orders would be taken to the market right away (potentially in smaller parcels), smaller orders would sit on the broker's desk, waiting for other similar orders to fill up a "round lot"—the minimum order size executable on an exchange. Smaller customers were thus often at a disadvantage, waiting for execution of their orders while the favorable market price slipped away.

4. Once the order or several sequential orders comprised the order size acceptable to the broker, the broker would route the order to the appropriate exchange.

5. Next, human representatives of the exchange, known as "specialists," would match the order and send the trade acknowledgments back to the broker. It is well understood that the specialists often created preferential terms for some of their connections, at the expense of orders of others. Such behavior rewarded investment in connections and chummy networks, and resulted in exclusive Wall Street cliques capable of significant price discrimination for in-group versus out-of-group customers. Even though exchanges operated as not-for-profit organizations, influence peddling was common, and the markets were a long way away from anything resembling an equal playing field for all participants.

6. The broker notified the client of execution and collected his commissions and oversized bonuses. The brokers presided over the power of the markets and were compensated as kings.

Figure 1.3 illustrates the traditional investing process prevalent circa 1970s.

Fast-forward 40-something years ahead, and the balance of power has shifted. Customers have increased their expertise in quantitative analysis and are often better equipped for research than brokers. Brokers' area of expertise has decreased in scope from the all-encompassing sell-side research into securities behavior to a more narrow, albeit still important area of algorithmic execution designed to help clients

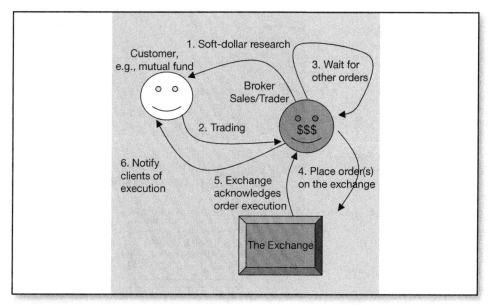

FIGURE 1.3 Broker-centric Investing Process Prevalent before Electronization

navigate the choppy intraday trading waters. With such buy-side investors, the market flow evolves according to the process in Figure 1.4:

1. Customers, not brokers, generate research based on forecasts of securities movements and their existing allocations, all within the quantitative portfolio management framework.
2. The customer places an order via electronic networks, greatly reducing errors and misunderstandings. The order instantaneously arrives on the broker's desktop.
3. The customer or the broker selects the broker's optimal execution algorithm designed to minimize the customer's execution costs and risk, speed up execution whenever possible, and minimize observability of the customer's trading actions.
4. Selected algorithm electronically parcels out the customer's order and routes the order slices to relevant exchanges and other trading venues.
5. Trading venues match the customer's order slices and acknowledge execution.
6. The broker sends the order acknowledgment back to the customer, and receives his considerably lower commission. (In 1997, the lowest broker commission on retail trades was offered by Merrill Lynch, and the commission was $70 per trade. Today, Interactive Brokers charges about $0.70 per trade, a 100-fold reduction in transaction costs available to clients.)

Some customers go even further and prefer to do away with broker service altogether, building their own execution algorithms, keeping a higher share of the profits. Plummeting costs of technology have enabled fast distribution of tick data to all interested parties, and now customers, not just brokers, can watch and time markets and generate short-term forecasts of market behavior. Customers taking the largely

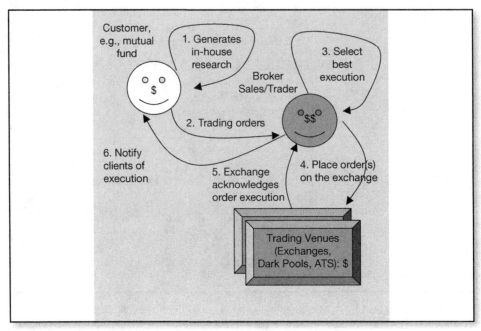

FIGURE 1.4 Modern Investing Process, Scenario 1: Brokers Provide Best Execution for Clients' Orders

broker-independent route are said to engage in "direct access" to the markets, and their execution process consists of the following steps:

1. The broker grants the customer a privilege to access the exchange directly for a negotiated per-trade or per-volume fee. To grant access, the broker may allow the customer to use the broker's own identification with a specific exchange. The customer's order routing systems then use the broker's identification in order messaging with the exchange.
2. Customer computer systems or human analysts generate a high- or low-frequency portfolio allocation decision that involves one or more trading orders.
3. Customer uses his own order splitting and routing algorithms to optimally place his orders directly with exchanges and other trading venues.
4. One or several exchanges and trading venues match the orders, acknowledg execution directly to client.
5. The broker receives settlement information and charges the client for the privilege of using the broker's direct access identification.

Figure 1.5 summarizes these steps.

■ Media, Modern Markets, and HFT

While the market-wide changes have disturbed the status quo on the broker-dealer side and squeezed many a broker out of business, the changes to the society at large have been mostly positive, depositing the saved dollars directly into investor pockets. Gone are the multimillion-dollar bonuses of many brokers taking phone orders

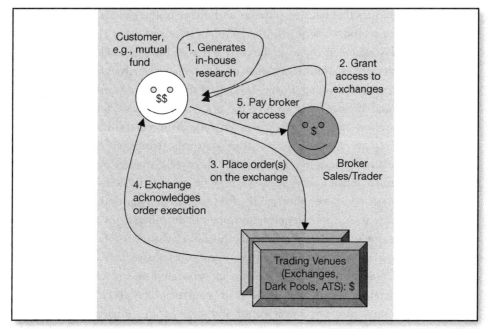

FIGURE 1.5 Modern Investing Process, Scenario 2: Clients Decide on Best Execution, Access Markets Directly

and watching markets on their computer screens. The money has been redirected to bank shareholders and end investors.

Clearly, not everyone is happy about such shifts in the industry, and the least happy bunch happens to be brokers losing their income to automation. Stripped of the ability to extract easy money out of investors' pockets, brokers have been the most vocal opponents of high-frequency trading. Brokers like Arnuk and Saluzzi (2012), for example, denounce automation, yet wax eloquent about those manual error-prone days when investors were not allowed on exchanges and brokers were the fat cats of the world.

Some brokers, whose lifestyle has been significantly reduced by technology, attempt to demonize HFT with an even more sinister goal in mind: they are seeking to lure in investors to their outfits still charging exorbitant transaction costs under the guise of protecting the poor investor lambs from the HFT predators. Investors should take time to compare costs of trading through a broker versus other available options. Chapters 5, 12, and 15 of this book provide specific information to enable low-frequency investors to estimate the risk of potentially adverse HFT, and take educated steps to managing said risk, without relying on self-serving hype of selected brokers who refuse to catch up on technical innovation, resorting to scare tactics at the expense of their clients instead. The remainder of this chapter is devoted to explaining the evolutionary nature of HFT and the definitions and overview of strategies that fall under the HFT umbrella.

■ HFT as Evolution of Trading Methodology

Brokers who speak loudly against the HFT tend to rely on technical analysis in making their decisions of when to enter or exit a position. Technical analysis was one of the earliest techniques that became popular with many traders and is, in many ways, a direct precursor to today's sophisticated econometrics and other HFT techniques.

Technical analysts came in vogue in the early 1910s and sought to identify recurring patterns in security prices. Many techniques used in technical analysis measure current price levels relative to the rolling moving average of the price, or a combination of the moving average and standard deviation of the price. For example, a technical analysis technique known as moving average convergence divergence (MACD) uses three exponential moving averages to generate trading signals. Advanced technical analysts would look at security prices in conjunction with current market events or general market conditions to obtain a fuller idea of where the prices may be moving next.

Technical analysis prospered through the first half of the twentieth century, when trading technology was in its telegraph and pneumatic-tube stages and the trading complexity of major securities was considerably lower than it is today. The inability to transmit information quickly limited the number of shares that changed hands, curtailed the pace at which information was incorporated into prices, and allowed charts to display latent supply and demand of securities. The previous day's trades appeared in the next morning's newspaper and were often sufficient for technical analysts to successfully infer future movement of the prices based on published information. In post-WWII decades, when trading technology began to develop considerably, technical analysis developed into a self-fulfilling prophecy.

If, for example, enough people believed that a "head-and-shoulders" pattern would be followed by a steep sell-off in a particular instrument, all the believers would place sell orders following a head-and-shoulders pattern, thus indeed realizing the prediction. Subsequently, institutional investors have moved to high-frequency econometric modeling using powerful computer technology, trading away technical patterns. By now, technical analysis at low frequencies, such as daily or weekly intervals, is marginalized to work only for the smallest, least liquid securities, which are traded at very low frequencies—once or twice per day or even per week.

Some technical analysis techniques, such as momentum or Bollinger bands, have been successfully adopted and extended by modern-day quants in all investing frequencies. It has long been shown that human investors tend to pour money into strategies that worked in recent months. As a result, strategies working in the past month are also likely to work the following month, forming a tradable momentum that can be detected using simple technical moving-average-based indicators, as well as more complex quantitative tools. Similarly, Bollinger bands detect deviation of prices the prespecified number of standard deviations away from the mean. The concept of statistical arbitrage extended Bollinger band principle to detect, for example, deviation of price differences from their long-running means. In this trading exercise, commonly known as pairs trading, traders identify the overpriced and underpriced financial instruments when the price of one instrument exceeds the price of another by the prespecified number of standard deviations of price difference changes. More generally, quants use Bollinger band ideas to pinpoint mean-reverting processes and trade financial instruments with the expectation that the measured average quantity will stay stable, or "stationary" in the language of statistics.

Another important investing and trading technique, known as fundamental analysis, originated in equities in the 1930s when traders noticed that future cash flows, such as dividends, affected market price levels. The cash flows were then discounted back to the present to obtain the fair present market value of the security. Graham and Dodd (1934) were the earliest purveyors of the methodology and their approach is still popular. Over the years, the term *fundamental analysis* expanded to include pricing of securities with no obvious cash flows based on expected economic variables. For example, fundamental determination of exchange rates today implies equilibrium valuation of the rates based on macroeconomic theories.

Fundamental analysis developed through much of the twentieth century. Today, fundamental analysis refers to trading on the expectation that the prices will move to the level predicted by supply-and-demand relationships, the fundamentals of economic theory. In equities, microeconomic models apply; equity prices are still most often determined as present values of future cash flows. In foreign exchange, macroeconomic models are most prevalent; the models specify expected price levels using information about inflation, trade balances of different countries, and other macroeconomic variables. Derivatives are traded fundamentally through advanced econometric models that incorporate statistical properties of price movements of underlying instruments. Fundamental commodities trading analyzes and matches available supply and demand.

Various facets of fundamental analysis are inputs into many high-frequency trading models, alongside market microstructure. For example, event arbitrage consists of trading the momentum response accompanying the price adjustment of the security in response to new fundamental information. The date and time of the occurrence of the news event is typically known in advance, and the content of the news is usually revealed at the time of the news announcement. In high-frequency event arbitrage, fundamental analysis can be used to forecast the fundamental value of the economic variable to be announced, in order to further refine the high-frequency process.

Like selected technical models, some fundamental models were adopted by quants who extended the precision of their models, and often dramatically sped up calculation of the relevant values. Fair values of equities following an earnings announcement were recomputed on the fly, enabling quants to reap the profits, at the expense of fundamental traders practicing longhand analysis in Excel spreadsheets.

Speed, in fact, became the most obvious aspect of quant competition. Whoever was able to run a quant model the fastest was the first to identify and trade on a market inefficiency and was the one to capture the biggest gain. To increase trading speed, traders began to rely on fast computers to make and execute trading decisions. Technological progress enabled exchanges to adapt to the new technology-driven culture and offer docking convenient for trading. Computerized trading became known as *systematic trading* after the computer systems that processed run-time data and made and executed buy-and-sell decisions.

High-frequency trading developed in the 1990s in response to advances in computer technology and the adoption of the new technology by the exchanges. From the original rudimentary order processing to the current state-of-the-art all-inclusive trading systems, HFT has evolved into a billion-dollar industry.

To ensure optimal execution of systematic trading, algorithms were designed to mimic established execution strategies of traditional traders. To this day, the term *algorithmic trading* usually refers to the automated "best execution" process—that is, the optimization of buy-and-sell decisions once these buy-and-sell decisions were made by another part of the systematic trading process or by a human portfolio manager. Algorithmic trading may determine how to process an order given current market conditions: whether to execute the order aggressively (on a price close to the market price) or passively (on a limit price far removed from the current market price), in one trade or split into several smaller "packets." As mentioned previously, algorithmic trading does not usually make portfolio allocation decisions; the decisions about when to buy or sell which securities are assumed to be exogenous.

The advances in computer technology over the past decades have enabled fully automated HFT, fueling the profitability of trading desks and generating interest in pushing the technology even further. Trading desks seized upon cost savings realized from replacing expensive trader head count with less expensive trading algorithms along with other advanced computer technology. Immediacy and accuracy of execution and lack of hesitation offered by machines as compared with human traders has also played a significant role in banks' decisions to switch away from traditional trading to systematic operations. Lack of overnight positions has translated into immediate savings due to reduction in overnight position carry costs, a particular issue in crisis-driven tight lending conditions or high-interest environments.

Banks also developed and adopted high-frequency functionality in response to demand from buy-side investors. Institutional investors, in turn, have been encouraged to practice high-frequency trading by the influx of capital following shorter lock-ups and daily disclosure to investors. Both institutional and retail investors found that investment products based on quantitative intraday trading have little correlation with traditional buy-and-hold strategies, adding pure return, or alpha, to their portfolios.

Under the Dodd-Frank Act, banks were forced to close many of the proprietary trading operations, but not HFT. In certain banks, the formerly prop-trading HFT is alive and well in the market-making function, where it is now run with client rather than bank capital and is often referred to as *prehedging*.

As computer technology develops further and drops in price, high-frequency systems are bound to take on an even more active role. Special care should be taken, however, to distinguish HFT from electronic trading, algorithmic trading, and systematic trading. Figure 1.6 illustrates a schematic difference between high-frequency, systematic, and traditional long-term investing styles.

Systematic trading refers to computer-driven trading decisions that may be held a month or a day or a minute and therefore may or may not be high frequency. An example of systematic trading is a computer program that runs daily, weekly, or even monthly; accepts daily closing prices; outputs portfolio allocation matrices; and places buy-and-sell orders. Such a system is not a high-frequency system.

Another term often mentioned in conjunction but not synonymous with HFT is *electronic trading*. Electronic trading refers to the ability to transmit the orders electronically as opposed to telephone, mail, or in person. Since most orders in today's financial markets are transmitted via computer networks, the term *electronic trading* is rapidly becoming obsolete.

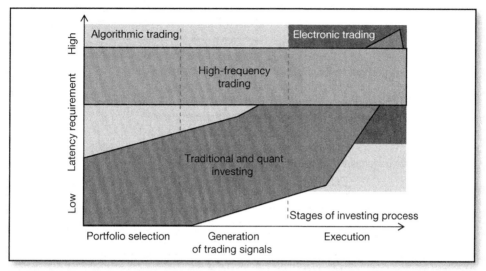

FIGURE 1.6 HFT versus Algorithmic (Systematic) Trading and Traditional Long-Term Investing

Algorithmic trading is more complex than electronic trading and can refer to a variety of algorithms spanning order-execution processes as well as high-frequency portfolio allocation decisions. The execution algorithms are designed to optimize trading execution once the buy-and-sell decisions have been made elsewhere. Algorithmic execution makes decisions about the best way to route the order to the exchange, the best point in time to execute a submitted order if the order is not required to be executed immediately, and the best sequence of sizes in which the order should be optimally processed. Algorithms generating HFT signals make portfolio allocation decisions and decisions to enter or close a position in a particular security. For example, algorithmic execution may determine that a received order to buy 1 million shares of IBM is best handled using increments of 100-share lots to prevent a sudden run-up in the price. The decision fed to the execution algorithm, however, may or may not be high frequency. An algorithm deployed to generate HFT signals, however, would generate the decision to buy the 1 million shares of IBM. The high-frequency signals would then be passed on to the execution algorithm that would determine the optimal timing and routing of the order.

Successful implementation of HFT requires both types of algorithms: those generating HFT signals and those optimizing execution of trading decisions. This book covers both groups of algorithms: those designed for generation of trading signals (Chapters 8 through 11) and those for order execution designed to conceal information within (Chapter 15). Chapter 14 of the book also includes latest algorithms for managing risk of HFT operations.

The intent of algorithmic execution is illustrated by the results of a survey conducted by Automated Trader in 2012. Figure 1.7 shows the full spectrum of responses from the survey. In addition to the previously mentioned factors related to adoption of algorithmic trading, such as performance management and reporting, both buy-side and sell-side managers also reported their use of the algorithms to be driven by trading decision and portfolio management needs.

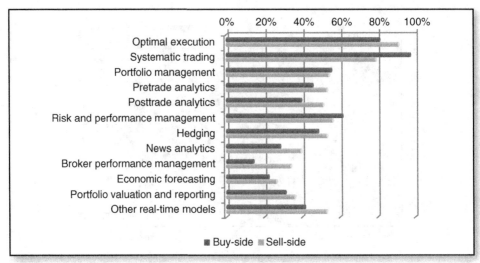

FIGURE 1.7   Reasons for Using Algorithms in Trading
Source: Automated Trader Survey, 2012

True HFT systems make a full range of decisions, from identification of under-priced or overpriced securities through optimal portfolio allocation to best execution. The distinguishing characteristic of HFT is the short position holding times, one day or shorter in duration, usually with no positions held overnight. Because of their rapid execution nature, most HFT systems are fully systematic and are also examples of systematic and algorithmic trading. All systematic and algorithmic trading platforms, however, are not high frequency.

Ability to execute an order algorithmically is a prerequisite for HFT in a given financial instrument. As discussed in Chapter 3, some markets are not yet suitable for HFT, inasmuch as most trading in those markets is performed over the counter (OTC). According to research conducted by Aite Group, equities are the most algorithmically executed asset class, with over 50 percent of the total volume of equities expected to be handled by algorithms by 2010. As Figure 1.8 shows, equities are closely followed by futures. Advances in algorithmic execution of foreign exchange, options, and fixed income, however, have

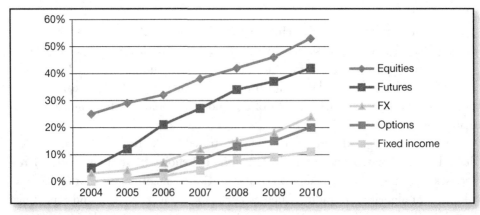

FIGURE 1.8   Adoption of Algorithmic Execution by Asset Class
Source: Aite Group

been less visible. As illustrated in Figure 1.8, the lag of fixed-income instruments can be explained by the relative tardiness of electronic trading development for them, given that many of them are traded OTC and are difficult to synchronize as a result.

While research dedicated to the performance of HFT is scarce relative to data on long-term buy-and-hold strategies, anecdotal evidence suggests that most computer-driven strategies are high-frequency strategies. Systematic and algorithmic trading naturally lends itself to trading applications demanding high speed and precision of execution, as well as high-frequency analysis of volumes of tick data. Systematic trading, in turn, has been shown to outperform human-led trading along several key metrics. Aldridge (2009b), for example, shows that systematic funds consistently outperform traditional trading operations when performance is measured by Jensen's alpha (Jensen, 1968), a metric of returns designed to measure the unique skill of trading by abstracting performance from broad market influences. Aldridge (2009b) also shows that the systematic funds outperform nonsystematic funds in raw returns in times of crisis. That finding can be attributed to the lack of emotion inherent in systematic trading strategies as compared with emotion-driven human traders.

Furthermore, computers are superior to humans in such basic tasks as information gathering and lightning-fast analysis of a multitude of quotes and news. Physiologically, the human eye cannot capture more than 50 data points per second, as evidenced by an entirely different industry—cinematography. In modern movies, the human eye is exposed to only 24 frames per second, which appear seamless to most moviegoers. Even then, the majority of images displayed on sequential frames involve continuously moving objects. In comparison, modern financial information incorporates drastically bouncing quotes, the number of which can easily exceed 1,000 per second for just one financial instrument. Detecting inter-instrument information spillovers involves processing data for multiple assets and asset classes, as discussed in Chapter 15. Where efficient processing of high volumes of information is key to profitable trading, technology-averse humans have little chance of succeeding. HFT takes over.

■ What Is High-Frequency Trading?

High-frequency trading is an umbrella term comprising several groups of strategies. Given the breadth of HFT, various market participants have somewhat divergent opinions of what HFT actually stands for. This section discusses common definitions of HFT:

■ *A definition of HFT that includes all activity utilizing fast algorithmic execution.* For example, the Technology Subcommittee of the U.S. Commodity Futures Trading Commission (CFTC), tasked with compiling a working definition of HFT, came back with the following draft definition in June 2012:

High-frequency trading is a form of automated trading that employs:

■ Algorithms for decision making, order initiation, generation, routing, or execution, for each individual transaction without human direction;

- low-latency technology that is designed to minimize response times, including proximity and co-location services;
- high speed connections to markets for order entry; *and*
- high message rates (orders, quotes or cancellations).

Such definition captures many high-frequency traders, yet also includes 95 percent of investors using algorithmic technology to execute their orders. Even a "mom-and-pop" retail investor entrusting his broker to execute his order in the most efficient algorithmic manner becomes a high-frequency trader under the definition proposed by the CFTC's subcommittee on HFT. Not surprisingly, this definition generated strong dissent from many members of the subcommittee itself.

- *The definition of HFT as a latency-sensitive subset of algorithmic trading.* Gomber, Arndt, Lutat, and Uhle (2011) proposed to define HFT as shown in Figure 1.9. Under such definition, HFTs are algo traders "on steroids," utilizing super-fast technology to speed up algorithmic processes and drive models in supersonic time. Interestingly, also under this definition, the HFTs do not engage in portfolio construction or management, but generate trading signals, validating models, and execute trades in any one security.

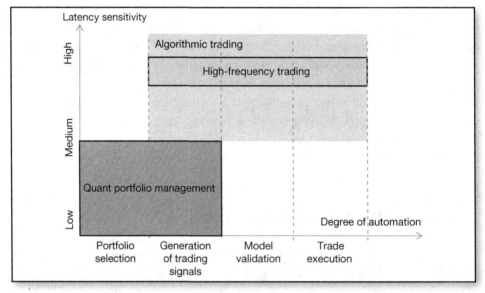

FIGURE 1.9   HFT vs. Algorithmic Trading and Quant Portfolio Management
Source: Gomber, Arndt, Lutat and Uhle (2011)

- *The definition of HFT based on holding period of capital throughput.* A survey of hedge-fund managers, conducted by FINalternatives in 2009, generated the following definition of HFT:

    High-frequency trading comprises

- Systematic,
- Quant-based models

- With holding periods from a fraction of a second to one day (no positions held overnight).

  The survey was based on nearly 300 responses from hedge fund managers who subscribe to FINalternatives (close to 10,000 questionnaires were sent out). It is also worth noting that at the time, a prominent multibillion-dollar Greenwich-based hedge fund launched a high-frequency fund with an average position holding period of three days, a far departure from submicrosecond frequencies often mentioned in connection with HFT. The fund was later retracted.

- *The definition of HFT based on their observed market activity.* Kirilenko, Kyle, Samadi, and Tuzun (2011) identify high-frequency traders as market participants that generate high market volume, all the while holding low inventory. The researchers use the definition to distinguish HFT from other market participants:

  - Intermediaries, characterized by low inventory, but not high trading volume.

  - Fundamental buyers, who are consistent net buyers intraday.

  - Fundamental sellers, who are consistent net sellers within a given day.

  - Small traders, generating low volume.

  - Opportunistic traders, loosely defined as all other traders, not fitting the definition of HFT or other categories above.

  Such definition may rely on somewhat arbitrary cutoffs of low inventory and high volume.

  The definition of HFT based on behavior unattainable by human market participants. A common definition used by brokers to segment their clients into HFT and non-HFT, this definition calls for attribution of trading activity of each specific account into human feasible and human infeasible. For example, an account generating 200 orders per second would be deemed HFT, as would an account that consistently succeeds at locking in a penny gain day-in and day-out.

  This book considers all of the definitions discussed here.

While a concrete definition of HFT has proven to be a challenge, most market participants are comfortable with the range of strategies deployed by HFT, summarized in Figure 1.10.

■ What Do High-Frequency Traders Do?

Despite the disagreements about the precise definition of HFT, most market participants agree that HFT strategies fall into the following four broad classes:

1. Arbitrage
2. Directional event-based trading
3. Automated market making
4. Liquidity detection

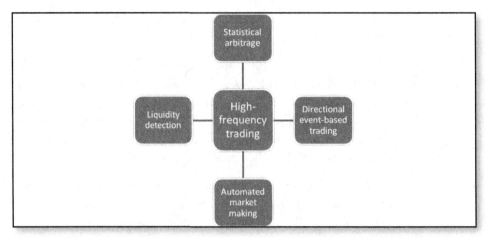

FIGURE 1.10 Major Categories of HFT Strategies

Arbitrage strategies trade away price deviations from long-running equilibria or relative asset mispricing, and can include multiple asset classes, as well as multiple exchanges. Many HF arbitrage strategies detect price discrepancies in multiple securities, as discussed in Chapter 8. Several strategies arbitrage prices of the same asset trading on different exchanges, are known as *latency arbitrage strategies,* and are discussed in Chapter 12. Most arbitrage strategies are based on assumptions of mean-reversion of asset prices.

Statistical arbitrage models comprise a range of models, including cross-asset models, where financial securities have strong statistical relationships. All the models included in the book are deep-rooted in economic theories, ruling out spurious statistical relationships often developed using plain data mining and also known as the Spaghetti Principle of Modeling (if one throws a plate of spaghetti filled with data against the wall of statistics, something may stick; what sticks, however, may not have any sound reason for sticking and is likely to fall apart in production). For example, bonds and interest rate futures have been shown to possess considerable dependencies, and their values, as a result, tend to move in tandem. When prices of bonds or interest rate futures deviate from their long-running price equilibrium for no obvious reason, statistical arbitrage trading may be feasible via buying the instrument with a lower-than-expected price relative to the other instrument(s), and selling the instrument with a higher-than-expected price relative to the other instrument(s). Chapter 8 details many economic models, as well as the model estimation techniques and known results.

Directional strategies identify short-term trend or momentum. This class of high-frequency strategies includes event-driven strategies, discussed in Chapter 9, other strategies based on predictable short-term price movements, discussed in Chapter 11, as well as the controversial ignition strategies, discussed in Chapter 12. Event arbitrage models show the methodology as well as performance of trading on predictable and recurrent effects of news. Various types of news used in event arbitrage are showcased in Chapter 9, which also includes references to the latest relevant studies as well as specific practical examples.

Automated market-making strategies comprise perhaps the most traditional trading strategies, encompassing automated market making, a cost-effective and accurate alternative to human broker-dealers, discussed in detail in Chapter 10. The category of automated market making and liquidity provision includes both inventory-driven and information-driven approaches. Inventory-driven methods tend to focus on joint minimization of the inventory risk and market risk, ensuring that the positions are within a trader's risk tolerance limits given market conditions, and hedged where appropriate. Information-driven market-making models are built with the goal of minimizing the risk of adverse selection, the risk of taking an opposite position to a better-informed party. To minimize the number of such losing positions, high-frequency traders can deploy a wide range of models that help forecast short-term directionality of markets, track the number of well-informed market players in the market waters, and even help forecast impending lumps and shortages of liquidity, covered in Chapter 11. These techniques allow traders to choose the quantities and levels of aggressiveness of their orders based on expectations of surplus or dearth of liquidity.

Perhaps least palatable to the low-frequency investors are liquidity detection strategies, like pinging (also known as sniffing and sniping), quote stuffing, and spoofing, addressed in Chapter 12. While this book focuses on explaining sound HFT strategies, the book attempts to draw a balanced perspective and include the methodology behind controversial HFT as well. "Pinging" has been shown to exist on selected venues (pinging was detected in dark pools). The nature of other strategies like "ignition strategies" have been mostly speculative, and no credible evidence of strategy existence has been produced to date. Still, the hypothetical strategies like ignition strategies have been included for completeness, accompanied by a brief analysis of their feasibility, properties, and impact on the broader markets.

How Many High-Frequency Traders Are There?

The number of high-frequency traders largely depends on the definition of HFT used. As mentioned earlier, under the CFTC draft definition proposed in June 2012, 19 out of every 20, or 95 percent of all investors and traders would qualify as HFT. Kirilenko, Kyle, Samadi, and Tuzun (2011), define HFTs as traders who produce large trading volume while holding little inventory, and find that HFTs account for about 30 percent of volume in the Standard & Poor's (S&P) 500 E-Mini markets. Aldridge (2012a) estimates that HFTs comprise just 25 to 30 percent in EUR/USD foreign exchange futures and that in the most liquid exchange-traded fund, the S&P 500 SPDR (NYSE:SPY), high-frequency traders on average represent fewer than 20 percent of market participants.

Major Players in the HFT Space

Many HFT participants prefer to stay out of the limelight, all the while generating considerable profits. The most well-known HFT outfits include Getco, Renaissance Capital, and DE Shaw. Lesser-known but still very profitable players dedicated to HFT include specialist firms like IV Capital, DKR Fusion, and WorldQuant.

The line between HFT and other forms of trading, however, can be blurred. As mentioned earlier, HFT, and specifically automated market making, are becoming staples on most trading desks in all the major banks. And the advantages of such developments are easy to see: the new automated market-making "robots" are considerably more accurate, inexpensive, and reliable than their human counterparts. Likewise, HFT can seamlessly blend in with activities of statistical arbitrage. In Canada, for example, banks often list most of their HFT in the statistical arbitrage category in the banks' annual reports.

■ Organization of This Book

This book is written with the explicit goal of providing the latest, yet applied and ready-to-implement information to management and employees that are interested in starting or enhancing their high-frequency trading operations, individuals and institutions seeking to protect their and their clients' trading activity against high-frequency traders, as well as casual observers, seeking to better understand modern financial markets.

Chapters 2 through 5 of the book explain the present-day frontiers in financial markets. Chapter 2 describes technological evolution that has enabled algorithmic and high-frequency trading. Chapters 3 through 5 lay the foundation of analysis via description of modern microstructure, high-frequency data, and trading costs.

Chapters 6 and 7 delve into the economics of high-frequency trading. Chapter 6 describes methodologies for evaluating performance and capacity of HFT strategies, and Chapter 7 outlines the business case of HFT.

Chapters 8 through 12 and 14 through 16 are devoted to actual implementation of HFT. Chapters 8 through 12 dissect core models of today's high-frequency strategies. Chapter 14 focuses on risk measurement and management of high-frequency trading as well as portfolio construction. Chapters 15 and 16 discuss the nuts-and-bolts in implementation of HFT systems, as well as best practices in running and monitoring HFT systems.

Chapters 13 and 15 focus on regulation of HFT and mitigation of HFT externalities. Chapter 13 presents a summary of current regulatory thought on HFT, discusses models for detection of HFT market manipulation, as well as mathematics of foreseeing market-wide events like flash crashes. Chapter 15 of the book offers solutions for low-frequency traders concerned about the impact of HFT on modern markets. Chapter 15 discusses the latest order slicing techniques and their respective ability to avoid information-prying HFTs, and may also prove useful to high-frequency traders seeking to further expand capacity of their trading systems.

■ Summary

- High-frequency trading is an organic evolution of trading technology.
- The technological evolution of financial markets created ability to replace human-driven intermediation function with cost-effective technology, returning broker compensation to end investors and bank shareholders.

- High-frequency trading strategies are well defined, and most of them are beneficial to the markets.

■ End-of-Chapter Questions

1. Describe the major groups of today's market participants. What role do they play? How do they interact?
2. What are the core groups of strategies deployed by high-frequency traders?
3. How do high-frequency trading strategies relate to other trading strategies, such as technical analysis, fundamental analysis, and quant strategies?
4. What are the major changes that have occurred in the financial markets over the past 40 years?
5. What is algorithmic trading?
6. How do end investors benefit from high-frequency trading?

CHAPTER 2

Technological Innovations, Systems, and HFT

Technological innovation leaves the most persistent mark on the operations of financial markets. While the introduction of new financial instruments, such as EUR/USD in 1999, created large-scale one-time disruptions in market routines, technological changes have a subtle and continuous impact on the markets. Over the years, technology has improved the way news is disseminated, the quality of financial analysis, and the speed of communication. The adoption of technology in financial services, however, was greatly aided by the ever-plummeting costs of technological improvements. This chapter examines the key developments that have occurred in technology over the past several decades in the context of enabling modern financial landscape.

■ A Brief History of Hardware

Trading was institutionalized during the Roman Empire, when the first exchange in currency in designated locations can be noted (benches or "bancas" were the direct precursors of today's banks). Gradual change guided the operations of trading firms until the technological revolution of the twentieth century enabled the current state of trading with rapid exchanges of information. As Figure 2.1 illustrates, over the past 100 years or so the computational speed available to traders has increased exponentially, while the cost of computing has been falling steadily since the 1980s, after reaching its peak.

The price decline in computer technology has been spectacular over the past 20 years. A computer system with 2 gigabytes of memory (RAM), 300 gigabytes of hard drive space, and a 2-gigahertz processor cost several million dollars in 1995, and was big enough to require its own room. In 2012, a computer with identical specifications not only fits in a standard desktop case, it can also be found for as little as $400 in any neighborhood Best Buy or other computer store.

The decline in the cost of computing can be largely traced to the efficiency of scale in production of computer chips overseas. The demand for the increasingly accessible and cheaper technology has, surprisingly, been driven not by the financial services practitioners, but rather by more casual users of computer technology with considerably thinner wallets. Over the past two decades, the latter demanders for cost-efficient technology happened to be video game players, whose sheer scale and desire for lifelike graphics has fueled the surge in mass production and plummeting prices of fast technology. Financial firms have reaped the benefits of innovation and cost efficiencies created by the activity of the video gaming industry.

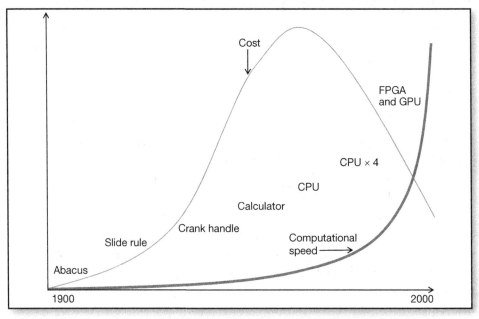

FIGURE 2.1 Evolution of Speed and Costs of Technology over the Twentieth Century

As shown in Figure 2.1, today's advanced technologies comprise multicore central processing units (CPUs), field programmable gate arrays (FPGAs), graphics processing units (GPUs), and the so-called massively parallel architecture chips. A CPU is the brain of the computer and decides how to store information in memory. Multicore CPUs use a shared memory for fast inter-CPU communication, while each individual CPU schedules tasks and performs computations on a given process branch or "thread." Sample architecture of a multicore CPU is shown in Figure 2.2. At the time this book was written, a multicore CPU could cost $100 and higher.

Unlike CPUs, where the majority of the space on the chip is occupied by memory and scheduler functions, the space on a sample GPU is largely devoted to the computational operations, performed in the so-called arithmetic logic units (ALUs). To further maximize efficiency of each chip, process threads are executed in parallel batches of identical size. These batches of threads are called *warps*. To minimize

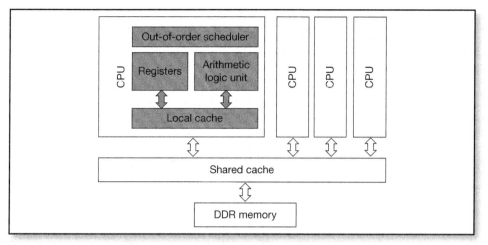

FIGURE 2.2 Architecture of a Sample Multicore CPU
Source: Thomas, Howes and Luk (2009)

latency, however, care should be taken to ensure that the threads of the process are similar in terms of the number of loops and conditional exits. In other words, programming expertise is required to ensure that GPUs are deployed with maximum efficiency. Figure 2.3 illustrates sample architecture of the GPU. A popular model of a GPU is Nvidia GTX series, which can retail for $100 to $700 per card.

FPGAs are an entirely different class of chips that do not have any fixed instruction set architecture. Instead, an FPGA provides a blank slate of bitwise functional units that can be programmed to create any desired circuit or processor. Some FPGAs

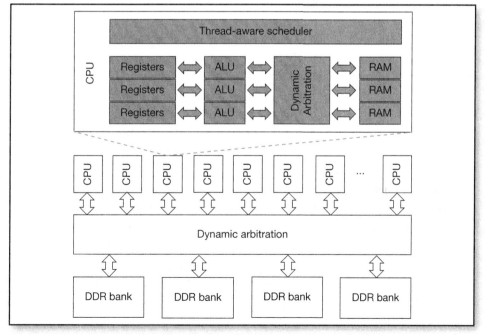

FIGURE 2.3 Architecture of a Sample GPU
Source: Thomas, Howes and Luk (2009)

contain a number of dedicated functional units, such as multipliers and memory blocks. Most of the area of an FPGA, however, is dedicated to the routing infrastructure the run-time connectivity of the FPGA's functional units. Figure 2.4 shows the architecture of a sample FPGA chip.

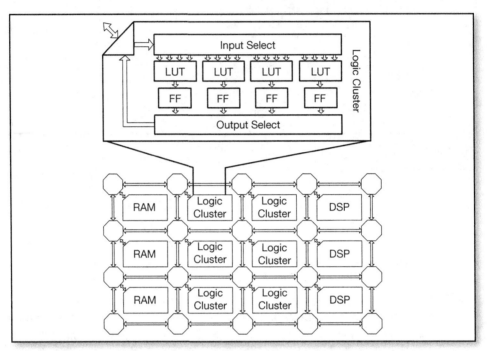

FIGURE 2.4   Architecture of a Sample FPGA Chip
Source: Thomas, Howes and Luk (2009)

The main distinction of FPGAs is that the programming code is written directly onto the chip from the outset. FPGAs are programmed using special programming languages, such as Verilog or VHDL. The languages are similar to C programming language and are easy to learn. A special FPGA programming device translates Verilog or VHDL into Assembly language understood by the FPGA chips. In the absence of FPGAs, trading programs need to be compiled and translated to the computer chips like CPUs during program run time, requiring additional computer operations and eating into the latency. The process of programming an FPGA is rather straightforward and inexpensive. While there exists a significant variation in costs of blank FPGA chips and Verilog or VHDL compilers and simulators, quality inexpensive options are commonly available, once again produced to satisfy demand of video gamers. A blank FPGA chip may cost anywhere from $4 to $5,000. The Verilog software and simulators may be free ("open-source") or $20,000. The software is then downloaded onto the chip, using the process specific to the chip manufacturer. Programming of FPGA chips is often taught in undergraduate electrical engineering programs, and tends to be easy to learn. However, achieving a state-of-the-art FPGA system may require arranging FPGAs in a format known as *massively parallel processor array configuration,* demanding advanced understanding of hardware and software optimization.

Performance-wise, FPGAs tend to be superior to GPUs and CPUs, particularly when used to simultaneously process a limited number of time series. Figure 2.5 shows a graphical comparison of efficiency of key hardware models. The horizontal axis of the figure shows the "input" size, or the number of independent variables simultaneously fed into the algorithm. The vertical axis shows the number of computer "cycles" required to perform an operation involving the given number of inputs. As Figure 2.5 illustrates, an FPGA posts best results when the number of inputs is less than 2,000. When the number of inputs exceeds this threshold, the speed of an FPGA becomes comparable to that of a GPU.

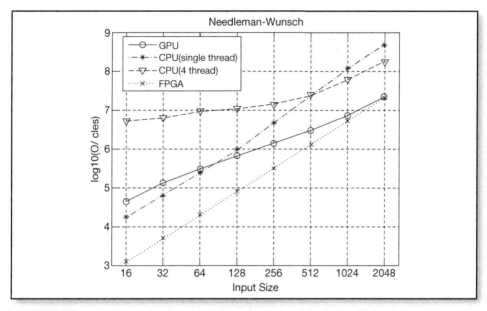

FIGURE 2.5   Comparative Performance of FPGA, GPU, Single CPU, and Quad CPU Architectures
Source: Thomas, Howes and Luk (2009)

The choice of a chip itself is not the single determinant of the speed of the computer program. The speed of each computer cycle is determined by the so-called oscillator crystal within each machine and, most important, organization of the program's algorithm.

■ Messaging

Hardware is just one of many components of computer technology necessary for achieving successful trading. Another crucial component is messaging, enabling communication among hardware and software modules of various market participants. Just as speed is important in hardware, it is also important in messaging. In fact, it is the speed of messaging that presents a hurdle or a bottleneck for trading communication.

Messaging Protocols

Trading messaging is comprised of three levels of protocols, shown in Figure 2.6. The most basic level of communication enables data streaming and is known as the User Datagram Protocol (UDP). UDP is the "bare bones" data communication protocol, lean in its implementation, and utilizing the fewest number of bytes and messages to identify and deliver the stream of data. As a result, UDP is very fast, but does not guarantee delivery of sent data. UDP is the same technology as the one used to stream games and movies over the Internet, where loss of one packet here and there does not significantly impact the viewer's experience. In trading, UDP is sometimes used to transmit quotes, the data that are refreshed continuously, and are, therefore, not very sensitive to lost information. If a particular quote sent from an exchange fails to reach a trader, the resulting impact may be deemed minimal: a new revised quote is already on the way, retiring the lost quote upon hitting the trader's account.

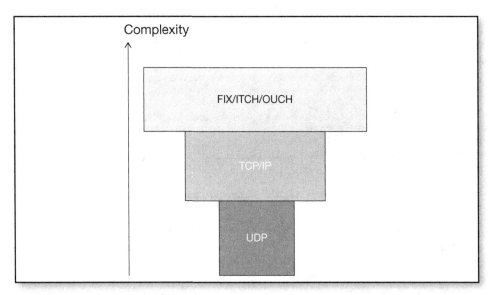

FIGURE 2.6 Three Levels of Complexity of Communication Protocols Used in Trading

The integrity of the quote process, however, can matter in trading model development. A trading algorithm developer may rely on the quote stream idiosyncrasies to generate predictive signals about impending market movements. If the structure of the historical quote stream used in model development differs significantly from that of the quote stream encountered by the trader "in production" environment, the calculated forecasts may cease working. Care should be taken to ensure that the data used in simulation and back-test of the algorithms is structurally compatible to the data received in production environment. At a minimum, the algorithm designer should ascertain that the frequency of quotes received in production matches that in the historical data used in the back-test. More complicated data tests can also be performed. For example, a rolling autocorrelation metric can be computed on the two sets of data, and the distribution of the resulting metrics should be comparable for successful algorithm design and implementation.

The next level of complexity in communication protocols is Transmission Control Protocol/Internet Protocol (TCP/IP). TCP/IP is another standard Internet communication protocol, presently used in most e-mail and Web-browsing communication. Unlike the UDP, where individual packets of information do not carry any identifying monikers, all packets of a TCP/IP transmission are sequentially numbered, the total number of bytes within each packet is counted, and undelivered or corrupt data is re-sent. As a result, TCP/IP provides a more secure framework for information delivery, and is used to transmit orders, order acknowledgments, execution acknowledgments, order cancellations, and similarly important information. As a trade-off, TCP/IP tends to be three times slower than UDP. Figure 2.7 summarizes common usage of UDP, TCP/IP and FIX in trading communication.

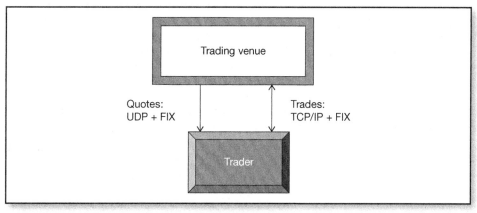

FIGURE 2.7 Common Use of Protocols in Trading Communication

Both the UDP and TCP/IP, however, require an additional layer of communication to standardize messages of the trading process. Protocols like Financial Information eXchange (FIX), ITCH, OUCH, and FAST are used on top of UDP and TCP to transmit data in a standardized machine-readable format. FIX protocol is a free XML-based text specification for quote, order, trade and related message transmission. The FIX protocol comprises data field definitions, enumerations, and various components, forming messages. Each message is then populated with the user-generated data. Each field of the message, including the version of FIX used, the time stamp, and other information, is separated from the following field by binary 1.

```
8=FIX.4.2 | 9=309 | 35=S | 34=5015 | 52=20070731-15:25:20 |
131=1185895365 | 301=0 | 55=USD/CAD | 167=FOR | 15=USD |
132=1.065450 | 133=1.065850 | 134=5000000.0 | 135=5000000.0 |
647=2000001.0 | 648=2000001.0 | 188=1.06545 | 190=1.06585 |
60=20070731-15:25:20 | 40=H | 64=20070801 | 10=178
```

FIGURE 2.8 Sample FIX Message

Figure 2.8 illustrates a sample FIX message, transmitting a quote for USD/CAD exchange rate. The shown quote contains the following information:

- Version of FIX, "FIX.4.2" (field number 8)

- The time stamp of the message, "20070731-15:25:20" (field number 52)

- Security identifier, "USD/CAD" (field number 55)

- Security type, "FOR" for foreign exchange (field number 167)

- Base currency, "USD" for U.S.$ (field number 15)

- Best bid and best ask (fields 132 and 133, respectively)

- Sizes at the best bid and best ask (fields 134 and 135)

Transmission speed of communication messages depends on several factors:

- Size of message

- Connection bandwidth

- TCP/IP and UDP "window" sizes, specifying how many bytes market participants are willing to send and receive at per message "slice." Once the system of one market participant sends out a message, the message is sliced into the individual parcels of a specified window length, a message header is attached to each parcel, and the messages are sent out on their route. The UDP message header typically identifies the destination, and consists of just 8 bytes. The TCP/IP message header includes the sender and destination identifications, parcel sequence number, and the total number of parcels comprising the message, among other variables. The standard TCP/IP header is 20 bytes. The FIX header can be much more elaborate, and is often in excess of 100 bytes.

While FIX is widely used, it is slow in comparison with Nasdaq's protocols known as ITCH and OUCH. The binary nature of ITCH and OUCH ensures that the messages arrive in the machine-readable format, using no processing time to convert them from text to binary and back. In addition to the binary format, ITCH and OUCH messages have a fixed message length, enabling faster transmission. OUCH is the order entry protocol, while ITCH is the outbound quote and trade-data dissemination specification. Yet ITCH and OUCH support only a limited number of messages. OUCH provides the platform for:

- Order entry.

- Replacement and cancellations.

- Receipt of execution acknowledgements.

ITCH is built for fast and lean quote and past trade data dissemination, and is able to transmit:

- Order-level data.

- Trade messages.

- Net order imbalance data.

- Administrative messages.

- Event controls, such as start of day, end of day, and emergency market halt/resume.

For more complex messages, ITCH- and OUCH-enabled market participants are often required to use FIX.

Core Message Architecture

Tick information is transmitted among market participants using one or several quote messaging specifications. FIX, ITCH, OUCH, and FAST are just a few messages languages enabling transmission of critical trading information. Despite their complicated acronyms, messaging is built around strikingly simple architecture, as illustrated in Figure 2.9.

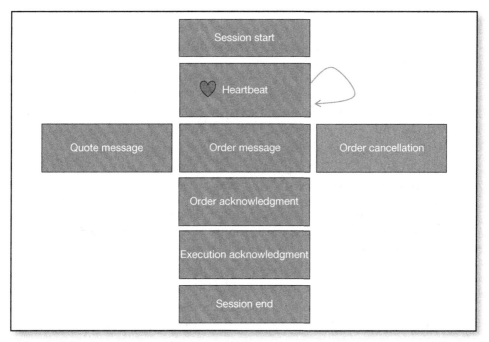

FIGURE 2.9   Core Message Architecture in Trading

As shown in Figure 2.9, every stream of quote and trade communication includes the following key messages:

1. *Session start* is the message sent in the beginning of every communication session, sometimes only once a day. The session start message notifies relevant market participants that the entity is open for trading and desires to establish a communication stream.

2. *Heartbeat* is a recurrent message that notifies the participant's communication parties that the participant is online, in a state of good technological health, and open for business. Parties that fail to receive their communication partners'

heartbeat messages for a preconfigured period of time often shut down the communication channel. The communication channel may then be reinstated using the "session start" sequence.

3. *Quote* message is a message carrying quote information, such as best bid and ask prices and sizes. Level II data, like the depth of the order book behind the best bid and ask quotes, may also be transmitted using quote messages.

4. *Order* message is used to transmit actual order information. A typical order message includes a buy or sell identifier, an order type—a market, limit or other specification, order size, and a desired execution price and validity period (day, good-till-canceled) in the case of limit orders.

5. *Order cancellation* message includes the unique identifier of the previously placed order that now needs to be canceled.

6. *Order acknowledgment* and *order cancellation acknowledgment* messages include confirmations of order placement or order cancellation, respectively.

7. *Execution acknowledgment* messages specify the details of execution: time of execution, obtained price, and execute quantity.

8. *Session end* message informs parties that a given trading entity has stopped trading and quoting for the day.

The resulting trade messaging flow comprises intuitive methodology to deliver effective, reliable, and traceable communication. Most trading outfits log their daily communication for easy reconciliation and fast identification of potential issues, such as network connectivity problems, algorithm errors, and the like.

Speed and Security

Neither TCP/IP nor UDP incorporate encryption. In other words, most TCP/IP and UDP messages are sent via Internet networks in plain text. FIX provides optional encryption at a considerable latency. While ITCH and OUCH send messages in a binary format, most Nasdaq OMX messages are still sent unencrypted over the Internet networks.

What kind of risk do market participants face by sending unencrypted messages? To answer this question, one needs to consider the current layout and flow of the Internet traffic. Today, most Internet traffic in the world flows through about 80 "core" nodes. These nodes, such as major Internet service providers (ISPs) like Verizon, have some security measures in place, limiting the incidence of spying activity at these nodes. At the same time, nodes can be quite congested, slowing down messaging traffic without consideration to its urgency.

If the core nodes were to fail, 70 percent of Internet traffic would flow through peer-to-peer networks, redundant backup structures in which the traffic would hop from one local user to another, in a distributed fashion. While the peer-to-peer network configuration can allow the network participants to observe each other's traffic and read unencrypted messages in full, the peer-to-peer communication is sufficiently randomized to prevent any peer party to accumulate the entire message flow. Still, peer-to-peer networks may be vulnerable to malicious intent, and the resulting potential hijacking of the order flow could destroy markets and cause tremendous losses for all market participants.

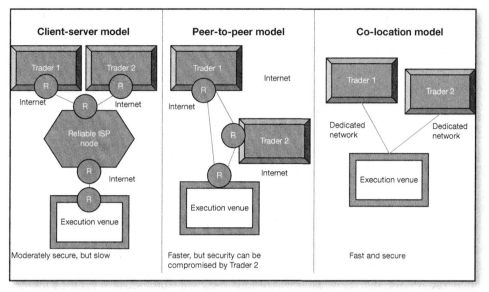

FIGURE 2.10 Messaging Architecture in Client-Server, Peer-to-Peer, and Co-location Models

Figure 2.10 describes three common Internet communication models prevalent in trading, including the so-called co-location model. In the co-location model, traders' servers are housed in the same secure facility as the exchange's matching servers. In the co-location scenario, trading servers have dedicated network access to the exchange servers. The dedicated network access comprises a private secure communication line from the trading servers directly to the exchange, minimizing the risk of malicious intervention and ensuring a safe environment for all market participants. Co-location also provides such benefits as speed advantage: the servers of a Chicago trader co-located with Nasdaq, for example, would allow the trader to shave anywhere from 17 to 22 milliseconds in a round-trip order latency due to the physical distance between New York and Chicago, all in addition to the immeasurable savings resulting from the security of the co-located trading connection. Figure 2.11 summarizes latency among selected co-location centers worldwide.

	New York, NY	Washington, DC	Toronto, Canada	Chicago, IL	London, U.K.	Frankfurt, Germany	Sao Paolo, Brazil	Tokyo, Japan
Newark, NJ	0.314	3.400	9.470	15.175	65.763	74.383	109.414	141.640
New York, NY		4.057	9.784	15.291	65.533	74.153	109.100	141.756
Washington, DC			13.270	14.175	69.083	78.164	111.960	140.640
Toronto, ON				10.795	75.233	83.853	118.884	136.910
Chicago, IL					80.740	89.360	123.485	127.595
London, U.K.						8.620	183.253	215.825
Frankfurt, Germany							183.253	215.825
Sao Paolo, Brazil								249.950

FIGURE 2.11 Latency Incurred by Electronic Signals Traveling over Optical Fiber Networks between Pairs of Locations

Within most co-location data centers, servers are positioned at various distances from the exchange server itself, raising natural concerns about "fairness" of connections of all traders co-located in a given facility. A physical distance difference of as little as 100 feet may result in one microsecond (one millionth of a second) time delay on every message sent and received, giving traders co-located near the exchange servers a potential advantage. To address such issues, the Nasdaq co-location center guarantees an equidistant length of fiber-optic cable from the servers to the exchange to the servers of each trader co-located in the Nasdaq's facility. The cable lengths are identical down to the millimeter, and can be seen coiled near the servers of traders physically close to servers of the exchange.

Although some market participants believe co-location to be unaffordably expensive, the real numbers point to the opposite. At a data center in Secaucus, New Jersey, for example, a private company, Equinix, offers co-location-equivalent proximity services with the minimum monthly charges broken down as follows:

- A cabinet for the trader's hardware equipped with biometric security scanners and air-conditioning runs $1,500 per month.

- A 20-amp 120-volt primary power source costs $350 per month.

- An additional 20-amp 120-volt power source designed for redundancy costs an additional $175 per month.

- Finally, a connection to the ultra-fast communication network linking various data centers around the world runs an additional $325 per month.

The grand total of the proximity setup adds up to just $2,350 per month, a negligible cost for any serious investor.

Network Throughput

The messaging architecture is a resource available to all market participants, yet it is not free to all. Exchanges, for example, have to continuously enhance their infrastructure to ensure that the bandwidth of their connections is broad enough to allow uninhibited message traffic among all interested traders. Perhaps the biggest challenge to exchanges and other order-matching venues is the sheer volume of order cancellations. According to Hautsch and Huang (2011), on Nasdaq, 95 percent of all limit orders are canceled within one minute from the time the orders are placed. Hasbrouck and Saar (2011) report similar activity grouped into brisk order placement and cancellation "runs." While this activity may seem malicious to an uninitiated observer, the explanation for such behavior is quite simple: as described in detail in Chapters 10, automated market makers need to quote close to the market price—"stay on top of the book"—in order to be successfully and promptly matched, thus ensuring a steady revenue stream. Once the market moves away from the quotes of the market maker, it is in the best interests of the market maker to cancel the orders and to resubmit them at the new best bid and best offer prices. In addition, as explained in Chapter 12, on exchanges with time-price priority of limit order books, market participants may place and then innocuously cancel excessive numbers limit orders to secure their execution priority, in a practice known as "layering."

In such dynamics, many trading venues are caught within a vicious circle: on the one hand, they are competing to attract the market makers, but on the other, many order-cancelling market makers are eroding network resources, resulting in missed quotes and other delays for all market participants. Even the co-location does not help fully navigate the bandwidth issue, as co-location space also faces capacity constraints: Nasdaq has seen so much demand in its co-location hangar in Mahwah, New Jersey, that it is reportedly running out of space to offer to the parties interested in co-locating there. As discussed in Chapters 3 and 12, a promising solution to the network bandwidth issue, known as *pro-rata execution*, has been developed and implemented at selected exchanges.

■ Software

High-frequency trading systems are ultimately software applications deployed over hardware and messaging described above. As with any software system, an HFT system begins with an idea, known as an *algorithm* in computer-science lingo, that is subsequently coded in a chosen computer language into a full-blown software program. The term *algorithm* is properly defined as logic, or a sequence of high-level actions, developed to explain to a computer how to implement a given task at hand. The algorithm does not delve into the details of actual coding or programming the system, but may still take into account the idiosyncrasies of the hardware and messaging structure on which the algorithm will be ultimately implemented. Algorithms are often visualized in diagrams. The key elements of the algorithm diagrams are summarized in Figure 2.12.

The algorithm elements shown in Figure 2.12 will be used throughout the book to explain algorithm designs of common HFT strategies. Figure 2.13 illustrates the step-by-step process of the following simple market-making algorithm:

1. Begin program.
2. Check market conditions: Are market conditions suitable for market making?
3. If yes, start market making.
4. If no, wait one minute.
5. Repeat step 2.

The algorithm presented in Figure 2.13 is "nested," or comprises two additional algorithms marked in Figure 2.13 only as "Check market conditions" and "Start market making." The nested tasks can be the critical "secret sauce" that distinguishes good HFT systems from bad ones. Usually, the tasks are designed on the basis of advanced research, where the task is selected among several competing ideas given

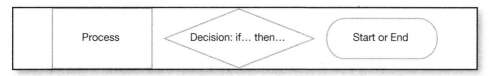

FIGURE 2.12   Common Elements of an Algorithm

positive results of rigorous testing. The two nested tasks shown in Figure 2.13 are explained in detail in Chapter 15.

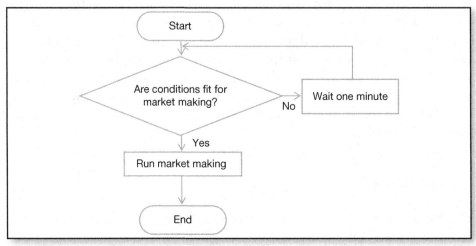

FIGURE 2.13   Sample Market-Making Algorithm

The term *algorithm* is often used synonymously with the terms *high-frequency trading, systematic trading, electronic trading,* and *low-latency trading.* The distinctions among the terms, however, are significant enough to warrant some explanation. A *system* usually refers to a highly methodical approach to a process. Systematic trading, therefore, is following some rigid frameworks, but does not have to be fully automated. A trader can be considered systematic if he manually places trades when certain indicators form a specific pattern. The term *systematic* was coined to distinguish traders practicing methodical allocations from traders using their intuition or discretion, and hence known as *discretionary* traders. All high-frequency and algorithmic traders are also systematic.

The term *electronic* describes the execution preferences of the trader: whether he chooses to place orders electronically or, perhaps, over the telephone. All high-frequency trading, algorithmic trading, and low-latency trading are necessarily electronic, but systematic trading may involve nonelectronic components. The reverse, however, does not have to be the case; many electronic trading systems route only orders that may or may not be placed algorithmically. As most markets and traders are moving on to electronic platforms, however, the term *electronic trading* is becoming implicit and obsolete.

Low-latency trading refers to trading that utilizes fast connectivity between traders and exchanges. As described in the previous section, latency measures the time distance between the trader and the exchange. Most latency measurements are currently recorded in microseconds. High-frequency trading systems often also happen to be low-latency, but the reverse does not have to hold: low-latency systems are often deployed by low-frequency traders to obtain better prices on trades.

Once an algorithm is designed, it is broken down into components and coded in a language understood by computers. The goal of coding is to accurately translate the logic of the algorithm into computer "speak" and, in the process, to create as little delay as possible during "run time," when the computer will read and interpret the code. The code written directly to FPGA chips is presently the fastest. Still, many high-frequency traders deploy standard non-FPGA architecture and rely on languages such as C++ and Java to code their systems. While C++ remains the fastest computer language easily understood by humans, many systems are coded in Java with workarounds of its slowest components. Thus, for example, the famed Nasdaq OMX system is reportedly coded in Java with Java garbage collection disabled and replaced with C++-like direct memory access for increased speed. Chapter 16 describes best practices of coding implementation.

The code outlining the actual trading logic of an algorithm tends to be quite short. In many successful cases, the trading logic comprises as few as 50 lines of code. In addition to the actual decisions to buy and sell, however, every HFT system incorporates supporting quote data retrieval functionality that may number in 10,000+ lines of code, as well as the trade send-off and acknowledgment receipt applications that can also take as much as 5,000 lines of code. Perhaps the most lengthy, yet mandatory, component of each HFT system is its risk management checks and balances, which can total 50,000+ lines of code. Risk management of HFT is discussed in detail in Chapter 14 of this book.

■ Summary

Algorithmic execution is inseparable from today's markets. It is a necessary function that delivers considerable value to all investors, large and small. With plummeting technology costs, most investors today can afford to build and use advanced algos, including algos designed for high-frequency trading, previously available only to a select few market participants. Services such as co-location provide added benefits of security and speed.

■ End-of-Chapter Questions

1. Would you encrypt your trading orders before transmitting them to the execution venue over the Internet? Explain.
2. Mr. Smith has read about the "arms race" of computer technology in the financial services industry and decides to invest into the latest super computer to increase the odds of fast order transmission. Is Mr. Smith's investment justified? Where does most message congestion occur in the cyber-universe today?
3. What is co-location?
4. On average, how much slower is the transmission of trade order messages in comparison with quote messages?
5. What is a heartbeat?
6. The best offer on exchange A contains 300 units of instrument X, the best offer on exchange B contains 500 units, and the best offer on exchange C contains just 100 units. Your customer wants you to buy 550 units on his behalf. How would you break up the customer's order and send them to exchanges under the minimal impact algorithm?

CHAPTER 3

Market Microstructure, Orders, and Limit Order Books

The study of market microstructure originated over four decades ago, and the core principles remain true today: most market participants rely on limit orders and market orders. These core order types remain most used despite an explosion of various derivative order types. Despite the continuity of these key principles still, much has changed. In the 1980s At one time, the peculiarities differentiating tick data dynamics from daily and monthly data were observed, but there was no way to incorporate the differences into a trading strategy. Today, that tick data can be captured easily and trades initiated quickly, it is possible to build trading strategies taking into account market microstructures. This chapter delves into the modern microstructure of markets, describing orders, matching processes, and rebate structures, among other issues defining today's markets.

Types of Markets

Financial markets are venues that allow investors and other market participants to buy and sell securities with a peace of mind that all transactions will be properly accounted and settled. In this respect, financial markets are not that different from markets for other nonfinancial products, such as a neighborhood grocer. When a customer enters a grocery store, he expects immediate execution of his transaction, an exchange of his money for merchandise—food. The grocer's cash register takes on the settlement function: the receipt itemizes the produce the customer bought and the total amount of money the grocer collected, nowadays most often from the customer's account rather than in cash form.

Furthermore, the grocery customer expects that the food he acquires is in good condition and that the transaction is permanent: that the grocer has full rights to sell the customer the product. Most centralized financial markets incorporate similar quality control for financial products: the products offered for purchase and sale on the floors of each market tend to be standardized, and their quality can be ensured via a thorough prelaunch due-diligence process as well as via the real-time data distribution to all market participants. For example, futures contracts traded on exchanges have a specific well-defined structure. Initial public offerings for stocks tend to be well scrutinized. Yet, just like grocers do not evaluate suitability of particular foods to each person, financial markets are unaware of a client's risk profile or accreditation, leaving the risk of investing decisions to the traders themselves.

Since the beginning of trading history, most financial and nonfinancial markets have been organized by product type. In nonfinancial settings, stores carrying lumber differ from stores selling clothes. Food markets used to be highly fragmented by type as well: fishmongers, bakers, butchers, and ice-cream makers all used to have their own shops, if not districts. Similarly, financial markets have been historically organized by the type of the traded instrument, each trading only equities, futures, options, or other securities. Recently, however, nonfinancial markets have been gearing toward megastores to increase their efficiency and take advantage of common distribution and procurement frameworks and skills. Similarly, many trading venues are now venturing in the cross-asset space, with the traditional foreign exchange player iCap launching a fixed-income trading offering, and equity exchange Best Alternative Trading Systems (BATS) considering entering the foreign exchange trading space.

The history of the financial exchanges is not always linear. The New York Stock Exchange (NYSE), for example, was first formed as a for-profit entity at the end of the eighteenth century, when two dozen stockbrokers signed an agreement to stop undercutting each other's commissions and instead retain at least 0.25 percent of each trade. In subsequent years, as the U.S. economy grew, more public listings became available, and the interest in investing grew from the U.S. public, stockbroking became increasingly lucrative and seats on the NYSE rose in value.

During major recessions, however, lavish lifestyles of stockbrokers drew the scrutiny of money-losing investors and regulators. In 1934, in the midst of the Great Depression, the NYSE was required to register and accept oversight from the then newly formed U.S. Securities and Exchange Commission (SEC). In 1971, during the post–Vietnam War recession, the NYSE was converted into a not-for-profit entity in a bid to cap excessive compensation of brokers and transfer some of their intake to the investors. The nonprofit mandate failed to live up to its expectation, with exchange-registered brokers creating a secondary market for their seats on the exchange that by the 1990s had reached multiple-million-dollar price tags.

The past two decades have witnessed increasing competition in the exchange space, and these competitive market forces appear to have succeeded in helping investors retain a larger share their earnings away from brokers. New exchanges, such as Nasdaq, deployed technology in lieu of bonus-collecting human traders, transferring some of the resulting savings into the pockets of investors and producing other benefits in the process. Technology has lowered error rates, increased execution times, and, perhaps most importantly, increased transparency of process to investors. Other early exchanges, such as the Chicago Mercantile Exchange, followed trajectories similar to that of NYSE, and today face competition from relatively new exchange entrants, such as the Intercontinental Commodity Exchange (ICE).

Today's equity markets comprise over a dozen various exchange venues, run by now-industry stalwarts such as the NYSE and Nasdaq, and relatively recent arrivals, such as BATS, DirectEdge, and others. Since all equity exchanges are subject to U.S. SEC oversight and trade standardized products, exchanges presently compete to differentiate their offerings mainly on liquidity and costs. In a bid to attract liquidity (more on this later in this chapter), most exchanges have done away with membership fees and now offer free registration. In addition, equity exchanges are differentiating themselves on price structures, not only rewarding large traders but also segmenting traders based on whether they place market orders or limit orders.

In addition to the regular exchanges, a new breed of matching venues has emerged, known as *dark pools.* Unlike an exchange, where the entire limit order book is available for observation, dark pools do not disclose their limit order books, instead keeping them "in the dark." Trading in a dark limit order book has appealed to large investors who are concerned about the information they may reveal by placing their orders in a traditional exchange, a *lit* market. Liquidnet is an example of an equities dark pool.

■ Limit Order Books

The cumulative trade size of all limit orders available to meet incoming market orders at any given time on a specific trading venue is known as *liquidity.* The larger the number of limit order traders available on the exchange, and the larger the size of each trader's limit orders, the more liquid the given trading venue. Liquidity is also necessarily finite in today's markets: the number of limit orders is measurable, and each limit order has a finite size. Liquidity was first defined by Demsetz (1968).

To account for limit orders, the majority of contemporary exchanges are organized as so-called centralized limit order books (CLOBs), also referred to as a double-sided auction. The CLOBs were pioneered in the United States in the early 1970s and adopted in Europe in the 1980s. In a CLOB model, all incoming limit orders are recorded in a "book": a table with columns corresponding to sequential price increments, and rows recording sizes of limit orders posted at each price increment. Figure 3.1 illustrates the idea. The limit order book information can be distributed to all other market participants as Level II data, discussed in detail in Chapter 4.

In theory, limit order books are often assumed to be symmetric about the market price, with the distribution of limit buy orders mirroring that of limit sell orders. Furthermore, in many risk management applications, order books are also assumed

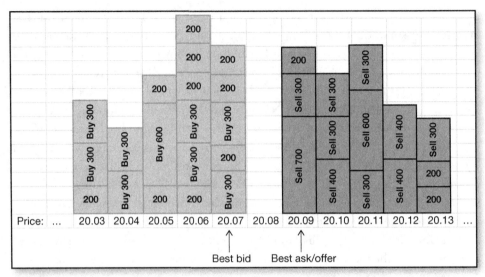

FIGURE 3.1 Sample Snapshot of a Limit Order Book. All limit buy orders are on the left-hand side of the book; all limit sell orders are on the right-hand side of the book.

to follow normal bell-curve distributions. Neither of the assumptions tends to hold: order books are seldom normal and are often asymmetric.

As Figure 3.2 shows, when a new limit order arrives, it is placed into a *limit order queue* corresponding to its price. Since all prices in today's markets are subject to a minimum increment, or *tick*, price-based bins are clearly delineated. The limit buy orders at the highest price form the best bid, with the price of these orders reflected in the best bid price, and the aggregate size reported as the best bid size. Similarly, the limit sell orders posted at the lowest price form the best ask, with respective price and size information. Best ask is sometimes referred to as *best offer*. At any given moment of time, there exists a finite aggregate size of all limit orders posted at each price.

When a market buy order arrives, it is matched with the limit sell orders, beginning with those placed at the best ask price. If the size of the incoming market buy order is greater than the size of the best ask queue, the market order "sweeps" through other offer queues in the direction of increasing price, "eating up" liquidity available at those price ticks. Sweeping leaves a significant gap in limit orders on the ask side, instantaneously increasing the bid-ask spread, and potentially inducing slippage in subsequent market buy orders. The order-matching process is similar for market sell orders that end up matched with the available limit buy orders aggregated on the bid size of the book. Limit buy orders with the prices equal or higher than the prevailing best bid are executed like market buy orders. Similarly, low-priced limit sell order are usually treated as market sell orders.

If the size of the incoming buy order is smaller than the size of the best ask, and the aggregate best ask queue is composed of several limit sell orders placed at the best ask price, the decision of which of the limit sell orders is matched against the market buy order may differ from one exchange to another. While most exchanges at present practice price-time priority, also known as the first-in-first-out (FIFO)

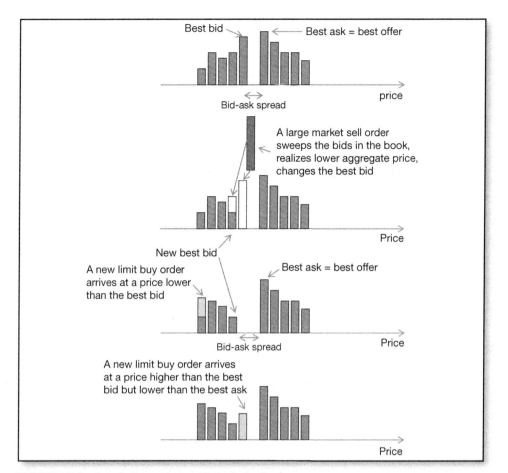

FIGURE 3.2 Sample Dynamics in a Limit Order Book

execution schedule for limit orders, several other exchanges now match a fixed proportion of each limit order at a given price in a process known as pro-rata matching.

In time-price priority, or FIFO, execution, the limit order that arrived first is also the first of that price bin to be matched with the incoming market order. Figure 3.3 illustrates the FIFO matching process. FIFO, known as the continuous auction, has been shown to enhance transparency of trading via the following measures (see Pagano and Roell, 1996; Jain, 2005; and Harris, 2003):

- Reducing information asymmetry—all traders have access to the limit order book information.

- Enhancing liquidity—a CLOB structure incentivizes traders to add limit orders, thereby increasing market liquidity.

- CLOB's organization supports efficient price determination by providing a fast and objective order-matching mechanism.

- Uniform rules for all market participants ensure operational fairness and equal access.

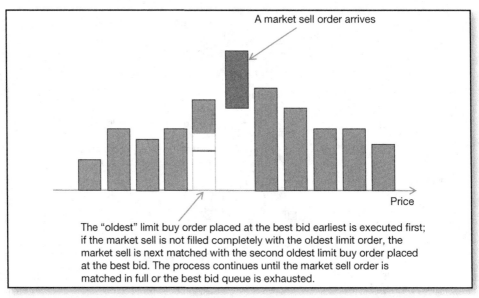

A market sell order arrives

Price

The "oldest" limit buy order placed at the best bid earliest is executed first; if the market sell is not filled completely with the oldest limit order, the market sell is next matched with the second oldest limit buy order placed at the best bid. The process continues until the market sell order is matched in full or the best bid queue is exhausted.

FIGURE 3.3 Price-Time Priority Execution

While most execution venues are based on FIFO, some exchanges, like Chicago Mercantile Exchange (CME), Chicago Board Options Exchange (CBOE), Philadelphia Stock Exchange (PHLX), and Intercontinental Commodity Exchange (ICE) have switched to pro-rata execution schedules. CME's pro-rata schedule matches an incoming market buy order with a fixed proportion of each limit order posted at the best ask. Similarly, an incoming sell order is matched with equal fractions of all of the limit orders posted at the best bid. The larger the limit order at the best bid and the best ask, therefore, the larger the fill of that order. Figure 3.4 shows the pro-rata process.

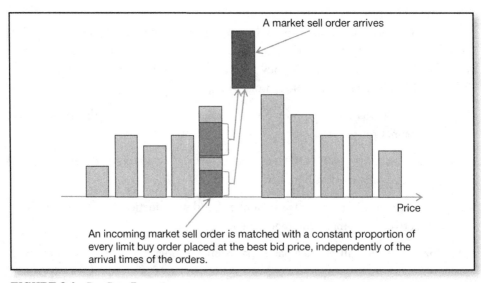

A market sell order arrives

Price

An incoming market sell order is matched with a constant proportion of every limit buy order placed at the best bid price, independently of the arrival times of the orders.

FIGURE 3.4 Pro-Rata Execution

The main advantage of the pro-rata matching from the exchange point of view is the built-in incentives for traders to place large limit orders, and, therefore, to bring liquidity to the exchange. The pro-rata matching encourages traders to post large limit orders without special compensation like rebates discussed below, thereby increasing exchange profitability. In addition, pro-rata matching eliminates incentives to place and then cancel limit orders with the intent to secure time priority of execution, reducing message traffic to and from the exchange.

In a nutshell, the pro-rata incentive works as follows: a trader desiring to execute a limit order knows that only a fraction of his order will be filled under the pro-rata schedule. The exact size of the filled portion of the order will depend on the cumulative size of limit orders placed at the same price by other limit order traders. The higher the aggregate size of limit orders in a specific price bin, the lower the percentage of all orders that will be filled in response to an incoming market order of the opposite sign. To increase his chances of filling the entire order, therefore, the trader is likely to place a limit order with a larger size than his intended order, with the explicit hope that the fraction of the order that will get filled is of the exact size as his intended order.

■ Aggressive versus Passive Execution

Orders can be described as passive or aggressive. Aggressive orders do not mean malicious orders, and passive orders do not indicate orders that are destined to be taken advantage of. Instead, the aggressiveness or passivity of orders refers to the proximity of the order price to the prevailing market price. Figure 3.5 illustrates the concept.

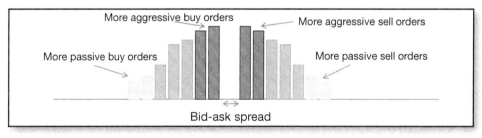

FIGURE 3.5 Aggressive and Passive Orders: An Illustration

A limit order far away from the market price (a low-priced limit buy order, or a high-priced limit sell order) is considered passive. The closer the limit order is to the market price, the more aggressive is the order. A market order is the most aggressive order, "crossing the spread" to be matched with the best-priced limit order on the opposite side of the limit order book. Limit orders crossing the spread are treated like market orders in the execution queue, and are also considered aggressive.

While market orders enjoy immediate and nearly guaranteed fills, market orders cross and pay the spread, incur transaction fees of the exchange and broker-dealers, and face price uncertainty. In today's markets, price uncertainty can be the costliest component associated with the market order execution. From the time the market order is placed to the time the execution is recorded, the market price may "slip," resulting in worse execution than the prevailing price at the time the market order was placed. The slippage may be due to several factors:

- Several market orders may arrive at the exchange and be executed between the time a given market order is placed and the time it is executed. Each of the arriving market orders may deplete the matching liquidity in the order book, adversely moving the market price. Such a situation is particularly common at times of news releases, when many traders and their algorithms simultaneously process information and place orders in the same direction.

- A market order that is large relative to the available depth of the order book may sweep through the book, executing fractional pieces of the order against limit orders at different price levels.

- Additional market conditions, such as market disruptions, may also result in significant slippage.

By contrast, the price of a limit order is fixed when the order is placed. A limit order is added to the limit order book, where it "sits" until the prevailing market price reaches it and a market order is executed against it. Limit orders also generally avoid "crossing the spread," a cost of paying the market spread incurred by market orders. Highly aggressive limit orders executed as market orders cross the spread, but obtain as good or better execution price than their specified limit price. Limit orders are also subject to positive or negative transaction costs, which vary from one trading venue to another.

For all their price advantages, limit orders are subject to an important risk—the risk of nonexecution. A limit order is executed only when it is matched with a market order of the opposite direction. A market price may quickly move away from a limit order, leaving it unexecuted. An unexecuted limit order may present a particular problem when placed to close a position, and misses the opportunity to eliminate market risk of the trade. And yet, unexecuted limit orders placed to open a position also incur a cost, that of the opportunity to engage in the trading strategy.

■ Complex Orders

In response to competition from new entrants in the matching business, trading venues have diversified their order offerings. For example, in response to competition from dark pools, selected exchanges expanded the number of available orders, creating so-called *iceberg orders*. Iceberg orders allow limit-order traders to display only a portion of their order in the limit order book, and keep the rest of their liquidity in the dark. In FIFO limit order books, iceberg orders are executed on a time priority basis: when matched against a smaller order, the nonexecuted part of the iceberg is being placed back at the end of their limit-order book queue. Unlike the orders in a dark pool, the size information of an iceberg is revealed after the iceberg is matched in part or in full: the matched size is disseminated to other traders as a trade tick. As a rule, iceberg orders cost more than do limit and market orders.

Other specialized orders have sprung up as well, to generate additional revenues from higher transaction costs and to serve the following potential needs of customers:

- *Limit risk.* Most trading venues and broker-dealers now offer a range of orders for containing market risk. The order examples include hard and trailing stop orders, where the position is liquidated when a price move exceeds the predetermined threshold in the adverse direction (see Chapter 14 for more information on stops).

- *Speed of execution.* Orders in this category try to enable the fastest execution possible and include, in addition to the vanilla market order, a market-on-close order that often guarantees to catch the closing price, a midpoint match order that bests the best bid limit order by attempting to negotiate crossing only half of the prevailing spread, and the sweep-to-fill order simultaneously clears the order book of the size requested in the order. The sweep-to-fill order may be executed faster than the market order, since a large market order is often executed by sweeping the limit order book gradually over time.

- *Price improvement.* Such orders include a block order in options that improves the price by obtaining large-volume discounts on transaction costs.

- *Privacy.* Privacy-providing orders deliver dark liquidity, and include iceberg orders and hidden orders, among others. The hidden order, as its name suggests, is not displayed in the limit order books. The iceberg order displays a limited portion of the order in the limit order book, as discussed in the beginning of this section.

- *Time to market.* Orders in the time-to-market group include fill-or-kill orders for market orders desiring the most immediate liquidity. A fill-or-kill order is canceled if the matching liquidity is not immediately available. Conversely, a good-till-canceled limit order falling in the same order category is kept in the limit order book until it is canceled or another maximum period of time set by the trading venue (e.g., a quarter).

- *Advanced trading.* These orders include additional quantitative triggers, such as implied volatility in options.

- *Algorithmic trading.* Orders in this category offer execution via order-slicing algorithms, such as percentage of volume (POV), described in detail in Chapter 17.

■ Trading Hours

Traditionally, many trading venues operated from 9:30 a.m. to 4:00 p.m. Eastern time. In today's globalized markets, more effort is placed on expanding accessibility of trading. As a result, many exchanges today offer premarket trading and afterhours trading, cumulatively known as *extended-hours trading.* Extended hours in equities, for example, allow market access from 4:00 a.m. to 8:00 p.m. Eastern time. The extended-hours volume is considerably thinner than that observed during the normal trading hours. Still, selected brokers use the after-hours trading to fill their customers' market-on-close orders.

Modern Microstructure: Market Convergence and Divergence

The electronization of markets has left an indelible footprint on all modern markets, streamlining some aspects of trading and fragmenting others. Among the trends in market convergence are the following developments:

- Most markets today can be accessed via Financial Information eXchange (FIX) messaging protocol. The FIX protocol is an XML-like specification that allows market participants to send and receive quotes, orders, and order cancellation and execution acknowledgments, among other messages necessary for fast and efficient trading. The FIX protocol is administered by an independent not-for-profit body, further facilitating proliferation of the protocol.

- Most markets worldwide are now designed as limit order books (LOBs). The Singaporean Stock Exchange was one of the last entities to use a different market structure, but converted to LOB in the past decade.

Among the key trends in market divergence is the progressing fragmentation of markets among the asset classes:

- Equities are subject to the National Best Bid and Offer (NBBO) rule, whereas all equities are to be executed at the aggregated and disseminated NBBO or better price. If the exchange is unable to execute an incoming market order at the NBBO, the exchange is obligated to route the order to an exchange with NBBO quotes.

- Futures exchanges do not have centralized pricing, but are subject to unique margining and daily mark-to-market requirements.

- Foreign exchange markets do not have centralized quotes or exchanges at all. All trades are continued to be negotiated over the counter (OTC), even though many OTC platforms are now fully electronic. Yet selected large market participants may be granted access to an interdealer network, an exchange-like entity.

- Option markets are numerous, with little activity on average.

- Following the Dodd-Frank regulation, new asset classes such as fixed income and swaps will be coming online or expanding in electronic forms. Each of the asset classes has distinct peculiarities, resulting in further fragmentation of the overall securities frontier.

Fragmentation exists within each asset class as well. The following sections discuss peculiarities within selected asset classes.

Fragmentation in Equities

U.S. equities can be traded in dark pools and on lit exchanges. Dark pools are exchange-like entities where the order book is "dark"—not displayed to any participant of that pool. According to Pragma Securities (2011), about 22 percent of the U.S. aggregate equity volume is presently traded in the dark pools. The singular advantage of dark pools lies in their ability to match large orders without revealing information associated with the order size, as the orders are not observable. The frequently cited disadvantages of dark pools include the lack of transparency and related issues. Unlike "lit" exchanges, dark pools do not offer differentiated pricing for limit and market orders—the dark pool limit order book is not disclosed to market participants.

The remaining 78 percent of the U.S. equity volume is executed on "lit" exchanges—venues where the order book is fully transparent and can be disseminated in full to interested market participants. But even within the lit markets category, the landscape is quite fragmented as the exchanges compete to set optimal fees.

In the lit exchanges, the U.S. equities are required to be executed at the NBBO or better quotes, compiled from the best bid and ask quotes available on all the member exchanges and disseminated by the Securities Information Processor (SIP). The aggregated best quotes are then disseminated back to exchanges as NBBO references. The NBBO execution rule was put forth by the Securities and Exchange Commission (SEC) in 2005 under the Regulation NMS, with the explicit purpose of leveling the playing field: under the NBBO rule, every best limit order, whether placed by a large institution or an individual investor, has to be displayed to all market participants. (Prior to the NBBO rule, individual investors were at the mercy of broker-dealers, who often failed to route investors' limit orders to exchanges, even when said limit orders were at the top of the market—better than the best quote available at the time.) Under the NBBO rule, exchanges that cannot execute at the NBBO due to the dearth of liquidity are required to route incoming market orders to other exchanges where the NBBO is available. As a result, traders placing market orders on lit exchanges are guaranteed that their orders are executed at the best possible prices available nationwide. Dark pools are exempt from the NBBO requirement.

Under the NBBO rule, exchanges can match trades only when they can execute at the NBBO, that is, when the NBBO-priced limit orders are recorded within their limit order books. Such NBBO limit orders can be achieved using two distinct approaches:

1. The exchange can compete to attract the top-of-the-book liquidity—limit orders priced at NBBO or better.
2. The exchange can compete to attract market orders, while simultaneously serving as a proprietary market maker posting NBBO limit orders.

The two business models of exchanges readily translate into the new fee structures of exchanges. In addition to clearing fees, exchanges now offer divergent pricing for suppliers of liquidity and takers of liquidity. Depending on whether the exchange follows the business model 1 or 2, the exchange may pay liquidity providers for posting limit orders, or pay takers of liquidity for bringing in market orders. Such payments, amounting to negative transaction costs, are known as *rebates*.

The two different business models have driven the exchanges into two distinct camps, "normal" and "inverted" exchanges, based on their fee structure. The normal exchanges offer the following fees: normal exchanges charge traders for placing market orders, taking away liquidity, and offer rebates for placing limit orders, bringing in liquidity. The NYSE, for example, charges $0.21 for a 100-share market order, and pays anywhere from $0.13 to $0.20 for a 100-share limit order. The exact value of the NYSE rebate is determined by the aggregate monthly volume of the trader—the higher the volume, the higher the rebate. The NYSE fee structure displayed online on May 14, 2012, is shown in Figure 3.6.

In contrast, the so-called "inverted" exchanges pay traders small rebates to remove liquidity (place market orders), and charge fees to place limit orders. Boston Exchange (Nasdaq OMX BX) is an example of an inverted exchange. There, traders with market orders for fewer than 3.5 million shares per day are paid $0.0005 per share, while traders placing market orders for 3.5 million or more shares per day are paid $0.0014 per share. Traders adding displayed limit orders under 25,000 per day are charged $0.0015 to $0.0018 per share. Yet, large limit order traders—traders placing limit orders for 25,000 shares per day or more—are paid rebates at the rate of $0.0014 per share. The snapshot of distribution of trading costs on the BX as of October 10, 2012, is shown in Figure 3.7.

As a result of the regulatory framework and pricing divergence among equity exchanges in the United States, various exchanges show different rates of availability

NYSE Arca Rates per 100 Shares					
		TAPE A (NYSE-LISTED)			
Tier	Tier Requirement(s)	Rebate for Adding[1]	Fee for Removing	Routing to NYSE[2]	Routing to Other Venues
Tier 1	NYSE Arca Daily Adding as of % of US CADV in excess of 0.70%	$ (0.30)	$ 0.30	$0.21/$0.23	$ 0.30
Tier 2	NYSE Arca Daily Adding as of % of US CADV in excess of 0.30%	$ (0.29)	$ 0.30	$0.21/$0.23	$ 0.30
Tier 3	NYSE Arca Daily Adding as of % of US CADV in excess of 0.20%	$ (0.25)	$ 0.30	$0.21/$0.23	$ 0.30
Step-Up Tier 1	NYSE Arca Daily Adding as % of US CADV in excess of 0.15% over the	$ (0.295)	$ 0.30	$0.21/$0.23	$ 0.30

FIGURE 3.6 Fee Structure of Orders Placed and Routed to and from NYSE
Source: NYSE web site

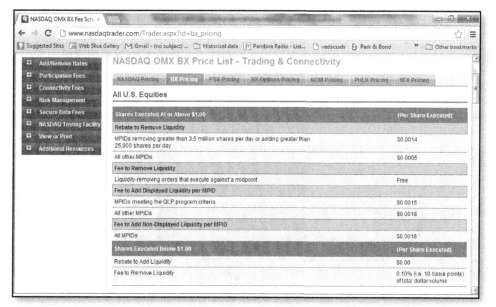

FIGURE 3.7 Fees on Nasdaq OMX BX, an Inverted Exchange
Source: Nasdaq web site

of NBBO on their order books as well as different market shares. As the intuition would suggest, the exchanges able to provide the highest occurrence of NBBO quotes are the ones able to secure the highest market share. Figure 3.8 displays the relationship between the NBBO availability rates and the market share rates. As shown in Figure 3.8, Nasdaq and NYSE on average have the highest availability of NBBO and obtain the highest share of trades.

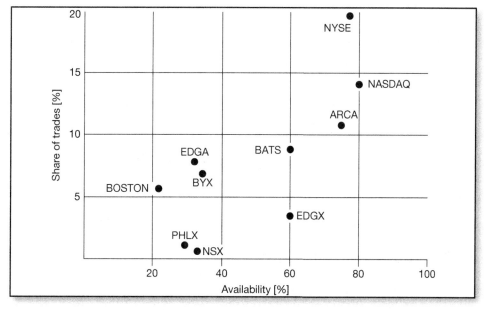

FIGURE 3.8 Availability of NBBO versus Share Volume
Source: Pragma Securities (2011)

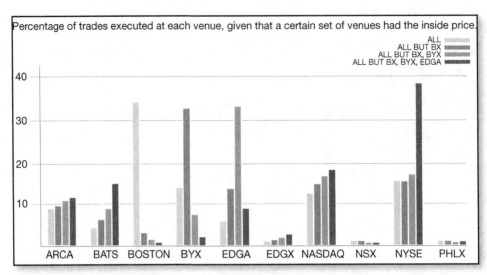

FIGURE 3.9 Percentage of Trades Executed at Each Trading Venue When NBBO Is Present at Certain Venues

Source: Pragma Securities (2011)

Figure 3.9 illustrates what happens when the NBBO is available on all or only some exchanges. When the best bid and the best ask at NBBO are available on all exchanges, over 30 percent of trade volume is executed at the BX, where the inverted fee structure attracts market order traders seeking NBBO liquidity. When every exchange except for BX has the NBBO limit orders, a similarly high number trades is routed to the BATS Y-Exchange (BYX). BYX, like BX, offers inverted fee structure, but with much smaller fees and rebates for removing liquidity. When the NBBO is not available solely on BX and BYX, the 30+ percent market share moves to Direct Edge's EDGA, an exchange with normal but low fee structure. When the NBBO is available everywhere except for BX, BYX, and EDGA, the trading volume moves on largely to the NYSE, although Nasdaq and BATS also benefit from the flow. The economic incentives associated with inverted price structures clearly work: the asymmetric order flow enjoyed by BX creates the first-taker advantage for Nasdaq, the parent company of BX.

High market share of trades does not alone contribute to the profitability of the exchange, as other fees can provide significant contributions to the bottom line of the exchanges. For example, both normal and inverted exchanges charge traders' fees for routing orders to other trading venues when the NBBO is not available on the current exchange. Thus, even an exchange with lowest proportion of NBBO can remain profitable by attracting enough orders and charging fees for routing said orders elsewhere.

■ Fragmentation in Futures

Futures exchanges operated in a manner similar to equity exchanhes, but without rebate pricing implemented or foreseeable at the time this book was written. In a bid to attract liquidity, and unlike the rebate structure prevalent in equities, futures exchanges have been deploying pro-rata matching, discussed earlier. Other differences among futures exchanges are predominantly based on their operational and risk management decisions, such as when to draw the circuit breakers and so on, described in detail in Chapter 13.

Fragmentation in Options

Various options exchanges have sprung up over the past decade. A majority of the exchanges, however, operate on similar principles and are driven by the same group of market makers.

Due to the sheer number of options with different expiration dates and strike price combinations, most options are barely traded. The same 10 or so broker-dealers tend to provide liquidity on most equity options markets, with large spreads being common.

The relative lack of activity in options trading enables market surveillance for insider information. A large trade in the long-dated option or an option with a strike price far away from the current market price of the underlying usually represents a bet on someone's special knowledge, not yet revealed to the rest of the markets.

Fragmentation in Forex

In Forex, interdealer brokers begin competing with broker-dealers for direct access to end traders. The traditionally interdealer brokers Currenex and iCAP, for example, now accept selected institutional customers. In breaking with other exchanges, iCAP offers a 250-microsecond validity on all of its top-of-the-book foreign exchange (forex) quotes.

Fragmentation in Fixed Income

While most fixed income traditionally traded OTC, some signs point to a potential near-term exchange-ization of the fixed-income market. Thus, iCAP has planned to launch a fixed-income matching engine using the Nasdaq OMX technology. The iCAP offering would further target institutional investors by providing a one-second validity of all top-of-the-book quotes.

Fragmentation in Swaps

Swaps have also traditionally traded OTC, with privately negotiated contracts. Under the Dodd-Frank Act, swaps are required to be standardized and traded electronically on exchanges. A new class of trading venues, collectively known as *swaps execution facilities* (SEFs), was jointly shaped by the industry and regulators at the time this book was written.

Summary

Modern markets are complex businesses ever concerned with streamlining their operations with the goal of delivering the most immediate, cost-effective service to their customers. The competition of trading venues has led to the innovation and evolution in methods, pricing, and service models of exchanges and alternative trading systems. While technology remains the key driver in development of faster and leaner offerings, the solutions are becoming more customer-centric, producing trading products customized to clients' unique execution needs.

End-of-Chapter Questions

1. What is the difference between the normal and inverted exchanges?
2. What type of orders would you use to buy a large quantity? Why?
3. You are given the task of developing an algorithm optimizing liquidation (selling) of a large equity position. Your aim is to develop an algorithm that maximizes execution costs while minimizing speed of liquidation process. How would you develop such an algorithm giving normal and inverted price structures of modern equity exchanges?
4. You are receiving Level I and Level II data on a certain futures contract from a well-known exchange. At 13:45:00:01:060 GMT, the aggregate liquidity reported at the best bid of 12.7962 comprises 325 contracts. The next tick of data is a trade print with a timestamp of 13:45:00:01:075 GMT, recording a trade of 900 contracts at 12.7962. The following tick is a 13:45:00:01:095 GMT quote citing the best bid of 12.7962 with the size of 325 contracts. What has happened in the market from 13:45:00:01:060 GMT to 13:45:00:01:095 GMT?
5. The current right-hand side of the limit order book for a particular stock on a given exchange shows the following information: Best Ask: 100 shares at 35.67, 200 shares at 35.68, 100 shares at 35.69. What is the average price per share you are likely to receive on your market buy order of 250 shares if the National Best Bid is advertised as 35.67? What if the National Best Bid is 35.65 instead?
6. Is an iceberg order passive or aggressive?
7. The last recorded trade price in a given options market is 2.83. The prevailing best bid is 2.65 and the prevailing best ask is 2.90. Is a limit order to buy 10 contracts at 2.85 passive or aggressive? Why?
8. A quantitative researcher ("quant") develops his investing models using daily closing prices. What order types should an execution trader use to execute the quant's buy-and-sell decisions?

CHAPTER 4

High-Frequency Data[1]

Trade and quote information is often distributed in Level I or Level II formats. Level I quotes include the best bid price, best ask price, best bid size, best ask size, and last trade price and size, where available. Level II quotes include all changes to the order book, including new limit order arrivals and cancellations at prices away from the market price. This chapter describes the details of data quotations and sampling methodologies and contrasts the data with their low-frequency counterparts.

What Is High-Frequency Data?

High-frequency data, also known as *tick data,* are records of live market activity. Every time a customer, a dealer, or another entity posts a so-called limit order to buy s units of a specific security with ticker X at price q, a bid quote $q_{t_b}^b$ is logged at time t_b to buy $S_{t_b}^b$ units of X. Market orders are incorporated into tick data in a different way, as discussed in this chapter.

When the newly arrived bid quote $q_{t_b}^b$ has the highest price relative to all other previously arrived bid quotes in force, $q_{t_b}^b$ becomes known as "the best bid" available at time t_b. Similarly, when a trading entity posts a limit order to sell s units of X at price q, an ask quote $q_{t_a}^a$ is logged at time t_a to sell $S_{t_a}^a$ units of X. If the latest $q_{t_a}^a$ is lower than all other available ask quotes for security X, $q_{t_a}^a$ becomes known as "the best ask" at time t_a.

What happens to quotes from the moment they arrive largely depends on the venue where the orders are posted. Best bids and asks posted directly on an exchange will be broadcast to all exchange participants and other parties tracking quote data. In situations when the new best bid exceeds the best ask already in force on the exchange, $q_{t_b}^b \geq q_{t_a}^a$, most exchanges will immediately "match" such quotes, executing a

---

[1] A version of this chapter appears in F. Fabozzi, ed., *Encyclopedia of Financial Models* (3 volume set) (Hoboken, NJ: John Wiley & Sons, 2012).

trade at the preexisting best ask, $q_{t_a}^a$ at time t_b. Conversely, should the newly arrived best ask fall below the current best bid, $q_{t_a}^a \le q_{t_b}^b$, the trade is executed at the preexisting best bid, $q_{t_b}^b$ at time t_a.

Most dark pools match bids and asks by "crossing the spread," but may not broadcast the newly arrived quotes (hence the mysterious moniker, the "dark pools"). Similarly, quotes destined for the interdealer networks may or may not be disseminated to other market participants, depending on the venue.

Market orders contribute to high-frequency data in the form of "last trade" information. Unlike a limit order that is an order to buy a specified quantity of a security at a certain price, a market order is an order to buy a specified quantity of a security at the best price available at the moment the order is "posted" on the trading venue. As such, market orders are executed immediately at the best available bid or best ask prices, with each market buy order executed at the best ask and each market sell matched with the best bid, and the transaction is recorded in the quote data as the "last trade price" and the "last trade size."

A large market order may need to be matched with one or several best quotes, generating several "last trade" data points. For example, if the newly arrived market buy order is smaller in size than that of the best ask, the best ask quote may still remain in force on most trading venues, but the best ask size will be reduced to reflect that the portion of the best ask quote has been matched with the market order. When the size of the incoming market buy order is bigger than the size of the corresponding best ask, the market order consumes the best ask in its entirety, and then proceeds to be matched sequentially with the next available best ask until the size of the market order is fulfilled. The remaining lowest-priced ask quote becomes the best ask available on the trading venue.

Most limit and market orders are placed in so-called "lot sizes": increments of certain number of units, known as a lot. In foreign exchange, a standard trading lot today is US$5 million, a considerable reduction from a minimum of $25 million entertained by high-profile brokers just a few years ago. On equity exchanges, a lot can be as low as one share, but dark pools may still enforce a 100 share minimum requirement for orders. An order for the amount other than an integer increment of a lot size, is called "an odd lot."

Small limit and market "odd lot" orders posted through a broker-dealer may be aggregated, or "packaged," by the broker-dealer into larger-size orders in order to obtain volume discounts at the orders' execution venue. In the process, the brokers may "sit" on quotes without transmitting them to an executing venue, delaying execution of customers' orders.

■ How Is High-Frequency Data Recorded?

The highest-frequency data are a collection of sequential "ticks," arrivals of the latest quote, trade, price, order size, and volume information. Tick data usually has the following properties:

- A timestamp
- A financial security identification code

- An indicator of what information it carries:

  - Bid price

  - Ask price

  - Available bid size

  - Available ask size

  - Last trade price

  - Last trade size

- Security-specific data, such as implied volatility for options

- The market value information, such as the actual numerical value of the price, available volume, or size

A timestamp records the date and time at which the quote originated. It may be the time at which the exchange or the broker-dealer released the quote, or the time when the trading system has received the quote. At the time this article is written, the standard "round-trip" travel time of an order quote from the ordering customer to the exchange and back to the customer with the acknowledgment of order receipt is 15 milliseconds or less in New York. Brokers have been known to be fired by their customers if they are unable to process orders at this now standard speed. Sophisticated quotation systems, therefore, include milliseconds and even microseconds as part of their timestamps.

Another part of the quote is an identifier of the financial security. In equities, the identification code can be a ticker, or, for tickers simultaneously traded on multiple exchanges, a ticker followed by the exchange symbol. For futures, the identification code can consist of the underlying security, futures expiration date, and exchange code.

The last trade price shows the price at which the last trade in the security cleared. Last trade price can differ from the bid and ask. The differences can arise when a customer posts a favorable limit order that is immediately matched by the broker without broadcasting the customer's quote. Last trade size shows the actual size of the last executed trade.

The best bid is the highest price available for sale of the security in the market. The best ask is the lowest price entered to buy the security at any particular time. In addition to the best bid and best ask, quotation systems may disseminate "market depth" information: the bid and ask quotes entered posted on the trading venue at prices worse than the best bid and ask, as well as aggregate order sizes corresponding to each bid and ask recorded on the trading venue's "books." Market depth information is sometimes referred to as the Level II data and may be disseminated as the premium subscription service only. In contrast, the best bid, best ask, last trade price, and size information ("Level I data") is often available for a small nominal fee.

Panels A and B of Figure 4.1 illustrate a 30-second log of Level I high-frequency data recorded by New York Stock Exchange (NYSE) Arca for Standard & Poor's Depositary Receipts (SPDR) S&P 500 exchange-traded fund (ETF; ticker SPY) from 14:00:16:400 to 14:02:00:000 GMT on November 9, 2009. Panel A shows quote

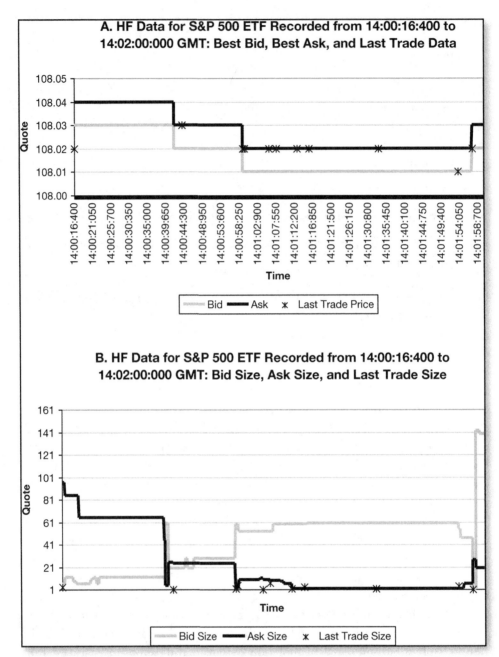

FIGURE 4.1   Level I High-Frequency Data Recorded by NYSE Arca for SPY from 14:00:16:400 to 14:02:00:000 GMT on November 9, 2009. Data source: Bloomberg

data: best bid, best ask and last trade information, while panel B displays corresponding position sizes (best bid size, best ask size, and last trade size).

■ Properties of High-Frequency Data

High-frequency securities data have been studied for many years. Yet they are still something of a novelty to many academics and practitioners. Unlike daily or monthly data sets commonly used in much of financial research and related applications, high-frequency data have distinct properties, which simultaneously can be advantageous and intimidating to researchers. Table 4.1 summarizes the properties of high-frequency data. Each property and its advantages and disadvantages are discussed in detail later in the article.

TABLE 4.1 Summary of Properties of High-Frequency Data

Property of HF Data	Description	Pros	Cons
Voluminous	Each day of high-frequency data contains the number of observations equivalent to 30 years of daily data.	Large numbers of observations carry lots of information.	High-frequency data are difficult to handle manually.
Subject to bid-ask bounce	Unlike traditional data based on just closing prices, tick data carry additional supply-and-demand information in the form of bid and ask prices and offering sizes.	Bid and ask quotes can carry valuable information about impending market moves, which can be harnessed to the researcher's advantage.	Bid and ask quotes are separated by a spread. Continuous movement from bid to ask and back introduces a jump process, difficult to deal with through many conventional models.
Not normally or lognormally distributed	Returns computed from tick are not normal or lognormal.	Many tradable models are still to be discovered.	Traditional asset pricing models assuming lognormality of prices do not apply.
Irregularly spaced in time	Arrivals of tick data are asynchronous.	Durations between data arrival carry information.	Most traditional models require regularly spaced data; need to convert high-frequency data to some regular intervals, or "bars" of data. Converted data are often sparse (populated with zero returns), once again making traditional econometric inferences difficult.
Do not include buy or sell trade direction information	Level I and Level II data do not include information on whether the trade was a result of a market buy or a market sell order	Data are leaner without trade direction information; trade information is more difficult for bystanders to extract.	The information on whether a trade is buyer initiated or seller initiated is a desired input in many models.

High-Frequency Data Are Voluminous

The nearly two-minute sample of tick data for SPY shown in Figure 4.1 contained over 2,000 observations of Level I data: best bid quotes and sizes, best ask quotes and sizes, and last trade prices and sizes. Table 4.2 summarizes the breakdown of the data points provided by NYSE Arca for SPY from 14:00:16:400 to 14:02:00:000 GMT on November 9, 2009, and SPY, Japanese yen futures, and a euro call option throughout the day on November 9, 2009. Other Level I data omitted from Table 4.2 include cumulative daily trade volume for SPY and Japanese yen futures, and "greeks" for the euro call option. The number of quotes observed on November 9, 2009, for SPY alone would comprise over 160 years of daily open, high, low, close, and volume data points, assuming an average of 252 trading days per year.

Quote Type	SPY, 14:00:16:400 to 14:02:00:000 GMT	SPY, All Day	USD/JPY Dec. 2009 Futures, All Day	EUR/USD Call Expiring Dec. 2009 with Strike Price of 1.5100, All Day
TABLE 4.2	**Summary Statistics for Level I Quotes for Selected Securities on November 9, 2009**			
Best bid quote	4 (3%)	5,467 (3%)	6,320 (5%)	1,521 (3%)
Best bid size	36 (29%)	38,948 (19%)	39,070 (32%)	5,722 (11%)
Best ask quote	4 (3%)	4,998 (2%)	6,344 (5%)	1,515 (3%)
Best ask size	35 (28%)	38,721 (19%)	38,855 (32%)	5,615 (11%)
Last trade price	6 (5%)	9,803 (5%)	3,353 (3%)	14 (0%)
Last trade size	20 (16%)	27,750 (14%)	10,178 (8%)	25 (0%)
Total	125	203,792	123,216	49,982

The quality of data does not always match its quantity. Centralized exchanges generally provide accurate data on bids, asks, and size. U.S. equity exchanges are required by law to archive and maintain reliable records of every tick of data, as well as to submit best quotes within one minute of their occurrence to the U.S. centralized ticker tape known as the *Securities Information Processor* (SIP). The information on the limit order book beyond the best bid and best offer is known as Level II data and can be obtained via special subscription.

In decentralized markets, such as foreign exchange and the interbank money market, no market-wide quotes are available at any given time. In such markets, participants are aware of the current price levels, but each institution quotes its own prices adjusted for its order book. In decentralized markets, each dealer provides his own tick data to his clients. As a result, a specific quote on a given financial instrument at any given time may vary from dealer to dealer. Reuters, Telerate, and Knight Ridder, among others, collect quotes from different dealers and disseminate them back, improving the efficiency of the decentralized markets.

There are generally thought to be three anomalies in interdealer quote discrepancies. First, each dealer's quotes reflect that dealer's own inventory. For example, a dealer that has just sold a customer $100 million of USD/CAD would be eager to diversify the risk of his position and avoid selling any more of USD/CAD. Most dealers, however, are obligated to transact with their clients on tradable quotes. To incite his clients to place sell orders on USD/CAD, the dealer temporarily raises the bid quote on USD/CAD. At the same time, to encourage his clients to withhold placing buy orders, the dealer raises the ask quote on USD/CAD. Thus, dealers tend to raise both bid and ask prices whenever they are short in a particular financial instrument and lower both bid and ask prices whenever they are disproportionately long in a financial instrument.

Second, in an anonymous marketplace, such as a dark pool, dealers as well as other market makers may "fish" for market information by sending indicative quotes that are much off the previously quoted price to assess the available demand or supply.

Third, Dacorogna et al. (2001) note that some dealers' quotes may lag real market prices. The lag is thought to vary from milliseconds to a minute. Some dealers quote moving averages of quotes of other dealers. The dealers who provide delayed quotes usually do so to advertise their market presence in the data feed. This was particularly true when most order prices were negotiated over the telephone, allowing a considerable delay between quotes and orders. Fast-paced electronic markets discourage lagged quotes, improving the quality of markets.

High-Frequency Data Are Subject to the Bid-Ask Bounce

In addition to trade price and volume data long available in low-frequency formats, high-frequency data comprise bid and ask quotes and their associated order sizes. Bid and ask data arrive asynchronously and introduce noise in the quote process.

The difference between the bid quote and the ask quote at any given time is known as the bid-ask spread. The bid-ask spread is the cost of instantaneously buying and selling the security. The higher the bid-ask spread, the higher the gain the security must produce in order to cover the spread along with other transaction costs. Most low-frequency price changes are large enough to make the bid-ask spread negligible in comparison. In tick data, however, incremental price changes can be comparable or smaller than the bid-ask spread.

Bid-ask spreads usually vary throughout the day. Figure 4.2 illustrates the average bid-ask spread cycles observed in the institutional EUR/USD market for the last two weeks of October 2008. As Figure 4.2 shows, the average spread increases significantly during Tokyo trading hours, when the market is quiet. The spread then reaches its lowest levels during the overlap of the London and New York trading sessions, when the market has many active buyers and sellers. The spike in the spread over the weekend of October 18–19, 2008, reflects the market concern over the subpoenas issued on October 17, 2009, to senior Lehman executives in a case relating to potential securities fraud at Lehman Brothers.

Bid-ask spreads typically increase during periods of market uncertainty or instability. Figure 4.3, for example, compares average bid-ask spreads on EUR/USD in the stable market conditions of July–August 2008 and the crisis conditions of September–October 2008. As the figure shows, the intraday spread pattern is persistent in both crisis and normal market conditions, but the spreads are significantly higher during crisis months than during normal conditions at all hours of the day. As Figure 4.3 also shows, the spread increase is not uniform at all hours of the day. The average hourly EUR/USD spreads increased by 0.0048 percent (0.48 basis points or pips) between the hours of 12 GMT and

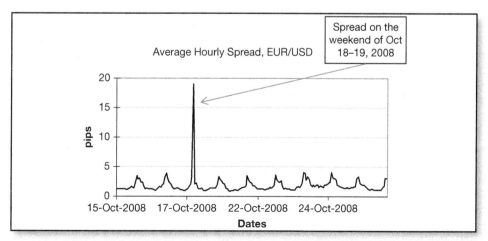

FIGURE 4.2 Average Hourly Bid-Ask Spread on EUR/USD Spot for the Last Two Weeks of October 2008 on a Median Transaction Size of US$5 Million

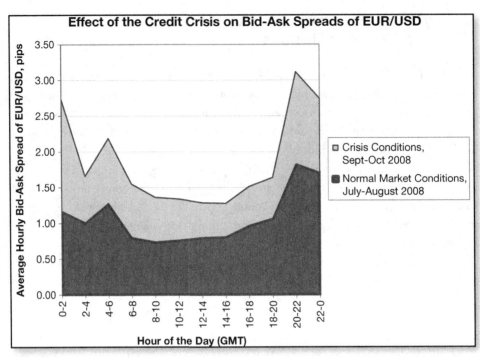

FIGURE 4.3 Comparison of Average Bid-Ask Spreads for Different Hours of the Day during Normal Market Conditions and Crisis Conditions

16 GMT, when the London and New York trading sessions overlap. From 0 to 2 GMT, during the Tokyo trading hours, the spread increased by 0.0156 percent, over three times the average increase during the New York/London hours.

As a result of increasing bid-ask spreads during periods of uncertainty and crises, the profitability of high-frequency strategies decreases during those times. For example, high-frequency EUR/USD strategies running over Asian hours incurred significantly higher costs during September and October 2008 as compared with normal market conditions. A strategy that executed 100 trades during Asian hours alone resulted in 1.56 percent evaporating from daily profits due to the increased spreads, while the same strategy running during London and New York hours resulted in a smaller but still significant daily profit decrease of 0.48 percent. The situation can be even more severe for high-frequency strategies built for less liquid instruments. For example, bid-ask spreads for NZD/USD (not shown) on average increased three times during September–October in comparison with market conditions of July–August 2008.

While tick data carry information about market dynamics, it is also distorted by the same processes that make the data so valuable in the first place. Dacorogna et al. (2001) report that sequential trade price bounces between the bid and ask quotes during market execution of orders introduce significant distortions into estimation of high-frequency parameters. Corsi, Zumbach, Muller, and Dacorogna (2001), for example, show that the bid-ask bounce introduces a considerable bias into volatility estimates. The authors calculate that the bid-ask bounce on average results in –40 percent first-order autocorrelation of tick data. Corsi et al. (2001) as well as Voev and Lunde (2007) propose to remedy the bias by filtering the data from the bid-ask noise prior to estimation.

In addition to real-time adjustments to bid-ask data, researchers deploy forecasting techniques to estimate the impending bid-ask spread and adjust for it in models ahead of time. Future realizations of the bid-ask spread can be estimated using the model suggested by Roll (1984), where the price of an asset at time t, p_t, is assumed to equal an unobservable fundamental value, m_t, offset by a value equal to half of the bid-ask spread, s. The price offset is positive when the next market order is a buy, and negative when the trade is a sell, as shown in equation (3):

$$p_{t.} = m_t + \frac{s}{2} I_t \tag{3}$$

$$\text{where } I_t = \begin{cases} 1, & \textit{market buy at ask} \\ -1, & \textit{market sell at bid} \end{cases}$$

If either a buy or a sell order can arrive next with equal probability, then $E[I_t] = 0$, and $E[\Delta p_t] = 0$, absent changes in the fundamental asset value, m_t. The covariance of subsequent price changes, however, is different from 0:

$$\text{cov}\left[\Delta p_t, \Delta p_{t+1}\right] = E\left[\Delta p_t \Delta p_{t+1}\right] = -\frac{s^2}{4} \tag{4}$$

As a result, the future expected spread can be estimated as follows:

$$E[s] = 2\sqrt{-\text{cov}\left[\Delta p_t, \Delta p_{t+1}\right]} \text{ whenever } \text{cov}\left[\Delta p_t, \Delta p_{t+1}\right] < 0$$

Numerous extensions of Roll's model have been developed to account for contemporary market conditions along with numerous other variables. Hasbrouck (2007) provides a good summary of the models.

To use standard econometric techniques in the presence of the bid-ask bounce, many practitioners convert the tick data to "midquote" format: the simple average of the latest bid and ask quotes. The midquote is used to approximate the price level at which the market is theoretically willing to trade if buyers and sellers agreed to meet each other halfway on the price spectrum. Mathematically, the midquote can be expressed as follows:

$$\hat{q}_{t_m}^m = \frac{1}{2}\left(q_{t_a}^a + q_{t_b}^b\right) \text{ where } t_m = \begin{cases} t_a, \text{if } t_a \geq t_b \\ t_b, \textit{otherwise} \end{cases} \tag{5}$$

The latter condition for t_m reflects the continuous updating of the mid-quote estimate: $\hat{q}_{t_m}^m$ is updated whenever the latest best bid, $q_{t_b}^b$, or best ask quote, $q_{t_a}^a$, arrives, at t_b or t_a respectively.

Another way to sample tick quotes into a cohesive data series is by weighing the latest best bid and best ask quotes by their accompanying order sizes:

$$\tilde{q}_t^s = \frac{q_{t_b}^b s_{t_a}^a + q_{t_a}^a s_{t_b}^b}{s_{t_a}^a + s_{t_b}^b} \tag{6}$$

where $q_{t_b}^b$ and $S_{t_b}^b$ is the best bid quote and the best bid available size recorded at time t_b (when $q_{t_b}^b$ became the best bid), and $q_{t_a}^a$ and $S_{t_a}^a$ is the best bid quote and the best bid available size recorded at time t_a.

High-Frequency Data Are Not Normal or Lognormal

Many classical models assume lognormality of prices, allowing price diffusion models to work seamlessly, and resulting in several pricing models, such as Black-Scholes, to be considered fair approximations of market evolutions of related financial instruments. A necessary condition for lognormality of prices is the normal distribution of sequential price changes. As this section shows, however, sequential changes in most of the tick data, like midquotes and size-weighted quotes and trades, do not follow normal distribution, yet distribution of sequential trade ticks is close to that of normal. Trade tick data are, therefore, the best choice for modelers assuming lognormal prices.

Figure 4.4 compares the histograms of simple returns computed from midquote (panel A), size-weighted midquote (panel B) and trade-price (panel C) processes for SPDR S&P 500 ETF data recorded as they arrive throughout November 9, 2009. The data neglect the time difference between the adjacent quotes, treating each sequential quote as an independent observation. Figure 4.5 contrasts the quantile distribution plots of the same data sets with the quantiles of a standard normal distribution.

As Figures 4.4 and 4.5 show, the basic midquote distribution is constrained by the minimum "step size": the minimum changes in the midquote can occur at half-tick increments (at present, the minimum tick size is $0.01 in equities). The size-weighted midquote forms the most continuous distribution among the three distributions discussed. Figure 4.5 confirms this notion further and also illustrates the fat tails present in all three types of data distributions.

As clearly shown in Figure 4.5, of the three methodologies, tick-by-tick trade returns most closely fit the normal distribution, when heavy tails past four standard deviations are ignored. Midquote values and size-weighted midquotes alike begin to deviate from normality at just two standard deviations, while trade returns follow the normal up to four standard deviations.

High-Frequency Data Are Irregularly Spaced in Time

Most modern computational techniques have been developed to work with regularly spaced data, presented in monthly, weekly, daily, hourly, or other consistent intervals. The traditional reliance of researchers on fixed time intervals is due to:

- Relative availability of daily data (newspapers have published daily quotes since the 1920s).

- Relative ease of processing regularly spaced data.

- An outdated view that "whatever drove security prices and returns, it probably did not vary significantly over short time intervals." (Goodhart and O'Hara 1997, pp. 80–81)

By contrast, high-frequency observations are separated by varying time intervals. One way to overcome the irregularities in the data are to sample it at certain

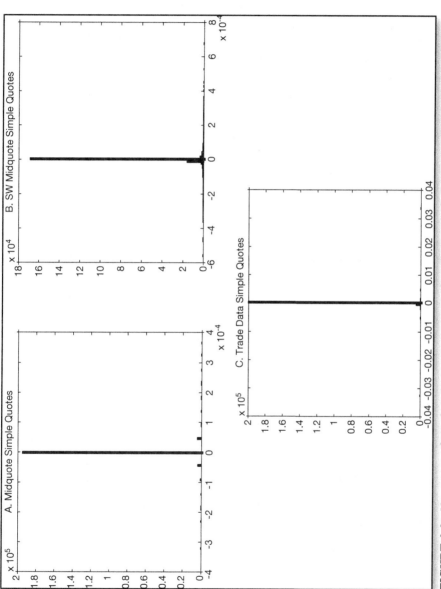

FIGURE 4.4 Histograms of Simple Returns Computed from Midquote (Panel A), Size-Weighted Midquote (Panel B) and Trade Price (Panel C) Processes for SPY Data Recorded as They Arrive throughout November 9, 2009

Panel A: Midquote simple returns

Panel B: Size-weighted midquote simple returns

Panel C: Last trade price simple returns

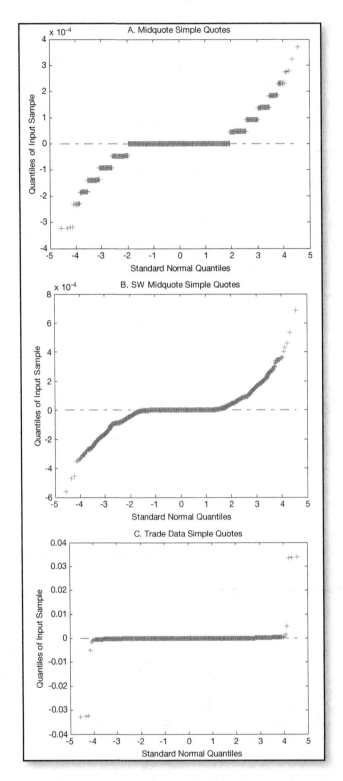

FIGURE 4.5 Quantile Plots of Simple Returns of Midquote (Panel A), Size-Weighted Midquote (Panel B) and Trade-Price (Panel C) Processes for SPY Data Recorded as They Arrive throughout November 9, 2009

Panel A: Midquote returns
Panel B: Size-weighted midquote returns
Panel C: Trade price returns

predetermined periods of time—for example, every hour or minute. For example, if the data are to be converted from tick data to minute "bars," then under the traditional approach, the bid or ask price for any given minute would be determined as the last quote that arrived during that particular minute. If no quotes arrived during a certain minute, then the previous minute's closing prices would be taken as the current minute's closing prices, and so on. Figure 4.7, panel A illustrates this idea. This approach implicitly assumes that in the absence of new quotes, the prices stay constant, which does not have to be the case.

Dacorogna et al. (2001) propose a potentially more precise way to sample quotes: linear time-weighted interpolation between adjacent quotes. At the core of the interpolation technique is an assumption that at any given time, unobserved quotes lie on a straight line that connects two neighboring observed quotes. Figure 4.6, panel B illustrates linear interpolation sampling.

As shown in Figure 4.6, panels A and B, the two quote-sampling methods produce quite different results.

Mathematically, the two sampling methods can be expressed as follows:
Quote sampling using closing prices:

$$\hat{q}_t = q_{t,last} \tag{7}$$

Quote sampling using linear interpolation:

$$\hat{q}_t = q_{t,last} + (q_{t,next} - q_{t,last}) \frac{t - t_{last}}{t_{next} - t_{last}} \tag{8}$$

where $\hat{q}_t$ is the resulting sampled quote, t is the desired sampling time (start of a new minute, for example), t_{last} is the timestamp of the last observed quote prior to the sampling time t, $q_{t,last}$ is the value of the last quote prior to the sampling time t, t_{next} is the timestamp of the first observed quote after the sampling time t, and $q_{t,next}$ is the value of the first quote after the sampling time t.

Figures 4.7 and 4.8 compare histograms of the midquote data sampled as closing prices and interpolated, at frequencies of 200 ms and 15 s. Figure 4.9 compares quantile plots of closing prices and interpolated distributions. As Figures 4.7 and 4.8 show, oft-sampled distributions are sparse, that is, contain more zero returns than distributions sampled at lower frequencies. At the same time, returns computed from interpolated quotes are more continuous than closing prices, as Figure 4.9 illustrates.

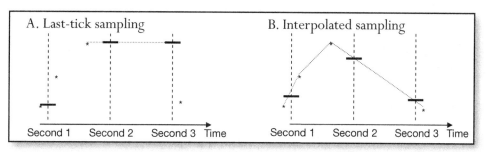

FIGURE 4.6 Data-Sampling Methodologies

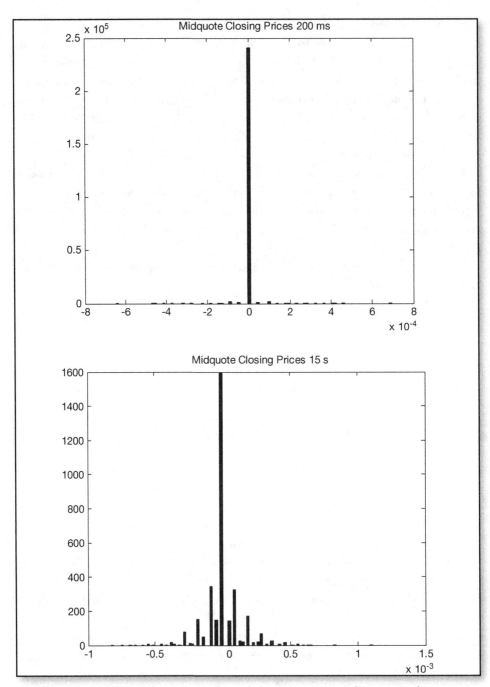

FIGURE 4.7 Midquote "Closing Quotes" Sampled at 200-ms (top) and 15-s Intervals

Instead of manipulating the interquote intervals into the convenient regularly spaced formats, several researchers have studied whether the time distance between subsequent quote arrivals itself carries information. For example, most researchers agree that intertrade intervals indeed carry information on securities for which short sales are disallowed; the lower the intertrade duration, the more likely the yet-to-be-observed good news and the higher the impending price change.

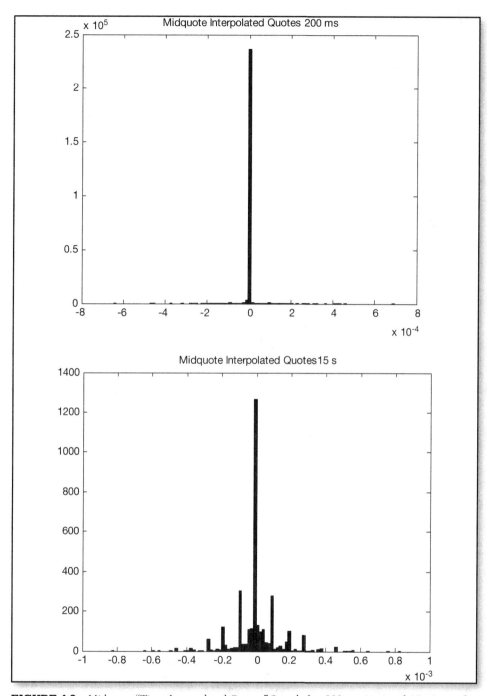

FIGURE 4.8 Midquote "Time-Interpolated Quotes" Sampled at 200-ms (top) and 15-s Intervals

Duration models are used to estimate the factors affecting the time between any two sequential ticks. Such models are known as quote processes and trade processes, respectively. Duration models are also used to measure the time elapsed between price changes of a prespecified size, as well as the time interval between predetermined trade volume increments. The models working with fixed price are known as *price processes;* the models estimating variation in duration of fixed volume increments are known as *volume processes.*

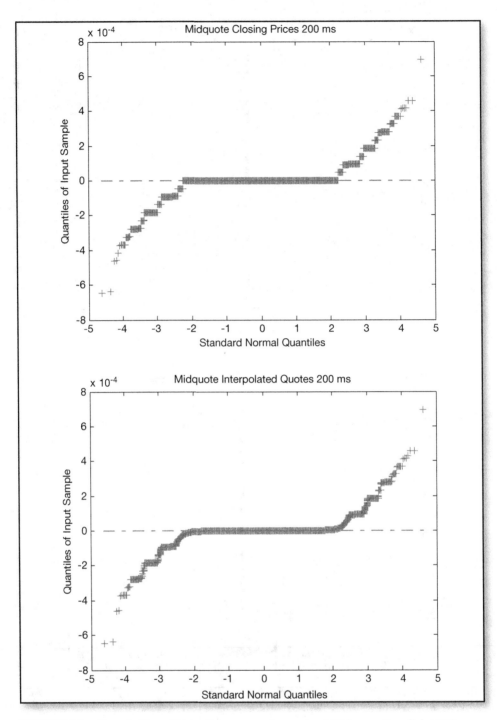

FIGURE 4.9   Quantile Plots: Closing Prices versus Interpolated Midquotes Sampled at 200 ms

Durations are often modeled using Poisson processes that assume that sequential events, like quote arrivals, occur independently of one another. The number of arrivals between any two time points t and $(t + \tau)$ is assumed to have a Poisson distribution. In a Poisson process, λ arrivals occur per unit time. In other words, the arrivals occur at an average rate of $(1/\lambda)$. The average arrival rate may be assumed to hold constant, or it may vary with time. If the average arrival rate is constant, the probability of observing exactly κ arrivals between times t and $(t + \tau)$ is

$$P[(N(t+\tau) - N(t)) = k] = \frac{1}{k!} e^{-\lambda \tau} (\lambda \tau)^k, \quad k = 0, 1, 2, \ldots \qquad (9)$$

Diamond and Verrecchia (1987) and Easley and O'Hara (1992) were the first to suggest that the duration between subsequent ticks carries information. Their models posit that in the presence of short-sale constraints, intertrade duration can indicate the presence of good news; in markets of securities where short selling is disallowed, the shorter the intertrade duration, the higher the likelihood of unobserved good news. The reverse also holds: in markets with limited short selling and normal liquidity levels, the longer the duration between subsequent trade arrivals, the higher the probability of yet-unobserved bad news. A complete absence of trades, however, indicates a lack of news.

Easley and O'Hara (1992) further point out that trades that are separated by a time interval have a much different information content than trades occurring in close proximity. One of the implications of Easley and O'Hara (1992) is that the entire price sequence conveys information and should be used in its entirety whenever possible, strengthening the argument for high-frequency trading.

Table 4.3 shows summary statistics for a duration measure computed on all trades recorded for SPY on May 13, 2009. As Table 4.3 illustrates, the average intertrade duration was the longest outside of regular market hours, and the shortest during the hour preceding the market close (3:00 to 4:00 p.m. ET).

The variation in duration between subsequent trades may be due to several other causes. While the lack of trading may be due to a lack of new information, trading inactivity may also be due to low levels of liquidity, trading halts on exchanges,

TABLE 4.3 Hourly Distributions of Intertrade Duration Observed on May 13, 2009, for SPY

| Hour (ET) | No. of Trades | Intertrade Duration (milliseconds) | | | | |
		Average	Median	Std. Dev.	Skewness	Kurtosis
4:00–5:00 a.m.	170	19,074.58	5,998	47,985.39	8.430986	91.11571
5:00–6:00 a.m.	306	11,556.95	4,781.5	18,567.83	3.687372	21.92054
6:00–7:00 a.m.	288	12,606.81	4,251	20,524.15	3.208992	16.64422
7:00–8:00 a.m.	514	7,096.512	2,995	11,706.72	4.288352	29.86546
8:00–9:00 a.m.	767	4,690.699	1,997	7,110.478	3.775796	23.56566
9:00–10:00 a.m.	1,089	2,113.328	1,934	24,702.9	3.5185	24.6587
10:00–11:00 a.m.	1,421	2,531.204	1,373	3,409.889	3.959082	28.53834
11:00–12:00 p.m.	1,145	3,148.547	1,526	4,323.262	3.240606	17.24866
12:00–1:00 p.m.	749	4,798.666	1,882	7,272.774	2.961139	13.63373
1:00–2:00 p.m.	982	3,668.247	1,739.5	5,032.795	2.879833	13.82796
2:00–3:00 p.m.	1,056	3,408.969	1,556	4,867.061	3.691909	23.90667
3:00–4:00 p.m.	1,721	2,094.206	1,004	2,684.231	2.9568	15.03321
4:00–5:00 p.m.	423	8,473.593	1,500	24,718.41	7.264483	69.82157
5:00–6:00 p.m.	47	73,579.23	30,763	113,747.8	2.281743	7.870699
6:00–7:00 p.m.	3	1,077,663	19,241	1,849,464	0.707025	1.5

and strategic motivations of traders. Foucault, Kadan, and Kandel (2005) consider that patiently providing liquidity using limit orders may itself be a profitable trading strategy, as liquidity providers should be compensated for their waiting. The compensation usually comes in the form of a bid-ask spread and is a function of the waiting time until the order limit is "hit" by liquidity takers; lower intertrade durations induce lower spreads. However, Dufour and Engle (2000) and Hasbrouck and Saar (2002) find that spreads are actually higher when traders observe short durations, contrasting the time-based limit order compensation hypothesis.

In addition to durations between subsequent trades and quotes, researchers have been modeling durations between fixed changes in security prices and volumes. The time interval between subsequent price changes of a specified magnitude is known as *price duration*. Price duration has been shown to decrease with increases in volatility. Similarly, the time interval between subsequent volume changes of a prespecified size is known as the *volume duration*. Volume duration has been shown to decrease with increases in liquidity.

Using a variant of the volume-duration methodology, Easley, Lopez de Prado, and O'Hara (2011) propose volume-based sampling of high-frequency data. In the volume-based approach, the researchers define a clock unit as a "bucket" of certain trade volume, say 50 futures contracts. The volume clock then "ticks" whenever the bucket is filled. Thus, the 50-contract volume clock advances whenever 50 single-contract trades arrive in sequence. The 50-contract volume clock advances twice when a 100-contract trade is executed.

The information content of quote, trade, price, and volume durations introduces biases into the estimation process, however. If the available information determines the time between subsequent trades, time itself ceases to be an independent variable, introducing substantial endogeneity bias into estimation. As a result, traditional estimates of variance of transaction prices are too high in comparison with the true variance of the price series.

■ Most High-Frequency Data Do Not Contain Buy-and-Sell Identifiers

Neither Level I nor Level II tick data contain identifiers specifying whether a given recorded trade was a result of a market buy order or a market sell order, yet some applications call for buy-and-sell trade identifiers as inputs into the models. To overcome this challenge, four methodologies have been proposed to estimate whether a trade was a buy or a sell from Level I data:

- Tick rule

- Quote rule

- Lee-Ready rule

- Bulk volume classification

The tick rule is one of the three most popular methodologies used to determine whether a given trade was initiated by a buyer or a seller, in the absence of such information in the data set. The other two popular methods are the quote rule and the Lee-Ready rule, after Lee and Ready (1991). The newest method is the bulk volume classification (BVC), due to Easley, Lopez de Prado, and O'Hara (2012).

According to the tick rule, the classification of a trade is performed by comparing the price of the trade to the price of the preceding trade; no bid or offer quote information is taken into account. Each trade is then classified into one of the four categories:

- *Uptick,* if the trade price is higher than the price of the previous trade.

- *Downtick,* if the trade price is lower than the price of the previous trade.

- *Zero-uptick,* if the price has not moved, but the last recorded move was an uptick.

- *Zero-downtick,* if the price has not moved, but the last recorded move was a downtick.

If the trade's price differs from that of the previous trade, the last trade is classified as an uptick or a downtick, depending on whether the price has moved up or moved down. If the price has not moved, the trade is classified as a zero-uptick or a zero-downtick, depending on the direction of the last nonzero price change. According to Ellis, Michaely, and O'Hara (2000), in 1997–1998, the tick rule correctly classified 77.66 percent of all Nasdaq trades. Figure 4.10 illustrates the tick rule.

The low proportion of correctly classified trades may be due to specifically to regulatory issues in equities. For example, Asquith, Oman, and Safaya (2008) report that the observed misclassifications are due at least in part to regulations requiring that short sales of stocks be executed on the uptick or zero-uptick (known as the *uptick rule*), the rule the Securities and Exchange Commission (SEC) repealed in 2007. Because nearly 30 percent of equity trades are short sales, Asquith et al. (2008) suggest that regulation-constrained short sales alone may be responsible for the observed errors in trade classification. In the absence of short-sale constraints, all of the preceding trade classifications are likely to be much more precise. On futures data, free from the uptick rule, Easley et al. (2012) indeed find that the tick rule delivers much higher accuracy in classifying trades into buyer initiated and seller

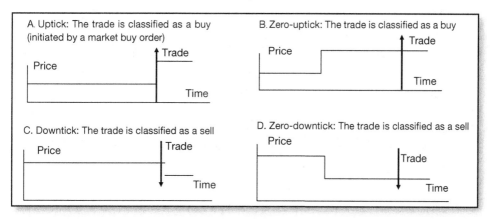

FIGURE 4.10 An Illustration of the Tick Rule, Used to Classify Trades into Buys and Sells

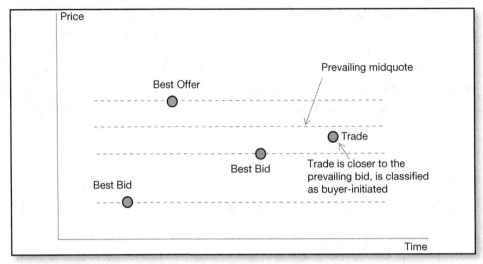

FIGURE 4.11 Example of the Quote Rule Classification

initiated. According to Easley et al. (2012) calculations, the tick rule correctly classifies 86.43 percent of all trades of E-mini futures on the S&P 500.

The quote rule is another way to classify quotes also documented by Lee and Ready (1991) and Ellis et al. (2000). Under this rule, a trade is a buy (sell) if the trade price is above (below) the average of the bid and the ask quotes prevailing at the time. If the trade price happens to be exactly at the midpoint of the prevailing bid and ask, the trade is not classified. While the quote rule is used often and has been shown to correctly classify 76.4 percent of all trades on Nasdaq (see Ellis et al., 2000), the definition of *prevailing quote* may be subject to interpretation and can potentially deliver a worse result than the tick rule. For example, Lee and Ready (1991) point out that quotes and trades are often reported out of sequence, making determination of the prevailing quote difficult. Specifically, they show that with the introduction of electronic books, quotes are often recorded ahead of the trades that triggered them. They propose to mitigate this situation by using the quotes at least five seconds ahead to classify trades. In 1991, five seconds was Nasdaq's median delay in reporting trades. However, the validity of the rule may have deteriorated over the past two decades as markets gained considerable speed since Lee and Ready's study was published. Figure 4.11 shows an example of the quote rule classification.

The so-called Lee-Ready rule classifies trades first using the quote rule. The trades occurring at the midpoint between the prevailing bid and ask quotes are not classified under the quote rule, and are subsequently classified using the tick rule. Once again, Lee and Ready (1991) emphasize matching trades with quotes that occurred at least five seconds prior in order to avoid erroneous sequencing of quotes. Dufour and Engle (2000) follow the five-second rule, while Ellis et al. (2000) object to it, showing that the trade reporting delay may differ depending on the end user's system. Ignoring the five-second delay, Ellis et al. (2000) show that the Lee-Ready rule correctly classifies just 81.05 percent of all trades as either buy or sell-initiated, a small improvement over the tick classification.

To further increase the accuracy of trade classification, Easley et al. (2012) propose a methodology that produces a probabilistic estimate of a particular volume generated by a market buy or a market sell order. The rule, named *bulk volume classification*, works as follows: for every unit of time or volume (a "volume bar," say every 100 shares traded), BVC assigns the probability of the observed volume being a buy as follows:

$$Pr(V_\tau = B) = Z\left(\frac{P_\tau - P_{\tau-1}}{\sigma \Delta P}\right) \tag{10}$$

where:

V_τ is the total volume observed during time or volume interval τ.

$P_\tau - P_{\tau-1}$ is the price difference observed between the two subsequent time or volume bars, $\tau - 1$ and τ.

$\sigma \Delta P$ is the standard deviation of sequential time or volume-clock based price changes.

Z is the pdf of a standard normal distribution.

The buyer-initiated trade volume can then be estimated as

$$V_\tau^B = V_\tau Z\left(\frac{P_\tau - P_{\tau-1}}{\sigma \Delta P}\right) \tag{11}$$

According to the BVC, the probability of a specific volume's being generated by a market sell order then becomes:

$$Pr(V_\tau = S) = 1 - Pr(V_\tau = B) = 1 - Z\left(\frac{P_\tau - P_{\tau-1}}{\sigma \Delta P}\right) \tag{12}$$

And the respective size of the seller-initiated volume is then

$$V_\tau^S = V_\tau\left(1 - Z\left(\frac{P_\tau - P_{\tau-1}}{\sigma \Delta P}\right)\right) \tag{13}$$

Easley et al. (2012) apply the BVC methodology to E-mini futures and show that the BVC rule correctly classifies 86.6 percent of all trades when time bars are used, and 90.7 percent of all trades when the volume clock is used instead of the time-based clock.

■ Summary

Tick data differ dramatically from low-frequency data. Utilization of tick data creates a host of opportunities not available at lower frequencies. A multitude of possible sampling and interpolation techniques creates diverse angles for data exploration.

Various methods of organizing and interpreting the discreet ticks of data deliver different statistical properties of the resulting time series.

■ End-of-Chapter Questions

1. What are the key properties of high-frequency data?
2. What types of data messages are most frequent?
3. What data sampling technique produces high-frequency time series most closely fitting the normal distribution?
4. What are the key differences between the tick trade classification rule and quote rule, Lee-Ready rule, and bulk volume classification rule?
5. Consider a trade executed at time t at 17.01, the best bid quote prevailing at time t. The previous trade, executed at time $t-1$, was executed at 17.00. Should the trade at time t be classified as buyer initiated or seller initiated under the quote rule? How should the trade completed at time t be classified under the tick rule?

CHAPTER 5

Trading Costs

Trading costs can make or break the profitability of a high-frequency trading strategy. Transaction costs that may be negligible for long-term strategies are amplified dramatically in a high-frequency setting.

This chapter focuses on the transparent and implicit costs that impact high-frequency trading.

■ Overview of Execution Costs

According to classical finance, markets are seamless, that is, they possess the following characteristics:

- Markets are uniform in their structure.

- Markets are consolidated; a price of a specific financial instrument is instantaneously updated wherever the instrument is traded.

- Prices immediately reflect all fundamental information.

- No transaction costs exist.

- Orders of all sizes can be executed instantaneously—markets are infinitely liquid, with each price queue in the limit order book containing infinite number of limit orders.

- Traders have unlimited borrowing power.

- No short-sale constraints exist.

- Market price is invariant to order size.

In real life, securities markets have frictions: prices incorporate information over time, markets differ in their structure and depth, markets can be highly fragmented, and issues like transaction costs further distort markets away from their textbook-perfect models. Costs known prior to trading activity are referred to as *transparent* or *explicit,* and costs that have to be estimated are known as *latent* or *implicit.* Likewise, the transparent costs are known with certainty prior to trading, and implicit costs are not known before trading takes place, yet implicit costs can be estimated from the costs' historical distribution inferred from the data of past trades.

■ Transparent Execution Costs

Transparent execution costs are generally known ahead of trading; they comprise broker commissions, exchange fees, and taxes. This section considers each of the transparent costs in detail.

Broker Commissions

Brokers charge commissions for

- Providing connectivity to exchanges, dark pools, and other trading venues.
- Facilitating "best execution" of client orders: executing client orders according to client specifications.
- Serving as the opposite side, or counterparty, to clients' orders in over-the-counter (OTC) arrangements.
- Providing custody of assets.
- Clearing trades from their execution to settlement and reporting trading activity.
- Delivering leverage and margin to clients.
- Other custom services.

Some broker-dealers may charge their customers additional fees for access to streaming market data and other premium information, such as proprietary research. Paid-for broker research is becoming increasingly obsolete as customers compete by retaining secrecy of their investment strategies. And while best execution presently accounts for a significant percentage of revenues for many brokers, clients with understanding of high-frequency data often choose to move away from brokers' best execution models, preferring to build their proprietary execution engines in-house instead. The latest best execution models are discussed in Chapters 15 of this book.

Broker fees can be fixed per order or month, or variable per trade size, trade value, or monthly volume. Broker commissions may also depend on the total business the broker receives from a given firm, various trade "bundling" options, and the extent of "soft-dollar," or implicit, transactions that the broker provides in addition to direct execution services. Broker commissions are negotiated well in advance of execution. The differences in cost estimates from one executing broker to another can be significant and are worth understanding to ensure favorable pricing.

Figure 5.1 shows the broker costs for metals trading offered by Interactive Brokers.

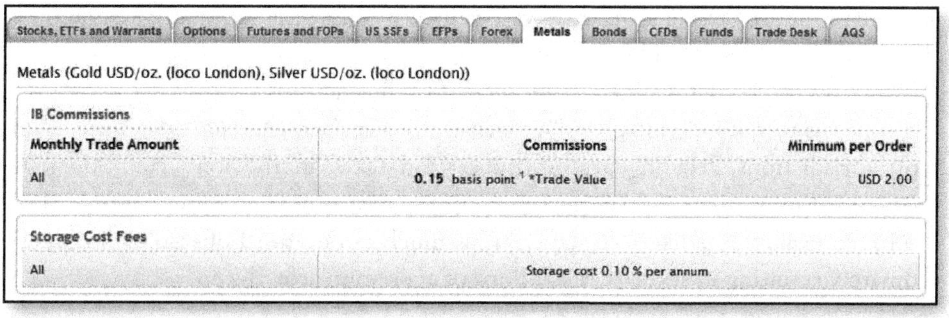

| Stocks, ETFs and Warrants | Options | Futures and FOPs | US SSFs | EFPs | Forex | **Metals** | Bonds | CFDs | Funds | Trade Desk | AQS |

Metals (Gold USD/oz. (loco London), Silver USD/oz. (loco London))

IB Commissions		
Monthly Trade Amount	**Commissions**	**Minimum per Order**
All	0.15 basis point [1] *Trade Value	USD 2.00

Storage Cost Fees	
All	Storage cost 0.10 % per annum.

FIGURE 5.1 Broker Commissions on Metal Trading Offered by Interactive Brokers
Source: Interactive Brokers web site

Exchange Fees

Exchanges match orders from different broker-dealers or electronic communication networks (ECNs) and charge fees for their services. The core product of every exchange is the liquidity, or presence of open buy-and-sell interest, that traders are looking to transact on the exchange.

Liquidity is created by open limit orders; limit buy orders placed at prices below the current ask provide liquidity, as do limit sell orders placed at prices above the current bid. Market orders, on the other hand, are matched immediately with the best limit orders available on the exchange, consuming liquidity. Limit orders can also consume liquidity; a limit buy placed at or above the market ask price will be matched immediately with the best available limit sell, thus removing the sell order from the exchange. Similarly, a limit sell placed at or below the market bid price will be immediately matched with the best available bid, as a market sell would.

To attract liquidity, exchanges may charge fees or pay rebates for orders consuming liquidity or for orders supplying liquidity. As discussed in Chapter 3, exchanges that charge for liquidity-removing orders and pay for liquidity-supplying orders are known as *normal* exchanges. Exchanges that pay for orders that remove liquidity and charge for orders that supply liquidity are called *inverted*. At the time this book was written, most U.S. equity exchanges deployed rebates in either normal or inverted models. Selected exchange ECNs in other countries now also offer rebate-based programs.

Exchange fees and fees of other trading venues can also vary by order type. Complicated orders, such as hidden-size orders like iceberg orders, or algo-enabled orders, like volume-weighted average price (VWAP) orders, carry associated cost premium.

Like broker commissions, exchange fees are negotiated in advance of execution.

Taxes

According to Benjamin Franklin, "in this world nothing can be said to be certain, except death and taxes." Taxes are charged from the net profits of the trading operation by the appropriate jurisdiction in which the operation is domiciled. High-frequency trading generates short-term profits that are usually subject to the full tax rate, unlike investments of one year or more, which fall under the reduced-tax capital gains umbrella in most jurisdictions. A local certified or chartered accountant should be able to provide a wealth of knowledge pertaining to proper taxation rates. Appropriate tax rates can be determined in advance of trading activity.

Proposals to tax individual trading transactions surface and fade over time, with most jurisdictions deciding against transaction taxes in the long run. Aldridge (2012b) estimates that a 0.05 percent tax imposed on every transaction of IBM stock, for example, is likely to wipe out as much as one third of trading volumes, ultimately resulting in severe contractions of economic growth.

■ Implicit Execution Costs

At the tick level of data, transparent costs are being increasingly dominated by implicit costs of the opportunity cost of investment, the bid-ask spread, latency or slippage, and related market impact. Additional implicit costs tracked by researchers and traders include the costs of price appreciation and market timing.

Bid-Ask Spreads

Bid-ask spreads are not known in advance. Instead, they are stochastic or random variables that are best characterized by the shape of the distribution of their historical values.

The bid-ask spread is the difference between the best ask and the best bid at any given point in time, and represents the cost of instantaneous liquidation of a trading position. The spread can also be seen as the premium paid by traders desiring immediate execution via market orders. On the flip side of the argument, the spread is the compensation paid to the patient traders providing liquidity through limit orders. The limit order traders take considerable risk of entering a losing position in the markets, the risk that increases with market volatility. As a result, limit traders' compensation also has to rise in times of higher uncertainty, a fact reflected in variability of the bid-ask spread in relation to volatility. Bid-ask spreads are discussed in detail in Chapter 4.

Slippage or Latency Costs

Latency cost, commonly known as *slippage,* is the adverse change in the market price of the traded security that occurs from the time an investment decision is made until the time the trade is executed. Slippage often accompanies market orders and refers to the difference between the best quote observed by the trader immediately prior to placing the order and the realized market price. The following example illustrates the concept of the latency cost or slippage. The trading strategy identifies a stock (e.g., IBM) to be a buy at $56.50, but by the time the market buy order is executed, the market price moves up to $58.00. In this case, the $1.50 differential between the desired price and the price obtained on execution is the cost of latency.

In the media, slippage is often portrayed as the evidence of the great divide between the haves and have-nots of the technological arms race. In reality, slippage is not solely dependent on the speed of trading activity. Instead, slippage is also a direct function of the a) liquidity available in the market and b) the number of market orders that have arrived to consume that liquidity. When many market participants simultaneously place market orders, the orders erode the finite liquidity and move the market price at high speeds in the process, as Figure 5.2 illustrates. As a result, slippage is typically larger during periods of high trading activity, for example, at market open

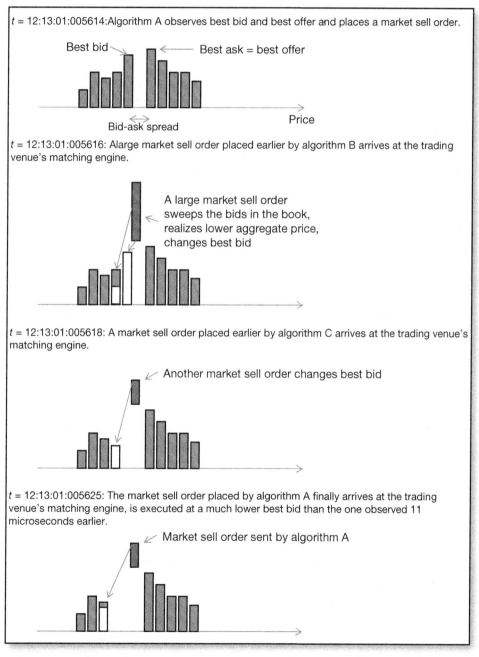

FIGURE 5.2 Slippage Illustration

and market close times, as well as times immediately following major macroeconomic announcements. The activity of other market participants can be forecasted in a probabilistic framework in the context of market impact, discussed next.

Still, latency due to technology alone can have a substantial impact on traders' performance. Stoikov and Rolf (2012), for example, find that ultra-fast trading infrastructure delivers significant profitability under certain forecasting assumptions. Specifically, Stoikov and Rolf (2012) define cost of latency as the expected value of dollar-denominated savings resulting from executing with slow and fast (low-latency) infrastructures:

$$COL = \mathbb{E}\,[S_{t+l} - S_t] \tag{1}$$

where S_{t+l} is the price obtained at time t with latency l and S_t is the price obtained on the same financial instrument at the same time t when latency l approaches zero. The authors observe that the cost of 10 milliseconds of communication delay is about twice that of an algorithm configured to run on only 1 millisecond of latency. In turn, 100 milliseconds of latency result in threefold latency cost as compared to that of an algo using 1 millisecond execution latency. An algorithm using infrastructure with a delay of 1 minute incurs an associated cost of four times greater than the algorithm with just 1 millisecond latency.

The shortcomings of technology resulting in latency costs may or may not reside in the trader's domain. Specifically, latency can occur in any of the following nodes of order routing:

1. *Trader's systems.* Slow systems and network architecture cause delays in processing and interpreting quotes.
2. *Networks.* Congestion and interruptions in network communications may disrupt timely execution and can delay transmission of orders. In addition, geographic differences between the location of the trader's servers and the location of the execution venue can cause latency by virtue of physical communication delays. Distances increase the time each quote or trade has to travel to their destinations, increasing trading latency. Latencies between major financial centers of the world are reported in Chapter 2. Co-location and private network connections with trading venue servers may help alleviate these issues.
3. *Broker-dealers.* Delays in broker-dealer routing engines prompted innovations of direct market access.
4. *Execution venues.* Execution venues may experience overloads of simultaneous orders resulting in an order-processing backlog and subsequent delay in execution. Such situations most often occur in high-volatility environments.

While latency costs are random and cannot be known with precision in advance of a trade, distribution of latency costs inferred from past trades can produce the expected cost value to be used within the trading strategy development process. Fast infrastructure, backup communication systems, and continuous human supervision of trading activity can detect network problems and route orders to their destinations along alternative backup channels, ensuring a continuous transmission of trading information.

Price Appreciation and Timing Risk Costs

Both price appreciation and timing risk costs describe market risk incurred during execution of a large position broken down into a series of child orders (see Chapter 15 for a discussion of child orders).

The price appreciation cost refers to the forecasted loss of investment value during the execution of a large position. The timing cost refers to random, unforecasted price movement ahead of execution of a child order.

The following EUR/USD trade illustrates the concept of a price appreciation cost. A trading strategy determines that EUR/USD is undervalued at 1.3560, and a buy order of $100 million EUR/USD is placed that must be executed over the next three minutes. The forecast turns out to be correct, and EUR/USD appreciates to 1.3660 over the following two minutes. The price appreciation cost is therefore 50 bps per minute. The price appreciation cost is due to the fundamental appreciation of price, not the trading activity in EUR/USD.

The cost of timing risk describes by how much, on average, the price of the traded security can randomly appreciate or depreciate within 1 second, 10 seconds, 1 minute, and so on from the time an investment decision is made until the market order is executed. The timing risk cost applies to active market timing activity, usually executed using market orders. The timing risk cost does not apply to limit orders, where the execution price is fixed.

Opportunity Costs

The opportunity cost is the cost associated with inability to complete an order. Most often, opportunity cost accompanies limit order–based strategies, when the market price does not cross the specified limit price. However, market orders can also fail to execute, for example, when the market does not have the liquidity sufficient to fulfill the order. On a U.S. equity exchange, a market order may fail to execute when the exchange does not have the limit orders posted at the National Best Bid and Offer (NBBO), as discussed in Chapter 3. The opportunity cost is measured as the profit expected to be generated had the order been executed.

Market Impact Costs

Market impact cost measures the adverse change in the market price following an order. Market impact is rapidly becoming the dominant transaction cost. In equities, according to the ITG Global Trading Cost Review (2010), market impact consumed 0.387 percent of the total dollar amount traded. Per report, the total amount of trading costs averaged 0.476 percent of turnover, with only 0.089 percent of the dollar volume spent on commissions. These figures were comparable in the U.S., EU, U.K., and Japanese equity markets; higher transaction costs were reported in emerging markets. In futures, both market impact and transaction costs appear lower, yet market impact costs still dominate: according to Aldridge (2012c), market impact observed in Eurobund futures (FGBL) on Eurex is 0.020 percent of the dollar volume.

Institutional transaction costs in the futures and forex markets tend to be in the $5 to $10 per every $1 million volume traded, or 0.0005 to 0.0010 percent of executed dollar volume. This section considers the cause and estimation of market impact.

■ Background and Definitions

All trades and orders convey information. The mere fact that a trader is placing his own money or reputation on the line to bet on a particular direction of the market informs other market participants of the trader's belief.

The information contained in a trade observation is much more potent than that in an opinion of a news analyst. Analysts are typically compensated via a salary, often irrespective of whether their prognoses come true. At the same time, traders are usually compensated via a percentage of profits they derive from their trading, with each trade having direct implications on the trader's welfare. As a result, trades are viewed as potent signals about beliefs of impending market moves. The larger the order, the more credible the trading signal.

Both aggressive and passive orders (market orders and limit orders) are credible signals—market orders are commitments to buy or sell a security immediately at the best market price, and limit orders are commitments to buy or sell at a predefined price when the opposite market trade is available. As such, both market orders and limit orders emit market impact. Unlike market orders, however, limit orders can be canceled. As a result, limit orders make less credible signals than market orders, and the intensity and even the direction of market and limit orders may differ.

The idea of an order as a credible signal was first published in 1971. The thought of signaling in the markets was so revolutionary at the time that the author of the research dared to publish the theory only under an assumed name, Bagehot, after a famous English nineteenth-century journalist covering topics in economics.

The mere existence of market impact runs against core principles of classical finance. In the idealized financial world, under the concept of market efficiency, considered to be the optimal steady state in most classical asset pricing models, the following conditions are assumed to hold:

- Everyone simultaneously receives the same information.

- Everyone interprets information in identical way.

- Only the fundamental information, such as earnings announcements or interest rates, affects security prices. Past price trends and other nonfundamental information has no relevance to security prices.

- All the relevant information is impounded into prices immediately upon information arrival, resulting in a sharp step function of security prices moving from one fundamental level to the next. Trades themselves carry no information, as all the information is already contained in prices. Figure 5.3 illustrates the perfect markets' response to an arrival of positive fundamental news, as well as to periods without any news arrivals.

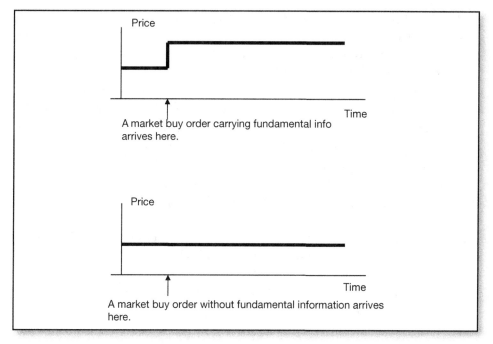

FIGURE 5.3 Classical Finance View on How Perfect Markets Incorporate Fundamental Information

In reality, traders interpret news differently, a result of divergent investment horizons, education, effort and experiences. On the subject of the impending price movement, opinions of long-term investors are likely to differ from those of short-term investors (see Hasbrouck, 1991, for example), a fact that has allowed both short-term and long-term investors to coexist without eating each other's proverbial lunch. Similarly, investors deploying technical market analysis disagree with quants and fundamental analysts. Traders poring over the information 15 hours a day are also likely to have an opinion different from a casual investor briefly analyzing his mutual fund statements only quarterly. Finally, a seasoned professional may have a point of view divergent from that of a newbie. All of these factors contribute to the markets' deviation from idealized conditions, and make trades and even orders able to carry information to other market participants.

In addition, most information is impounded into prices gradually, as first noted by Kyle (1985), and not instantaneously, as the study of classical finance would prefer. Every trade is a result of a buy order meeting a sell order. Often, a trade is a product of one market order meeting an opposing limit order, although two price-meeting limit orders of opposite direction may also be matched to form a trade. A trade is a product of opposing forces: supply and demand, and, in theory, each trade does not move the markets much. In the short-term reality, however, the opposite holds:

- Market buy orders are on average followed by a rise in prices of the traded securities, while market sell orders on average result in lower prices.

■ Limit buy-and-sell orders also generate a market impact in anticipation of a future trade (see Harris, 1997; Parlour and Seppi, 2007; Boulatov and George, 2008; and Rosu, 2010). As a result, limit orders have also been shown to be followed by a persistent price change (see Eisler, Bouchaud, and Kockelkoren, 2009; and Hautsch and Huang, 2011). While a completed trade is an irreversible and most credible signal, limit orders are cancelable indications of trading interest, and, as a result, are smaller in magnitude than that for market orders. Hautsch and Huang (2011) and Aldridge (2012c) estimate the market impact of a limit order to be about 25 percent of that of a similar market order. The direction of the price change following a limit order may be reversed relative to that of a comparable market order, depending on how far is the limit order price away from the market price.

Figure 5.4 illustrates gradual adjustment of prices in response to positive news and no news observed in actual trading conditions. When positive news arrives, the market price tends to overshoot its fundamental level, with the overshoot component gradually settling or decaying to its fundamental level.

Information leakage accompanying orders and trades is hardly new: for years, broker-dealers and other market participants with access to tick-level data competed on being able to "read the ticker tape" and infer short-term price forecasts from that. By continuously watching the ticker tape, manual market makers would learn the information content of trades and adjust their quotes according to their short-term predictions—in the process resembling a manual variant of today's high-frequency trading. As markets become increasingly computerized, however, the ticker tape is moving increasingly fast, and it is now literally impossible for a human eye to parse ticker-tape information in real time.

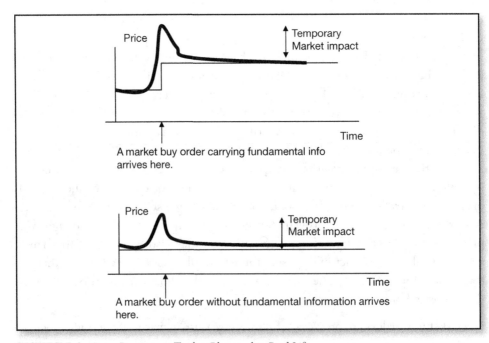

FIGURE 5.4 Price Reaction to Trades Observed in Real Life

This phenomenon of real-life price changes following news and orders is known as *market impact* (MI). MI can be attributed to several factors including:

- In the trading world with heterogeneous traders possessing different beliefs and information, MI is the negotiation or tâtonnement process via which traders' information and beliefs are impounded into the security prices.

- Both market and limit orders represent traders' commitments of money and reputation, and therefore form credible signals to other market participants who may choose to trade in the same direction.

- Every market buy (sell) order temporarily depletes liquidity supply on the ask (bid) side of the order book, driving the next market buy (sell) order to be matched against a higher (lower) best available limit order price.

■ Estimation of Market Impact

The metric of MI answers the question, "How much would the trader move the price if he were to make the trade?" Figure 5.5 illustrates the MI determination for a single order. The impact of the order incoming to the exchange at time t^*, for example, can be measured as the price change observed after time t^* relative to the last trade price recorded before t^*, as illustrated in Figure 5.5. The selected postorder reference trade time t can be measured in clock time, trade time, tick time, or volume time. In clock time, time t is selected as x time units, say 10 seconds, post order arrival time t^*. In trade time, the MI is measured y number of trades following the order observed at t^*. In tick time, the impact is computed z ticks, quote revisions or trades, past the order. Finally, in volume time, the impact is measured when the aggregate trade volume following the order of interest reaches at least V trading units (e.g., shares or contracts). Tick-time and trade-time MI is computationally easier to estimate than clock-time or volume-time impact.

While the exact impact following a future trade can never be known in advance of the trade, the *expected* MI can be estimated using historical data and trade-specific characteristics. The logic for estimating expectation of MI is similar to the logic used to forecast price levels: while the exact future price can never be pinpointed with full precision,

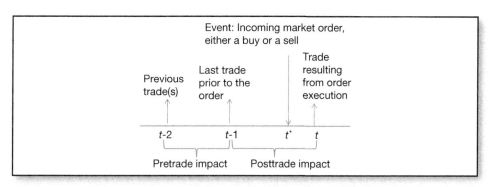

FIGURE 5.5 Estimation of Market Impact for an Order Arriving at an Exchange at Time t^*

an expectation of the future price can be formed based on some auxiliary metrics. The expected MI can be measured in an event-study framework using recent historical data.

MI can turn a profitable strategy into a losing one. A strategy that relies on repeating trades, for example, may be distorted by MI, with sequential trades obtaining much worse prices than expected.

As noted earlier, MI is a function of order size: the larger the trade, the more credible the information conveyed by the trade, the higher the impact the trade generates. The exact evolution or functional form of MI is important: a trader can increase the size of his investment while remaining profitable when the MI grows slowly with trade size (see Farmer, Gerig, Lillo, and Waelbroeck, 2009). Glosten (1987) and Easley and O'Hara (1987) were the first to note that MI can be broken down into two distinct functional parts: permanent and temporary MI. Permanent MI impounds fundamental information into prices in a manner consistent with the classical financial theory and the efficient market hypothesis (see Fama, 1970). Temporary MI is the noise component that first overshoots the fundamental price level and then decays with time until the fundamental price level is reached.

The precise shapes of permanent and temporary MI functions have been subjects of competing theories. Breen, Hodrick and Korajczyk (2002) and Kissell and Glantz (2002), for example, suggested that MI is a linear function of the order size ($MI_t \propto V_{t*}$). Lillo, Farmer, and Mangegna (2003), however, detected a power law specification ($MI_t \propto (V_{t*})^\beta$). The latest research on the topic (see Huberman and Stanzl, 2004; and Gatheral, 2009), however, reconciles the linear and power-law specifications by finding an order-size-based linear relationship for the permanent MI and time-based power-law decay for temporary impact, as shown in Figure 5.6.

For market orders, the MI appears strongly concave in the order size, and the signs of market orders are autocorrelated in time: market buy orders tend to follow other market buy orders, and vice versa. A model unifying the preceding facts expresses the MI function as follows (Eisler, Bouchaud, and Kockelkoren, 2009):

$$P_t = \sum_{t^*<t} [G(t,t^*)\epsilon t^*(v_{t*})^\theta + n_{t*}] + P_\infty \tag{2}$$

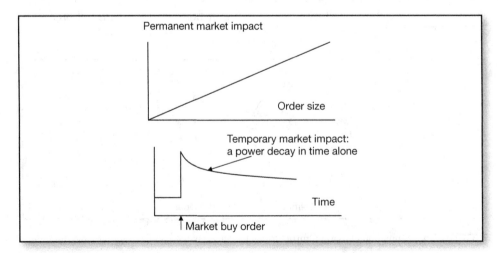

FIGURE 5.6 Functional Form of Market Impact: Permanent and Temporary Components

where:

v_{t^*} is the volume of the trade at time t^*

ϵ_{t^*} is the sign of the trade at time t^*

n_{t^*} is the independent noise term that models any price change not induced by news

$G(t, t^*)$ is the propagator function, which describes, on average, how prices respond to a single trade over time; $G(t, t^*)$ decays with time

The MI of an individual order recorded at time t^* is then

$$MI_{t^*} = G(t,t^*)\epsilon_{t^*}(v_{t^*})^{\theta} + n_{t^*} \qquad (3)$$

The MI propagator function $G(t,t^*)$ has to decay with time, and in a specific way, to satisfy the high autocorrelation of direction of subsequent trades. If G did not decay, price returns would be proportional to the signs of the trades and returns would be highly autocorrelated in time. According to Eisler, Bouchaud and Kockelkoren (2009), G decays as follows:

$$G(t,t^*) \sim |t-t^*|^{-\beta} \qquad (4)$$

where $= \dfrac{1-\gamma}{2}$, and $\gamma < 1$ is the decay parameter in the correlation of subsequent trade signs:

$$C(l) = (\epsilon_t \epsilon_{t+l}) \sim (l)^{-\gamma} \qquad (5)$$

$G(t, t^*)$ further has the following boundary properties:

$$G\left(t \to t^*\right) = \frac{\partial p_t}{\partial \xi_t} \qquad (6)$$

where $\xi_t = \epsilon_t v_t^{\theta} \sim N(0,\sigma)$ is normally distributed with mean zero and standard deviation σ.

In addition to trade size and time, however, MI has been empirically shown to depend on other variables. In equities, MI has been shown to depend on:

- Intertrade durations (see Dufour and Engle, 2000)

- Stock-specific characteristics, such as industry and earnings of the issuing company (see Breen, Hodrick, and Korajchyk, 2002; Lillo, Farmer, and Mantegna, 2003; and Almgren, Thum, Hauptmann, and Li, 2005)

- Volatility and spread (Ferraris, 2008)

In futures, MI has been found to vary with:

- Liquidity (see Burgardt, Hanweck, and Lei, 2006)

- Intertrade durations and volatility (see Aldridge, 2012c)

The size and the direction of MI of a limit order has been found to depend on the size of the order as well as on the order's proximity to the best quote on the opposing side of the market. For buy limit orders placed on Nasdaq within the spread (see Hautsch and Huang, 2011, for details), orders than went on to be matched with the best ask experienced a positive MI, just as market buy orders would. Buy limit orders placed within the spread that became the best bid quotes on average experienced a negative MI of the size comparable to that of the orders matched with the best ask. The MI of a limit buy order that was posted inside the spread and became the best bid, however, varied with the size of the order:

- Small-sized buy limit orders, with a size matching the depth at the bid, placed inside the spread that became best bids were on average followed by *negative* MI.

- Midsized (seven times larger than depth at the bid) were followed by a small *positive* MI, about 20 percent of the absolute MI experienced by small orders.

- Large orders (15 times larger than depth at the bid) were followed by a medium *positive* MI, about 50 percent of the absolute MI experienced by small orders.

Figure 5.7 summarizes the findings.

■ Empirical Estimation of Permanent Market Impact

Data Preparation

MI can be estimated using both Level I and Level II tick data, as well as data containing trade stamps only. Level II data allow one to precisely pinpoint arrivals of limit and market orders: an increase in the aggregate size at a specific price level on the bid size indicates an arrival of a limit buy order. A decrease in the top-of-the-book liquidity on the bid side indicates an arrival of a market sell order.

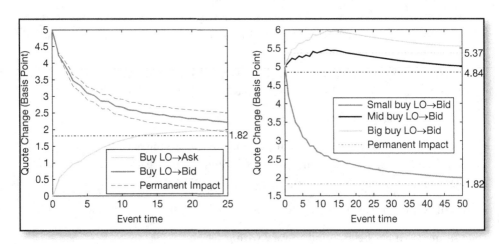

FIGURE 5.7 Market Impact of Limit Orders Observed on Nasdaq
Source: Hautsch and Huang (2011)

When using Level I or trade data, however, one comes across the challenge of separating buyer- and seller-initiated orders and trades. Over the years, researchers have developed several methodologies to separate buys and sells: tick, quote, Lee-Ready, and bulk volume classification, discussed in detail in Chapter 4.

Basic Estimation Model

Data points separated into buys and sells are ready for estimation of permanent MI. Under the assumption of linear functional form, the permanent MI can be estimated using a linear regression with the following specification:

$$\Delta P_{t,\tau} = \alpha_\tau + \beta_\tau V_t + \beta_{\tau-1} V_{t+1} + \ldots + \beta_1 V_{t+\tau-1} + \varepsilon_{t,\tau} \tag{7}$$

where t is the time of the trade, τ is the number of posttrade ticks or time units in the event window at which the trade impact is measured, V_t is the size of the trade observed at time t, and $\Delta P_{t,\tau}$ is the normalized price change from time t to time τ and can be expressed as shown in equation (8):

$$\Delta P_{t,\tau} = \ln(P_\tau) - \ln(P_t) \tag{8}$$

Figures 5.8 and 5.9 show $\widehat{\alpha}_5$ and $\widehat{\beta}_5$ estimated five trade ticks following each trade on tick data of every trading day in 2009 and 2010 for Eurobund futures (FGBL), per Aldridge (2012c). As Figure 5.8 and 5.9 show, buyer-initiated trades

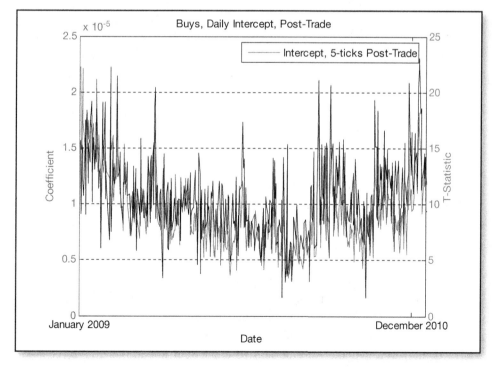

FIGURE 5.8 Daily Intercept $\widehat{\alpha}_5$ of Model (7) Estimated on Buyer-Initiated Trades in Eurobund Futures, 2009–2010

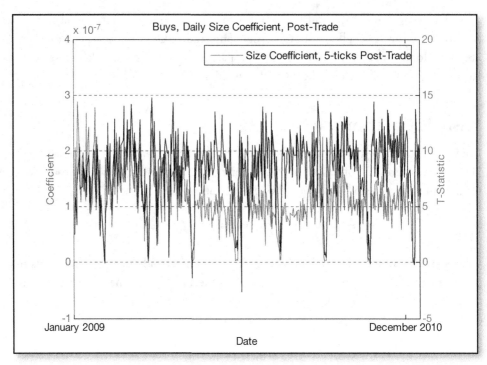

FIGURE 5.9 Daily Size Coefficient $\widehat{\beta}_s$ of Model (7) Estimated on Buyer-Initiated Trades in Eurobund Futures, 2009–2010

display the following properties. The 5-tick market impact of buy trades exhibits very strong positive dependency on trade size: the t-statistics of $\widehat{\beta}_5$ often reach 10, as shown on the right axis of Figure 5.9, indicating that the dependency on trade size is 99.999 percent statistically significant. While the MI's dependency on trade size is highly persistent, the actual value of the coefficient estimate, $\widehat{\beta}_5$, is small: as the left axis shows, $\widehat{\beta}_5$ is on the order of 10^{-7}, in other words, for every 100 contracts of Eurobund futures traded, the futures price directly attributable to the trading size on average rose by only 0.001 percent five ticks after each trade. The observed results are largely invariant from one day to the next, with clear exceptions at the end of each quarter when the statistical significance of the estimates appears to dip to zero, possibly due to regular rollovers of futures.

Figure 5.8 plots daily estimates of $\widehat{\alpha}_s$, the average increase in FGBL price observed following buyer-initiated trades that cannot be attributed to trade sizes. As the $\widehat{\alpha}_s$ value (left) axis in Figure 5.8 shows, the average size-independent component of price increase following buy trades is on the order of 10^{-5}, or about 100 times larger than the price change attributable to trade size. As such, the size-independent market impact dominates size-dependent impact for trades under 100 Eurobund futures contracts, resulting in the following Eurobund-futures specific feature: FGBL trades of 1 or 100 contracts incur comparable market impact! Trades larger than 100 FGBL contracts, however, generate substantial size-dependent impact. The observed size-independent impact $\widehat{\alpha}_s$ is highly statistically persistent, with accompanying t-ratios ranging from about 5 to 20, as the right axis of Figure 5.8 notes. Seller-initiated trades incur a similar scale of market impact, yet in the opposite direction, as Figures 5.10 and 5.11 show.

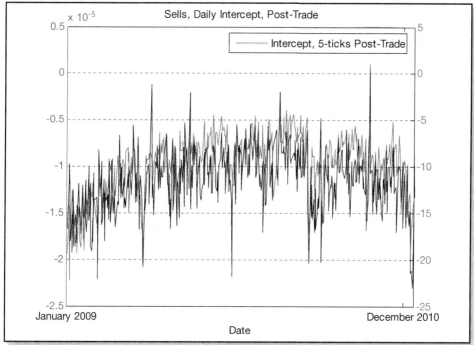

FIGURE 5.10 Daily Intercept $\widehat{\alpha}_s$ of Model (7) Estimated on Seller-Initiated Trades in Eurobund Futures, 2009–2010

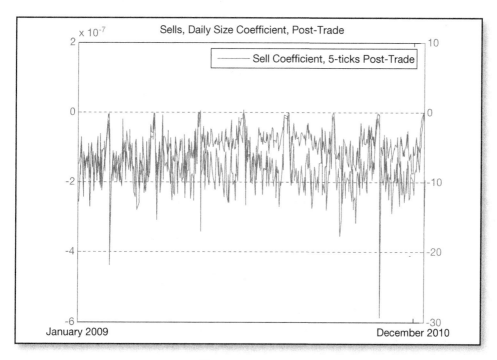

FIGURE 5.11 Daily Size Coefficient $\widehat{\beta}_s$ of Model (7) Estimated on Seller-Initiated Trades in Eurobund Futures, 2009–2010

The statistical meaningfulness, or the explanatory power, of model in the equation (7) applied to buyer-initiated trades is quite low, however, as measured by the adjusted R-squared of the model and ranging from 1 to 2 percent, as Figure 5.12 illustrates. To put the 1 to 2 percent adjusted R-squared in perspective, though, one needs to consider the adjusted R-squared on predictive power of generalized autoregressive conditional heteroskedasticity (GARCH), a popular volatility estimation model used in many commercial applications. The R-squared of predictive power of GARCH usually hits only about 5 percent. In other words, while the R-squared of the model of equation (7) is quite low in principle, it is comparable to R-squared estimates of other popular models.

Additional Explanatory Variables The strong significance of the intercept $\widehat{\alpha}_s$ in the model of equation (7) invites questions about what kind of additional variables, if any, can help the unexplained variation captured by $\widehat{\alpha}_s$. Commercial models for estimation of market impact often deploy additional explanatory variables, such as the observed spread, short-term volatility, and intertrade durations. To analyze the potential impact of these variables, one can extend the model of equation (7) as follows:

$$\Delta P_{t,\tau} = \alpha_\tau + \beta_{V,\tau} V_t + \beta_{\sigma,\tau} \widehat{\sigma}_t + \beta_{S,\tau} \widehat{S}_t + \beta_{T,\tau} \widehat{T}_t + \varepsilon_{t,\tau} \qquad (9)$$

where:

- As before, $\Delta P_{t,\tau}$ represents the τ-tick change in price,

$$\Delta P_{t,\tau} = \ln(P_\tau) - \ln(P_{t-\tau}) \qquad (10)$$

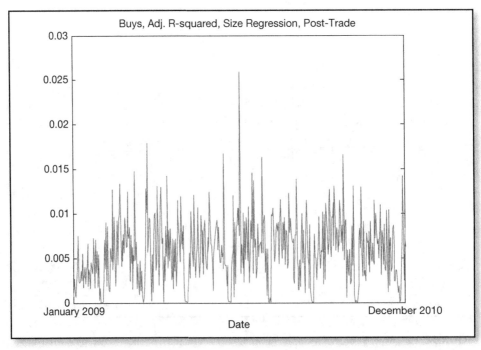

FIGURE 5.12 Explanatory Power of the Linear Market Impact Estimator of Equation (7)

- V_t denotes the size of the trade recorded at t

- $\hat{\sigma}_t$ is the estimate of short-term volatility, and can be measured in several ways, as standard deviation, or as a log change of high and low prices during a predefined pretrade period beginning $\tau*$ ticks before the trade tick t, as first suggested by Garman and Klass (1980):

$$\sigma_t = \ln\left(P_{High,[t-\tau*,t-1]}\right) - \ln\left(P_{Low,[t-\tau*,t-1]}\right) \tag{11}$$

- $\hat{S}_t$ is the average spread observed during the $\tau*$ ticks preceding each trade. In data containing quotes, the average spread is the mean difference between the best offer and the best bid:

$$S_t = \frac{1}{\tau-1} \sum_{j=t-\tau}^{t-1} Ask_j - Bid_j \tag{12}$$

- When quote data is unavailable, the average effective spread can still be estimated by assuming that sequential price changes occur at intervals equal to the effective spread. Such an assumption generally holds true whenever a buy follows a sell and vice versa, as the market buy is executed at the best ask, and the market sell hits the best bid. The resulting expression for the average effective spread is shown in equation (19), an approximation noted by Aldridge (2012c):

$$S_t = \frac{1}{\tau-1} \sum_{j=t-\tau}^{t-1} |\ln(P_j) - \ln(P_{j-1})| \; where \; P_j \neq P_{j-1} \tag{13}$$

- Finally, $\hat{T}_t$ is the average clock time between every two subsequent trades:

$$T_t = \frac{1}{\tau-1} \sum_{j=t-\tau}^{t-1} t_j - t_{j-1} \tag{14}$$

Aldridge (2012c) estimates equation (9) in FGBL data. In FGBL, the additional explanatory variables influence the resulting market impact, but do not eliminate the statistical significance of the intercept, or change the value of the trade size coefficient, $\beta_{V,\tau}$. The impact of intertrade durations, $\hat{T}_t$, is consistent with that described by Dufour and Engle (2000): MI is lower when average intertrade durations are shorter. According to Dufour and Engle (2000), the observation is likely due to the following: shorter intertrade durations allow more gradual impounding of information into prices, resulting in lower price changes in response to each trade.

Causality   The estimates of MI coefficients obtained from models of equations (7) and (9) can be questioned from the following perspective: since MI is measured several ticks after each trade, is it possible that other trade ticks determine the impact and its relationship with trading volume? For example, could the size of a trade truly impact the size and directions of the following trades, which in turn would exaggerate market impact and make it appear dependent on the original trade size, instead of the follow-up trade sizes?

To answer these questions, one can deploy the so-called vector autoregressive (VAR) model (different from value-at-risk, VaR, model), first proposed by Hasbrouck (1991), and later extended by Dufour and Engle (2000). The VAR model answers the following key cause-and-effect question: does MI influence direction of subsequent trades, or does direction and size of trades influence MI to a greater degree? In addition, the VAR model allows us to test for auxiliary effects, such as any persistent irregularities during different times of day.

The Dufour and Engle (2000) specification of the VAR model that ascertains causality within five ticks from the time of each trade can be written as follows:

$$\Delta P_t = \sum_{j=1}^{5} a_j \Delta P_{t-j} + \sum_{t=8}^{18} \gamma_t D_{t,i} + \sum_{j=0}^{5} b_j Q_{i-j} + \varepsilon_i \tag{15}$$

$$Q_i = \sum_{j=1}^{5} c_j \Delta P_{t-j} + \sum_{t=8}^{18} \delta_t D_{t,i} + \sum_{j=1}^{5} d_j Q_{i-j} + \vartheta_i \tag{16}$$

where

R_i is the instantaneous market impact following a trade tick i, calculated as a one-tick log return, that is, as a difference of logarithms of the price of tick i, and the price of the previous trade tick i-1.

$$\Delta P_t = \ln(P_t) - \ln(P_{t-1}) \tag{17}$$

Q_i is the direction of the trade i, with $Q_i = 1$ when a trade is a result of a buy market order, and $Q_i = -1$ for seller-initiated trades

$D_{t,i}$ is a "dummy" variable indicating the hour of the day:

$$D_{t,i} = \begin{cases} 1, \text{if trade } i \text{ occurs in hour } t \\ 0, \text{otherwise} \end{cases} \tag{18}$$

b_j and d_j, in turn, are functions of trade size:

$$b_j = \alpha_j + \beta_j \ln(V_j) \tag{19}$$

$$d_j = \theta_j + \rho_j \ln(V_j) \tag{20}$$

Equation (15) measures dependency of posttrade one-tick MI R_i on the following data: lagged one-tick market impact of five preceding trades, time of day when each trade occurred, contemporaneous and lagged direction of five preceding trades, Q, and the product of contemporaneous and lagged trade direction and trade size QV. Equation (16) considers how well the same explanatory variables predict the direction of the next trade. In other words, equation (16) considers whether the past five one-tick returns, time of day, directions and sizes of the previous five trades can predict the direction of the impending trade.

Tables 5.2 and 5.3 show results of estimation of equations (15) and (16), respectively, on Eurobund futures data for May 6, 2009, a regular trading day exactly one

TABLE 5.2 Results of OLS Estimation of VAR model, Equation (15), on Eurobund futures (FGBL) Trade Tick Data for May 6, 2009 R_i

Independent Variable: R_{i-j}		Independent Variable: Q_{i-j}		Independent Variable: $V_i Q_{i-j}$	
		α_0	4.1 E-05 (67.4)	β_0	1.9 E-07 (25.9)
a_1	0.347 (71.1)	α_1	−1.3 E-05 (−18.6)	β_1	8.5 E-09 (1.0)
a_2	0.151 (29.0)	α_2	−2.8 E-06 (−3.9)	β_2	2.7 E-08 (3.5)
a_3	0.080 (15.2)	α_3	2.7 E-06 (3.8)	β_3	2.5 E-08 (3.2)
a_4	0.061 (11.8)	α_4	7.7 E-06 (11.0)	β_4	8.4 E-09 (1.0)
a_5	−0.306 (-62.5)	α_5	−2.4 E-05 (−37.6)	β_5	−1.1 E-07 (−14.8)
		Adj. R^2 = 46.25%			

Dependent variable is the one-tick return, R_i. T-statistics are reported in parentheses, bold-font values represent statistical significance of 99.999 percent and higher. *Source: Aldridge (2012d)*.

year prior to the "flash crash." As shown in Table 5.2, instantaneous MI is indeed determined by MI accompanying previous trades, contemporaneous and lagged trade sign, and concurrent trade size. Trade sizes of previous trades have shown to produce little impact on future MI. The hourly dummy variable measuring the effects of the time of day was statistically significant only for the 10 to 11 GMT time period. The trades executed between 10 and 11 GMT had a lower market impact than trades executed at other hours of the day. This could, potentially be due to price trending in response to macroeconomic news. Interestingly, the explanatory power of the regression, measured by Adj. R^2, was 46.25 percent—a substantial figure.

As Table 5.3 shows, neither the trade size nor the market impact generated by past trades (except the most recent trade) play a significant role in determining direction of upcoming trades. Instead, the direction of the subsequent trades is almost entirely determined by the direction of immediately preceding trades, buy or sell, independent of the size of those trades or the market impact each of the preceding trades generates. Specifically, according to the estimates presented in Table 5.3, on May 6, 2009, an FGBL trade immediately following a buy had a 46.2 percent likelihood of also being a buy; while a trade following two consecutive buys had a 62.5 percent probability of being a buy. A trade following three consecutive buys was 69.3% likely to be buyer initiated, and after four sequential buy trades, the probability of observing a buy rose to 72.5 percent, a large number. The hourly dummy in the trade

TABLE 5.3 Results of OLS Estimation of VAR Model, Equation (16), on FGBL Trade Tick Data for May 6, 2009 Q_i

Independent Variable: R_{i-j}		Independent Variable: Q_{i-j}		Independent Variable: $V_i Q_{i-j}$	
c_1	−841.5 (−18.1)	θ_1	0.462 (75.8)	ρ_1	2.0 E-04 (2.8)
c_2	−94.1 (−1.8)	θ_2	0.163 (24.6)	ρ_2	1.6 E-04 (2.1)
c_3	184.5 (3.6)	θ_3	0.068 (10.1)	ρ_3	1.4 E-04 (1.9)
c_4	55.7 (1.1)	θ_4	0.032 (4.7)	ρ_4	1.3 E-04 (1.8)
c_5	−10.2 (−0.2)	θ_5	0.010 (1.7)	ρ_5	2.4 E-04 (3.3)
		Adj. R^2 = 39.29%			

Dependent variable is trade direction, Q_i. T-statistics are reported in parentheses and bold-font values represent statistical significance of 99.999 percent and higher. *Source: Aldridge (2012d)*.

sign equation happened to be only significant from 16 to 17 GMT (11:00 a.m. to noon ET). The hourly dummy from 16 to 17 GMT was positive, indicating a preponderance of buy FGBL trades during that hour on May 6, 2009. As with the estimates of the return equation (15), equation (16) showed a high adjusted R^2 of nearly 40 percent, indicating a high explanatory power of the given variables.

A question that begs further investigation is whether market conditions change dramatically one year later during the flash crash of May 6, 2010. Tables 5.4 and 5.5 present the answers: May 6, 2010 (flash crash), values exhibit little difference from a regular market day May 6, 2009, one year prior.

As shown in Aldridge (2012c), estimates of equation (15) recorded on May 6, 2009, are very similar to those estimated on the data of the flash crash, implying that the MI model performs well in most market conditions. As Aldridge (2012c) also shows, the model of equation (15) makes robust out-of-sample predictions of future market impact, delivering 99.9 percent accurate predictions of MI based on parameters estimated as much as 30 minutes ahead of a given trade.

■ Summary

Transaction costs present a considerable hurdle for high-frequency trading systems. Among all costs, however, market impact accounts for the most significant proportion of costs. Understanding and measuring the current cost structure is imperative to designing profitable systems.

■ End-of-Chapter Questions

1. What costs are present in the financial markets?
2. What are latent costs? How do they differ from transparent costs?
3. Which type of cost is most dominant in today's markets?
4. What kind of tax structure do high-frequency traders face?
5. What is market impact? Why does it exist?
6. Can market impact following a market buy order be zero? Explain.
7. Can expected market impact of a buy order be negative? Explain.
8. What is a permanent market impact? How different is it from temporary market impact?
9. What market impact accompanies limit orders?

CHAPTER 6

Performance and Capacity of High-Frequency Trading Strategies

O ver the past few years, several studies attempted to measure high-frequency trading (HFT) performance and capacity. The results vary from author to author. Many different metrics have been developed over time to illuminate a strategy's performance. This chapter summarizes the most popular approaches for performance measurement and discusses strategy capacity and the length of time required to evaluate a strategy. The chapter also discusses estimation of capacity and illustrates capacity of HFT with specific examples.

■ Principles of Performance Measurement

One can manage only something measurable. Performance measurement is therefore a critical function of investment management and of HFT. While many metrics developed for standard investment management apply well in a high-frequency setting, several other metrics have been developed specifically to evaluate HFT activity.

At the heart of a successful investment management of HFT lie three P's:

■ Precision

■ Productivity

■ Performance

The first P, precision of mathematical metrics, refers to the exactitude required to quickly and reliably separate winning strategies from the losing ones. Statistical tools also help ascertain whether a strategy apparent profitability is a short-term fluke or a statistically solid predictor of performance.

Standardized metrics, when applied uniformly across all investment strategies, deliver the second P, productivity of the investment process. Statistical tools are highly scalable and can be rapidly deployed to optimize a diverse array of investing ideas.

The third P, performance, is particularly relevant to high-frequency systems. In an environment where data points from multiple sources arrive with nanosecond frequency, proper measuring systems are necessary. Monitoring systems equipped with the latest portfolio tracking and risk-management capabilities are critical for effective and sustainable investing.

The three P's share one key requirement: data. The simplest, least processed, data, such as tick data, is most informative and has consequently proven to be very valuable. Trade-by-trade data can reveal the short-term risks of the trading strategy, and to allow risk-mitigating approaches for strategy improvement. Additionally, most granular data allows to quickly and accurately identify strategy dependencies on specific market events or financial instruments, feeding back into strategy development and forming stronger, longer-lasting trading systems. Finally, tick data allow investment managers to monitor and evaluate performance of trading strategies in real time without losing the opportunity to limit losses and enhance profitability along the way.

■ Basic Performance Measures

Return

Trading strategies may come in all shapes and sizes, but they share one characteristic that makes comparison across different strategies feasible—return. Return can be expressed as a dollar difference in prices but is most often considered as a percentage change in value. The resulting dimensionless measure is independent of the price level of the financial instrument under consideration and allows easy cross-strategy and cross-asset comparison of performance:

$$R_{t1} = \frac{P_{t1}}{P_{t0}} - 1 \tag{1}$$

Simple return of equation (1) is illustrated in Figure 6.1.

An equivalent log return metric is shown in equation (2):

$$r_{t1} = \ln\left(P_{t1}\right) - \ln\left(P_{t0}\right) \tag{2}$$

It can be shown that at high frequencies, simple returns of equation (1) are nearly identical to log returns defined by equation (2). The choice of the return metric is often dependent on the application and mathematics of the estimation models.

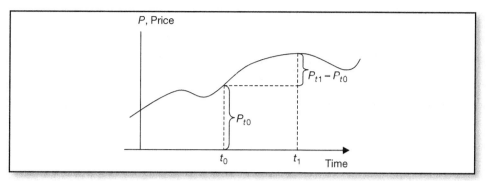

FIGURE 6.1 Illustration of a Simple Return

Volatility

Volatility of returns measures how much the return moves up and down around its average value. The movement of returns, often known as *dispersion,* is often taken as a measure of risk. Figures 6.2 and 6.3 illustrate low-volatility and high-volatility conditions, drawn comparatively to each other.

At least a dozen measures of volatility exist, each metric assessed over a specific period of time: round-trip trade, minute, day, month, and so on. The most common measures of volatility include:

Simple standard deviation of returns is by far the most popular measure of volatility.

$$\hat{\sigma}_t^2 = \frac{1}{N}\sum_{i=1}^{N}\left(R_{t-i} - \overline{R_t}\right)^2 \tag{3}$$

where $\overline{R_t}$ is a simple average of N observations preceding time t.

- Weighted average deviation, emphasizing later observations, is also used often:

$$\hat{\sigma}_t^2 = \frac{\sum_{i=1}^{N} w_i \left(R_{t-i} - \overline{R_t}\right)^2}{\sum_{i=1}^{N} w_i} \tag{4}$$

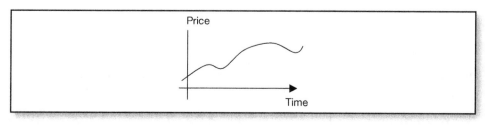

FIGURE 6.2 Example of a Low-Volatility Market Condition

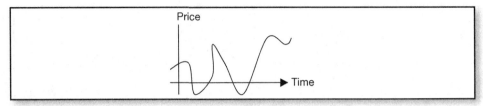

FIGURE 6.3 Example of a High-Volatility Condition

where $\bar{R} = \dfrac{\sum_{i=1}^{N} w_i R_{t-i}}{\sum_{i=1}^{N} w_i}$, and w_i is the "data importance" weight corresponding

to each individual returns R_i. All w_i are often chosen to add up to 1 and to increase toward the most current observation:

$$\sum_{i=1}^{N} w_i = 1 \qquad (5)$$

$$w_i > w_{i+1} > w_{i+2} > \cdots > w_{i+N} \qquad (6)$$

- Average of open, high, low, and close prices is another metric of volatility

$$\hat{\sigma}_t = \frac{P_{t-N} + \max\left(P_{\tau \in t-N, t-1}\right) + \min\left(P_{\tau \in t-N, t-1}\right) + P_{t-1}}{4} \qquad (7)$$

- High minus low recorded during a specific period of time is useful in analyses where many lagged variables are present. The high minus low metric avoids endogeneity problem inherent with standard deviation and lagged returns: since standard deviation is computed from lagged returns, the analysis comparing lagged returns and standard deviation is faulty by design.

$$\hat{\sigma}_t = \max\left(P_{\tau \in t-N, t-1}\right) - \min\left(P_{\tau \in t-N, t-1}\right) \qquad (8)$$

- Average square returns recorded over a certain period of time is yet another metric of volatility. This one has been shown to work particularly well with applications like generalized autoregressive conditional heteroskedasticity (GARCH) (see Bollerslev, 2005):

$$\hat{\sigma}_t^{\,2} = \frac{1}{N} \sum_{i=1}^{N} \left(R_{t-i}\right)^2 \qquad (9)$$

Drawdown

Drawdown is a measure of historical loss. It is recorded as a maximum loss relative to the highest previous value, the latter often referred to as the *water mark*. Investment managers typically receive performance fees only after they exceed the highest water mark on record.

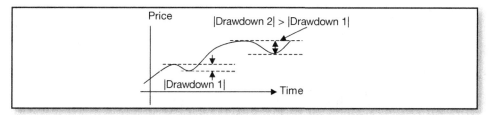

FIGURE 6.4 Maximum Drawdown Computation, Scenario 1

Maximum drawdown identifies the biggest drop of price or value in history of the investment, and helps illustrate potential downside risk. Figures 6.4 and 6.5 illustrate computation of maximum drawdown.

Formally, maximum drawdown is a measure of tail risk popular among practitioners that documents the maximum severity of losses observed in historical data. As such, maximum drawdown records the lowest peak-to-trough return from the last global maximum to the minimum that occurred prior to the next global maximum that supersedes the last global maximum. The global maximum measured on the past data at any point in time is known as *high water mark*. A drawdown is then the lowest return in between two successive high water marks. The lowest drawdown is known as the maximum drawdown:

$$\text{max } Drawdown = \max_{\tau} P_{t_i \in \tau} - \min_{\tau} P_{t_j \in \tau} \Big| \forall t_1 < t_2 \qquad (10)$$

In risk management, the concept of maximum drawdown is closely related to value-at-risk, a measure of worst quantity of losses, described in detail in Chapter 14.

Win Ratio

Win ratio explains what portion of the trades, trading days or trading months ended profitably:

$$WinRatio = \frac{\#\,Trading\ Periods \big|_{Gain>0}}{Total\,\#\,Trading\ Periods} \qquad (11)$$

Win ratios help compare accuracy of predictive signals of strategies: better forecasts result in higher win ratios. Win ratios also help in monitoring run-time

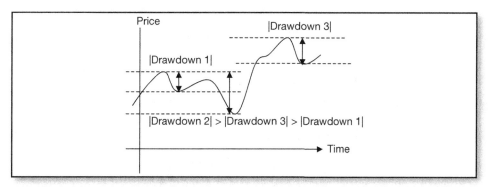

FIGURE 6.5 Maximum Drawdown Computation, Scenario 2

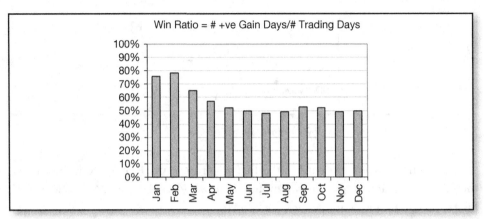

FIGURE 6.6 A Decline in Win Ratio Shown May Indicate that the Strategy Is Reaching Capacity

performance. As a simplest metric, win ratio can be used to assess whether present performance record is consistent with prior performance. A decline in the win ratio may indicate that the strategy is reaching capacity, as Figure 6.6 illustrates.

Similar, but more advanced, tests for evaluating consistency of run-time performance are described in Chapter 14.

Average Gain/Loss

Average gain and average loss are two metrics, statistically closely related to maximum drawdown. The average loss is also a close cousin of the concept of expected loss, discussed in Chapter 14. The average gain measures the average profitability of the strategy when a positive result is recorded. Similarly, the average loss computes the average total for all trades, days or months when the strategy delivered negative performance.

Considered in conjunction with the win ratio, average gain and loss metrics may deliver additional insights. For example, a strategy with high win ratio may tolerate lower average gain relative to the observed average loss, while low win ratio requires a high average gain as compared with the average loss. The outcomes of various win ratio and average gain/loss combinations are shown in Figure 6.7.

Formally, for the strategy to deliver positive performance, the following inequality must hold:

$$\mathbb{E}[R] \geq (WinRatio) * \mathbb{E}[Gain] + (1 - WinRatio) * \mathbb{E}[Loss] \qquad (12)$$

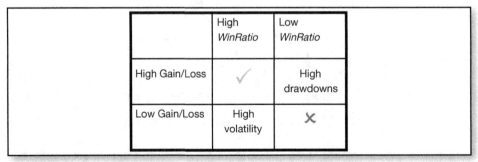

FIGURE 6.7 Outcomes of Win Ratio and Average Gain/Loss Combinations

The inequality of equation (12) can be used as first step litmus test for evaluating performance of candidate investing strategies and manager credibility.

Correlation

Correlation measures co-movement of strategy returns with those of another strategy or financial instrument:

$$\rho_{1,2} = \sum_t \left(R_{1,t} - \mathbb{E}[R_1] \right) \left(R_{2,t} - \mathbb{E}[R_2] \right) \tag{13}$$

When two strategies with low correlation are combined in a portfolio, traditional portfolio management theory suggests that the resulting portfolio is diversified (i.e., allows one strategy to pull up returns when performance of another strategy temporarily declines).

Simple correlation, however, may no longer be sufficient in delivering robust measurements of co-movement of financial instruments. The main problem with simple correlation is the following observation: prices of financial instruments display increasingly divergent correlations in rising and in falling markets. Specifically, when broad market indices rise (a market entity such as Standard & Poor's [S&P] 500, for example) correlations vary from any two financial instruments to any other two financial instruments. When the broad market indices fall, however, returns of most financial instruments become highly correlated. Such divergent correlation in different states of the markets is known as the *asymmetric* or *tail correlation* that can be computed by dividing the data sample into points when price returns of one of the instruments measured are positive and negative:

$$\rho_{1,2}\Big|_{R_1 > 0} = \sum_t \left(R_{1,t} - \mathbb{E}[R_1] \right) \left(R_{2,t} - \mathbb{E}[R_2] \right)\Big|_{R_1 > 0} \tag{14}$$

$$\rho_{1,2}\Big|_{R_1 < 0} = \sum_t \left(R_{1,t} - \mathbb{E}[R_1] \right) \left(R_{2,t} - \mathbb{E}[R_2] \right)\Big|_{R_1 < 0} \tag{15}$$

In both equations (14) and (15) financial instrument 1 is taken as a reference. Equation (14) computes the correlation for the "up" states of returns of financial instrument 1, while equation (15) does the same for the "down" states. A strategy delivering returns negatively correlated to those of the existing portfolio helps buffer core portfolio's losses in the "down" states, and is much more valuable than the strategy delivering positively correlated returns and thereby amplifying losses of wider portfolio.

Alpha and Beta

Alpha and beta are two now-mainstay measures of investment performance that are equally well suited for evaluation of high-frequency strategies. At its most basic level, alpha measures the return achieved by the strategy abstracted of any influences by the reference portfolio or the broader markets, measured by, say, the S&P 500 index. Thus, alpha reflects the performance of the strategy that is independent of the prevailing market conditions. A positive alpha is desirable. Strategies with a negative alpha are generally avoided, unless the negative-alpha strategy signals can be profitably used to trade "in reverse"—buy when the strategy advises to sell and vice versa.

Beta, however, is a multiplier that measures exactly how the strategy responds to the current market trends. A positive beta indicates that the strategy is likely to deliver positive performance when the reference portfolio rises in value. A negative beta shows that, on average, the strategy is likely to perform better when the reference portfolio declines. Depending on the investor's cumulative portfolio, either positive or negative beta may be preferable.

Alpha and beta are estimated using a linear regression (OLS):

$$R_{i,t} = \alpha_i + \beta_i R_{p,t} + \varepsilon_{i,t} \tag{16}$$

where $R_{i,t}$ is the return on a high-frequency strategy i observed over a unit of time t, $R_{p,t}$ is the return on the reference portfolio observed over the same period of time, α_i and β_i are the parameters to be estimated, and $\varepsilon_{i,t}$ is the "statistical estimation error" specific to each observation when equation (16) is applied to data. By the assumptions of the model of equation (16), the errors $\varepsilon_{i,t}$ average to zero.

Figure 6.8 graphically illustrates alpha and beta, as computed from a scatterplot of returns: the returns of the reference portfolio are plotted along the horizontal axis, and the contemporaneous returns on the HF strategy are plotted along the vertical axis. When a straight line is fitted through the data, the slope of the line is beta. Alpha is the intercept, or the point where the line intersects the vertical axis.

Skewness and Kurtosis

Skewness and kurtosis are additional parameters used to describe the distribution of returns of the strategy. *Skewness* describes the tendency of the strategy to deliver positive or negative returns. Positive skewness of a return distribution implies that the strategy is more likely to post positive returns than negative returns. Figure 6.9 illustrates possible skewness scenarios.

Kurtosis measures the likelihood of extreme occurrences, that is, of severely positive and severely negative returns relative to normal returns. When kurtosis is

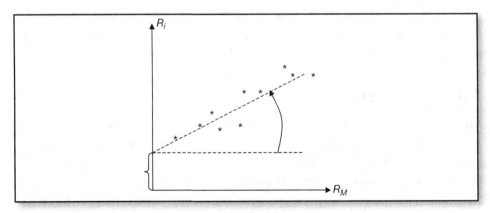

FIGURE 6.8 Graphical Representation of Alpha and Beta

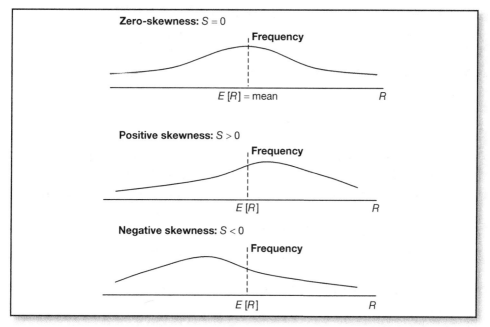

FIGURE 6.9 Skewness Values and Their Meaning in Distribution of Returns

high, extreme returns are likely. When kurtosis is low, extreme returns are unlikely. Figure 6.10 illustrates the idea of kurtosis.

The average return, volatility, and maximum drawdown over a prespecified window of time measured at a predefined frequency are the mainstays of performance comparison and reporting for different trading strategies. In addition to the average return, volatility, and maximum drawdown, practitioners sometimes quote skewness and kurtosis of returns when describing the shape of their return distributions. As usual, skewness illustrates the position of the distribution relative to the

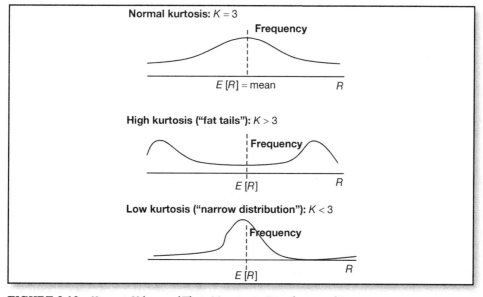

FIGURE 6.10 Kurtosis Values and Their Meaning in Distribution of Returns

return average; positive skewness indicates prevalence of positive returns, while negative skewness indicates that a large proportion of returns is negative. Kurtosis indicates whether the tails of the distribution are normal; high kurtosis signifies "fat tails," a higher-than-normal probability of extreme positive or negative events.

■ Comparative Ratios

While average return, standard deviation, and maximum drawdown present a picture of the performance of a particular trading strategy, the measures do not lend to an easy point comparison among two or more strategies. Several comparative performance metrics have been developed in an attempt to summarize mean, variance, and tail risk in a single number that can be used to compare different trading strategies. Table 6.1 summarizes the most popular point measures.

TABLE 6.1	Performance Measure Summary	
Sharpe ratio (Sharpe, 1966)	$SR = \dfrac{E[r] - r_f}{\sigma[r]}$, where $$E[r] = \frac{r_1 + \cdots + r_T}{T}$$ $$\sigma[r] = \sqrt{\frac{(r_1 - E[r])^2 + \cdots + (r_T - E[r])^2}{T-1}}$$ The Sharpe ratio of high-frequency trading strategies: $SR = \dfrac{E[r]}{\sigma[r]}$	Adequate if returns are normally distributed.
Treynor ratio (Treynor, 1965)	$Treynor_i = \dfrac{E[r_i] - r_f}{\beta_i}$ β_i is the regression coefficient of trading returns on returns of the investor's reference portfolio, such as the market portfolio.	Adequate if returns are normally distributed and the investor wishes to split his holdings between one trading strategy and the market portfolio.
Jensen's alpha (Jensen, 1968)	$\alpha_i = E[r_i] - r_f - \beta_i(r_M - r_f)$ β_i is the regression coefficient of trading returns on returns of the investor's reference portfolio, such as the market portfolio.	Measures trading return in excess of the return predicted by CAPM. Adequate if returns are normally distributed and the investor wishes to split his holdings between one trading strategy and the market portfolio, but can be manipulated by leveraging the trading strategy.

Measures based on lower partial moments (LPMs):

LPM of order n for security i:

$$LPM_{ni}(\tau) = \frac{1}{T}\sum_{t=1}^{T}\max[\tau - r_{it}, 0]^n$$

where τ is the minimal acceptable return;

n is the moment: $n = 0$ is the shortfall probability, $n = 1$ is the expected shortfall, $n = 2$ for $\tau = E[r]$ is the semivariance.

According to Eling and Schuhmacher (2007), more risk-averse investors should use higher-order n.

LPMs consider only negative deviations of returns from a minimal acceptable return. As such, LPMs are deemed to be a better measure of risk than standard deviation, which considers both positive and negative deviations (Sortino and van der Meer, 1991). Minimal acceptable return can be zero, risk-free rate, or average return.

| TABLE 6.1 | (Continued) |

Omega (Shadwick and Keating, 2002; Kaplan and Knowles, 2004)	$\Omega_i = \dfrac{E[r_i] - \tau}{LPM_{1i}(\tau)} + 1$	$E[r_i] - \tau$ is the average return in excess of the benchmark rate.
Sortino ratio (Sortino and van der Meer, (1991)	$Sortino_i = \dfrac{E[r_i] - \tau}{\left(LPM_{2i}(\tau)\right)^{1/2}}$	
Kappa 3 (Kaplan and Knowles, 2004)	$K3_i = \dfrac{E[r_i] - \tau}{\left(LPM_{3i}(\tau)\right)^{1/3}}$	
Upside Potential ratio (Sortino, van der Meer, and Plantinga, 1999)	$UPR_i = \dfrac{HPM_{1i}(\tau)}{\left(LPM_{2i}(\tau)\right)^{1/2}}$ where HPM = higher partial moment $HPM_{ni}(\tau) = \dfrac{1}{T}\sum_{t=1}^{T}\max[r_{it} - \tau, 0]^n$	According to Eling and Schuhmacher (2007), this ratio gains from the consistent application of the minimal acceptable return τ in the numerator as well as in the denominator.

Measures based on drawdown: frequently used by CTAs, according to Eling and Schuhmacher (2007, p.5), "because these measures illustrate what the advisors are supposed to do best—continually accumulating gains while consistently limiting losses (see Lhabitant, 2004)." MD_{i1} denotes the lowest maximum drawdown, MD_{i2} the second lowest maximum drawdown, and so on.

Calmar ratio (Young, 1991)	$Calmar_i = \dfrac{E[r_i] - r_f}{-MD_{i1}}$	MD_{i1} is the maximum drawdown.
Sterling ratio (Kestner, 1996)	$Sterling_i = \dfrac{E[r_i] - r_f}{-\dfrac{1}{N}\sum_{k=1}^{N} MD_{ij}}$	$-\dfrac{1}{N}\sum_{k=1}^{N} MD_{ij}$ is the average maximum drawdown.
Burke ratio (Burke, 1994)	$Burke_i = \dfrac{E[r_i] - r_f}{\left[\sum_{k=1}^{N}\left(MD_{ij}\right)^2\right]^{1/2}}$	$\left[\sum_{k=1}^{N}\left(MD_{ij}\right)^2\right]^{1/2}$ is a type of variance below the Nth largest drawdown; accounts for very large losses.

Value-at-risk–based measures.

Value-at-risk (VaR_i) describes the possible loss of an investment, which is not exceeded with a given probability of $1 - \alpha$ in a certain period. For normally distributed returns, $VaR_i = -(E[r_i] + z_\alpha \sigma_i)$, where z_α is the α-quantile of the standard normal distribution.

Excess return on value at risk (Dowd, 2000)	$Excess\ R\ on\ VaR = \dfrac{E[r] - r_f}{VaR_i}$	Not suitable for non-normal returns.
Conditional Sharpe ratio (Agarwal and Naik, 2004)	$Conditional\ Sharpe = \dfrac{E[r] - r_f}{CVaR_i}$ $CVaR_i = E[-r_{it} \mid r_{it} \le -VaR_i]$	The advantage of CVaR is that it satisfies certain plausible axioms (Artzner et al., 1999).

(Continued)

TABLE 6.1	(Continued)

Modified Sharpe ratio (Gregoriou and Gueyie (2003)	$\text{Modified Sharpe} = \dfrac{E[r] - r_f}{MVaR_i}$ Cornish-Fisher expansion is calculated as follows: $MVaR_i = -(E[r_i] + \sigma_i(z_\alpha + (z_\alpha^2 - 1)S_i/6$ $+ (z_\alpha^3 - 3z_\alpha)EK_i/24 - (2z_\alpha^3 - 5z_\alpha)S_i^2/36))$ where Si denotes skewness and EK_i the excess kurtosis for security i (Favre and Galeano, 2002).	Suitable for non-normal returns.

The first generation of point performance measures were developed in the 1960s and include the Sharpe ratio, Jensen's alpha, and the Treynor ratio. The Sharpe ratio is probably the most widely used measure in comparative performance evaluation; it incorporates three desirable metrics—average return, standard deviation, and the cost of capital borrowed for strategy leverage.

The Sharpe ratio was designed in 1966 by William Sharpe, later a winner of the Nobel Memorial Prize in Economics; it is a remarkably enduring concept used in the study and practice of finance. A textbook definition of the Sharpe ratio is

$SR = \dfrac{\bar{R} - R_F}{\sigma_R}$, where $\bar{R}$ is the annualized average return from trading, σ_R is the

annualized standard deviation of trading returns, and R_F is the risk-free rate (e.g., Fed Funds) that is included to capture the opportunity cost as well as the position carrying costs associated with the trading activity. It should be noted that in most instruments HFT with no positions carried overnight, the position carrying costs are zero. Therefore, the high-frequency Sharpe ratio is computed as follows:

$$SR = \dfrac{\bar{R}}{\sigma_R}$$

What makes the Sharpe ratio an appealing measure of performance, in comparison with, say, raw absolute return? Surprisingly, the Sharpe ratio is an effective metric for selecting mean-variance efficient securities.

Consider Figure 6.11, for example which illustrates the classic mean-variance frontier. In the figure, the Sharpe ratio is the slope of the line emanating from the risk-free rate and passing through a point corresponding to a given portfolio (M for market portfolio), trading strategy, or individual security. The bold line tangent to the mean-variance set of all portfolio combinations is the efficient frontier itself. It has the highest slope and, correspondingly, the highest Sharpe ratio of all the portfolios in the set. For any other portfolio, trading strategy, or individual financial instrument A, the higher the Sharpe ratio, the closer the security is to the efficient frontier.

Sharpe himself came up with the metric when developing a portfolio optimization mechanism for a mutual fund for which he was consulting. Sharpe's mandate was to develop a portfolio selection framework for the fund with the following

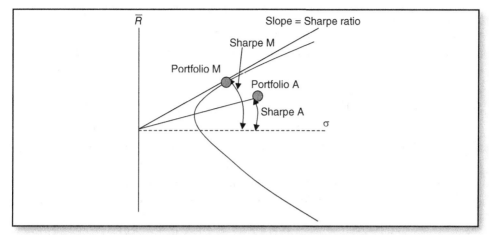

FIGURE 6.11 Sharpe Ratio as a Mean-Variance Slope. The market portfolio has the highest slope and, correspondingly, the highest Sharpe ratio.

constraint: no more than 5 percent of the fund's portfolio could be allocated to a particular financial security. Sharpe then created the following portfolio solution: he first ranked the security universe on what now is known as Sharpe ratio, then picked the 20 securities with the best performance according to the Sharpe ratio measure, and invested 5 percent of the fund into each of the 20 securities. Equally weighted portfolio allocation in securities with the highest Sharpe ratios is just one example of a successful Sharpe ratio application.

Jensen's alpha is a measure of performance that abstracts from broad market influences, capital asset pricing model (CAPM)-style. Jensen's alpha implicitly takes into consideration the variability of returns in co-movement with chosen market indices.

The third ratio, the Treynor ratio, measures the average return in excess of the chosen benchmark per unit of risk proxied by beta from the CAPM estimation.

While these three metrics remain popular, they do not take into account the tail risk of extreme adverse returns. Brooks and Kat (2002), Mahdavi (2004), and Sharma (2004), for example, present cases against using Sharpe ratios on non–normally distributed returns. The researchers' primary concerns surrounding the use of the Sharpe ratio are linked to the use of derivative instruments that result in an asymmetric return distribution and fat tails. Ignoring deviations from normality may underestimate risk and overestimate performance. New performance measures have been subsequently developed to capture the tail risk inherent in the returns of most trading strategies.

A natural extension of the Sharpe ratio is to change the measure of risk from standard deviation to a drawdown-based methodology in an effort to capture the tail risk of the strategies. The Calmar ratio, Sterling ratio, and Burke ratio do precisely that. The Calmar ratio, developed by Young (1991), uses the maximum drawdown as the measure of volatility. The Sterling ratio, first described by Kestner (1996), uses the average drawdown as a proxy for volatility. Finally, the Burke ratio, developed by Burke (1994), uses the standard deviation of maximum drawdowns as a volatility metric.

In addition to ignoring the tail risk, the Sharpe ratio is also frequently criticized for including positive returns in the volatility measure. The argument goes that only the negative returns are meaningful when estimating and comparing performance of trading strategies. In response, a "Greek" class of ratios extended the Sharpe ratio by replacing volatility with the average metrics of adverse returns only. These adverse return metrics are known as lower partial moments (LPMs) and are computed as regular moments of a distribution (i.e., mean, standard deviation, and skewness), except that the data used in computation comprises returns below a specified benchmark only. Thus, a metric known as Omega, developed by Shadwick and Keating (2002) and Kaplan and Knowles (2004), replaces the standard deviation of returns in the Sharpe ratio calculation with the first LPM, the average of the returns that fell below the selected benchmark. The Sortino ratio, developed by Sortino and van der Meer (1991), uses the standard deviation of the returns that fell short of the benchmark, the second LPM, as a measure of return volatility in the Sharpe ratio calculation. The Kappa 3 measure, developed by Kaplan and Knowles (2004), replaces the standard deviation in the Sharpe ratio with the third LPM of the returns, the skewness of the returns below the benchmark. Finally, the Upside Potential ratio, produced by Sortino, van der Meer, and Platinga (1999), measures the average return above the benchmark (the first higher partial moment) per unit of standard deviation of returns below the benchmark.

Value-at-risk (VaR) measures, discussed in detail in Chapter 14, also gained considerable popularity as metrics able to summarize the tail risk in a convenient point format within a statistical framework. The VaR measure essentially identifies the 90 percent, 95 percent, or 99 percent Z-score cutoff in distribution of returns (the metric is also often used on real dollar distributions of daily profit and loss). A VaR companion measure, the conditional VaR (CVaR), also known as expected loss (EL), measures the average value of return within the cutoff tail. Of course, the original VaR assumes normal distributions of returns, whereas the returns are known to be fat-tailed. To address this issue, a modified VaR (MVaR) measure was proposed by Gregoriou and Gueyie (2003) and takes into account deviations from normality. Gregoriou and Gueyie (2003) also suggest using MVaR in place of standard deviation in Sharpe ratio calculations.

How do these performance metrics stack up against each other? It turns out that all metrics deliver comparable rankings of trading strategies. Eling and Schuhmacher (2007) compare hedge fund ranking performance of the 13 measures listed and conclude that the Sharpe ratio is an adequate measure for hedge fund performance.

■ Performance Attribution

Performance attribution analysis, often referred to as "benchmarking," goes back to the arbitrage pricing theory of Ross (1977) and has been applied to trading strategy performance by Sharpe (1992) and Fung and Hsieh (1997), among others. In a nutshell, performance attribution notes that t-period return on strategy i that invests into individual securities with returns r_{jt} in period t, with $j = 1, \ldots, J$, has an underlying factor structure:

$$R_{it} = \sum_j x_{jt} r_{jt} \tag{17}$$

where x_{jt} is the relative weight of the jth financial security in the portfolio at time t, $\sum_j x_{jt} = 1$. The jth financial security, in turn, has a period-t return that can be explained by K systematic factors:

$$r_{jt} = \sum_k \lambda_{jk} F_{kt} + \varepsilon_{jt} \tag{18}$$

where F_{kt} is one of K underlying systematic factors in period t, $k = 1, \ldots, K$, λ is the factor loading, and ε_{jt} is the security j idiosyncratic return in period t. Following Sharpe (1992), factors can be assumed to be broad asset classes, as well as individual stocks or other securities. Combining equations (17) and (18), we can express returns as follows:

$$R_{it} = \sum_{j,k} x_{jt} \lambda_{jk} F_{kt} + \sum_j x_{jt} \varepsilon_{jt} \tag{19}$$

reducing the large number of financial securities potentially underlying strategy i's returns to a small group of global factors. Performance attribution to various factors then involves regressing the strategy's returns on a basket of factors:

$$R_{it} = \alpha_i + \sum_k b_{ik} F_{kt} + u_{it} \tag{20}$$

where b_k measures the performance of the strategy that can be attributed to factor k, α_i measures the strategy's persistent ability to generate abnormal returns, and u_{it} measures the strategy's idiosyncratic return in period t.

In the performance attribution model, the idiosyncratic value added of the strategy is the strategy's return in excess of the performance of the basket of weighted strategy factors.

Fung and Hsieh (1997) find that the following eight global groups of asset classes serve well as performance attribution benchmarks:

- Three equity classes: MSCI U.S. equities, MSCI non–U.S. equities, and IFC emerging market equities

- Two bond classes: JPMorgan U.S. government bonds and JPMorgan non–U.S. government bonds

- One-month Eurodollar deposit representing cash

- The price of gold proxying commodities and the Federal Reserve's trade-weighted dollar index measuring currencies in aggregate.

Performance attribution is a useful measure of strategy returns for the following reasons:

- The technique may accurately capture investment styles of black-box strategies in addition to the details reported by the designer of the strategy.

- Performance attribution is a measure of true added value of the strategy and lends itself to easy comparison with other strategies.

- Near-term persistence of trending factors allows forecasting of strategy performance based on performance attribution (see, for example, Jegadeesh and Titman, 2001).

The bottom line in the performance attribution analysis is this: if the high-frequency strategy under consideration exhibits high dependency on a benchmark, it may be cheaper to invest into the benchmark instead of the HF strategy, particularly when development and transaction costs as well as the associated risks are taken into account. That is, when the performance attribution beta is high, and alpha is low, it might be more effective to invest into the benchmark, particularly when any one of the following conditions holds:

- Investing into benchmark can be passive or simply costs less in terms of aggregate transaction costs.

- The benchmark has lower drawdown risk.

- The benchmark is more liquid than the instrument traded in the HFT strategy, and the benchmark therefore faces a lower liquidation risk.

■ Capacity Evaluation

Over the past few years, HFT strategies have been erroneously called low-capacity strategies. One study, for example, based its low-capacity conclusions for HFT on a major gaffe—an assumption that all high-frequency traders solely use market orders to complete their trades. In such an analysis, market impact dominates and multiplies in fast trading, leaving high-frequency traders unable to profitably enter or liquidate their positions. The maximum capacity of a high-frequency market-order trading strategy then amounts to the liquidity available at the best bid or best offer at a specific time when each market sell or buy order, respectively, is placed.

In reality, as later chapters of this book describe, most HFT strategies place and execute limit orders, with very few market orders placed in the mix. Market orders in HFT are generally used at times when markets take an unexpected wrong turn and the trader's inventory has to be liquidated—fast.

Limit orders generate much smaller market impact than do market orders, as Chapter 5 of this book explains. Still, even strategies relying solely on limit orders do not enjoy infinite capacity since two variables in addition to market impact also adversely affect performance of HFT strategies. These variables are probability of execution and transparent execution costs.[1]

Transparent execution costs, also described in Chapter 5 of this book, affect the profitability of round-trip trades, yet are predictable as they tend to be known ahead of each trade. Execution costs on selected venues may be positive or negative, depending on the venue's business model.

---

[1] Strategy capacity has been shown to be a function of trading costs and asset liquidity by Getmansky, Lo, and Makarov (2004).

The probability of execution is simple for market orders: it is always close to 1. The probability of execution of limit orders, however, is not known with certainty at the time the order is placed. For a limit order to be executed, it needs to

1. Become the best available price—best bid or best ask—the process also known as "reaching the top of the book."
2. Be matched with or *crossed* by a market order or an aggressive limit order.

As a result, the probability of execution for limit orders is variable and depends on the following factors:

- The distance of the limit order price from the market price.
- Market volatility.
- The number of other limit orders available at the same price or closer to market.
- The size of the limit order.
- The rate of arrival of same-side limit orders.
- The rate of arrival of opposing market orders and aggressive limit orders.

A limit order placed far away from the market price faces a tangible risk of nonexecution: the market price may never reach limit orders placed far away from the market. The probability of the market price crossing the limit order, in turn, depends on the market volatility—the higher the volatility, the more likely is the market price to hit the level specified by the limit order. The congestion of limit orders also matters, as each limit placed at a given price will be stored in a queue and executed according to a scheme specific to the execution venue; as discussed in Chapter 3, the most common matching schemes are the first-in-first-out (FIFO) and pro-rata algorithms. Under the FIFO arrangements, the larger limit orders face a larger risk of nonexecution: large limit orders may be only partially executed before the market moves away, leaving some of the limit order in the queue. With a pro-rata algorithm, the opposite holds: all orders are executed on a fixed proportion of their sizes; small orders may take a long time to execute in full.

The higher the number of other limit orders arriving at the same price as the trader's close to market price, the steeper the competition for market orders, and the less likely the limit order to be matched. However, the higher the arrival rate of opposing market orders, the higher the probability of execution.

Algebraically, the maximum size of a limit order (capacity) S deployed by a high-frequency strategy can be expressed as follows:

$$\max S \text{ s.t.} \sum_t \left[S Q_t \left(1 + MI_{t-1}\right) P_t \operatorname{Pr}_t \left(Execution\right) - C_t \right] \geq 0 \text{ and } \sum_t Q_t = 0 \quad (21)$$

where

S is the size of each order in the strategy, assuming the strategy can be executed using trades of equal size S.

Q_t is the direction of the order placed at time t: $Q_t = 1$ when the order is a buy, and $Q_t = -1$ when the order is a sell.

MI_{t-1} is the market impact generated by the previous order placed by the HFT strategy, and impacting the market conditions at time t; only the market impact that has not fully decayed by time t needs to be considered.

P_t is the price of the order or, in case of a market order, the price obtained upon execution.

$\Pr_t(Execution)$ is the probability that the order placed at time t will be executed; this probability can be assumed to be 1 for market orders.

Finally, C_t is the cost of execution of the order placed at time t; this cost includes broker fees and other costs discussed in Chaper 5 of this book that affect the bottom-line profitability of high-frequency strategies.

As shown in Chapter 5, market impact (MI) can be probabilistically estimated. In addition to the magnitude of MI following an average order, the probability of execution can be estimated as well by noting the statistics of when a market price crosses limit orders placed at various points away from the market. Assuming that the trade signals of an HFT system deliver credibly positive results, the capacity of the system is then determined by a trade-off between market impact and probability of execution.

To further increase the capacity of an HFT strategy, market and limit orders may be potentially sequenced. Figure 6.12 shows a decision tree for evaluating the optimal capacity of an HF trading system.

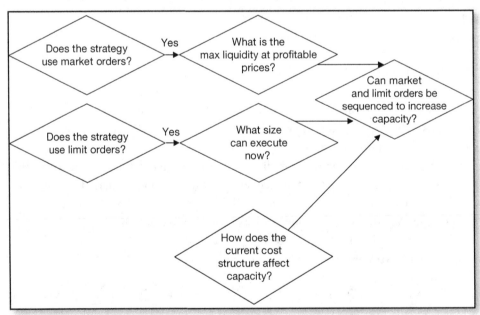

FIGURE 6.12 Basic Framework for Evaluating Capacity of HFT Strategies

Ding et al. (2008) conjecture that when the amount of capital deployed is lower than the strategy capacity, the strategy performance may be positively related to its capitalization. However, once capitalization exceeds strategy capacity, performance becomes negatively related to the amount of capital involved. Chapter 15 discusses the latest research on optimizing order execution and potentially increasing strategy capacity further.

Length of the Evaluation Period

Most portfolio managers face the following question in evaluating candidate trading strategies for inclusion in their portfolios: how long does one need to monitor a strategy in order to gain confidence that the strategy produces the Sharpe ratio advertised?

Some portfolio managers have adopted an arbitrarily long evaluation period: six months to two years. Some investors require a track record of at least six years. Yet others are content with just one month of daily performance data. It turns out that, statistically, any of the previously mentioned time frames is correct if it is properly matched with the Sharpe ratio it is intended to verify. The higher the Sharpe ratio, the shorter the strategy evaluation period needed to ascertain the validity of the Sharpe ratio.

If returns of the trading strategy can be assumed to be normal, Jobson and Korkie (1981) showed that the error in Sharpe ratio estimation is normally distributed with mean zero and standard deviation

$$s = [(1/T)(1 + 0.5SR^2)]^{1/2}.$$

For a 90 percent confidence level, the claimed Sharpe ratio should be at least 1.645 times greater than the standard deviation of the Sharpe ratio errors, s. As a result, the minimum number of evaluation periods used for Sharpe ratio verification is

$$T_{min} = (1.645^2/SR^2)(1 + 0.5SR^2).$$

The Sharpe ratio SR used in the calculation of T_{min}, however, should correspond to the frequency of estimation periods. If the annual Sharpe ratio claimed for a trading strategy is 2, and it is computed based on the basis of monthly data, then the corresponding monthly Sharpe ratio SR is $2/(12)^{0.5} = 0.5774$. However, if the claimed Sharpe ratio is computed based on daily data, then the corresponding Sharpe ratio SR is $2/(250)^{0.5} = 0.1054$. The minimum number of monthly observations required to verify the claimed Sharpe ratio with 90 percent statistical confidence is then just over nine months for monthly performance data and just over eight months for daily

TABLE 6.2	Minimum Trading Strategy Performance Evaluation Times Required for Verification of Reported Sharpe Ratios	
Claimed Annualized Sharpe Ratio	No. of Months Required (Monthly Performance Data)	No. of Months Required (Daily Performance Data)
0.5	130.95	129.65
1.0	33.75	32.45
1.5	15.75	14.45
2.0	9.45	8.15
2.5	6.53	5.23
3.0	4.95	3.65
4.0	3.38	2.07

performance data. For a claimed Sharpe ratio of 6, less than one month of daily performance data is required to verify the claim. Table 6.2 summarizes the minimum performance evaluation times required for verification of performance data for key values of Sharpe ratios.

◼ Alpha Decay

In addition to the performance metrics outlined earlier, HFT strategies can be evaluated on the basis of alpha decay, the erosion of alpha with time. The erosion of alpha may be due to the lack of execution in strategies relying on limit orders, or due to the poor latency infrastructure used for transmission of market orders. In either case, alpha decay can be measured and forecasted.

The alpha decay observed due to latency can be estimated as a distribution of market impact costs observed in a particular financial instrument a finite period of time after each trading decision was made.

Alpha decay of a strategy using limit orders measures the opportunity cost associated with failure to execute on trading signals of the strategy. Alpha decay is strategy specific and should be assessed based on the signals generated by the given strategy.

◼ Summary

Statistical tools for strategy evaluation allow managers to assess the feasibility and appropriateness of high-frequency strategies to their portfolios. As traders' and investment managers' understanding of HFT deepens, new metrics are deployed to capture the variability among HFT strategies. As a quick test of strategy feasibility, the Sharpe ratio remains the favorite.

◼ End-of-Chapter Questions

1. What is the Sharpe ratio? What are its drawbacks? How can it be enhanced?
2. What is the Sortino ratio?
3. Suppose a performance attribution analysis on a given high-frequency trading strategy finds strong dependence of trading gains on changes in the S&P 500. What are the implications for the trading strategy? Discuss.
4. Why does market impact enter calculation of strategy capacity? Why does probability of execution?
5. What is alpha decay and why does it exist?

CHAPTER 7

The Business of High-Frequency Trading

Contrary to popular belief, the business of high-frequency trading (HFT) is not entirely the business of trading, nor is it a business of pure research. Instead, most of HFT is the business of technology. As such, the economics of building an HFT operation differ considerably from those of a traditional trading floor. This chapter explains the economic nuts and bolts of a successful HFT organization.

■ Key Processes of HFT

The central value proposition of HFT is enabled by tick-by-tick data processing and high capital turnover. The technology behind identifying small changes in the quote stream is what differentiates this business and enables a trader to send rapid-fire signals to open and close positions.

Processing every tick of data on multiple financial instruments is possible only via automated trading. Evaluating data separated by microseconds, interpreting reams of market information, and making trading decisions in a consistent continuous manner is too complex a task for a human brain. Affordable fully automated HFT systems, however, can make fast, efficient, and emotionless decisions.

Figure 7.1 illustrates a sample deceivingly simple process used to develop HFT systems. Just like any software development activity, the HFT process begins with a concept of the final product: a trading idea that becomes a quantitative model. The concept, or a prototype, may be a 20-line piece of code written in a modeling language, such as MatLab, and shown to produce hypothetical profitability on a selection of data.

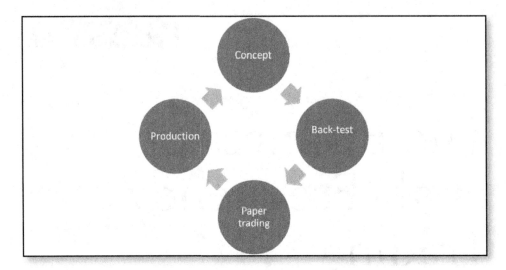

FIGURE 7.1 Algorithm Design and Reevaluation Process

The next step is a back-test: a process whereby the concept is tested on a large volume of tick data. Two years is generally considered a sufficient amount of tick data to ascertain validity of the concept. Back-test best practices are discussed in Chapter 16 of this book. The model is tested on "out-of-sample" or "clean" swath of data, a series of quotes and trades unused in the initial proof of concept activity. If the model performs satisfactorily out-of-sample, the model is moved into paper trading. Models that fail the back-test are generally discarded.

Following a successful back-test, the models are moved into the preproduction or paper-trading phase. Paper trading emulates real-time trading activity without placing actual orders, but keeps track of the orders in a program-generated log. Except for the order-placement functionality, the paper-trading phase is typically a fully programmed HFT system. As such, the paper-trading stage is a perfect "sandbox" for testing all other aspects of the HFT system: data receipt and processing, run-time generation of trading signals, position accounting, archiving of data, and risk management. To ascertain the correctness of the paper HFT system, the back-test algorithm is typically run at the end of each trading day on data collected in paper trading—any deviations observed between the back-test and paper trading are noted and investigated.

When paper trading and the back-test are properly programmed, both should deliver identical results. A month of clean paper trading fully reconciled with back-test results is usually considered to be sufficient to move the system into a low-amount live trading or "production."

The transition to production is often loaded with its own set of challenges, described in detail in Chapter 16. Trade execution and real-time portfolio accounting can be complex coding exercises, and have to be executed perfectly to avoid unexpected malfunctions and losses. Extended production runs with little capital at stake help iron out various code issues and ensure a smooth and effective trading functionality.

This section demonstrates that in the development of a successful HFT system, human time is functionally split as follows:

- Quant HFT model development/proof of concept including back-tests: 15 percent

  Quant HFT models, the core examples of which are described in Chapters 8 through 11 of this book, are the road maps for trading. The output of quant models is a set of persistent indicators built to identify trading opportunities.

- Risk management principles, model validation and policy development: 10 percent

  Competent risk management, discussed in Chapter 14, prevents seemingly harmless glitches in the code, market data, market conditions, or the like from throwing off trading dynamics and causing large losses. The objective of risk management is to assess the extent of potential damages and to create infrastructure to mitigate damaging conditions during run-time, and to build a system of warnings, failure breaks, and processes with the goal to eliminate or limit the potential damage. Some risk management processes may be built into the code, while others require a human presence to ensure a failure-safe operation.

- Coding of trading and risk-management infrastructure: 40 percent

  Coding trading and risk-management signals comprises the primary focus of HFT development. High-frequency execution systems tend to be complex entities that detect and react to a variety of market conditions. Most HFT systems today are built to be "platform independent"—that is, to incorporate flexible interfaces to multiple broker-dealers, electronic communication networks (ECNs), and exchanges. This independence is accomplished through the use of the Financial Information eXchange (FIX) language, a special sequence of codes optimized for financial trading data. With FIX, at the flip of a switch the routing can be changed from one executing broker to another or to several brokers simultaneously. Best coding practices are described in Chapter 16.

  FIX can be quite cumbersome, as discussed in Chapter 2. To counteract the delay in speed induced by the complexities of FIX, several providers have rolled out proprietary communication protocols and application programming interfaces (APIs). The proprietary structures also have the effect of making it difficult for traders to switch platforms, thus capturing the audience. The extent of work required to adapt to a given platform can be extensive, however, and some providers even offer monetary incentives for traders interested in building out connectivity. Some divisions of Deutsche Börse, for example, may offer as much as $65,000 to prospective traders to defray the interface implementation costs.

- System testing: 20 percent

  System testing is another critical component, discussed in detail in Chapter 16. To ensure thorough testing, the system is run through various scenarios, or "scripts." Professional software testers are typically deployed to examine each block of code, to compare its performance with its stated mandate, and to document all discrepancies, known as "bugs." Testers are often compensated about one third as much as coders. Separating coding and testing duties also ensures proper testing, free of face-saving whitewashing gaffes that can ultimately cost the business significant money.

- Run-time monitoring: 5 percent

    Run-time monitoring is another HFT task requiring personnel. The task of monitoring a well-defined HFT system with clear risk management parameters and escalation procedures is not particularly involved, but requires close attention to detail. Separate personnel are typically tasked with the duty of watching the systems and ensuring that run-time performance remains within acceptable limits. Best practices for HFT monitoring are discussed in Chapter 16.

- Compliance and other administrativia: 10 percent

    Compliance and other administrative tasks are a function of all trading businesses. Keeping track of regulatory guidelines, documentation, and all other related activities is a full-time job.

The proportion of time spent on each task outlined here varies with the stage of HFT business development, as shown in Figure 7.2. In the start-up phase, HFT businesses tend to be data and programming centered. In the ramp-up stage, testing, risk management, and monitoring take the majority of effort. Finally, in steady-state production, it is monitoring, compliance, and other administrative tasks that take the majority of time.

In the traditional broker-dealer world, where the word *technology* is often associated only with new shiny gadgets provided by technology teams far removed from business, tasks such as system testing and policy development may seem like an unnecessary expense. By separating technology from the business, the management creates an impression that traders need not feel accountable for the systems they are using. Real-life examples, such as the Knight Capital fiasco that occurred in the summer of 2012, have shown that thorough testing, compliance, and monitoring of HFT systems are key to the long-term profitability of the business. These functions follow directly from the best practices of software development, discussed in detail in Chapter 16.

As Figure 7.2 illustrates, development of an HFT business follows a process unusual for most traditional trading desks. Designing new HFT strategies is costly; executing and monitoring finished high-frequency products costs close to nothing. By contrast, a traditional proprietary trading businesses incurs fixed costs from the

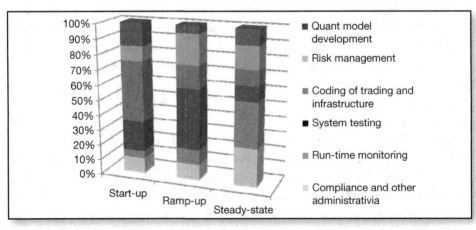

FIGURE 7.2 Allocation of Man-Hours during Different Phases of HFT Development

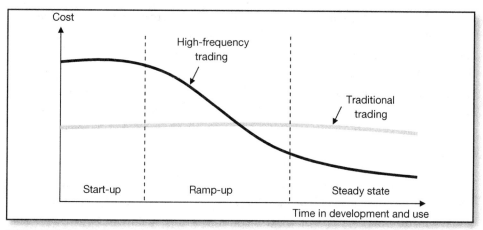

FIGURE 7.3 The Economics of High-Frequency versus Traditional Trading Businesses

moment an experienced senior trader with a proven track record begins running the trading desk and training promising young apprentices, through the time when the trained apprentices replace their masters.

Figure 7.3 illustrates the cost curves for rolling out computerized and traditional trading systems. The cost of traditional trading remains fairly constant through time. With the exception of trader "burnouts" necessitating hiring and training new trader staff, costs of staffing the traditional trading desk do not change. Developing computerized trading systems, however, requires an up-front investment that is costly in terms of labor and time. One successful trading system takes on average 36 months to develop. The costs of computerized trading decline as the system moves into production, ultimately requiring a small support staff that typically includes a dedicated systems engineer and a performance-monitoring agent. Both the systems engineer and a monitoring agent can be responsible for several trading systems simultaneously, driving the costs closer to zero.

■ Financial Markets Suitable for HFT

A wide range of securities and market conditions fit the profile for trading at high frequencies. Some securities markets, however, are more appropriate than others.

To be appropriate for this type of trading, two requirements must be met: the ability to quickly move in and out of positions and sufficient market volatility to ensure that changes in prices exceed transaction costs. The volatilities of different markets have been shown to be highly interrelated and dependent on the volume of macroeconomic news reaching the markets. The ability to quickly enter into positions as well as to close them is in turn determined by two factors: market liquidity and availability of electronic execution.

Liquid assets are characterized by readily available supply and demand. Liquid securities such as major foreign exchange pairs are traded 24 hours a day, 5 days a week. Less liquid securities, such as penny stocks, may trade only once every few days. Between trades, the prices of illiquid assets may change substantially, making less liquid securities more risky as compared with more liquid assets.

High-frequency strategies focus on the most liquid securities; a security requiring a holding period of 10 minutes may not be able to find a timely reasonably-priced counterparty in illiquid markets. While longer-horizon investors can work with either liquid or illiquid securities, Amihud and Mendelson (1986) show that longer-horizon investors optimally hold less liquid assets. According to these authors, the key issue is the risk/return consideration; longer-term investors (already impervious to the adverse short-term market moves) will obtain higher average gains by taking on more risk in less liquid investments.

A perfectly liquid market is the one where the quoted bid or ask price can be achieved irrespective of the quantities traded (see Bervas, 2006, for detailed treatment of the subject). Market liquidity depends on the presence of limit-order traders in the market, as well as the counterparties' willingness to trade. The market participants' willingness to trade in turn depends on their risk aversions and expectations of impending price movements, along with other market information.

One way to compare the liquidity of different securities is to use the average daily volume of each security as the measure of liquidity. In terms of daily average trading volume, foreign exchange is the most liquid market, followed by recently issued U.S. Treasury securities, then equities, options, commodities, and futures. Swaps, traditionally traded over the counter (OTC), but entering the electronic era under the Dodd-Frank Act, are on their way to become the most liquid and optimal market for HFT.

Economics of HFT

Costs of Doing HFT Business

The cost drivers in an HFT business are data, labor, equipment and software, trading costs, administrative and legal costs, and, most important, trading losses. Effective risk management, monitoring, and compliance frameworks, discussed in Chapters 14 and 16 are required to limit the latter. This section describes the costs of doing business that are not attributable to risk.

Costs of Data

Data tend to be either very expensive or entirely free. Multiple companies, like Reuters and Bloomberg, offer tick data for sale for a significant premium. Broker-dealers and trading venues may offer quality tick data free of charge to prospective traders. Start-up HFT firms will need to obtain at least two years of historical data in the instrument of choice to generate initial trading models.

Hardware As discussed in Chapter 2, hardware costs are the least prominent component of HFT operating expenses. The most basic, yet effective, HFT setup involves computers commonly available at retail stores. A professional operating system, like Windows 7 or Red Hat Linux, is necessary for thorough configuration and remote access. It is wise to purchase separate machines for development, testing, and production, to minimize incidents of unintentional code manipulation and over-loads of processing power.

Connectivity Connectivity is important for any successful HFT operation: a fast connection with a sufficient bandwidth ensures that the trading operation receives the fullest set of quotes and trades: as described in Chapter 2, quotes in particular can be lost in cyberspace congestion. Connectivity options involve

- Co-location
- Proximity
- Run-of-the-mill connections

Co-location or "colo" is offered by exchanges and other trading venues in their dedicated facilities, and typically includes a secure "cage" for the HFT server, a power source, and an actual network "wire" connecting the HFT and the exchange servers, most often via a dedicated line. High-frequency traders are free to configure the server anyway they like, and may include remote accessibility.

Proximity services are similar to co-location, except they are run by third-party companies with access to facilities located close to trading venues, but not in the same facility as trading venues. Like co-location, proximity offers a cage for servers, a power source, and a fast wire (typically, a fiber-optic hookup). The wire, however, connects to the exchange via the general Internet, making proximity less secure than co-location.

Finally, a shoestring HFT start-up can survive on a premium cable network as well until its systems become consistently profitable. The common network, however, is subject to extreme congestion, resulting in serial quote losses and information and trading delays.

Software HFT operations deploy the following software that may or may not be built in-house:

- Computerized generation of trading signals is the core functionality of an HFT system. The generator accepts and processes tick data, generates port-folio allocations and trade signals, and records profit and loss (P&L). Genera-tors are most often built in-house and kept in utmost secrecy. The secrecy requirement stems from purely competitive business considerations: every investment strategy has a finite capacity, and a competitor armed with a gen-erator code is bound to significantly diminish or outright destroy profitability of an HFT strategy.
- Computer-aided analysis is done with financial modeling software deployed by HFT operations to build new trading models. MatLab and R have emerged as the industry's most popular quantitative modeling choices. MatLab can be pricey, but is well known in the industry. R, however, is free: it is an open-source software that is efficient, and, best of all, can be extended with proprietary libraries. Citi-group, for example, now runs almost all of its modeling in R.

- Internet-wide information-gathering software facilitates high-frequency fundamental pricing of securities. Promptly capturing rumors and news announcements enhances forecasts of short-term price moves. Thomson Reuters, Dow Jones, and newcomers like RavenPack, SemLab and AbleMarkets.com offer a range of products that deliver real-time news in a machine-readable format.

- Trading software incorporates optimal execution algorithms for achieving the best execution price within a given time interval. This software enables traders to time trades, decide on market aggressiveness, and size orders into optimal lots. Development and per-trade licensing of best execution algorithms is now the bread and butter of many broker-dealers. Yet independent companies have sprung up to help investors distribute their orders in the most efficient manner. For example, the New York–based MarketFactory provides a suite of software tools to help automated traders get an extra edge in the foreign exchange market. Furthermore, an increasing number of traditional buy-side investors, like large pension funds and hedge funds, have developed their own suites of best execution algorithms in a bid to bypass broker-dealers altogether. Chapter 15 discusses the latest developments in best execution.

- Run-time risk management applications ensure that the system stays within pre-specified behavioral and P&L bounds, as discussed in detail in Chapter 14. Such applications may also be known as system-monitoring and fault-tolerance software and are often built in-house, but are generic enough to buy off the shelf. The advantage of buying third-party risk software is the reliability of the modules. The third-party software undergoes diligent review by multiple customers and, as a result, may be more sound than anything built in-house.

- Desktop and mobile applications designed for monitoring performance of HFT systems are a must for all modern HFT organizations. Any issues, breaches of risk limits, power outages, or any other problems should be immediately related to responsible parties. Like risk-management systems, performance monitoring and compliance systems tend to be generic enough to warrant purchasing well-tested third-party software.

- Real-time third-party research can stream advanced information and forecasts. Sometimes, these forecasts can be incorporated into a trading system in a useful manner. For example, a forecast that warns of an imminent crash can be used to enhance a liquidity provision HFT system. AbleMarkets.com and HFTindex.com provide this kind of information.

Electronic Execution HFT practitioners may rely on their executing brokers and ECNs to quickly route and execute their trades. Goldman Sachs and Credit Suisse are often cited as broker-dealers dominating electronic execution. UBS, Barclays and Quantitative Brokers have been the go-to venues for foreign exchange and fixed income.

Execution providers typically charge a per-trade fee, known in advance. The total costs may, however, include other unobservable components that vary from broker to broker, as Chapter 5 describes in detail. Understanding the cost structure of execution is especially important in high-frequency settings where the sheer number of transactions can eliminate gains.

Custody and Clearing In addition to providing connectivity to exchanges, broker-dealers typically offer special "prime" services that include safekeeping of trading capital (known as *custody*) and trade reconciliation (known as *clearing*). Both custody and clearing involve a certain degree of risk. In a custody arrangement, the broker-dealer takes the responsibility for the assets, whereas in clearing, the broker-dealer may act as insurance against the default of trading counterparties. Broker-dealers and trading venues charge custody and clearing fees.

Staffing Costs Initial development of high-frequency systems is both risky and pricey, and the staff required to design trading models needs to understand PhD-level quantitative research in finance and econometrics. In addition, programming staff should be experienced enough to handle complex issues of system interoperability, computer security, and algorithmic efficiency.

Administrative and Legal Costs Like any business in the financial sector, high-frequency traders need to make sure that "all i's are dotted and all t's are crossed" in legal and accounting departments. Qualified legal and accounting assistance is therefore indispensable for building a capable operation.

Capitalization of HFT

As with any other form of trading, an HFT firm can be capitalized with equity and leverage. The initial equity normally comprises contributions from the founders of the firm, private equity capital, private investor capital, or capital of the parent company. The amount of the initial equity required depends on many factors, but can be approximated using the following variables:

- Profitability of the HFT strategy to be traded with live capital.
- Cost structure of the trading operation.
- Sharpe ratio of the strategy.
- Maximum drawdown of the strategy.

The profitability of the HFT strategy describes the "gross" return on every dollar invested. The gross return does not account for trading costs and presents a high-level picture of potential profitability. During the earliest stages of investment, back-test performance can be used as potential future performance. Great caution, however, should be used: back-tests often fail to account for basic costs and market impact of the strategy itself, reducing production profitability. Worst of all, back-tests can be simply wrong, either due to unrealistic assumptions or coding mistakes that may not be exposed until the code is transferred into production.

Strategies that do well in gross performance terms are subject to significant costs. In high-frequency settings, per-trade gains are typically small compared to the transaction costs, which can easily annihilate any semblance of profitability. This is particularly true in the start-up phases of operation, when the traded notional is often small. As described in Chapter 5, trading costs are often larger when the traded amount is small and vice versa. For example, a common retail brokerage charges $20 per every leg of the trade with notional of $40,000 and less, or more than 0.05 percent of the notional. And every trade has two legs: one to open a position, and one to close, emptying a retail trader of 0.1 percent per every round-trip trade. At the same time, a large institution faces costs of as little as $3 or $5 for every $1 million traded—just 0.0005 percent of the notional, a cost 100 times smaller than the one offered to the retail investors.

When the available capital is small, it often can be "levered." Leverage most often refers to borrowed funds collateralized by the traded financial instruments. Thus, with a 1:9 leverage, a $100,000 investment becomes $1 million trading notional, possibly obtaining lower transaction costs and retaining better profitability. In addition, leverage helps multiply gains of the strategy. A 0.1 percent return on $100,000 is $100 without leverage. When the strategy is traded with a 1:9 leverage, the $0.1 percent return becomes a $1 million × 0.1 percent = $1,000 or 1 percent return on the $100,000 investment, a significant improvement. Of course, when the strategy loses money, its losses are also multiplied accordingly: what is a $100 loss in an unlevered $100,000 notional extends to a $1,000 loss with a 1:9 leverage.

Broker-dealers are the most natural providers of leverage: they can observe the trader's positions in real time and ensure return of their capital by liquidating said trader's positions. Liquidation happens when the trader's account value falls below a safety collateral value known as *margin*. Margin requirements vary from broker to broker, but typically designate a certain percentage of the traded notional to be in the account at all times. Margin requirements are not, however, written in stone and can be negotiated on an account-by-account and even situation-by-situation basis.

To avoid liquidation, traders can optimize the leverage that works best for each strategy. Maximum drawdown and Sharpe ratio metrics help traders determine how much leverage the trader can afford given the volatility of his strategy and the maximum downside recorded in historical data.

In addition to leverage, later-stage equity can be a source of trading capital, and it can be obtained from established institutions, such as bank asset management divisions, fund-of-funds, pension funds, large hedge funds interested in boosting their performance, and the like.

From the perspective of a large institutional investor, possibly looking to invest into a high-frequency operation, most HFT tends to fall into the category of "alternative" investments. The term *alternative investments* describes most strategies under a broader hedge fund umbrella; the term is used to distinguish strategies from "traditional" investments, such as long-only mutual funds and bond portfolios. As a result of its alternative status, HFT strategies are candidates for inclusion in larger institutional portfolios. To qualify for institutional investment, HFT managers need to deliver a one- to three-year auditable performance track record of 8 to 12 percent per annum, with as little volatility as possible.

The compensation of HFTs then follows the hedge fund model: HFT managers are paid management and performance fees. Management fees are typically fixed percentages of the notional amount invested. The performance fees are percentages of the gain above the previous highest value of the fund shares, known as *high water mark*. Just as with any other hedge fund manager, the performance fee is paid to a high-frequency manager only when the manager increases (or has increased) the value of the fund shares, creating an incentive to outperform.

Due to its relative novelty, HFT is often treated as an "emerging manager" business. The "emerging" label typically results in higher perceived risk as far as strategy longevity is concerned, from the institutional investor's point of view. This, in turn, translates into higher performance, but lower management fees. Where an arbitrary hedge fund may command 2 percent management fee and 20 percent performance fee (the classic "2-and-20" model), high-frequency traders often offer a "1-and-30" model, with 1 percent of all assets under management serving as a compensation for administrative activity, and 30 percent of above-the-highest-water mark gains paid as a performance incentive.

Leverage of HFT

How much leverage can an HFT business sustain and remain viable? The quick answer to this question depends on two performance variables characteristic to each HFT strategy: Sharpe ratio and maximum drawdown. The beauty of the Sharpe ratio lies in its invariance with respect to leverage: a Sharpe ratio of an unlevered HFT strategy is exactly the same as the Sharpe ratio of an HFT strategy levered 100 times. This is due to the structure of the high-frequency Sharpe ratio: no levered HFT positions are held overnight, so the HFT Sharpe ratio does not include the risk-free rate in the numerator, as pointed out in Chapter 6. When the Sharpe ratio increases, the expected return in the numerator and the volatility in the denominator of the ratio increase proportionally by the amount of leverage, L:

$$SR^{HFT} = \frac{\mathbb{E}\left[R_{annualized}\right]}{\sigma\left[R_{annualized}\right]} = \frac{\mathbb{E}\left[R_{annualized}\right] \times L}{\sigma\left[R_{annualized}\right] \times L} \tag{1}$$

The expected return of the high-frequency operation must take into account the costs of doing business, so the Sharpe ratio of an HFT business is adjusted for expenses:

$$SR^{HFT\ Ops} = \frac{\mathbb{E}\left[R_{annualized}\right] \times L \times (Capital) - (Annualized\ Expenses)}{\sigma\left[R_{annualized}\right] \times L \times (Capital)} \tag{2}$$

or, using daily data, and assuming 250 trading days per year:

$$SR^{HFT\ Ops} = \frac{\mathbb{E}\left[R_{daily}\right] \times L \times \left(Capital\right) - \left(Daily\ Expenses\right)}{\sigma\left[R_{daily}\right] \times L \times \left(Capital\right)} \sqrt{250} \tag{3}$$

Expressions in equations (2) and (3) have to be positive for a profitable business, yet the leverage value L cannot be increased infinitely. Annualized volatility is only the average measure of return variability. The actual realizations of losses can be much more severe. To determine the minimum Sharpe ratio $SR^{HFT\ Ops}$ required for a stable operation, a maximum drawdown comes in as a convenient metric.

Assuming that the historical maximum drawdown can occur in 10 percent of worst-case scenarios, the required Sharpe ratio $SR^{HFT\ Ops}$ is related to the number of standard deviations the historical maximum drawdown lies away from the mean of returns:

$$\frac{Max\$\$Drawdown}{Capital} > SR^{HFT\ Ops} \times \sigma\left[R_{annualized}\right] \times L - 1.645 \times \sigma\left[R_{annualized}\right] \times L \quad (4)$$

from where the minimum $SR^{HFT\ Ops}$ can be obtained as

$$SR^{HFT\ Ops}_{min} = \frac{Max\$\$Drawdown/Capital + 1.96 \times \sigma\left[R_{annualized}\right] \times L}{\sigma\left[R_{annualized}\right] \times L} \quad (5)$$

For a levered strategy to remain solvent, the Sharpe ratio takes into account operating costs $SR^{HFT\ Ops}$ that have to exceed SR^{HFTOps}_{min} determined by equation (5). Figure 7.4 presents gross cumulative performance of a sample high-frequency strategy. The strategy delivers a gross Sharpe ratio of 2.78 with a maximum drawdown of 0.93 percent incurred in July 2012, and daily volatility of 0.15 percent computed over the sample history of the strategy. The minimum operational Sharpe ratio $SR^{HFT\ Ops}$ this strategy delivers when levered has to exceed SR^{HFTOps}_{min} of equation (5), computed to be 1.41. If this particular strategy is allocated $10 million in capital and allowed a nine-to-one leverage, $L = 10$, then the maximum daily spending of the operation cannot exceed $13,730, or $3,432,729 for 250 trading days per year. This number is considerably smaller than the number computed from the daily average return: if the risk of going bankrupt via maximum drawdown is ignored completely, then the expected levered performance is computed as the annualized average daily return multiplied by capital and leverage:

$$E\left[Gain_{naive}\right] = E\left[R_{daily}\right] \times 250 \times Capital \times Leverage \quad (6)$$

If computed using equation (6), the naïve gain works out to be nearly $6,959,034—a misleading number to spend when the risk of drawdown is taken into account.

If a stricter performance measure is required, whereby the observed maximum drawdown occurs in less than 5 percent of all cases, equation (5) can be rewritten as

$$SR^{HFT\ Ops}_{min} = \frac{MaxDrawdown/Capital + 1.96 \times \sigma\left[R_{annualized}\right] \times L}{\sigma\left[R_{annualized}\right] \times L} \quad (7)$$

where number of standard deviations where maximum drawdown is located has changed from 1 to 3. For the $10 million capital deployed in strategy with the

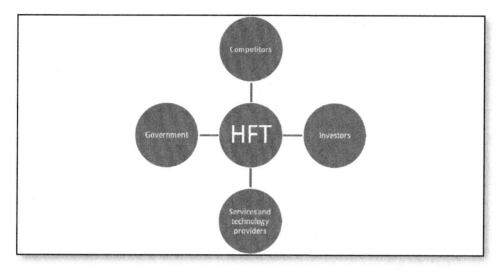

FIGURE 7.4   HFT Industry Participants

minimum operational Sharpe ratio of 2.41, for example, the maximum allowable annual expense is $931,801.

An HFT operation is more likely to survive and prosper if it has leverage and high Sharpe ratios. High leverage increases the likelihood of covering costs, and the high Sharpe ratio reduces the risk of a catastrophic loss.

■ Market Participants

Like any other industry, HFT is subject to outside forces and influences. Figure 7.4 summarizes the playing field of HFT. The remainder of the section discusses market participants in detail.

Competitors

HFT firms compete with other, more traditional, investment management firms, as well as market-making broker-dealers. The competition with traditional mutual and hedge funds centers on attracting investment. The rivalry with quantitative hedge funds and other high-frequency trading firms also includes recruitment of talented and experienced strategists and technologists, as well as direct contest for market inefficiencies. Likewise, the battle with traditional non-HFT broker-dealers involves turf wars over "first dibs" access to profit opportunities in the traditional market-making arena.

Investors

Investors in HFT include funds-of-funds aiming to diversify their portfolios, hedge funds eager to add new strategies to their existing mix, and private equity firms seeing a sustainable opportunity to create wealth. Most investment banks offer leverage through their "prime" services.

Services and Technology Providers

Like any business, a high-frequency trading operation requires specific support services. Most common and, in many cases, critical providers to the high-frequency business community include providers of data, hardware, connectivity, software, execution, custody, clearing, staffing, and administrative and legal services, described in more detail earlier in this chapter.

Government

Several regulatory initiatives were under way around the world at the time this book was written. Chapter 13 summarizes the latest regulatory thought.

■ Summary

Developing a high-frequency business involves challenges that include issues surrounding the "gray box" or "black box" nature of many systems. The low transparency of fast and complex algorithm decisions requires diligent risk management and monitoring processes, and constant human supervision. The deployment and execution costs decrease considerably with time, leaving the profit-generating engines operating consistently, with no emotion, sickness, or other human factors. Well-designed and -executed high-frequency systems, capitalizing on multiple short-term moves of security prices, are capable of generating solid profitability in all types of electronic markets.

■ End-of-Chapter Questions

1. What are the key steps in algorithm development?
2. How much time is spent on monitoring in a stable HFT operation?
3. What kind of operational costs can an HFT with $100 million in capital and a net (after transaction costs) Sharpe ratio of 1.5 carry?
4. What is the minimum capital needed for a breakeven of an HFT with the following characteristics:
   a. Net (after transaction costs) Sharpe ratio of 2.8
   b. Three full-time officers earning $150,000 per year each
   c. Office overhead (office space, networking and computer expenses) of $72,000 per year
   d. Co-location of $36,000 per year
5. Who are the HFT industry participants?

CHAPTER 8

Statistical Arbitrage Strategies

Like human trading, high-frequency trading (HFT) strategies can be broken down into three major categories (per Harris, 1998):

1. *Statistical arbitrage or stat-arb, also known as value-motivated strategies.* Stat-arb traders wait for security prices to become cheap relative to their proprietary valuations of security based on fundamental or purely statistical indicators. These traders run models to determine the fair value of each financial instrument. Stat-arb traders might be traditional, low-frequency institutional money managers, as well as high-frequency managers, arbitraging short-term valuation discrepancies. Stat-arb traders may deploy market orders for fast-dissolving price discrepancies as well as limit orders to capture slowly evolving misvaluations (see Kaniel and Liu, 2006; and Angel, 1994).

2. *Directional strategies, also known as informed trading.* Directional traders successfully estimate the direction of an impending market move. Directional traders are often high-frequency money managers and other proprietary traders with superior access to information and skill in assessing immediate market situations. Their information can include analyses from paid-for news sources, like Bloomberg, not yet available to the general public; forecasts based on market microstructure; and other sources.

   Directional traders' forecasts tend to be time sensitive. Forecasts may be related to an event scheduled to occur at a specific time, after which the forecasts cease to be useful. Information obtained from premium sources may soon be distributed to the public, reducing its potency. As a result, directional traders are impatient and typically execute using market orders or "aggressive" limit orders set at prices close to market (see Vega, 2007). Directional event-based strategies are discussed in Chapter 9.

3. *Market-making, also known as liquidity trading.* Market makers have no material market insights and aim to profit from providing liquidity. When using high-frequency algorithms, liquidity traders deploy automated market-making strategies, discussed in Chapters 10 and 11. Market makers are most likely to use limit orders, although selected situations may call for market orders as well.

Figure 8.1 illustrates distributions of order aggressiveness and trader types relative to the market price in the limit order book.

Statistical arbitrage (stat-arb) exploded on the trading scene in the 1990s, with traders reaping double-digit returns using simple statistical phenomena. This chapter discusses common stat-arb strategies deployed in the HFT space.

Stat-arb is named after its primary function: detection of statistically persistent phenomena, most often, with fundamental roots. Such statistically persistent relationships may exist between the current price level of equity and the recently reported earnings of the traded company. The relationships may also be between price levels of multiple financial instruments, linked by some fundamental variables, the price level of one financial instrument and the volatility of another, and many other values.

The critical point in the identification process of financial instruments suitable for stat-arb is that the relationship among the variables has to hold with at least 90 or higher percent statistical confidence. This level of statistical confidence is observed when the numerical variation in the tested relationship remains within two standard deviations from its average value. Thus, in a way, stat-arb is a modern and sophisticated cousin of a technical analysis strategy utilizing "Bollinger bands" that showed a two-standard-deviation envelope around the simple moving average of the price, suggesting the likely near-term price path bounds.

Stat-arb models measuring statistical persistence of shown economic phenomena tend to have higher profitability and longer staying power than models detecting statistical persistence based on data mining alone. An example of stat-arb based on solid economic principles is the exchange-traded fund (ETF) or index arbitrage: by the Law of One Price of finance, a traded index or ETF should have the same price as a basket of individual financial instruments comprising the ETF

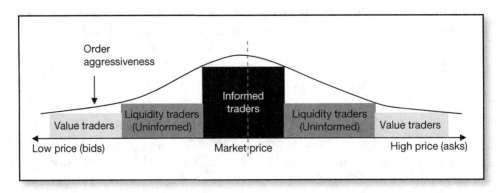

FIGURE 8.1 Graphical Representation of Order Aggressiveness and Trader Type Distributions in the Limit Order Book

and weighed accordingly. If a mismatch between the do-it-yourself basket and the traded ETF exists, a trader can profitably arbitrage the mismatch, as discussed later in this chapter.

By contrast, a statistical relationship observed between prices of two completely unrelated stocks may be purely random, or "spurious." While the relationship produces a highly significant statistical dependency, it can hardly be used to make meaningful predictions about future values of the stocks under consideration. From a trading strategy point of view, such a relationship is not too different from the statistical relationships shown by Challe (2003), who illustrates the following outrageous spurious relationship: a statistically significant link between the occurrence of sunspots and the predictability of asset returns.

This chapter explores techniques developed for detecting stat-arb relationships, as well as presents specific cases of proven dependencies.

Practical Applications of Statistical Arbitrage

General Considerations

The prices of two or more financial instruments traded in stat-arb models often will be fundamentally related in some fashion or other, but they can nevertheless span a variety of asset classes and individual names. In equities, the companies issuing securities may belong to the same industry and will therefore respond similarly to changes in the broad market. Alternatively, the securities may actually be issued by the same company. Companies often issue more than one class of shares, and the shares typically differ by voting rights. Even shares of the same class issued by the same company but trading on different exchanges may have profitable intraday deviations in prices. In foreign exchange, the pair of instruments chosen can be a foreign exchange rate and a derivative (e.g., a futures contract) on the same foreign exchange rate. The same underlying derivative trading strategy may well apply to equities and fixed-income securities. Passive indices, such as infrequently rebalanced ETFs, can be part of profitable trades when the index and its constituents exhibit temporary price deviations from equilibrium. In options, the pair of instruments may be two options on the same underlying asset but with different times to expiration.

This section discusses numerous examples of statistical arbitrage applied to various financial instruments. Table 8.1 itemizes the strategies discussed subsequently. The selected strategies are intended to illustrate the ideas of fundamental arbitrage. The list is by no means exhaustive, and many additional fundamental arbitrage opportunities can be found.

Equities

Examples of successful statistical arbitrage strategies involving fundamental equities models abound. This section reviews the following popular equity stat-arb trading strategies: pairs, different equity classes of the same issuer, market-neutral pairs trading, liquidity arbitrage, and large-to-small information spillovers.

TABLE 8.1

TABLE 8.1 Summary of Fundamental Arbitrage Strategies by Asset Class Presented in This Section

Asset Class	Fundamental Arbitrage Strategy
Equities	Pairs trading
Equities	Different equity classes of the same issuer
Equities	Risk arbitrage
Equities	Liquidity rbitragea
Foreign exchange	Triangular arbitrage
Foreign exchange	Uncovered interest parity (UIP) arbitrage
Indices and ETFs	Index composition arbitrage
Options	Volatility curve arbitrage
Cross-asset	Futures basis trading
Cross-asset	Futures/ETF arbitrage

Pairs Trading Pairs trading is the simplest and most commonly used stat-arb strategy. Mathematically, the steps involved in the development of stat-arb trading signals are based on a relationship between price levels or other variables characterizing any two financial instruments. A relationship based on price levels $S_{i,t}$ and $S_{j,t}$ for any two instruments i and j can be can be arrived at through the following procedure:

1. Identify the universe of liquid financial instruments: instruments that trade at least once within the desired trading frequency unit. For example, for hourly trading frequency choose securities that trade at least once every hour.

2. Measure the difference between prices of every two securities, i and j, identified in step (1) across time t:

$$\Delta S_{ij,t} = S_{i,t} - S_{j,t}, \ t \in [1,T] \tag{1}$$

where T is a sufficiently large number of daily observations. According to the central limit theorem (CLT) of statistics, 30 observations at selected trading frequency constitute the bare minimum. The intra-day data, however, may have high seasonality—that is, persistent relationships can be observed at specific hours of the day. Thus, a larger T of at least 30 daily observations is strongly recommended. For robust inferences, a T of 500 daily observations (two years) is desirable.

3. For each pair of securities, select the ones with the most stable relationship—security pairs that move together. To do this, Gatev, Goetzmann and Rouwenhorst (1999) perform a simple minimization of the historical differences in returns between every two liquid securities:

$$\min_{i,j} \sum_{t=1}^{T} (\Delta S_{ij,t})^2 \tag{2}$$

The stability of the relationship can also be assessed using cointegration and other statistical techniques.

Next, for each security i, select the security j with the minimum sum of squares obtained in equation (2).

4. Estimate basic distributional properties of the difference as follows.
   Mean or average of the difference:

$$E[\Delta S_t] = \frac{1}{T}\sum_{t=1}^{T}\Delta S_t$$

Standard deviation:

$$\sigma[\Delta S_t] = \frac{1}{T-1}\sum_{t=1}^{T}(\Delta S_t - E[\Delta S_t])^2$$

5. Monitor and act upon differences in security prices:
   At a particular time τ, if

$$\Delta S_\tau = S_{i,\tau} - S_{j,\tau} > E[\Delta S_\tau] + 2\sigma[\Delta S_\tau]$$

sell security i and buy security j. However, if

$$\Delta S_\tau = S_{i,\tau} - S_{j,\tau} < E[\Delta S_\tau] - 2\sigma[\Delta S_\tau]$$

buy security i and sell security j.
6. Once the gap in security prices reverses to achieve a desirable gain, close out the positions. If the prices move against the predicted direction, activate stop loss.

Instead of detecting statistical anomalies in price levels, statistical arbitrage can be applied to other variables, such as correlation between two securities and traditional fundamental relationships. The details of implementation of statistical arbitrage based on fundamental factors are discussed in detail in the following text.

Pairs-trading strategies can be trained to dynamically adjust to changing market conditions. The mean of the variable under consideration, to which the identified statistical relationships are assumed to tend, can be computed as a moving weighted average with the latest observations being given more weight than the earliest observations in the computation window. Similarly, the standard deviation used in computations can be computed using a limited number of the most recent observations, reflecting the latest economic environment.

Statistical relationships validated by academic research in economics and finance may consistently produce positive results for many traders. Thorough understanding of economic theory helps quantitative analysts distinguish between solid and arbitrary relationships and, in turn, improves the profitability and reduces risk of trading operations that use stat-arb methodology.

In addition to the issues embedded in the estimation of statistical relationships, statistical arbitrage strategies are influenced by numerous adverse market conditions.

Arbitraging Different Equity Classes of the Same Issuer It is reasonable to expect stocks corresponding to two common equity classes issued by the same company to be trading within a relatively constant price range from each other. Different classes of common equity issued by the same company typically diverge in the following two characteristics only: voting rights and number of shares outstanding.

Shares with superior voting rights are usually worth more than the shares with inferior voting rights or nonvoting shares, given that shares with wider voting privileges allow the shareholders to exercise a degree of control over the direction of the company—see Horner (1988) and Smith and Amoako-Adu (1995), for example. Nenova (2003) shows that the stock price premium for voting privileges exists in most countries. The premium varies substantially from country to country and depends on the legal environment, the degree of investor protection, and takeover regulations, among other factors. In countries with the greatest transparency, such as Finland, the voting premium is worth close to zero, whereas in South Korea, the voting premium can be worth close to 50 percent of the voting stock's market value.

Stocks with a higher number of shares outstanding are usually more liquid, prompting actively trading investors to value them more highly (see Amihud and Mendelson, 1986, 1989; Amihud, 2002; Brennan and Subrahmanyam, 1996; Brennan, Chordia, and Subrahmanyam, 1998; and Eleswarapu, 1997). At the same time, the more liquid class of shares is likely to incorporate market information significantly faster than the less liquid share class, creating opportunities for information arbitrage.

A typical trade may work as follows: if the price range widens to more than two standard deviations of the average daily range without a sufficiently good reason, it may be a fair bet that the range will narrow within the following few hours.

The dual-class share strategy suffers from two main shortcomings and may not work for funds with substantial assets under management (AUM).

1. The number of public companies that have dual share classes trading in the open markets is severely limited, restricting the applicability of the strategy. In January 2009, for example, Yahoo! Finance carried historical data for two equity classes for just eight companies trading on the New York Stock Exchange (NYSE): Blockbuster, Inc.; Chipotle; Forest City Entertainment; Greif, Inc.; John Wiley & Sons; K V Pharma; Lennar Corp.; and Moog, Inc.

2. The daily volume for the less liquid share class is often small, further restricting the capacity of the strategy. Table 8.2 shows the closing price and daily volume for dual-class shares registered on the NYSE on January 6, 2009. For all names, Class B daily volume on January 6, 2009, does not reach even one million in shares and is too small to sustain a trading strategy of any reasonable trading size.

TABLE 8.2 Closing Price and Daily Volume of Dual-Class Shares on NYSE on January 6, 2009

Company Name	Ticker Class A	Class A Close	Class A Volume (MM Shares)	Ticker Class B	Class B Close	Class B Volume (MM Shares)
Blockbuster, Inc.	BBI	1.59	2.947	BBI-B	0.88	0.423
Chipotle	CMG	60.38	0.659	CMG-B	55.87	0.156
Forest City Entertainment	FCE-A	8.49	1.573	FCE-B	8.41	0.008
Greif, Inc.	GEF	35.42	0.378	GEF-B	35.15	0.016
John Wiley & Sons	JW-A	36.82	0.237	JW-B	36.63	0.005
K V Pharma	KV-A	3.68	0.973	KV-B	3.78	0.007
Lennar Corp.	LEN	11.17	8.743	LEN-B	8.5	0.074
Moog, Inc.	MOG-A	37.52	0.242	MOG-B	37.9	0.000

Risk Arbitrage   Risk arbitrage or market-neutral arbitrage refers to a class of trading models that are based on classical equilibrium finance literature. At core, most market-neutral models are built on the capital asset pricing model (CAPM) developed by Sharpe (1964), Lintner (1965), and Black (1972).

The CAPM is based on the idea that returns on all securities are influenced by the broad market returns. The degree of the co-movement that a particular security may experience with the market is different for each individual security and can vary through time. For example, stocks of luxury companies have been shown to produce positive returns whenever the broad market produces positive returns as well, whereas breweries and movie companies tend to produce higher positive returns whenever the overall market returns are downward sloping.

The CAPM equation is specified as follows:

$$r_{i,t} - r_{f,t} = \alpha_i + \beta_i(r_{M,t} - r_{f,t}) + \varepsilon_t \tag{3}$$

where $r_{i,t}$ is the return on security i at time t, $r_{M,t}$ is the return on a broad market index achieved in time period t, and $r_{f,t}$ is the risk-free interest rate, such as Fed Funds rate, valid in time period t. The equation can be estimated using ordinary least squares (OLS) regression. The resulting parameter estimates, $\hat{\alpha}$ and $\hat{\beta}$, measure the abnormal return that is intrinsic to the security ($\hat{\alpha}$) and the security's co-movement with the market ($\hat{\beta}$).

The simplest example of CAPM-based pair arbitrage in equities is trading pairs with the same response to the changes in the broader market conditions, or beta, but different intrinsic returns, or alpha. This type of strategy is often referred to as a market-neutral strategy, with the idea that going long and short, respectively, in two securities with similar beta would neutralize the resulting portfolio from broad market exposure.

Often, the two securities used belong to the same or a similar industry, although this is not mandatory. The alpha and beta for two securities i and j are determined from the CAPM equation (3). Once the point estimates for alphas and betas of the two securities are produced, along with standard deviations of those point estimates, the statistical significance of difference in alphas and betas is then determined using the difference in the means test, described here for betas only:

$$\Delta\hat{\beta} = \hat{\beta}_i - \hat{\beta}_j \tag{4}$$

$$\hat{\sigma}_{\Delta\beta} = \sqrt{\frac{\sigma_{\beta i}^2}{n_i} + \frac{\sigma_{\beta j}^2}{n_j}} \tag{5}$$

where n_i and n_j are the numbers of observations used in the estimation of equation (3) for security i and security j, respectively.

The standard t-ratio statistic is then determined as follows:

$$Student\, t_\beta = \frac{\Delta\hat{\beta}}{\hat{\sigma}_{\Delta\beta}} \tag{6}$$

The difference test for alphas follows the same procedure as the one outlined for betas in equations (4) through (6).

As with other t-test estimations, betas can be deemed to be statistically similar if the t statistic falls within one standard deviation interval:

$$t_\beta \in [\Delta\hat{\beta} - \hat{\sigma}_{\Delta\beta}, \Delta\hat{\beta} + \hat{\sigma}_{\Delta\beta}] \tag{7}$$

At the same time, the difference in alphas has to be both economically and statistically significant. The difference in alphas has to exceed trading costs, TC, and the t-ratio has to indicate a solid statistical significance, with 95 percent typically considered the minimum:

$$\Delta\hat{\alpha} > TC \tag{8}$$

$$|t_\alpha| > [\Delta\hat{\alpha} + 2\hat{\sigma}_{\Delta\alpha}] \tag{9}$$

Once a pair of securities satisfying equations (7) through (9) is identified, the trader goes long in the security with the higher alpha and shorts the security with the lower alpha. The position is held for the predetermined horizon used in the forecast.

Variations on the basic market-neutral pair trading strategy include strategies accounting for other security-specific factors, such as equity fundamentals. For example, Fama and French (1993) show that the following three-factor model can be successfully used in equity pair trading:

$$r_{i,t} = \alpha_i + \beta_i^{MKT} MKT_t + \beta_i^{SMB} SMB_t + \beta_i^{HML} HML_t + \varepsilon_t \tag{10}$$

where $r_{i,t}$ is the return on stock i at time t, MKT_t is the time-t return on a broad market index, SMB_t (small minus big) is the time-t difference in returns between market indices or portfolios of small and big capitalization stocks, and HML_t (high minus low) is the return on a portfolio constructed by going long in stocks with comparatively high book-to-market ratios and going short in stocks with comparatively low book-to-market ratios.

Liquidity Arbitrage   In classical asset pricing literature, a financial security that offers some inconvenience to the prospective investors should offer higher returns to compensate investors for the inconvenience. Limited liquidity is one such inconvenience; lower liquidity levels make it more difficult for individual investors to unwind their positions, potentially leading to costly outcomes. On the flip side, if liquidity is indeed priced in asset returns, then periods of limited liquidity may offer nimble investors highly profitable trading opportunities.

In fact, several studies have documented that less liquid stocks have higher average returns: see Amihud and Mendelson (1986); Brennan and Subrahmanyam (1996); Brennan, Chordia, and Subrahmanyam (1998); and Datar, Naik, and Radcliffe (1998). Trading the illiquid stocks based exclusively on the information that they are illiquid, however, delivers no positive abnormal returns. The relatively high average returns simply compensate prospective investors for the risks involved in holding these less liquid securities.

Pastor and Stambaugh (2003), however, recognize that at least a portion of the observed illiquidity of financial securities may be attributed to market-wide causes. If the market-wide liquidity is priced into individual asset returns, then market illiquidity arbitrage strategies may well deliver consistent positive abnormal returns on the risk-adjusted basis.

Pastor and Stambaugh (2003) find that in equities, stocks whose returns have higher exposure to variability in the market-wide liquidity indeed deliver higher returns than stocks that are insulated from the market-wide liquidity. To measure sensitivity of stock i to market liquidity, Pastor and Stambaugh (2003) devise a metric γ that is estimated in the following OLS specification:

$$r^e_{i,t+1} = \theta + \beta r_{i,t} + \gamma \, sign(r^e_{i,t}).v_{i,t} + \tau_{t+1} \tag{11}$$

where $r_{i,t}$ is the return on stock i at time t, $v_{i,t}$ is the dollar volume for stock i at time t, and $r^e_{i,t}$ is the return on stock i at time t in excess of the market return at time t: $r^e_{i,t} = r_{i,t} - r_{m,t}$. The sign of the excess return $r^e_{i,t}$ proxies for the direction of the order flow at time t; when stock returns are positive, it is reasonable to assume that the number of buy orders in the market outweighs the number of sell orders, and vice versa. The prior time-period return $r_{i,t}$ is included to capture the first-order autocorrelation effects shown to be persistent in the return time series of most financial securities.

Large-to-Small Information Spillovers Equity shares and other securities with relatively limited market capitalization are considered to be "small." The precise cutoff for "smallness" varies from exchange to exchange. On the NYSE in 2002, for example, "small" stocks were those with market capitalization below $1 billion; stocks with market capitalization of $1 billion to $10 billion were considered to be "medium," and "large" stocks were those with market cap in excess of $10 billion.

Small stocks are known to react to news significantly more slowly than large stocks. Lo and MacKinlay (1990), for example, found that returns on smaller stocks follow returns on large stocks. One interpretation of this phenomenon is that large stocks are traded more actively and absorb information more efficiently than small stocks. Hvidkjaer (2006) further documents "an extremely sluggish reaction" of small stocks to past returns of large stocks and attributes this underreaction to the inefficient behavior of small investors.

A proposed reason for the delay in the response of small stocks is their relative unattractiveness to institutional investors who are the primary source of the information that gets impounded into market prices. The small stocks are unattractive to institutional investors because of their size. A typical size of a portfolio of a midcareer institutional manager is $200 million; if a portfolio manager decides to invest into small stocks, even a well-diversified share of an institutional portfolio will end up moving the market for any small stock significantly, cutting into profitability and raising the liquidity risk of the position. In addition, ownership of 5 percent or more of a particular U.S. stock must be reported to the Securities and Exchange Commission (SEC), further complicating institutional investing in small stocks. As a result, small stocks are traded mostly by small investors, many of whom use daily data and traditional "low-tech" technical analysis to make trading decisions.

The market features of small stocks make the stocks illiquid and highly inefficient, enabling profitable trading. Llorente, Michaely, Saar, and Wang (2002) studied further informational content of trade volume and found that stocks of smaller firms and stocks with large bid-ask spreads exhibit momentum following high-volume periods. Stocks of large firms and firms with small bid-ask spread, however, exhibit no momentum and sometimes exhibit reversals following high-volume time periods. Profitable trading strategies, therefore, involve trading small stocks based on the results of correlation or cointegration with lagged returns of large stocks as well as the volume of large and small stocks' records during preceding periods.

Foreign Exchange

Foreign exchange has a number of classic models that have been shown to work in the short term. This section summarizes statistical arbitrage applied to triangular arbitrage and uncovered interest rate parity models. Other fundamental foreign exchange models, such as the flexible price monetary model, the sticky price monetary model, and the portfolio model can be used to generate consistently profitable trades in the statistical arbitrage framework.

Triangular Arbitrage Triangular arbitrage exploits temporary deviations from fair prices in three foreign exchange crosses. The following example illustrates triangular arbitrage of EUR/CAD, following a triangular arbitrage example described by Dacorogna et al. (2001). The strategy arbitrages mispricings between the market prices on EUR/CAD and "synthetic" prices on EUR/CAD that are computed as follows:

$$EUR/CAD_{Sunthetic,bid} = EUR/USD_{Market,bid} \times USD/CAD_{Market,bid} \qquad (12)$$

$$EUR/CAD_{Sunthetic,ask} = EUR/USD_{Market,ask} \times USD/CAD_{Market,ask} \qquad (13)$$

If market ask for EUR/CAD is lower than synthetic bid for EUR/CAD, the strategy is to buy market EUR/CAD, sell synthetic EUR/CAD, and wait for the market and synthetic prices to align, then reverse the position capturing the profit. The difference between the market ask and the synthetic bid should be high enough to at least overcome two spreads—on EUR/USD and on USD/CAD. The USD-rate prices used to compute the synthetic rate should be sampled simultaneously. Even a delay as small as one second in price measurement can significantly distort the relationship as a result of unobserved trades that affect the prices in the background; by the time the dealer receives the order, the prices may have adjusted to their no-arbitrage equilibrium levels.

Uncovered Interest Parity Arbitrage   The uncovered interest parity (UIP) is just one such relation. Chaboud and Wright (2005) find that the UIP best predicts changes in foreign exchange rates at high frequencies and daily rates when the computation is run between 4:00 p.m. ET and 9:00 p.m. ET. The UIP is specified as follows:

$$1 + i_t = (1 + i_t^*)\frac{E_t[S_{t+1}]}{S_t} \qquad (14)$$

where i_t is the one-period interest rate on the domestic currency deposits, i_t^* is the one-period interest rate on deposits denominated in a foreign currency, and S_t is the spot foreign exchange price of one unit of foreign currency in units of domestic currency. Thus, for example, if domestic means United States–based and foreign means Swiss, the UIP equation, equation (14), can be used to calculate the equilibrium CHF/USD rate as follows:

$$1 + i_{t,USD} = (1 + i_{t,CHF}^*)\frac{E_t[S_{t+1,CHF/USD}]}{S_{t,CHF/USD}} \qquad (15)$$

The expression can be conveniently transformed to the following regression form suitable for linear estimation:

$$\ln(S_{t+1,CHF/USD}) - \ln(S_{t,CHF/USD}) = \alpha + \beta(\ln(1 + i_{t,USD}) - \ln(1 + i_{t,CHF}^*)) + \varepsilon_{t+1} \qquad (16)$$

A statistical arbitrage of this relationship would look into the statistical deviations of the two sides of equation (16) and make trading decisions accordingly.

Indices and ETFs

Index arbitrage is driven by the relative mispricings of indices and their underlying components. Under the Law of One Price, index price should be equal to the price of a portfolio of individual securities composing the index, weighted according to their weights within the index. Occasionally, relative prices of the index and the underlying securities deviate from the Law of One Price and present the following arbitrage opportunities. If the price of the index-mimicking portfolio net of transaction costs exceeds the price of the index itself, also net of transaction costs, sell the index-mimicking portfolio, buy index, hold until the market corrects its index pricing, then realize gain. Similarly, if the price of the index-mimicking portfolio is lower than that of the index itself, sell index, buy portfolio, and close the position when the gains have been realized.

Alexander (1999) shows that cointegration-based index arbitrage strategies deliver consistent positive returns and sets forth a cointegration-based portfolio management technique step by step:

1. A portfolio manager selects or is assigned a benchmark. For a portfolio manager investing in international equities, for example, the benchmark can be a European, Asian, or Far East (EAFE) Morgan Stanley index and its constituent indices. Outperforming the EAFE becomes the objective of the portfolio manager.

2. The manager next determines which countries lead EAFE by running the error-correcting model (ECM) with log(EAFE) as a dependent variable and log prices of constituent indices in local currencies as independent (explanatory) variables:

$$EAFE_t = \alpha + \beta_1 x_{1,t} + \ldots + \beta_n x_{n,t} + \varepsilon_t \qquad (17)$$

where the statistically significant $\beta_1 \ldots \beta_n$ coefficients indicate optimal allocations pertaining to their respective country indices $x_1 \ldots x_n$, and α represents the expected outperformance of the EAFE benchmark if the residual from the cointegrating regression is stationary. $\beta_1 \ldots \beta_n$ can be constrained in estimation, depending on investor preferences.

An absolute return strategy can further be obtained by going long in the indices in proportions identified in step 2 and shorting EAFE.

Options

In options and other derivative instruments with a nonlinear payoff structure, statistical arbitrage usually works between a pair of instruments written on the same underlying asset but having one different characteristic. The different characteristic is most often either the expiration date or the strike price of the derivative. The strategy development proceeds along the steps noted in the previous sections.

Cross-Asset

Statistical arbitrage is not limited to a single asset class. Instead, statistical arbitrage can apply to pairs consisting of a financial instrument and its derivative, or two financial instruments sharing fundamental values.

Basis Trading   Futures are financial instruments of choice in many cross-market stat-arb models. Futures prices are linear functions of the underlying asset and are easy to model:

$$F_t = S_t \, exp[r_t(T-t)] \qquad (18)$$

where F_t is the price of a futures contract at time t, S_t is the price of the underlying asset (e.g., equity share, foreign exchange rate, or interest rate) also at time t, T is the time the futures contract expires, and r_t is the interest rate at time t. For foreign exchange futures, r_t is the differential between domestic and foreign interest rates.

The statistical arbitrage between a futures contract and the underlying asset is known as "basis trading." As with equity pairs trading, the basis-trading process follows the following steps: estimation of the distribution of the contemporaneous price differences, ongoing monitoring of the price differences, and acting upon those differences.

Lyons (2001) documents results of a basis-trading strategy involving six currency pairs: DEM/USD, USD/JPY, GBP/USD, USD/CHF, FRF/USD, and USD/CAD. The strategy bets that the difference between the spot and futures prices reverts to its mean or median values. The strategy works as follows: sell foreign currency futures whenever the futures price exceeds the spot price by a certain predetermined level or more, and buy foreign currency futures whenever the futures price falls short of the spot price by at least a prespecified difference. Lyons (2001) reports that when the predetermined strategy trigger levels are computed as median basis values, the strategy obtains a Sharpe ratio of 0.4 to 0.5.

Futures/ETF Arbitrage   In response to macroeconomic news announcements, futures markets have been shown to adjust more quickly than spot markets. Kawaller, Koch, and Koch (1993), for example, show that prices of the S&P 500 futures react to news faster than prices of the S&P 500 index itself, in the Granger causality specification. A similar effect was documented by Stoll and Whaley (1990): for returns measured in 5-minute intervals, both S&P 500 and money market index futures led stock market returns by 5 to 10 minutes.

The quicker adjustment of the futures markets relative to the equities markets is likely due to the historical development of the futures and equities markets. The Chicago Mercantile Exchange, the central clearinghouse for futures contracts in North America, rolled out a fully functional electronic trading platform during the early 1990s; most equity exchanges still relied on a hybrid clearing mechanism that involved both human traders and machines up to the year 2005. As a result, faster information-arbitraging strategies have been perfected for the futures market, while systematic equity strategies remain underdeveloped to this day. By the time this book was written, the lead-lag effect between futures and spot markets had decreased from the 5- to 10-minute period documented by Stoll and Whaley (1990) to a 1- to 2-second advantage. However, profit-taking opportunities still exist for powerful HFT systems with low transaction costs.

Cointegration of Various Financial Instruments/Asset Classes   Stat-arb models can also be built on two or more financial instruments, potentially from drastically different asset classes. Often, such multi-instrument multiasset models are developed using cointegration. *Cointegration* refers to a condition whereby prices of two or more financial instruments move in tandem according to a simple specification, parameterized on historical data. A two-instrument cointegration model can be specified as follows:

$$P_{1,t} = \alpha + \beta P_{2,t} + \varepsilon_t \qquad (19)$$

where $P_{1,t}$ is the price of the first financial instrument, $P_{2,t}$ is the price of the second financial instrument under consideration, and α and β are coefficients in a simple OLS regression. Instruments 1 and 2 and said to be cointegrated whenever the generated error term ε_t is stationary, that is, mean reverting. Several tests for stationarity of error terms exist. Perhaps the simplest test works as follows: if at least 90 percent of error observations, ε_t, lie within two standard deviations of ε_t away from the mean of ε_t, the error series ε_t can be considered stationary.

To further fine-tune statistical dependencies between any two securities, a stat-arb researcher may include lagged realizations of price changes in a vector-autoregressive framework to detect stat-arb relationships several time periods ahead of trading time:

$$P_{1,t} = \alpha + \beta_0 P_{2,t} + \beta_1 (P_{2,t} - P_{2,t-1}) + \beta_2 (P_{2,t-1} - P_{2,t-2}) + \cdots + \beta_k (P_{2,t-k+1} - P_{2,t-k}) + \varepsilon_t$$
(20)

$$P_{2,t} = \gamma + \delta_0 P_{1,t} + \delta_1 (P_{1,t} - P_{1,t-1}) + \delta_2 (P_{1,t-1} - P_{1,t-2}) + \cdots + \delta_k (P_{1,t-k+1} - P_{1,t-k}) + \omega_t$$
(21)

The number of lags, k, used in the regressions (20) and (21), is typically determined based on statistical significance of the coefficients β_k and δ_k. As a rule of thumb, if the absolute value of t-ratios accompanying β_k and δ_k drop off to less than two, the of the kth lag is considered nonexistent, and the kth lag becomes the terminal lag in the regressions.

Yet another common way to enhance performance of stat-arb models is to extend the regression of equation (19) with additional financial instruments:

$$P_{1,t} = \alpha + \beta P_{2,t} + \gamma P_{3,t} + \cdots + \delta P_{n,t} + \varepsilon_t$$
(22)

As in equation (19), the key stat-arb criterion of the multi-instrument cointegration is the stationarity of the error terms, ε_t. Similar to equations (20) and (21), equation (22) can be extended to include lagged observations of prices.

■ Summary

Statistical arbitrage is powerful in high-frequency settings as it provides a simple set of clearly defined conditions that are easy to implement in a systematic fashion in high-frequency settings. Statistical arbitrage based on solid economic theories is likely to have longer staying power than strategies based purely on statistical phenomena.

■ End-of-Chapter Questions

1. What are the three types of traders present in financial markets? How do they differ and coexist?
2. What are the key principles behind statistical arbitrage? Discuss.
3. You are considering trading SPY and E-mini futures on the S&P 500 contracts in a stat-arb model. According to equation (18), prices of SPY and E-mini futures are theoretically linked by a mathematical relationship. Suppose that the short-term estimate of the cointegration models of equations (20) and (21) generates negative and statistically significant coefficients $\beta 1$ and $\delta 1$. How can SPY and E-mini futures on the S&P 500 be arbitraged in this scenario?

STATISTICAL ARBITRAGE STRATEGIES

4. Suppose that, over a long range, high-frequency returns on two stocks are linked by the market-neutral framework of equations (3) through (10) (same β, different α: $\alpha1 > \alpha2$). In the short term, however, this relationship has reversed, and now $\alpha2 > \alpha1$ over the past 30 minutes. How can one statistically arbitrage such an occurrence?

5. A particular ETF is updated daily. Suppose you are interested in arbitraging the ETF against the basket of securities it comprises. To do so, you run cointegration models pitching the high-frequency ETF returns against returns of a large universe of stocks and pick up some statistically significant dependencies. How do you arbitrage your findings?

CHAPTER 9

Directional Trading Around Events

Many traditional low-frequency quantitative models assume several idealized market conditions. The following condition is assumed particularly often: markets instantaneously incorporate all relevant public information as soon as the information is available. Fair long-term quantitative valuation, the theory goes, is feasible only when the prices always reflect all fundamental information (see rational expectations of Muth, 1961, and the efficient markets hypotheses, Fama, 1970, for details).

Anyone who has watched the evolution of real-life financial prices surrounding a major news release has noted that the price adjustment to news is hardly instantaneous. In fact, the news "impoundment" into prices can be described as follows: volatile swings of the price that eventually settle within a certain range. The price never settles on a constant price level because a degree of volatility, however small, accompanies all market conditions. The process of the market finding its optimal postannouncement price band is often referred to as *tâtonnement,* from the French for "trial and error."

The tâtonnement toward a new optimal price happens through the implicit negotiation among buyers and sellers that is occurring in the order flow.

With news reported instantly and trades placed on a tick-by-tick basis, high-frequency traders are ideally positioned to profit from the impact of announcements on markets. By arbitraging price fluctuations surrounding each news release, HFTs high-frequency strategies further deliver a common good: they bring real-life markets ever closer to their idealized state whereby all prices are instantaneously updated with the latest news. The high-frequency strategies presented in this chapter trade on the market movements surrounding market-wide events, such as news announcements and other occurrences.

Developing Directional Event-Based Strategies

Directional event-based strategies refer to the group of trading strategies that place trades on the basis of the markets' reaction to events. The events may be economic, industry, or even instrument-specific occurrences that consistently affect the instrument(s) of interest time and time again. For example, unexpected increases in the Fed Funds rates consistently raise the value of the U.S. dollar, simultaneously raising the rate for USD/CAD and lowering the rate for AUD/USD. The announcements of the U.S. Fed Funds decisions, therefore, are events that can be consistently and profitably arbitraged.

The goal of event arbitrage strategies is to identify portfolios that make positive profit over the time window surrounding each event. The time window is typically a time period beginning just before the event and ending shortly afterwards. For events anticipated ex-ante, such as scheduled economic announcements, the portfolio positions may be opened ahead of the announcement or just after the announcement. The portfolio is then fully liquidated shortly after the announcement.

Trading positions can be held anywhere from a fraction of a second to several hours and can result in consistently profitable outcomes with low volatilities. The speed of response to an event often determines the trade gain; the faster the response, the higher the probability that the strategy will be able to profitably ride the momentum wave to the post-announcement equilibrium price level. As a result, event arbitrage strategies are well suited for high-frequency applications and are most profitably executed in fully automated trading environments.

Developing an event arbitrage trading strategy harnesses research on equilibrium pricing and leverages statistical tools that assess tick-by-tick trading data and events the instant they are released. Further along in this chapter, we will survey academic research on the impact of events on prices; now we investigate the mechanics of developing an event arbitrage strategy.

Most event arbitrage strategies follow a three-stage development process:

1. For each event type, identify dates and times of past events in historical data.
2. Compute historical price changes at desired frequencies pertaining to securities of interest and surrounding the events identified in step 1.
3. Estimate expected price responses based on historical price behavior surrounding past events.

The sources of dates and times for specified events that occurred in the past can be collected from various Internet sites. Most announcements recur at the same time of day and make the job of collecting the data much easier. U.S. unemployment announcements, for example, are always released at 8:30 a.m. Eastern time. Some announcements, such as those of the U.S. Federal Open Markets Committee interest rate changes, occur at irregular times during the day and require greater diligence in collecting the data. Firms such as Reuters, Dow Jones, RavenPack, SemLab, HFTIndex.com and AbleMarkets.com distribute news and other tradeable data in machine-readable formats, further simplifying automation of event-driven trading strategies.

What Constitutes an Event?

The events used in event arbitrage strategies can be any releases of news about economic activity, market disruptions, and other events. The key requirement for event suitability is that the chosen events are repetitive. The recurrence of events allows researchers to estimate historical impact of the events and project the effect into the future.

All events do not have the same magnitude. Some events may have positive and negative impacts on prices, and some events may have more severe consequences than others. The magnitude of an event can be measured as a deviation of the realized event figures from the expectations of the event. In economics, the deviation is frequently referred to as a "surprise." The price of a particular stock, for example, should adjust to the net present value of its future cash flows following a higher- or lower-than-expected earnings announcement. However, if earnings are in line with investor expectations, the price should not move. Similarly, in the foreign exchange market, the level of a foreign exchange pair should change in response to an unexpected change—for example, in the level of the consumer price index (CPI) of the domestic country. If, however, the domestic CPI turns out to be in line with market expectations, little change should occur.

Market participants form expectations about event figures well before the formal statistics are announced. Many financial economists are tasked with forecasting inflation, earnings, and other figures based on other continuously observed market and political variables, as well as pure news. When event-related forecasts become available, market participants trade securities on the basis of the forecasts, impounding their expectations into prices well before the formal announcements occur.

One of the key steps in the estimation of news impact is separating the unexpected change, or news, from the expected and priced-in component. The earliest macroeconomic event studies (see Frenkel, 1981, and Edwards, 1982, for example) assumed that most economic news developed slowly over time, and the trend observed during the past several months or quarters was the best predictor of the value to be released on the next scheduled news release day. The news, or the unexpected component of the news release, was then the difference between the value released in the announcement and the expectation formed on the basis of autoregressive analysis.

Later researchers such as Eichenbaum and Evans (1993) and Grilli and Roubini (1993) have been using such a framework to predict the decisions of the central bankers, including the U.S. Federal Reserve. Once again, the main rationale behind the autoregressive predictability of the central bankers' actions is that the central bankers are not at liberty to make drastic changes to economic variables under their control, given that major changes may trigger large-scale market disruptions. Instead, the central bankers adopt and follow a longer-term course of action, gradually adjusting the figures in their control, such as interest rates and money supply, to lead the economy in the intended direction.

The empirical evidence of the impact of news defined in the autoregressive fashion shows that the framework indeed can be used to predict future movements of securities. Yet the impact is best seen in shorter terms. Almeida, Goodhart, and Payne (1998) documented a significant effect of macroeconomic news announcements on the USD/DEM exchange rate sampled at five-minute intervals. The authors found that news announcements pertaining to the U.S. employment and trade balance were particularly significant predictors of exchange rates, but only within two hours following the announcement. However, U.S. non-farm payroll and consumer confidence news announcements caused price momentum lasting 12 hours or more following an announcement.

Surprises in macroeconomic announcements can be measured relative to published averages of economists' forecasts. For example, every week *Barron's* and the *Wall Street Journal* publish consensus forecasts for the coming week's announcements, as do Bloomberg and Reuters. The forecasts are developed from a survey of field economists.

■ Forecasting Methodologies

Development of forecasts involves event studies on very specific trading data surrounding event announcements of interest. Event studies measure the quantitative impact of announcements on the returns surrounding the news event and are usually conducted as follows:

1. The announcement dates, times, and "surprise" changes are identified and recorded. To create useful simulations, the database of events and the prices of securities traded before and after the event should be very detailed, with events categorized carefully and quotes and trades captured at high frequencies. The surprise component can be measured in two ways:
   - ■ As the difference between the realized value and the prediction based on autoregressive analysis.
   - ■ As the difference between the realized value and the analyst forecast consensus.
2. The returns corresponding to the times of interest surrounding the announcements are calculated for the securities under consideration. For example, if the researcher is interested in evaluating the impact of CPI announcements on the 1-second change in USD/CAD, the one-second change in USD/CAD is calculated from 8:30:00 to 8:30:01 a.m. on historical data on past CPI announcement days. (The U.S. CPI announcements are always released at 8:30 a.m. ET.)
3. The impact of the announcements is then estimated in a simple linear regression:

$$R_t = \alpha + \beta \Delta X_t + \varepsilon_t$$

where R_t is the vector of returns surrounding the announcement for the security of interest arranged in the order of announcements ΔX_t is the vector of "surprise" changes in the announcements arranged in the order of announcements; ε_t is the idiosyncratic error pertaining to news announcements; α is the estimated intercept of the regression that captures changes in returns due to factors other than announcement surprises; and, finally, β measures the average impact of the announcement on the security under consideration.

Changes in equity prices are adjusted by changes in the overall market prices to account for the impact of broader market influences on equity values. The adjustment is often performed using the market model of Sharpe (1964):

$$R_t^a = R_t - \hat{R}_t \qquad (1)$$

where the "hat" notation expresses the average estimate and $\hat{R}_t$ is the expected equity return estimated over historical data using the market model:

$$R_t = \alpha + \beta R_{m,t} \varepsilon_t \qquad (2)$$

The methodology was first developed by Ball and Brown (1968), and the estimation method to this day delivers statistically significant trading opportunities.

During a typical trading day, numerous economic announcements are made around the world. The news announcements may be related to a particular company, industry, or country; or, like macroeconomic news, they may have global consequences. Company news usually includes quarterly and annual earnings releases, mergers and acquisitions announcements, new product launch announcements, and the like. Industry news comprises industry regulation in a particular country, the introduction of tariffs, and economic conditions particular to the industry. Macroeconomic news contains interest rate announcements by major central banks, economic indicators determined from government-collected data, and regional gauges of economic performance.

With the development of information technology such as RSS feeds, alerts, press wires, and news aggregation engines such as Google, it is now feasible to capture announcements the instant they are released. A well-developed automated event arbitrage system captures news, categorizes events, and matches events to securities based on historical analysis. Various companies offer machine-readable streams of data that can be readily parsed by a computer and used as an input to event-driven strategies. The companies with machine-readable offerings include Thomson Reuters, Dow Jones, and a large number of smaller players.

A Practical Example

The latest figures tracking U.S. inflation are released monthly at 8:30 a.m. on pre-specified dates. On release, USD/CAD spot and other USD crosses undergo an instantaneous one-time adjustment, at least in theory. Identifying when and how quickly the adjustments happen in practice, we can construct profitable trading strategies that capture changes in price levels following announcements of the latest inflation figures.

The first step in identification of profitable trading opportunities is to define the time period from the announcement to the end of the trading opportunity, known as the *event window*. We select data sample windows surrounding the recent U.S. inflation announcements in the tick-level data from January 2002 through August 2008. As all U.S. inflation announcements occur at 8:30 a.m. EST, we define 8:00 to 9:00 a.m. as the trading window and download all of the quotes and trades recorded during that time. We partition the data further into 5-minute, 1-minute, 30-second, and 15-second blocks. We then measure the impact of the announcement on the corresponding 5-minute, 1-minute, 30-second, and 15-second returns of USD/CAD spot.

According to the purchasing power parity (PPP), a spot exchange rate between domestic and foreign currencies is the ratio of the domestic and foreign inflation rates. When the U.S. inflation rate changes, the deviation disturbs the PPP equilibrium and the USD-based exchange rates adjust to new levels. When the U.S. inflation rate rises, USD/CAD is expected to increase instantaneously, and vice versa. To keep matters simple, in this example we will consider the inflation news in the same fashion as it is announced, ignoring the market's preannouncement adjustment to expectations of inflation figures.

The sign test then tells us during which time intervals, if any, the market properly and consistently responds to announcements during our "trading window" from 8 to 9 a.m. The sample includes only days when inflation rates were announced. The summary of the results is presented in Table 9.1.

Looking at five-minute intervals surrounding the U.S. inflation announcements, it appears that USD/CAD reacts persistently only to decreases in the U.S. inflation rate and that reaction is indeed instantaneous. USD/CAD decreases during the five-minute interval from 8:25 to 8:30 a.m. in response to announcements of lower inflation with 95 percent statistical confidence. The response may potentially support the instantaneous adjustment hypothesis; after all, the U.S. inflation news is released at 8:30 a.m., at which point the adjustment to drops in inflation appears to be completed. No statistically significant response appears to occur following rises in inflation.

Higher-frequency intervals tell us a different story—the adjustments occur in short-term bursts. At one-minute intervals, for example, the adjustment to increases in inflation can now be seen to consistently occur from 8:34 to 8:35 a.m. This postannouncement adjustment, therefore, presents a consistent profit-taking opportunity.

Splitting the data into 30-second intervals, we observe that the number of tradable opportunities increases further. For announcements of rising inflation, the price adjustment now occurs in four 30-second postannouncement intervals. For the announcements showing a decrease in inflation, the price adjustment occurs in one 30-second postannouncement time interval.

Examining 15-second intervals, we note an even higher number of time-persistent trading opportunities. For rising inflation announcements, there are five 15-second periods during which USD/CAD consistently increased in response to the inflation announcement between 8:30 and 9:00 a.m., presenting ready tradable opportunities. Six 15-second intervals consistently accompany falling inflation announcements during the same 8:30 to 9:00 a.m. time frame.

In summary, as we look at shorter time intervals, we detect a larger number of statistically significant currency movements in response to the announcements. The short-term nature of the opportunities makes them conducive to a systematic (i.e., black-box) approach, which, if implemented knowledgeably, reduces risk of execution delays, carrying costs, and expensive errors in human judgment.

TABLE 9.1	Number of Persistent Trading Opportunities in USD/CAD Following the U.S. Inflation Rate Announcements	
Estimation Frequency	U.S. Inflation Up	U.S. Inflation Down
5 minutes	0	0
1 minute	1	0
30 seconds	4	1
15 seconds	5	6

Tradable News

This section summarizes various event types and their impact on specific financial instruments. The impact of events is drawn from various academic sources. The time frames for the impact of the news may have shrunk considerably since the studies were first published due to proliferation of machine-readable news and general interest in this set of trading strategies. The described impact is, however, based on strong fundamental factors, and is likely to persist, even if for shorter periods of time. Some of the included studies estimate impact using low-frequency data; the high-frequency response of the variables used in studies tends to be comparable or even more pronounced.

Corporate News

Corporate activity such as earnings announcements, both quarterly and annual, significantly impacts equity prices of the firms releasing the announcements. Unexpectedly positive earnings typically lift equity prices, and unexpectedly negative earnings often depress corporate stock valuation.

Earnings announcements are preceded by analyst forecasts. The announcement that is materially different from the economists' consensus forecast results in a rapid adjustment of the security price to its new equilibrium level. The unexpected component of the announcements is computed as the difference between the announced value and the mean or median economists' forecast. The unexpected component is the key variable used in estimation of the impact of an event on prices.

Theoretically, equities are priced as present values of future cash flows of the company, discounted at the appropriate interest rate determined by the capital asset pricing model (CAPM), the arbitrage pricing theory of Ross (1977), or the investor-specific opportunity cost:

$$\text{Equity price} = \sum_{t=1}^{\infty} \frac{E[Earnings_t]}{(1+R_t)^t} \tag{3}$$

where $E[Earnings_t]$ are the expected cash flows of the company at a future time t, and R_t is the discount rate found appropriate for discounting time t dividends to present. Unexpected changes to earnings generate rapid price responses whereby equity prices quickly adjust to new information about earnings.

Significant deviations of earnings from forecasted values can cause large market movements and can even result in market disruptions. To prevent large-scale impacts of earnings releases on the overall market, most earnings announcements are made after the markets close.

Other firm-level news also affects equity prices. The effect of stock splits, for example, has been documented by Fama, Fisher, Jensen, and Roll (1969), who show that the share prices typically increase following a split relative to their equilibrium price levels.

Event arbitrage models incorporate the observation that earnings announcements affect each company differently. The most widely documented firm-level factors for evaluation include the size of the firm market capitalization (for details, see Atiase, 1985; Freeman, 1987; and Fan-fah, Mohd, and Nasir, 2008).

Industry News

Industry news consists mostly of legal and regulatory decisions along with announcements of new products. These announcements reverberate throughout the entire sector and tend to move all securities in that market in the same direction. Unlike macroeconomic news that is collected and disseminated in a systematic fashion, industry news usually emerges in an erratic fashion.

Empirical evidence on regulatory decisions suggests that decisions relaxing rules governing activity of a particular industry result in higher equity values, whereas the introduction of rules constricting activity pushes equity values down. The evidence includes the findings of Navissi, Bowman, and Emanuel (1999), who ascertained that announcements of relaxation or elimination of price controls resulted in an upswing in equity values and that the introduction of price controls depressed equity prices. Boscaljon (2005) found that the relaxation of advertising rules by the U.S. Food and Drug Administration was accompanied by rising equity values.

Macroeconomic News

Macroeconomic decisions and some observations are made by government agencies on a predetermined schedule. Interest rates, for example, are set by economists at the central banks, such as the U.S. Federal Reserve or the Bank of England. On the other hand, variables such as CPIs are typically not set but are observed and reported by statistics agencies affiliated with the countries' central banks.

Other macroeconomic indices are developed by research departments of both for-profit and nonprofit private companies. The ICSC Goldman store sales index, for example, is calculated by the International Council of Shopping Centers (ICSC) and is actively supported and promoted by the Goldman Sachs Group. The index tracks weekly sales at sample retailers and serves as an indicator of consumer confidence: the more confident consumers are about the economy and their future earnings potential, the higher is their retail spending and the higher is the value of the index. Other indices measure different aspects of economic activity ranging from relative prices of McDonald's hamburgers in different countries to oil supplies to industry-specific employment levels.

Table 9.2 shows an ex-ante schedule of macroeconomic news announcements for Tuesday, March 3, 2009, a typical trading day. European news is most often released in the morning of the European trading session while North American markets are closed.

TABLE 9.2 Ex-Ante Schedule of Macroeconomic Announcements for March 3, 2009

Time (ET)	Event	Prior Value	Consensus Forecast	Country
1:00 a.m.	Norway Consumer Confidence	−13.3		Norway
1:45 a.m.	GDP Q/Q	0.0%	−0.8%	Switzerland
1:45 a.m.	GDP Y/Y	1.6%	−0.1%	Switzerland
2:00 a.m.	Wholesale Price Index M/M	−3.0%	−2.0%	Germany
2:00 a.m.	Wholesale Price Index Y/Y	−3.3%	−6.3%	Germany
3:00 a.m.	Norway PMI SA	40.8	40.2	Norway
4:30 a.m.	PMI Construction	34.5	34.2	United Kingdom
7:45 a.m.	ICSC Goldman Store Sales			United States
8:55 a.m.	Redbook			United States
9:00 a.m.	Bank of Canada Rate	1.0%	0.5%	Canada
10:00 a.m.	Pending Home Sales	6.3%	−3.0%	United States
1:00 p.m.	Four-Week Bill Auction			United States
2:00 p.m.	Total Car Sales	9.6M	9.6M	United States
2:00 p.m.	Domestic Car Sales	6.8M	6.9M	United States
5:00 p.m.	ABC/*Washington Post* Consumer Confidence	v48	−47	United States
5:30 p.m.	AIG Performance of Service Index	41		Australia
7:00 p.m.	Nationwide Consumer Confidence	40	38	United Kingdom
7:30 p.m.	GDP Q/Q	0.1%	0.1%	Australia
7:30 p.m.	GDP Y/Y	1.9%	1.1%	Australia
9:00 p.m.	ANZ Commodity Prices	−4.3%		New Zealand

SA = seasonally adjusted; NSA = non–seasonally adjusted data.

Most macroeconomic announcements of the U.S. and Canadian governments are distributed in the morning of the North American session that coincides with afternoon trading in Europe. Most announcements from the Asia Pacific region, which includes Australia and New Zealand, are released during the morning trading hours in Asia.

Many announcements are accompanied by "consensus forecasts," which are aggregates of forecasts made by economists of various financial institutions. The consensus figures are usually produced by major media and data companies, such as Bloomberg LP, that poll various economists every week and calculate average industry expectations.

Macroeconomic news arrives from every corner of the world. The impact on currencies, commodities, equities, and fixed-income and derivative instruments is usually estimated using event studies, a technique that measures the persistent impact of news on the prices of securities of interest.

■ Application of Event Arbitrage

Event trading is applicable to many asset classes, yet the impact of each event may be different for every financial instrument. This section considers documented persistent impact of events on various financial instruments.

Foreign Exchange Markets

Market responses to macroeconomic announcements in foreign exchange were studied by Almeida, Goodhart, and Payne (1997); Edison (1996); Andersen, Bollerslev, Diebold, and Vega (2003); and Love and Payne (2008), among many others.

Edison (1996) finds that foreign exchange reacts most significantly to news about real economic activity, such as nonfarm payroll employment figures. In particular, Edison (1996) shows that for every 100,000 surprise increases in nonfarm payroll employment, USD appreciates by 0.2 percent on average. At the same time, the author documents little impact of inflation on foreign exchange rates.

Andersen et al. (2003) conducted their analysis on foreign exchange quotes interpolated based on timestamps to create exact five-minute intervals. The authors show that average exchange rate levels adjust quickly and efficiently to new levels according to the information releases. Volatility, however, takes longer to taper off after the spike surrounding most news announcements. The authors also document that bad news usually has a more pronounced effect than good news.

Andersen et al. (2003) use the consensus forecasts compiled by the International Money Market Services (MMS) as the expected value for estimation of surprise component of news announcements. The authors then model the five-minute changes in spot foreign exchange rate R_t as follows:

$$R_t = \beta_0 + \sum_{i=1}^{I} \beta_i R_{t-i} + \sum_{k=1}^{K} \sum_{j=0}^{J} \beta_{kj} S_{k,t-j} + \varepsilon_t, \ t = 1, \ldots, T \tag{4}$$

where R_{t-i} is i-period lagged value of the five-minute spot rate, $S_{k,t-j}$ is the surprise component of the kth fundamental variable lagged j periods, and ε_t is the time-varying volatility that incorporates intraday seasonalities. Andersen et al. (2003) estimate the impact of the following variables:

- GDP (advance, preliminary, and final figures)
- Nonfarm payroll
- Retail sales
- Industrial production
- Capacity utilization
- Personal income
- Consumer credit
- Personal consumption expenditures
- New home sales
- Durable goods orders
- Construction spending
- Factory orders
- Business inventories

- Government budget deficit
- Trade balance
- Producer price index
- Consumer price index
- Consumer confidence index
- Institute for Supply Management (ISM) index (formerly the National Association of Purchasing Managers [NAPM] index)
- Housing starts
- Index of leading indicators
- Target Fed Funds rate
- Initial unemployment claims
- Money supply (M1, M2, M3)
- Employment
- Manufacturing orders
- Manufacturing output
- Trade balance
- Current account
- CPI
- Producer prices
- Wholesale price index
- Import prices
- Money stock M3

Andersen, Bollerslev, Diebold, and Vega (2003) considered the following currency pairs: GBP/USD, USD/JPY, DEM/USD, CHF/USD, and EUR/USD from January 3, 1992, through December 30, 1998. The authors document that all currency pairs responded positively, with 99 percent significance, to surprise increases in the following variables: nonfarm payroll employment, industrial production, durable goods orders, trade balance, consumer confidence index, and the National Association of Purchasing Managers (NAPM) index. All the currency pairs considered responded negatively to surprise increases in the initial unemployment claims and money stock M3.

Love and Payne (2008) document that macroeconomic news from different countries affects different currency pairs. Love and Payne (2008) studied the impact of the macroeconomic news originating in the United States, the Eurozone, and the United Kingdom on the EUR/USD, GBP/USD, and EUR/GBP exchange-rate pairs. The authors find that the U.S. news has the largest effect on the EUR/USD, while GBP/USD is most affected by the news originating in the United Kingdom. Love and Payne (2008) also document the specific impact of the type of news from the three regions on their respective currencies; their findings are shown in Table 9.3.

Equity Markets

A typical trading day is filled with macroeconomic announcements, both domestic and foreign. How do the macroeconomic news impact equity markets?

TABLE 9.3	Effect of Region-Specific News Announcements on the Respective Currency, per Love and Payne (2008)		
	News Announcement Type		
Region of News Origination	Increase in prices or money	Increase of output	Increase in trade balance
Eurozone, Effect on EUR	Appreciation	Appreciation	
United Kingdom, Effect on GBP	Appreciation	Appreciation	Appreciation
United States, Effect on USD	Depreciation	Appreciation	Appreciation

According to classical financial theory, changes in equity prices are due to two factors: changes in expected earnings of publicly traded firms, and changes in the discount rates associated with those firms. Expected earnings may be affected by changes in market conditions. For example, increasing consumer confidence and consumer spending are likely to boost retail sales, uplifting earnings prospects for retail outfits. Rising labor costs, however, may signal tough business conditions and decrease earnings expectations as a result.

The discount rate in classical finance is, at its bare minimum, determined by the level of the risk-free rate and the idiosyncratic riskiness of a particular equity share. The risk-free rate pertinent to U.S. equities is often proxied by the three-month bill issued by the U.S. Treasury; the risk-free rate significant to equities in another country is taken as the short-term target interest rate announced by that country's central bank. The lower the risk-free rate, the lower is the discount rate of equity earnings and the higher are the theoretical prices of equities.

How does macroeconomic news affect equities in practice? Ample empirical evidence shows that equity prices respond strongly to interest rate announcements and, in a less pronounced manner, to other macroeconomic news. Decreases in both long-term and short-term interest rates indeed positively affect monthly stock returns with 90 percent statistical confidence for long-term rates and 99 percent confidence for short-term rates. (See Cutler, Poterba, and Summers, 1989, for example.) Anecdotal evidence suggests that most adjustments of prices occur within seconds or minutes of the announcement time.

Stock reaction to nonmonetary macroeconomic news is usually mixed. Positive inflation shocks tend to induce lower stock returns independent of other market conditions (see Pearce and Roley, 1983, 1985, for details). Several other macroeconomic variables produce reactions conditional on the contemporary state of the business cycle. Higher-than-expected industrial production figures are good news for the stock market during recessions but bad news during periods of high economic activity, according to McQueen and Roley (1993).

Similarly, unexpected changes in unemployment statistics were found to cause reactions dependent on the state of the economy. For example, Orphanides (1992) finds that returns increase when unemployment rises, but only during economic expansions. During economic contractions, returns drop following news of rising unemployment. Orphanides (1992) attributes the asymmetric response of equities to the overheating hypothesis: when the economy is overheated, increase in unemployment actually presents good news. The findings have been confirmed by Boyd, Hu, and Jagannathan (2005). The asymmetric response to macroeconomic news is not limited to the U.S. markets. Löflund and Nummelin (1997), for instance, observe the asymmetric response to surprises in industrial production figures in the Finnish equity market; they found that higher-than-expected production growth bolsters stocks in sluggish states of the economy.

Whether or not macroeconomic announcements move stock prices, the announcements are always usually surrounded by increases in market volatility. While Schwert (1989) pointed out that stock market volatility is not necessarily related to volatility of other macroeconomic factors, surprises in macroeconomic news have been shown to significantly increase market volatility. Bernanke and Kuttner (2005), for example, show that an unexpected component in the interest rate announcements of the U.S. Federal Open Market Committee (FOMC) increase equity return volatility. Connolly and Stivers (2005) document spikes in the volatility of equities comprising the Dow Jones Industrial Average (DJIA) in response to U.S. macroeconomic news. Higher volatility implies higher risk, and financial theory tells us that higher risk should be accompanied by higher returns. Indeed, Savor and Wilson (2008) show that equity returns on days with major U.S. macroeconomic news announcements are higher than on days when no major announcements are made. Savor and Wilson (2008) consider news announcements to be "major" if they are announcements of consumer price index (CPI), producer price index (PPI), employment figures, or interest rate decisions of the FOMC. Veronesi (1999) shows that investors are more sensitive to macroeconomic news during periods of higher uncertainty, which drives asset price volatility. In the European markets, Errunza and Hogan (1998) found that monetary and real macroeconomic news has considerable impact on the volatility of the largest European stock markets.

Different sources of information appear to affect equities at different frequencies. The macroeconomic impact on equity data appears to increase with the increase in frequency of equity data. Chan, Karceski, and Lakonishok (1998), for example, analyzed monthly returns for U.S. and Japanese equities in an arbitrage pricing theory setting and found that idiosyncratic characteristics of individual equities are most predictive of future returns at low frequencies. By using factor-mimicking portfolios, Chan et al. (1998) show that size, past return, book-to-market ratio, and dividend yield of individual equities are the factors that move in tandem ("covary") most with returns of corresponding equities. However, Chan et al. (1998, p. 182) document that "the macroeconomic factors do a poor job in explaining return covariation" at monthly return frequencies. Wasserfallen (1989) finds no impact of macroeconomic news on quarterly equities data.

Flannery and Protopapadakis (2002) found that daily returns on the U.S. equities are significantly impacted by several types of macroeconomic news. The authors estimate a generalized autoregressive conditional heteroskedasticity (GARCH) return model with independent variables and found that the following macroeconomic announcements have significant influence on both equity returns and volatility: CPI, PPI, monetary aggregate, balance of trade, employment report, and housing starts figures.

Ajayi and Mehdian (1995) document that foreign stock markets in developed countries typically overreact to the macroeconomic news announcements from the United States. As a result, foreign equity markets tend to be sensitive to the USD-based exchange rates and domestic account balances. Sadeghi (1992), for example, notes that in the Australian markets, equity returns increased in response to increases in the current account deficit, the AUD/USD exchange rate, and the real gross domestic product (GDP); equity returns decreased following news of rising domestic inflation or interest rates.

Stocks of companies from different industries have been shown to react differently to macroeconomic announcements. Hardouvelis (1987), for example, pointed out that stocks of financial institutions exhibited higher sensitivity to announcements of monetary adjustments. The extent of market capitalization appears to matter as well. Li and Hu (1998) show that stocks with large market capitalization are more sensitive to macroeconomic surprises than are small-cap stocks.

The size of the surprise component of the macroeconomic news impacts equity prices. Aggarwal and Schirm (1992), for example, document that small surprises, those within one standard deviation of the average, caused larger changes in equities and foreign exchange markets than did large surprises.

Fixed-Income Markets

Jones, Lamont, and Lumsdaine (1998) studied the effect of employment and PPI data on U.S. Treasury bonds. The authors find that while the volatility of the bond prices increased markedly on the days of the announcements, the volatility did not persist beyond the announcement day, indicating that the announcement information is incorporated promptly into prices.

Hardouvelis (1987) and Edison (1996) note that employment figures, PPI, and CPI move bond prices. Krueger (1996) documents that a decline in the U.S. unemployment causes higher yields in bills and bonds issued by the U.S. Treasury.

High-frequency studies of the bond market responses to macroeconomic announcements include those by Ederington and Lee (1993); Fleming and Remolona (1997, 1998, 1999); and Balduzzi, Elton, and Green (2001). Ederington and Lee (1993) and Fleming and Remolona (1998) show that new information is fully incorporated in bond prices just two minutes following its announcement. Fleming and Remolona (1999) estimate the high-frequency impact of macroeconomic announcements on the entire U.S. Treasury yield curve. Fleming and Remolona (1999) measure the impact of 10 distinct announcement classes: CPI, durable goods orders, GDP, housing starts, jobless rate, leading indicators, nonfarm payrolls, PPI, retail sales, and trade balance. Fleming and Remolona (1999) define the macroeconomic surprise to be the actual number released less the Thomson Reuters consensus forecast for the same news release.

All of the 10 macroeconomic news announcements studied by Fleming and Remolona (1999) were released at 8:30 a.m. The authors then measure the significance of the impact of the news releases on the entire yield curve from 8:30 to 8:35 a.m., and document statistically significant average changes in yields in

TABLE 9.4

TABLE 9.4	Effects of Macroeconomic News Announcements Documented by Fleming and Remolona (1999)		
Announcement	3-Month Bill	2-Year Note	30-Year Bond
CPI	0.593*	1.472**	1.296**
Durable goods orders	1.275**	2.180**	1.170**
GDP	0.277	0.379	0.167
Housing starts	0.670**	1.406**	0.731**
Jobless rate	−0.939*	−1.318**	−0.158
Leading indicators	0.411**	0.525*	0.271*
Nonfarm payrolls	3.831**	6.124**	2.679*
PPI	0.768**	1.879**	1.738
Retail sales	0.582*	1.428**	0.766**
Trade balance	−0.138	0.027	−0.062

The table shows the average change in percent in the yields of the 3-month U.S. Treasury bill, the 2-year U.S. Treasury note, and the 30-year U.S. Treasury bond, corresponding to a 1 percent "surprise" in each macroeconomic announcement. * and ** indicate statistical significance at the 95 percent and 99 percent confidence levels, respectively. The estimates were conducted on data from July 1, 1991, to September 29, 1995.

response to a 1 percent positive surprise change in the macro variable. The results are reproduced in Table 9.4. As Table 9.4 shows, a 1 percent "surprise" increase in the jobless rate led on average to a 0.9 percent drop in the yield of the 3-month bill with 95 percent statistical confidence and a 1.3 percent drop in the yield of the 2-year note with 99 percent confidence. The corresponding average drop in the yield of the 30-year bond was not statistically significant.

Futures Markets

The impact of the macroeconomic announcements on the futures market has been studied by Becker, Finnerty, and Kopecky (1996); Ederington and Lee (1993); and Simpson and Ramchander (2004). Becker, Finnerty and Kopecky (1996) and Simpson and Ramchander (2004) document that news announcements regarding the PPI, merchandise trade, nonfarm payrolls, and the CPI move prices of bond futures. Ederington and Lee (1993) find that news-induced price adjustment of interest rate and foreign exchange futures happens within the first minute after the news is released. News-related volatility, however, may often persist for the following 15 minutes.

Emerging Economies

Several authors have considered the impact of macroeconomic news on emerging economies. For example, Andritzky, Bannister, and Tamirisa (2007) study how macroeconomic announcements affect bond spreads. The authors found that the U.S. news had a major impact, whereas domestic announcements did not generate much effect. However, Nikkinen, Omran, Sahlström, and Äijö (2006) conducted similar analysis on equity markets and found that while mature equity markets respond almost instantaneously to U.S. macroeconomic announcements, emerging equity markets are not affected. Kandir (2008) estimated macroeconomic impact on the

Istambul Stock Exchange, and found that the Turkish lira/USD exchange rate, the Turkish interest rate, and the world market returns significantly affect Turkish equities, while domestic variables such as industrial production and money supply had little effect. Muradoglu, Taskin, and Bigan (2000) found that emerging markets were influenced by global macroeconomic variables, depending on the size of the emerging market under consideration and the degree of the market's integration with the world economy.

Association of Southeast Asian Nations (ASEAN) countries, however, appear to be influenced predominantly by their domestic variables. Wongbangpo and Sharma (2002) find that local gross national products (GNPs), CPIs, money supplies, interest rates, and the USD-based exchange rates of ASEAN countries (Indonesia, Malaysia, Philippines, Singapore, and Thailand) significantly influence local stock markets. At the same time, Bailey (1990) found no causal relation between the U.S. money supply and stock returns of Asian Pacific markets.

Commodity Markets

Empirical evidence in the commodity markets includes the findings of Gorton and Rouwenhorst (2006), who document that both real activity and inflation affect commodity prices. The effect of the news announcements, however, can be mixed; higher-than-expected real activity and inflation generally have a positive effect on commodity prices, except when accompanied by rising interest rates, which have a cooling impact on commodity valuations. See Bond (1984), Chambers (1985), and Frankel (2006) for more details on the relationship between commodity prices and interest rates.

Real Estate Investment Trusts

Equity real estate investment trusts (REITs) are fairly novel publicly traded securities, established by the U.S. Congress in 1960. The market capitalization of all U.S.-based REITs was about $9 million in 1991 and steadily grew to $300 billion by 2006. A REIT is traded like an ordinary equity, but it is required to have the following peculiar structure: at least 75 percent of the REIT's assets should be invested in real estate, and the REIT must pay out at least 90 percent of its taxable earnings as dividends. Because of their high payout ratios, REITs may respond differently to macroeconomic news announcements than would ordinary equities.

The impact of inflation on REIT performance has been documented by Simpson, Ramchander, and Webb (2007). The authors found that the returns on REITs increase when inflation unexpectedly falls as well when inflation unexpectedly rises. Bredin, O'Reilly, and Stevenson (2007) examine the response of REIT returns to unanticipated changes in U.S. monetary policy. The authors find that the response of REITs is comparable to that of equities—increase in the Federal Funds rates increases the volatility of REIT prices while depressing the REIT prices themselves.

▣ Summary

Directional trading around events generates profitability in narrow windows immediately following the news and preceding the reaction of other market participants. Estimation of the impact of historical announcements enable profitable trading decisions surrounding market announcements.

▣ End-of-Chapter Questions

1. Which of the following is/is not a tradable event in the HFT sense? Why?
   a. The S&P 500 registers a positive gain on market open relative to previous close.
   b. Announcement of the QE3 (quantitative easing led by the U.S. Fed).
   c. Regular announcement of employment figures.
2. What financial instruments can be traded on events in HFT setting?
3. Suppose a particular stock usually rises within 15 minutes of an announcement of positive changes to the U.S. nonfarm payroll. The latest announcement figures have just been released, and the change is negative. How can your system trade on the announcement?
4. Intuitively, why does something like a change in CPI affect futures prices in the short term?
5. Does high-frequency directional trading on events make markets more or less efficient?

CHAPTER 10

Automated Market Making—Naïve Inventory Models

Most high-frequency trading (HFT) systems are deployed to provide automated market-making services. Some 30 years ago, this activity was entirely human, but is now moving to a nearly fully computerized mode. This chapter considers the basic principles behind the successful market-making models.

■ Introduction

Every veteran trader can recount a story of a dominant human market maker who "owned" transactions in a particular financial instrument. These kingpins of financial markets generated heavy transaction-based profits for their employers, commanded extensive bonuses and lived luxurious lifestyles.

With rare exceptions, nearly all stories about these once-potent human traders end on the same sour note: "and then one day, the market turned against him, he suffered a major loss, and was fired the next day." An example of such a "burnout" was a trader in USD/CAD foreign exchange futures at a certain bank, who made markets for a long time and periodically enhanced his profitability and bonus by taking directional bets at his personal discretion. Once, the trader's bet fell radically off its mark, resulting in nearly instantaneous multimillion-dollar losses to his employer. The trader was immediately dismissed following the incident and was prohibited from ever again setting a foot on any trading floor.

Automated market making provides several advantages to the market-making institution as well as other market participants. First, automated market makers stay on script. Unlike human traders, properly programmed and tested computer systems do not deviate into discretionary actions. As a result, automated market makers reduce the incidence of market crashes and negative surprises for market makers' bottom line. Second, execution of automated market making is cost efficient: once the human-intensive programming and testing stages are completed (see Chapter 16 for details of HFT development processes), automated market makers require little compensation. The savings from head-count reductions are significant and are passed directly to the automated market makers' shareholders and clients in the form of enhanced profitability and reduced transaction costs.

Perhaps the best feature of market-making strategies is their scalability across various markets. Almost any market-making strategy running on an exchange equipped with a centralized limit order book can be run on another exchange, another financial instrument and even another asset class, provided that the new trading venue also deploys centralized limit order book methodology (see Chapter 3 for limit order book definitions and description). Most of today's exchanges in the world deploy the centralized limit order book model, making market-making technology extremely portable.

A market-making process works as follows: a market maker, whether human or computerized, posts limit buy and limit sell orders. Depending on market conditions and positions in the market maker's current portfolio, the market maker may choose to post only limit buy or only limit sell orders. Some market participants, however, consider market making to refer strictly to a continuous activity with open limit orders placed simultaneously on both sides of the market. *Liquidity provision* is a more general term describing market making as well as most limit order trading.

When the market price reaches the market maker's limit buy order with the highest price, this price becomes the best bid on that market, and is distributed to other market participants as a Level I "quote." Similarly, when the market maker's limit sell order is the lowest-priced limit sell order in the market, his order becomes a best offer or best ask, and is quoted to other market participants.

Market makers' orders are executed by virtue of being matched with incoming market orders of the opposite direction. The market maker's bids are said to be "hit" by market sell orders, and the market maker's ask or offer limit orders are said to be "lifted" by incoming market buy orders. With every executed limit order, the market maker accumulates or divests quantities of the traded financial instrument in his account. These quantities are known as *inventory*. Immediately upon acquiring the inventory, the market maker begins to manage it, to reduce risk and enhance profitability.

The two broad functions of a market maker are therefore:

- Manage inventory to ensure sufficient profitability.

- Keep track and respond to information in order to avoid being "run over" or "picked over" by the markets.

Too little inventory may be insufficient to generate a profit; too much inventory makes the trader risk inability to quickly liquidate his position and face a certain loss.

Market Making: Key Principles

In a nutshell, "market-making" describes placement of limit orders on both sides of the market price. A market maker placing a limit buy order just below the market price and a limit sell order just above the market price creates or "makes" the "market." When a market buy order arrives from another market participant, it is matched with the market maker's limit sell order, and the limit sell order is executed (i.e., a short position is recorded in the market maker's account). Similarly, if a market sell order arrives from yet another market participant, it is matched with the market maker's limit buy order, and a long position is added to the market maker's account. If the size of the long position neutralizes the size of the short position in the market maker's portfolio, the market maker collects the spread as a compensation for providing limit orders, or liquidity, to traders placing market orders. The market order traders are known as *liquidity takers*.

Of course, market making is subject to risk. As soon as the market maker places his limit orders, he immediately faces two types of risk:

- Inventory risk

- Risk of adverse selection

Inventory risk describes the potential loss the market maker might incur when the value of his inventory declines in price due to natural market movements. Thus, a market maker accumulating a long position (buying) in a downward-trending market is likely to experience a loss on his position, at least in the short term. In addition, inventory risk is incurred when the market maker wishes to close his positions, as the market maker may face competition from other parties looking to sell their positions at the same time, resulting in difficulties liquidating his inventory. Inventory risk also includes the opportunity costs reflecting the gains the market maker misses while waiting for execution of his limit orders.

The risk of adverse selection measures potential loss due to informational differences between the market maker and a market taker. When the market taker possesses better information set than the market maker, the market maker is likely to be entering the losing end of the trade. For example, when a market maker's limit buy order is matched with a market sell order, it is possible that the seller has better information than the market maker about the imminent direction of the market – in this case, down, and that the market maker is about to commit to a losing trade. Per Copeland and Galai (1983), all limit orders suffer from an informational disadvantage, whereby they are picked off by better-informed investors. While the risks of inventory and adverse selection can produce significant losses for the market makers, the risks can be profitably controlled.

Simulating a Market-Making Strategy

Trading with limit orders generates nonlinear payoffs; sometimes limit orders execute and sometimes they do not. As a result, limit orders are difficult to model. This section delves into the logistics of limit-order modeling.

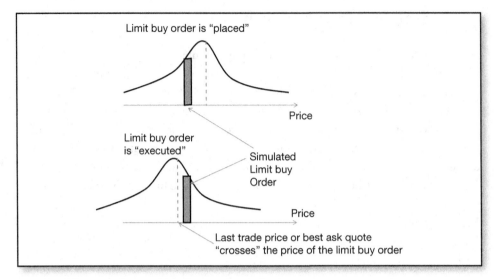

FIGURE 10.1 Mechanics of Simulating Limit Order Execution

Strategies that deploy market orders can be simulated with an assumption that each order is executed near the latest trade price observed in data at the time the simulated order is placed. By contrast, simulating execution of limit orders requires additional work. Most solid simulations consider a given limit order executed only when the best opposing quote reaches or crosses the limit order, in a process shown in Figure 10.1. A limit buy order is considered executed when the last trade price or the best ask quote falls below the price of the simulated limit order. A limit sell order can be marked processed whenever the last trade price or the best bid quote exceeds the price of the simulated limit order.

■ Naïve Market-Making Strategies

This section explains the details of practical market-making strategies that concern themselves only with effective management of inventory. Enhancements based on short-term directional market forecasts are discussed in Chapter 11.

Fixed Offset

The most naïve market-making strategy is continuously placing limit orders at a predetermined number of ticks away from the market price, on both sides of the market. Naturally, the probability of limit orders being executed depends on the limit order price proximity to the current market price. Limit orders placed at current market quotes are likely to be executed, whereas the probability of execution for passive limit orders, those far away from the market price, is close to zero. In most financial instruments, market makers are allowed to place limit orders only within 10 percent of the current market price, to prevent so-called "stub quotes" far away from the market from executing at times of extreme volatility.

The smaller the offset of a limit order from the market price in a naïve strategy, the higher the probability of order execution, and the more frequent the resulting reallocation of the market maker's capital. Frequency of trading has been shown to be key to market makers' profitability. The higher the number of times the market maker can "flip" his capital, the higher the cumulative spread the market-maker can capture, and the lower the risk the market maker bears waiting for execution of his orders. A study of market making on actively traded stocks on the Stockholm Stock Exchange, for example, found that the expected profit on limit orders increases when they are matched more frequently. The study, written by Sandas (2001), shows that market makers' profitability is not proportional to the time they spend providing liquidity; instead, market makers' profit is directly tied to the frequency with which their orders are executed.

By contrast, early market-making theories presumed that market makers were content to be compensated for time spent providing liquidity. The longer the waiting time until order execution, the thought went, the higher was the expected compensation to liquidity providers who did not change their limit order specifications once they submitted the orders. Such ideas were known as *static equilibrium models* and included Rock (1996), Glosten (1994), and Seppi (1997).

The assumptions of static equilibrium models reflected early exchange conditions. Changing the details of a limit order and canceling orders was prohibitively costly, and market makers indeed expected a tidy compensation for bearing the risk of ending up in an adverse position once their limit orders were hit. Limit order cancellations and revisions could be performed free of charge on most markets at the time this book was written. As a result, today's high-frequency market makers enjoy better profitability than their human market-making counterparts.

The ability to place orders at the best bid and best ask prices, however, may be limited by the speed of the HFT market maker's technology. Super-fast technology allows market makers to continually cancel and resubmit their limit orders to ensure their spot on the top of the book, high execution rates, and high profitability. Slower technology can still deliver profitable market-making strategies via larger offsets away from the going market price.

Volatility-Dependent Offset

To improve the fixed-offset strategy, one may vary the offset of limit orders with market conditions. One intuitive way to change the offset is to make it a function of volatility: in high-volatility conditions, limit orders farther away from the market are likely to be hit, generating higher premium for market makers. In low-volatility conditions, however, limit orders may need to be placed closer to the market to be executed. A sample determination of volatility-dependent offset is shown in equation (1):

$$offset_t = round\left(\frac{1}{T} \sum_{\tau=t-1}^{t-T} (P_\tau - P_{\tau-1})^2 \right) \tag{1}$$

Offset Is a Function of Order-Arrival Rate

Still another way to improve the naïve market making is to make the offset dependent on the arrival frequency of market orders. As Parlour and Seppi (2008) point out, limit orders compete with other limit orders, both existing and those submitted in the future. Furthermore, all limit orders execute against future market orders. The market order arrival rate, therefore, is an important determinant of market-making profitability.

The market orders can be assumed to arrive independently of one another, and with a great degree of randomness. Much like the arrival of subway trains or street cars, though, the randomness of order arrivals can be modeled using well-specified statistical distributions. Under the assumptions of exponentially-distributed inter-arrival times, for example, the market orders arrive to "hit the bid" and to "lift the ask" with a certain average rate, μ. The limit orders can be assumed to repopulate the top of the limit order book at an average rate λ. Probability of a top-of-the-book limit order being matched can then be expressed as a function of $\lambda = 1/\lambda$, $\mu = 1/\mu$ and a given interval of time, Δt:

$$P(hit, \Delta t) = 1 - P(not\ hit,\ \Delta t) = 1 - \exp\left(-\frac{\lambda}{\mu}\Delta t\right) \tag{2}$$

Parameters λ and μ can be calibrated on recent tick data. Level I data can be used to calibrate parameters for minimal time intervals, $\Delta t = 1$. When the best bid moves up or the size at the best bid increases, a new limit buy order is assumed to have arrived. When the best ask moves up or the size at the best ask decreases, a market buy order is recorded. Avellaneda and Stoikov (2008) present an example of strategy deploying arrival rates.

Another analytical model for determining the optimal offset of limit orders is due to Foucault, Kadan, and Kandel (2005). This model explicitly suggests whether a trader should place a passive or an aggressive limit order, and how many ticks away from the market price should the trader place his limit order. The model makes the following key assumptions:

- All other execution parameters have been selected.

- All traders in the market are free to switch from passive to aggressive execution, and vice versa.

The determining factor in whether or not a trader decides to place a passive or an aggressive order, is the so-called "reservation spread," defined as follows:

$$j^R = ceiling\left[\frac{\delta}{\mu\Delta}\right] \tag{3}$$

where

- δ is the market-maker's expected dollar-cost of execution that may incorporate expectations about market impact.

- Δ is the minimal tick size, say $0.01 for equities.

- μ is the arrival rate of matching market orders per unit of time; with $1/\mu$ representing the average time between two sequential order arrivals. If the model is used to determine levels of aggressiveness of limit buy orders, μ is the rate of arrival of market sell orders, computed as a number of market sell orders recorded per unit of time. In Foucault et al. (2005), all orders, both market and limit, are assumed to be of the same size.

Foucault et al. (2005) use the reservation spread j^R to establish a short-run equilibrium, where all traders achieve their optimality. To do so, Foucault et al. (2005) consider three different types of markets:

1. A market with identical (homogenous) traders.
2. A market with two different types of traders, facing diverging transaction costs.
3. A market with q different types of traders, with heterogeneous transaction costs.

The main intuition behind the model works as follows: The trader's reservation spread is the cost of executing the given order slice. If the current market spread is smaller than the trader's reservation spread, the trader can avoid additional costs associated with the risk of nonexecution, placing a market order. When the trader's execution costs per rate of arrival of opposing orders are smaller than the market spread, the trader places an aggressive limit order, shrinking the spread and further improving his cost structure by avoiding crossing the spread.

In a market with identical traders, all traders [1 . . . q] have the same transaction costs, and face common arrival rates for opposing orders, resulting in equal reservation spreads: $j_1^R = j_2^R = \ldots = j_q^R = j^R$. In such a market, each trader would submit a limit order j^R ticks away from the market whenever the inside market spread s is greater than j^R, and submit a market order otherwise. Such a market is characterized by a highly competitive outcome, with traders shrinking market spreads to the minimum tick size.

In a market with two traders facing different transaction costs, similar dynamics take place. Trader 1 places a limit order j_1^R ticks away from the market whenever the market spread s is larger than j_1^R. Similarly, trader 2 places a limit order j_2^R ticks away from the market whenever the market spread s is larger than j_2^R. Yet, when the market inside spread s exceeds j_1^R and $S < j_2^R$, trader 2 places a market order, while trader 1 places a limit order j_1^R ticks away from the market price, potentially shrinking the spread. In this market with identically sized orders, no trader ever places a limit order "behind" the market or farther away from the market than the spread.

In a market with [1 ... q] heterogeneous traders, $j_1^R < j_2^R < \cdots < j_q^R$, similar dynamics hold: whenever the market spread s is smaller than the ith trader reservation spread j_i^R, all traders [i, …, q] place market orders. All traders with reservation spread smaller than the market spread s, on the other hand, place limit orders at their reservation spread.

The differences in transaction costs of traders may be due to the following factors:

- Fees: Large institutional traders are likely to face lower fees than smaller traders.

- Market impact: Large child orders are expected to bear higher market impact than smaller order slices.

- Taxes: Individual investors may be subject to high marginal tax rates on their trading gains.

- Other quantifiable transaction costs.

The Foucault et al. (2005) model takes into account only the aggregate transaction cost facing a trader, and does not distinguish among various types of costs.

Key implications from Foucault et al. (2005) model, $j^R = ceiling\left[\dfrac{\delta}{\mu\Delta}\right]$, include the following observations:

- Higher market order arrival rates lead to lower reservation spreads, and as a result, lower market spreads. As a result, competing market orders are good for the markets, lowering the costs of overall trading.

- Lower trading costs also lead to lower spreads, suggesting that rebates help facilitate cheaper execution, not to make trading more expensive.

- High execution costs and low market order arrival rates, however, result in wide reservation spreads, and may destroy markets by creating no-trade voids. Such conditions can be observed in long-dated futures markets following the ban of stub quotes: due to the low demand and the resulting low number of orders, traders in long-dated futures have traditionally "quoted wide," at large deviations from the market. The so-called quote stuffing ban adopted in Europe and the United States in 2010–2011 prohibits traders from placing limit orders farther than 10 percent away from the prevailing market price, eliminating the ability to trade in naturally wide-quoted markets, and hurting farmers, agricultural processors, and other consumption traders in the process.

While the Foucault et al. (2005) model presents groundbreaking foundation for predicting micro-trader behavior, several assumptions of the model deviate from market reality and thus limit its applicability. For one, the model assumes that all limit and market orders are always of the same size, and that the arrival of the opposing market orders μ and the execution costs δ are invariant with time. As a result, all limit orders in the model shrink the spread, and no limit orders behind the market price are ever placed, an impractical consequence in many today's markets where the spread has already contracted to the size of the minimum tick allowed.

Trend-Dependent Offset

An improvement to basic market-making models may involve differentiation between trending and mean-reverting markets. In a mean-reverting market, the price bounces up and down within a range, reducing the risk of adverse selection and making such market conditions perfect for market making. In trending markets, however, a market maker needs to reduce the size of limit orders on the "wrong" side of the markets, hedge the exposure, or exit the markets altogether. To determine whether the market is trending, the systems may deploy directional analysis, like the event-based frameworks presented in Chapter 9 and intelligent forecasting discussed in Chapter 11.

■ Market Making as a Service

The key objective of market making was formally defined over 50 years ago as provision of "predictable immediacy" in supply and demand on security exchanges (see Demsetz, 1968). This predictable immediacy comprises *liquidity*."

Intuitively, a service adding liquidity is particularly useful, and the associated premium and the strategy profitability particularly high, whenever the liquidity levels are low. By reverse logic, whenever the liquidity levels are particularly high, aggressive liquidity-consuming orders may deliver better profitability.

Many measures of liquidity have been developed over the years. Among the most popular metrics are:

- The tightness of the bid-ask spread.

- Market depth at best bid and best ask.

- Shape of the order book.

- Price sensitivity to block transactions.

- Price sensitivity to order-flow imbalance.

- Price change per unit volume.

- Technical support and resistance levels.

- Market resilience.

The Tightness of the Bid–Ask Spread

The tightness of the bid-ask spread reflects the degree of competition among limit order–placing traders. The more traders are competing to post and execute limit orders, the closer will the traders post their limit orders to the market price, the tighter will be the resulting bid-ask spread. This metric is an easy liquidity test suitable for most markets, and particularly in markets with wide spreads, such as most U.S. equity options.

Market Depth at Best Bid and Best Ask

In many securities, the bid-ask spread often reaches its minimum value and stays at the minimum value through the most market hours. For example, in commonly traded

U.S. equities, the spread was often $0.01 at the time this book was written. In such conditions, the tightness of the bid-ask spread loses its potency, and the relative liquidity levels can be approximated using market depth at the best bid and the best ask. The sizes at the best bid and ask can be thought of as the sizes of limit orders of traders that desire to be at the top of the book, if the minimum tick size were smaller.

Shape of the Order Book

When available, Level II data can be used to calculate the exact amount of aggregate supply and demand available on a given trading venue. Using Level II data, supply and demand can be determined as the cumulative sizes of limit orders posted on the sell and buy sides of the limit order book, respectively

Shape of the order book also helps separate immediately available top-of-the-book liquidity from deeper-in-the-book "behind-the-market" liquidity. Such separation may be particularly interesting to market makers seeking to fine-tune their algorithms to post orders at selected price points. High liquidity observed deeper in the book may indicate presence of large investors. Academic research suggests that, when a large investor is present, all human and automated market makers choose to cater to that specific investor by placing aggressive limit orders on the opposite side of the limit order book. Handa, Schwartz, and Tiwari (2003), for example, find that when the order book is imbalanced due to the presence of a large investor, market makers on the opposing side of the book exert greater market power and obtain better prices from investors on the populous trading side.

Limit order books may also contain "holes," ranges of prices that are skipped by investors when submitting limit orders. Holes were empirically documented by Biais, Hillion, and Spatt (1995), among others. The impact of holes on trading has not been thoroughly studied.

Price Sensitivity to Block Transactions

When the Level II data are not available, the shape of the order book can still be estimated using techniques that hail from technical analysis, like support and resistance levels and moving averages. Due to the popularity of the support and resistance methodology, for example, many human traders as well as trading algos choose to place limit orders at the market support and resistance levels. Computing support and resistance helps pinpoint liquidity peaks without parsing cumbersome Level II information. This fact was first pointed out by Kavajecz and Odders-White (2004).

Mathematically, support and resistance levels are determined as linear projections of recent price minima in case of support, and maxima in case of resistance. To determine the support level one minute ahead, the algorithm would compute minimum prices within the past minute and the prior minute, and then project the minima trend one minute ahead:

$$SL_{t+1} = \min(P_t) + (\min(P_t) - \min(P_{t-1})) \tag{4}$$

Similarly, resistance level can be computed as:

$$RL_{t+1} = \max(P_t) + (\max(P_t) - \max(P_{t-1})) \tag{5}$$

In addition to support and resistance levels, indicators based on moving averages help identify the skewness of the order book. When a short-run moving average rises above a long-run moving average, the buy-side liquidity pool in the limit order book moves closer to the market price.

Kavajecz and Odders-White (2004) speculate that technical analysis remains popular in dark markets and markets without centralized order books, like foreign exchange, because the technical techniques help traders reverse-engineer unobservable limit order books and deploy profitable liquidity provision strategies.

Price Sensitivity to Order-Flow Imbalance

Price sensitivity to block transactions measures how the market price moves following an order. The main idea is that low liquidity makes a large market order "eat" through the limit order book, moving the market price substantially. Price sensitivity measures the relationship between the net directional trading volume and the price change induced by the trade size. The sensitivity parameter is known as *Kyle's lambda* after Kyle (1985):

$$\Delta P_t = \alpha + \lambda NVOL_t + \varepsilon_t \tag{6}$$

where ΔP_t is the change in market price from time $t - 1$ to time t due to the market impact of orders and $NVOL_t$ is the difference between sizes recorded at the best bid and best ask quotes at time t. Parameters α, λ, and ε_t are then components of the linear regression specification of equation (6): ε_t is the error term associated with each individual observation ΔP_t, α is the intercept of the regression, and λ is the Kyle's lambda, the parameter of interest, measuring the sensitivity of price changes to net volume imbalance. The lower the lambda, the less sensitive the price to large directional trades, and the higher the liquidity available on the trading venue.

Price Change per Unit Volume

A modified Kyle's lambda proposed by Aldridge (2012d) works as follows:

$$\Delta P_t = \alpha + \lambda(S_t^b - S_t^a) + \varepsilon_t \tag{7}$$

where ΔP_t is a change in prices on executed trades observed during predefined time period t, S_t^b is the aggregate volume of trades executed at the best bid that was in force at the time each trade was processed during period t, and S_t^a is the volume of trades matched at the best ask prevailing at trade time. The difference between $S_t^b - S_t^a$ can be interpreted as the net order flow imbalance observed during time period t: the volume executed at bid is likely to be generated by market sell orders, while the trades processed at ask are often a result of market buy orders.

Technical Support and Resistance Levels

Absolute price change per unit volume traded is yet another measure of liquidity:

$$\gamma_t = \frac{1}{D_t} \sum_{d=1}^{D_t} \frac{|r_{d,t}|}{v_{d,t}} \tag{8}$$

This metric is due to Amihud (2002) and is known as the illiquidity ratio. Similarly to Kyle's lambda, illiquidity ratio estimates size-induced change in price of the traded financial instrument. The smaller the average price change per unit of trading volume, the deeper is the available liquidity. While modified Kyle's lambda requires attribution of trades to prevailing bid and ask quotes, the metric of equation (8) assumes that the liquidity is balanced at all times, and accounts only for the absolute change in price per unit volume traded.

Market Resilience

Market resilience is yet another metric of liquidity and measures just how quickly the order book recovers its "shape" following a market order. Estimation of market resilience is discussed in Chapter 15 of this book.

■ Profitable Market Making

To ensure that the market-making operation is profitable, several key conditions must hold. The conditions, dating back to Garman (1976), relate the arrival rates of limit orders, probability of gain and loss, and prices of traded instruments.

Temporary imbalances between buy and sell orders are due to differences between the individual trader and the way a dealer optimizes his order flow, which may reflect underlying differences in budgets, risk appetite, access to markets, and a host of other idiosyncrasies. The individual trader optimization problems themselves are less important than the aggregated order imbalances that these optimization differences help create. The market maker's objective is to maximize profits while avoiding bankruptcy or failure. The latter arise whenever the market maker has no inventory or cash. Both buy and sell orders arrive as independent stochastic processes.

The model solution for optimal bid and ask prices lies in the estimation of the rates at which a unit of cash (e.g., a dollar or a "clip" of 10 million in foreign exchange) "arrives" to the market maker when a customer comes in to buy securities (pays money to the dealer) and "departs" the market maker when a customer comes in to sell (the dealer pays the customer). Suppose the probability of an arrival, a customer order to buy a security at the market ask price P_a is denoted λ_a. Correspondingly, the probability of departure of a clip from the market maker to the customer, or a customer order to sell securities to the market maker at the bid price P_b, can be denoted λ_b.

The solution is based on the solution to a classical problem known as the Gambler's Ruin Problem. In the dealer's version of the Gambler's Ruin Problem, a gambler, or a dealer, starts out with a certain initial wealth position and wagers (stays in business) until he loses all his money. This version of the Gambler's Ruin Problem is known as an unbounded problem. The bounded problem assumes that the gambler bets until he either loses all his money or reaches a certain level of wealth, at which point he exits.

Under the Gambler's Ruin Problem, the probability that the gambler will lose all his money is

$$\text{Pr}_{Failure} = \left(\frac{\text{Pr}(Loss) \times Loss}{\text{Pr}(Gain) \times Gain} \right)^{Initial\ Wealth} \tag{9}$$

where *Initial Wealth* is the gambler's start-up cash, Pr(*Loss*) is the probability of losing an amount (*Loss*) of the initial wealth, and Pr(*Gain*) is the probability of gaining an amount (*Gain*).

From the Gambler's Ruin Problem, we can see that the probability of failure is always positive. It can be further shown that failure is certain whenever the probability of losing exceeds the probability of gaining. In other words, the minimum condition for a positive probability of avoiding failure in the long term is Pr(*Gain*) > Pr(*Loss*).

Garman (1976) applies the Gambler's Ruin Problem to the market-making business in the following two ways:

1. The market maker fails if he runs out of cash.
2. The market maker fails if he runs out of inventory and is unable to satisfy client demand.

In modeling the Gambler's Ruin Problem for the market maker's ruin through running out of inventory, we assume that both the *Gain* and *Loss* variables are single units of the underlying financial asset. In other words,

$Gain = 1$
$Loss = 1$

In the case of equity, this unit may be a share of stock. In the case of foreign exchange, the unit may be a clip. Then, from the market maker's perspective, the probability of "losing" one unit of inventory is the probability of selling a unit of inventory, and it equals the probability λ_a of a buyer arriving. By the same logic, the probability of gaining one unit of inventory is λ_b, the probability of a seller arriving. The Gambler's Ruin Problem equation (9) now becomes

$$\lim_{t \to \infty} \text{Pr}_{Failure}(t) \approx \left(\frac{\lambda_a}{\lambda_b} \right)^{Initial\ Wealth / E_0(P_a, P_b)} \quad , \text{if } \lambda_b > \lambda_a$$

$$= 1, \text{ otherwise.} \tag{10}$$

where $E_0(P_a, P_b)$ is the initial average price of an underlying unit of inventory and $\frac{Initial\ Wealth}{E_0(P_a, P_b)}$ is the initial number of units of the financial instrument in possession of the market maker.

The Gambler's Ruin Problem is further applied to the market maker's probability of failure due to running out of cash. From the market maker's perspective, gaining a unit of cash—say a dollar—happens when a buyer of the security arrives. As before, the arrival of a buyer willing to buy at price P_a happens with probability λ_a. As a result, the market maker's probability of gaining a dollar is P_a. Similarly, the market maker's probability of "losing" or giving away a dollar to a seller of the security for selling the security at price P_b is λ_b. The Gambler's Ruin Problem now takes the following shape:

$$\lim_{t \to \infty} \Pr_{Failure}(t) \approx \left(\frac{\lambda_b P_b}{\lambda_a P_a} \right)^{InitialWealth} , \text{ if } \lambda_a P_a > \lambda_a P_b$$

$$= 1, \text{ otherwise.} \qquad (11)$$

For a market maker to remain in business, the first conditions of equations (10) and (11) need to be satisfied simultaneously. In other words, the following two inequalities have to hold contemporaneously:

$\lambda_b > \lambda_a$ and

$\lambda_a p_a > \lambda_a p_b$

For both inequalities to hold at the same time, the following must be true at all times: $p_a > p_b$, defining the bid-ask spread. The bid-ask spread allows the market maker to earn cash while maintaining sufficient inventory positions. The reverse, however, does not hold true: the existence of the bid-ask spread does not guarantee that the market maker satisfies profitability conditions of equation (11).

▮ Summary

Market making and any liquidity provision is a service to the markets and deserves compensation. Profitable automated market making is feasible with very simple models that only take into account inventory on the market maker's books. While Level II data is informative, and, therefore, desirable, the information delivered by Level II data can be extracted out of Level I data using simple techniques like technical analysis.

▮ End-of-Chapter Questions

1. What is market making? How does it differ from liquidity provision?
2. Why is market making inherently profitable?
3. What is the core market-making strategy? What are the common extensions?
4. What are the common measures of liquidity?
5. What are the minimum profitability conditions of market-making strategies?

CHAPTER 11

Automated Market Making II

Inventory market-making models, discussed in Chapter 10, explain and help manage transitory variations in prices resulting from the imbalances in a dealer's book, or portfolio. The models usually start with a "sweet spot" inventory, an inventory level sufficient to satisfy immediate client demand, and proceed to adjust the inventory according to client demand and the market's conditions. Such models do not consider actions and information available to other market participants.

By contrast, information-based market-making models addressed in this chapter carefully evaluate the trading patterns of various market participants, deduce the news available to them, and optimize market-making process by responding to available supply and demand in the markets. The models account for present and expected future trading, including the shape of limit order book, order flow, as well as histories of orders and trading outcomes.

■ What's in the Data?

Publicly available data carries information that is sufficient to detect short-term price movements and manage one's positions accordingly. This section presents four cases for illustration. The figures accompanying the cases show sample market situations observable by all market participants subscribing to Level I data from a given trading venue. The cases apply to all trading venues that deploy a centralized limit order book for its matching operation.

In all figures, the horizontal axis is time. The solid lines are the best bid and the best ask, a.k.a. best offer, observed at the given point in time, and the dashed line shows the midquote: the simple average between the best bid and the best ask. The stars indicate the price and timing of trades: some trades occur at ask, some at bid, and some may occur in the vicinity of either bid or ask.

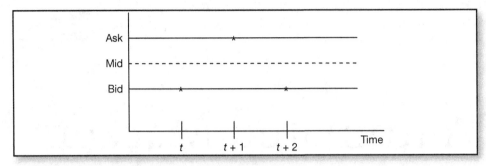

FIGURE 11.1   The Market Does Not Move in Response to Trades

Case 1: Market Does Not Move

In Figure 11.1, the trades are recorded in the following sequence: the first trade occurred at the best bid, then at the best ask, and finally at the best bid again. Neither the best bid nor the best ask moved. What is the dynamic at work in the market shown in Figure 11.1?

A short answer to this question is "none." In the market shown in Figure 11.1, nothing interesting or unusual is happening. The first order that arrived and resulted in the trade was a market sell—the trade was recorded at the bid, as market sell orders would be. The market sell order was smaller in size than the size at the best bid at the time the order arrived—following the trade, the best bid did not move. The order did not carry any information, at least not from the broader market perspective: the best bid and the best ask quotes remained at their original levels. Had other market participants been concerned about the specialized knowledge of the trader or the imminent movement of the market, they would have likely revised their quotes to minimize their risk.

Following the first sell order, Figure 11.1 shows that two additional orders are executed shortly afterward: a market buy order and a market sell order. The buy order is identified as such because it is recorded at the best ask—market buy orders would be matched with the ask side of the limit order book. The next trade is recorded at the best bid and, therefore, must be a sell. Once again, Figure 11.1 shows no changes in prices following either order, implying that

- The size of both orders was small in comparison with aggregate sizes at the best bid and the best ask.
- The orders were not perceived to have any special informational advantages.

Case 2: Market Moves and Rebounds

Figure 11.2 presents a different scenario: a trade is recorded at the bid. Following the bid, the quotes drop lower, yet gradually recovers over time.

The trade in Figure 11.2 occurred at the bid, and was, therefore, triggered by a market sell order. The subsequent drop in the quotes that was followed by gradual recovery suggests that:

1. The trade size was large relative to the size available at the best bid; the market sell order had to "sweep" through the book to be fully matched.

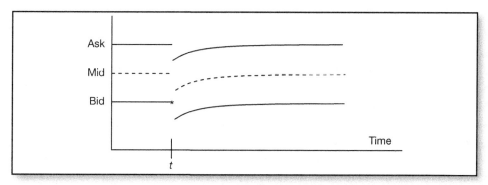

FIGURE 11.2   The Market Moves and Shortly Rebounds Following a Trade

2. Despite its large size, the trade did not move the fundamentals that drive the price—the quotes slowly recovered to their original levels; the trade carried no information.

In Figure 11.2, the best ask quote also drops following the sell. This may be due to the market makers' activity seeking to disgorge the inventory just acquired via the sell trade. By lowering the best ask quote, a market maker can promptly sell the newly purchased inventory, realizing a quick profit.

Case 3: A Trade Moves Markets

The trade in Figure 11.3 also occurred at the bid. Unlike Case 2 above, where the quotes recovered following the trade, in Figure 11.3 the trade substantially shifted both bid and ask quotes downward. No immediate recovery of quotes is observed.

The most likely explanation of market activity in Figure 11.3 is information. The trade once again came in at the bid and was hence a sell. The markets interpreted the sell, however, as a trade containing enough information to warrant a permanent price decline. Unlike Case 2 above, the quotes did not recover to their original levels, but instead remained at their new lows. The new persistent price level is most likely the result of fundamental information carried by the sell trade.

The market makers may determine that the sell trade possessed information in several ways. Often, the broker-dealer of the trader who placed the sell market order may observe that the trader possesses superior research skills and routinely places profitable orders ahead of other traders. In such situations, the trader's broker-dealer may be the first to adjust the quotes after the trade is executed to protect

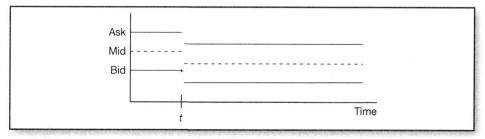

FIGURE 11.3   A Trade Moves Markets

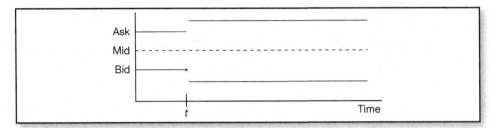

FIGURE 11.4 The Quotes Widen Following a Trade

himself against accepting further trades with a losing counterparty. Such activity is perfectly legal, and is often referred to as *prehedging*. Alternatively, the broker-dealer and other market participants may determine the probabilistic presence of informed traders through information-extracting models described later in this chapter.

Case 4: The Quotes Widen

Figure 11.4 illustrates yet another scenario: a case where spreads widen following a trade.

The scenario depicted in Figure 11.4 is most often a result of increased uncertainty in the markets. An example of such uncertainty can be the time preceding a major scheduled news announcement, where the news, once released, is likely to move the markets considerably one way or the other. Market makers' natural response is to avoid being run over by better-informed traders and to pull orders closest to the market price, a practice known as *quoting wide*, shown in Figure 11.4.

Cases 1 through 4 illustrate predictable market maker behavior following distinct situations. Other scenarios are also possible. Market makers' behavior following specific market events, observable in public quote data, helps automated trading systems to extract information available solely to other market makers.

■ Modeling Information in Order Flow

The remaining sections of the chapter describe four classes of techniques that have been developed to identify impending market moves based on the behavior of other market participants. The described models take into account:

- Order flow autocorrelation
- Order flow aggressiveness
- Shape of the order book
- Sequential evolution of quotes

Autocorrelation of Order Flow as a Predictor of Market Movement

Order flow is a result of end customers receiving and acting on information. Information models are trained to observe order flow and extract and then trade upon information available to various market participants.

Order flow is the difference in trade volume between trades initiated with market buy orders and trades triggered by market sell orders, all noted within a predetermined period of time. Trades begun with a market buy order are known as *buyer initiated*. Similarly, trading volume caused by market sell orders is referred to as *seller initiated*. Equation (1) illustrates the definition of order flow:

$$x_t = v_t^a - v_t^b \tag{1}$$

where v_t^a is the trading volume resulting from market buy orders being matched with the ask side of the order book, and v_t^b is the trading volume triggered by market sell orders hitting the bid side of the order book.

According to academic research, order flow is directly responsible for at least 50 percent of information impounded into market prices. Around news releases, order flow becomes highly directional. For example, Love and Payne (2008) estimate that following a major Eurozone and the U.S. news announcement, the order flow surrounding the EUR/USD exchange rate closely follows the directionality of the announcement. Thus, "good" U.S. news, expected to lift the U.S. dollar, is dominated by "buy U.S. dollar" or "sell Euro" orders. Other studies with similar findings about various securities include Lyons (1995), Perraudin and Vitale (1996), Evans and Lyons (2002a), and Jones, Kaul, and Lipson (1994).

According to Lyons (2001), order flow is informative for three reasons:

1. Order flow can be thought of as market participants exposing their equity to their own forecasts. Market orders are irrevocable commitments to buy or sell, and therefore carry most powerful information. Limit orders can also be executed and be costly and, as a result, carry information. Order flow therefore reflects market participants' honest beliefs about the upcoming direction of the market.
2. Order flow data is decentralized with limited distribution. Brokers can directly observe the order flow of their clients and interdealer networks. End investors seldom see any direct order flow at all, but can partially infer the order flow information from market data, as described in this section. Exchanges possess order flow data they receive from brokers and other market participant. The exchange data may, however, miss significant numbers of investor orders, as broker-dealers increasingly seek to match orders internally, in the process called *internalization of the order flow*. The internalization is presently viewed as a necessary function to contain broker costs by avoiding exchanges whenever possible. Because the order flow is not available to everyone, those who possess full order flow information or successfully model it are in a unique position to exploit it before the information is impounded into market prices.
3. Order flow shows large and nontrivial positions that will temporarily move the market regardless of whether the originator of the trades possesses any superior information, due to market impact. Once again, the traders observing or modeling the order flow are best positioned to capitalize on the market movements surrounding the transaction.

Lyons (2001) further distinguishes between transparent and opaque order flows, with transparent order flows providing immediate information, and opaque order flows failing to produce useful data or subjective analysis to extract market beliefs. According to Lyons (2001), order flow transparency encompasses the following three dimensions:

- Pretrade versus posttrade information
- Price versus quantity information
- Public versus dealer information

Brokers observing the customer and interdealer flow firsthand have access to the information pretrade, can observe both the price and the quantity of the trade, and can see both public and dealer information. End customers can generally see only the posttrade price information by the time it becomes public or available to all customers. Undoubtedly, dealers are much better positioned to use the wealth of information embedded in the order flow to obtain superior returns, given the appropriate resources to use the information efficiently.

Order Flow Is Directly Observable   As noted by Lyons (1995), Perraudin and Vitale (1996), and Evans and Lyons (2002b), among others, order flow was previously dispersed among market participants but can be viewed centrally by the broker-dealer or a trading venue. Order flow for a particular financial security at any given time is formally measured as the difference between buyer-initiated and seller-initiated trading interest. Order flow is sometimes referred to as *buying or selling pressure*. When the trade sizes are observable, the order flow can be computed as the difference between the cumulative size of buyer-initiated trades and the cumulative size of seller-initiated trades. When trade quantities are not directly observable (as is often the case in foreign exchange), order flow can be measured as the difference between the number of buyer-initiated trades and seller-initiated trades in each specific time interval.

Both trade-size-based and number-of-trades-based measures of order flow have been used in the empirical literature. These measures are comparable since most orders are transmitted in "clips," or parcels of a standard size, primarily to avoid undue attention and price run-ups that would accompany larger trades. Jones et al. (1994) actually found that order flow measured in number of trades predicts prices and volatility better than order flow measured in aggregate size of trades.

The importance of order flow in arriving at a new price level following a news announcement has been verified empirically. Love and Payne (2008), for example, examine the order flow in foreign exchange surrounding macroeconomic news announcements and find that order flow directly accounts for at least half of all the information impounded into market prices.

Love and Payne (2008) studied the impact of order flow on three currency pairs: USD/EUR, GBP/EUR, and USD/GBP. The impact of the order flow on the respective rates found by Love and Payne (2008) is shown in Table 11.1. The authors measure order flow as the difference between the number of buyer-initiated and the number of seller-initiated trades in each one-minute interval. Love and Payne (2008) document that at the time of news release from Eurozone, each additional buyer-initiated trade in excess of seller-initiated trades causes USD/EUR to increase by 0.00626 or 0.626 percent.

TABLE 11.1	Average Changes in One-Minute Currency Returns Following a Single Trade Increase in the Number of Buyer-Initiated Trades in Excess of Seller-Initiated Trades		
	USD/EUR Return	GBP/EUR Return	USD/GBP Return
Flow_t at a time coinciding with a news release from Eurozone	0.00626*	0.000544	0.00206
Flow_t at a time coinciding with a news release from the United Kingdom	0.000531	0.00339***	0.00322***
Flow_t at a time coinciding with a news release from the United States	0.00701***	0.00204	0.00342**

***, ** and * denote 99.9 percent, 95 percent, and 90 percent statistical significance, respectively.

Order Flow Is Not Directly Observable   Order flow is not necessarily transparent to all market participants. For example, executing brokers can directly observe buy-and-sell orders coming from their customers, but generally the customers can see only the bid and offer prices, and, possibly, the depth of the market.

As a result, various models have sprung up to extract order flow information from the observable data. The most basic algorithm tests autocorrelation of trade signs. First, the algorithm separates all trades recorded over the past period of time T, say, 30 minutes, into buys and sells. The identification of trades can be performed using the Lee-Ready or volume clock rule described in Chapter 4 of this book. Trades identified as buys are assigned "trade direction value" of $+1$, and each sell trades is noted as -1. Next, the algorithm computes the autocorrelation function (ACF) for lagged trade direction variable, x_t :

$$\rho_{t,t+\tau} = \frac{1}{N}\sum_{t=1}^{N} x_t x_{t+\tau} \qquad (2)$$

where t is the sequential number of a given trade tick in the chosen evaluation interval T, and N is the total number of ticks within the time interval. An ACF plot, linking the computed autocorrelation $\rho_{t,t+\tau}$ with a lag τ, reveals trade dependencies.

Figure 11.5 shows comparative autocorrelation figures for two financial instruments.

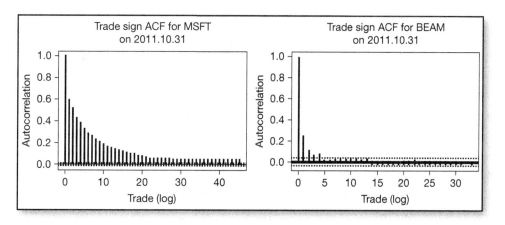

FIGURE 11.5   Autocorrelation of Order Flow Observed for Microsoft (MSFT) and Sunbeam (BEAM) on October 31, 2011
Source: Sotiropoulos, 2012.

Hasbrouck (1991), in estimating order autocorrelation, adjusts for returns caused by previously placed orders as well as effects of the time of day:

$$x_t = \alpha_x \sum_{k=1}^{K} \beta_k r_{t-k} + \sum_{m=1}^{M} \gamma_m x_{t-m} + \sum_{t=1}^{T} \delta D_t + \varepsilon_t \qquad (3)$$

where x_t is the order flow observed at time t, set to $+1$ when the given trade was estimated originate from a market buy order and -1 otherwise; r_t is a one-trade return; and D_t is the dummy indicator controlling for the time of day into which time t falls.

Ellul, Holden, Jain, and Jennings (2007) interpret short-term autocorrelation in high-frequency order flows as waves of competing order flows responding to current market events within liquidity depletion and replenishment. Ellul et al. (2007) confirm strong positive serial correlation in order flow at high frequencies, but find negative order firm correlation at lower frequencies. Other studies of order autocorrelation include Hedvall, Niemeyer, and Rosenqvist (1997); Ranaldo (2004); Hollifield, Miller, and Sandas (2004); Foucault, Kadan, and Kandel (2005); Rosu (2005); and Biais, Hillion, and Spatt (1995).

Order flow information is easy to trade profitably. A disproportionately large number of buy orders will inevitably push the price of the traded security higher; placing a buy order at the time a large buy volume is observed will result in positive gains. Similarly, a large number of sell orders will depress prices, and a timely sell order placed when the sell order flow is observed will generate positive results.

Order Aggressiveness as a Predictor of Market Movement

To extract the market information from the publicly available data, Vega (2007) proposes monitoring the aggressiveness of trades. Aggressiveness refers to the percentage of orders that are submitted at market prices, as opposed to limit prices. The higher the percentage of market orders, the more aggressive is the trader in his bid to capture the best available price and the more likely the trader is to believe that the price of the security is about to move away from the market price.

The results of Vega (2007) are based on those of Foster and Viswanathan (1996), who evaluate the average response of prices in a situation where different market participants are informed to a different degree. For example, before an expected economic announcement is made, it is common to see "a consensus forecast" that is developed by averaging forecasts of several market analysts. The consensus number is typically accompanied by a range of forecasts that measures the dispersion of forecasts by all analysts under consideration. For example, prior to the announcement of the January 2009 month-to-month change in retail sales in the United States, Bloomberg LP reported the analysts' consensus to be -0.8 percent, while all the analysts' estimates for the number ranged from -2.2 percent to 0.3 percent (the actual number revealed at 8:30 a.m. on February 12, 2009, happened to be $+1.0$ percent).

Foster and Viswanathan (1996) show that the correlation in the degree of informativeness of various market participants affects the speed with which information is impounded into prices, impacts profits of traders possessing information, and also determines the ability of the market participants to learn from each other. In other words, the narrower the analysts' forecast range, the faster the market arrives at fair market prices of securities following a scheduled news release. The actual announcement information enters prices through active trading. Limit orders result in more favorable execution prices than market orders; the price advantage, however, comes at a cost—the wait and the associated risk of nonexecution. Market orders, on the other hand, are executed immediately but can be subject to adverse pricing. Market orders are used in aggressive trading, when prices are moving rapidly and quick execution must be achieved to capture and preserve trading gains. The better the trader's information and the more aggressive his trading, the faster the information enters prices.

As a result, aggressive orders may themselves convey information about the impending direction of the security price move. If a trader executes immediately instead of waiting for a more favorable price, the trader may convey information about his beliefs about where the market is going. Vega (2007) shows that better-informed market participants trade more aggressively. Mimicking aggressive trades, therefore, may result in a consistently profitable trading strategy. Measures of aggressiveness of the order flow may further capture informed traders' information and facilitate generation of short-term profits.

Anand, Chakravarty, and Martell (2005) find that on the New York Stock Exchange (NYSE), institutional limit orders perform better than limit orders placed by individuals, orders at or better than market price perform better than limit orders placed inside the bid-ask spread, and larger orders outperform smaller orders. To evaluate the orders, Anand et al. (2005) sampled all orders and the execution details of a three-month trading audit trail on the NYSE, spanning November 1990 through January 1991.

Anand et al. (2005) use the following regression equation to estimate the impact of various order characteristics on the price changes measured as $Diff_t$, the difference between the bid-ask midpoints at times t and $t + n$:

$$Diff_t = \beta_0 + \beta_1 Size_t + \beta_2 Aggressiveness_t + \beta_3 Institutional_t + D_{1t} + \ldots + D_{n-1,t} + \varepsilon_t \quad (4)$$

where t is the time of the order submission, n equals 5 and then 60 minutes after order submission. $Size$ is the number of shares in the particular order divided by the mean daily volume of shares traded in the particular stock over the sample period. For buy orders, $Aggressiveness$ is a dummy that takes the value 1 if the order is placed at or better than the standing quote and zero otherwise. $Institutional$ is a dummy variable that takes the value 1 for institutional orders and 0 for individual orders. D_1 to D_{n-1} are stock-specific dummies associated with the particular stock that was traded.

Table 11.2, from Anand et al. (2005), summarizes the results of robustness regressions testing for a difference in the performance of institutional and individual orders. The regression equation controls for stock selection by institutional and individual traders. The dependent variable in the regression is the change in the bid-ask midpoint 5 and then 60 minutes after order submission.

TABLE 11.2	Summary of Robustness Regressions Testing for a Difference in the Performance of Institutional and Individual Orders			
	Intercept	Size	Aggressiveness	Institutional
Panel A: 97 stocks				
5 min after order placement	0.005	0.010*	0.016*	0.004*
60 min after order placement	0.020**	0.020*	0.012*	0.006*
Panel B: 144 stocks				
5 min after order placement	0.006	0.012*	0.014*	0.004*
60 min after order placement	0.021**	0.023*	0.012*	0.004*

*t-test significant at 1 percent; **t-test significant at 5 percent.

Reprinted from Amber Anand, Sugato Chakravarty, and Terrence Martell, "Empirical Evidence on the Evolution of Liquidity: Choice of Market versus Limit Orders by Informed and Uninformed Traders," *Journal of Financial Markets* (August 3, 2005): 21, with permission from Elsevier.

According to several researchers, market aggressiveness exhibits autocorrelation that can be used to forecast future realizations of market aggressiveness. The autocorrelation of market aggressiveness is thought to originate from either of the following sources:

- Large institutional orders that are transmitted in smaller slices over an extended period of time at comparable levels of market aggressiveness
- Simple price momentum

Research into detecting autocorrelation of market aggressiveness was performed by Biais et al. (1995), who separated orders observed on the Paris Bourse by the degree of aggressiveness—from the least aggressive market orders that move prices to the most aggressive limit orders outside the current book. The authors found that the distribution of orders in terms of aggressiveness depends on the state of the market and that order submissions are autocorrelated. The authors detected a "diagonal effect" whereby initial orders of a certain level of aggressiveness are followed by other orders of the same level of aggressiveness. Subsequent empirical research confirmed the findings for different stock exchanges. See, for example, Griffiths, Smith, Turnbull, and White (2000) for the Toronto Stock Exchange; Ranaldo (2004) for the Swiss Stock Exchange; Cao, Hansch, and Wang (2004) for the Australian Stock Exchange; Ahn, Bae, and Chan (2001) for the Stock Exchange of Hong Kong; and Handa et al. (2003) for the CAC40 stocks traded on the Paris Bourse.

Shape of the Order Book as a Predictor of Market Direction

Several studies have considered how the limit order book can be used to predict short-term price moves. Cao et al. (2004), for example, find that a liquidity peak close to the market price, for example, tends to push the market price away from the peak. However, a liquidity peak away from the market price tends to "pull" the market price toward the peak. Cohen, Maier, Schwartz, and Whitcomb (1981), call this phenomenon a "gravitational pull" of quotes. Figure 11.6 shows the sample evolution of the market depth and the associated liquidity.

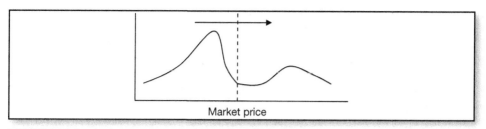

FIGURE 11.6 An Asymmetric Liquidity Peak Near the Market Price Tends to Push the Market Price Away from the Peak

Rosu (2005) determines that the shape of the limit order book depends on the probability distribution for arriving market orders. High probabilities of large market orders lead to hump-shaped limit order books. Foucault, Moinas, and Theissen (2005) find that the depth of the limit order book can forecast future volatility of asset prices: the lower the depth, the lower the expected volatility. Berber and Caglio (2004) find that limit orders carry private information around events such as earnings announcements: a concentration of limit orders far away from the current market price is likely to reflect someone's postannouncement valuation of the traded instrument.

Cont, Kukanov, and Stoikov (2011) suggest that even Level I data can be used to generate successful predictions of the impending price movements. To predict the price movement, Cont et al. (2011) define a new variable, order flow imbalance (OFI):

$$OFL_k = \sum_{n=N(t_k-1)+1}^{N(t_k)} e_n \qquad (5)$$

where e_n represents an instantaneous change in the top-of-the-book liquidity, and is defined as follows:

$$e_n = I_{\{P_n^B \geq P_{n-1}^B\}} q_n^B - I_{\{P_n^B \leq P_{n-1}^B\}} q_{n-1}^B - I_{\{P_n^A \leq P_{n-1}^A\}} q_n^A + I_{\{P_n^A \geq P_{n-1}^A\}} q_{n-1}^A \qquad (6)$$

where I is the indicator function, equal to 1 when the bracketed condition is true, and 0 otherwise, and q^B and q^A are the sizes at the best bid and the best ask, respectively.

Equations (5) and (6) can be interpreted as follows: Order Flow Imbalance depends on the instantaneous change in the top-of-the-book liquidity, which in turn depends on the tick-to-tick change in best bid and best offer prices. If the best bid price increased, the Order Flow Imbalance increases by the size at the *new* best bid. If the best bid price decreases from one tick to the next, the associated OFI is reduced by the best bid size recorded at the *previous* tick. Similarly, if the ask price decreases, the OFI is decremented by the size at the *new* best ask. If the ask price increases from last tick to the present tick, the OFI is increased by the size recorded at the *previous* best ask.

To ascertain predictive power of the OFI, Cont et al. (2011) next map the OFI figures vis-à-vis short-term price changes, and obtain a linear relationship, as shown in Figure 11.7.

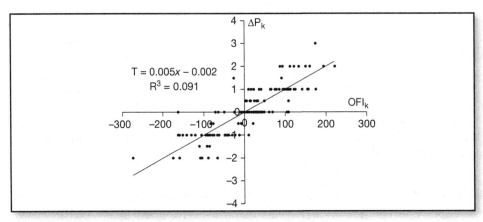

FIGURE 11.7 Order-Flow Imbalance versus Short-Term Price Changes
Source: Cont, Kukanov, and Stoikov (2011)

Evolution of Tick Data as a Predictor of Market Movement

The advanced class of information models specifically addresses the intent and future actions of various market participants. Such models include game-theoretic approaches to reverse-engineer quote and trade flows to discover the information a market maker possesses. Information models also use observed or inferred order flow to make informed trading decisions.

At their core, information models describe trading on information flow and possible informational asymmetries arising during the dissemination of information. Differences in information flow persist in different markets. Information flow is comparably faster in transparent centralized markets, such as most equity markets and electronic markets, and slower in the opaque markets, such as foreign exchange and over-the-counter (OTC) markets in bonds and derivatives.

Asymmetric information present in the markets leads to adverse selection, or the ability of informed traders to "pick off" uninformed market participants. According to Dennis and Weston (2001) and Odders-White and Ready (2006), the following measures of asymmetric information have been proposed over the years:

- Quoted bid-ask spread
- Effective bid-ask spread
- Information-based impact
- Adverse-selection components of the bid-ask spread
- Probability of informed trading

Quoted Bid-Ask Spread The quoted bid-ask spread is the crudest, yet most readily observable measure of asymmetric information. First suggested by Bagehot (1971) and later developed by numerous researchers, the bid-ask spread reflects the expectations of market movements by the market maker using asymmetric information. When the quoting dealer receives order flow that he suspects may come from an informed trader and may leave the dealer at a disadvantage relative to the market movements, the dealer increases the spread he quotes in order to compensate himself against potentially adverse uncertainty in price movements. As a result, the wider the quoted bid-ask spread, the higher is the dealer's estimate of information asymmetry between his clients and the dealer himself. Given that the dealer has the same access to public information as do most of the dealer's clients, the quoted bid-ask spread may serve as a measure of asymmetric information available in the market at large at any given point in time.

Effective Bid-Ask Spread   The effective bid-ask spread is computed as twice the difference between the latest trade price and the midpoint between the quoted bid and ask prices, divided by the midpoint between the quoted bid and ask prices:

$$S_t^e = \left(\frac{4S_t}{S_t^a + S_t^b} - 1 \right) \tag{7}$$

The effective spread measures how far, in percentage terms, the latest realized price fell away from the simple midquote. When markets are balanced and no information streams through, the true midquote is the natural trading price. When the limit order book is skewed or imbalanced in some other way, the traded price moves closer to the side with excess limit orders located at or near the top of the book.

Information-Based Impact   The information-based impact measure of asymmetric information is attributable to Hasbrouck (1991). Brennan and Subrahmanyam (1996) specify the following vector autoregressive (VAR) model for estimation of the information-based impact measure, λ:

$$V_{i,t} = \theta_{i,0} + \sum_{k=1}^{K} \beta_{i,k} \Delta P_{i,t-k} + \sum_{m=1}^{M} \gamma_{i,m} V_{i,t-m} + \tau_{i,t} \tag{8}$$

$$\Delta P_{i,t} = \phi_{i,0} + \phi_{i,1} sign(\Delta P_{i,t}) + \lambda_i \tau_{i,t} + \varepsilon_{i,t} \tag{9}$$

where $\Delta P_{i,t}$ is the change in price of security i from time $t-1$ to time t, $V_{i,t} = sign(\Delta P_{i,t}) \cdot v_{i,t}$, and $v_{i,t}$ is the volume recorded in trading the security i from time $t-1$ to time t. Brennan and Subrahmanyam (1996) propose five lags in estimation of equation (8): $K = M = 5$.

Adverse Selection Components of the Bid-Ask Spread   The adverse selection components of the bid-ask spread is attributable to Glosten and Harris (1988). The model separates the bid-ask spread into the following three components:

- Adverse selection risk
- Order-processing costs
- Inventory risk

Models in a similar spirit were proposed by Roll (1984); Stoll (1989); and George, Kaul, and Nimalendran (1991). The version of the Glosten and Harris (1988) model popularized by Huang and Stoll (1997) aggregates inventory risk and order-processing costs and is specified as follows:

$$\Delta P_{i,t} = (1 - \lambda_i) \frac{S_{i,t}}{2} sign(\Delta P_{i,t}) + \lambda_i \frac{S_{i,t}}{2} sign(\Delta P_{i,t}) \cdot v_{i,t} + \varepsilon_{i,t} \tag{10}$$

where $\Delta P_{i,t}$ is the change in price of security i from time $t-1$ to time t, $V_{i,t}=sign(\Delta P_{i,t})$. $v_{i,t}$, $v_{i,t}$ is the volume recorded in trading the security i from time $t-1$ to time t, $S_{i,t}$ is the effective bid-ask spread as defined previously, and λ_i is the fraction of the traded spread due to adverse selection.

Probability of Informed Trading Easley, Kiefer, O'Hara, and Paperman (1996) propose a model to distill the likelihood of informed trading from sequential quote data. The model reverse-engineers the quote sequence provided by a dealer to obtain a probabilistic idea of the order flow seen by the dealer.

The model is built on the following concept. Suppose an event occurs that is bound to impact price levels but is observable only to a select group of investors. Such an event may be a controlled release of selected information or a research finding by a brilliant analyst. The probability of such an event is α. Furthermore, suppose that if the event occurs, the probability of its having a negative effect on prices is δ and the probability of the event's having a positive effect on prices is $(1-\delta)$. When the event occurs, informed investors know of the impact the event is likely to have on prices; they then place trades according to their knowledge at a rate μ. Thus, all the investors informed of the event will place orders on the same side of the market—either buys or sells. At the same time, investors uninformed of the event will keep placing orders on both sides of the market at a rate ω. The probability of informed trading taking place is then determined as follows:

$$PI = \frac{\alpha\mu}{\alpha\mu + 2\omega} \tag{11}$$

The parameters α, μ and ω are then estimated from the following likelihood function over T periods of time:

$$L(B,S|\alpha,\mu,\omega,\delta) = \prod_{t=1}^{T} \ell(B,S,t|\alpha,\mu,\omega,\delta) \tag{12}$$

where $\ell(B,S,t|\alpha,\mu,\omega,\delta)$ is the likelihood of observing B buys and S sells within a specific period of time:

$$\ell(B,S,t|\alpha,\mu,\omega,\delta) = (1-\alpha)\left[\exp(-\omega T)\frac{(\omega T)^B}{B!}\right]\left[\exp(-\omega T)\frac{(\omega T)^S}{S!}\right]$$

$$+\alpha(1-\delta)\left[\exp(-(\omega+\mu)T)\frac{((\omega+\mu)T)^B}{B!}\right]\left[\exp(-\omega T)\frac{(\omega T)^S}{S!}\right] \tag{13}$$

$$+\alpha\delta\left[\exp(-\omega T)\frac{(\omega T)^B}{B!}\right]\left[\exp(-(\omega+\mu)T)\frac{((\omega+\mu)T)^S}{S!}\right]$$

Summary

Understanding the type and motivation of each market participant can unlock profitable trading strategies. For example, understanding whether a particular market participant possesses information about impending market movement may result in immediate profitability from either engaging the trader if he is uninformed or following his moves if he has superior information.

End of Chapter Questions

1. If the quotes widen following a trade, and then revert to their original levels, what can be said about the informational content of the trade? Explain.
2. What is order flow? How is it measured? How can it be estimated from tick data?
3. Does the order-flow imbalance metric developed by Cont, Kukanov, and Stoikov (2011) increase when the size at the best bid increases? Explain.
4. Suppose you observe a high autocorrelation of order flow in MSFT. Who is most likely trading and why? How can your algorithm utilize the information to generate positive gains?
5. What is adverse selection? When the risk of adverse selection falls, what does this mean for a market-making algorithm?

CHAPTER 12

Additional HFT Strategies, Market Manipulation, and Market Crashes

As Chapters 8 through 11 illustrate, high-frequency trading (HFT) by and large automates human trading. The opponents of HFT, however, perceive a range of adverse HFT outcomes that have the potential to negatively impact market dynamics. This chapter discusses these perceived threats in detail, along with methods that enable detection of high-frequency market manipulation and future market crashes.

Opinions on HFT continue to run the gamut. On one end of the spectrum we find employers in the financial services industry. Just open the "Jobs" page in "Money and Investment" section in the *Wall Street Journal,* and you will mostly find job postings seeking talent for HFT roles. The advertising employers are the whitest shoe investment banks like Morgan Stanley. These careful firms generally invest resources into something they deem worthwhile and legitimate. The extent of their hiring (often the only hiring advertised in the *Wall Street Journal*) implies that the industry is enormously profitable and here to stay.

At the other extreme we find individuals such as Mark Cuban, a successful Dallas-based businessman, who recently proclaimed that he is afraid of high-frequency traders. Mr. Cuban's fears are based on his belief that high-frequency traders are nothing more than "hackers," seeking to game the markets and take unfair advantage of systems and investors.

So how can Mr. Cuban and Morgan Stanley have such divergent views of the high-frequency world? For one, Mr. Cuban has likely fallen prey to some unscrupulous uncompetitive financial services providers making a scapegoat out of high-frequency traders. Opponents of high-frequency traders identify a range of purported HFT strategies that are supposedly evidence of how HFT destroys the markets. Purportedly malicious HFT strategies compiled by one of the workgroups of the Commodity Futures Trading Commission's (CFTC) subcommittee on HFT included such ominous names as *spread scalping, market ignition,* and *sniping,* just to name a few.

As this chapter shows, strategies thought to be malicious and often associated with HFT fall into one of the following categories:

- Legitimate strategies serving price discovery.
- Strategies not feasible in "lit" markets–regulated exchanges; the same strategies can be feasible in dark pools.
- Strategies that are a direct consequence of pump-and-dump activity, a market manipulation technique that is banned in most financial markets.

The CFTC subcommittee on HFT tasked with identifying undesirable HFT strategies identified the following instances:

- Latency arbitrage
- Spread scalping
- Rebate capture
- Quote matching
- Layering
- Ignition
- Pinging/Sniping/Sniffing
- Quote stuffing
- Spoofing
- Pump-and-dump manipulation
- Machine learning

Each of the proposed activities is discussed in detail in the following sections. While some market participants claim that HFTs can also manipulate markets via special front-running order types, such advanced orders typically carry a heavier price tag that annihilates any excess profitability of such orders in the long term, rendering the orders unprofitable to HFT. This chapter also discusses methodologies for detection of pump-and-dump activity.

■ Latency Arbitrage

Latency arbitrage is often pinpointed by the opponents of HFT as the most direct example of the technological arms race, and one without obvious consequences. To succeed in latency arbitrage, unlike other HFT strategies discussed in Chapters 8 through 11, deployment of the fastest technology is pivotal. Contrary to the belief of some, however, latency arbitrage has a well-defined market benefit, described next.

An important concept of financial theory is the Law of One Price. The Law states that in well-functioning markets, a given financial instrument always has the same price, regardless of the characteristics of markets where the financial instrument trades. The Law of One Price then serves to assure low-frequency investors that their trading will always be at the fair market price, no matter in which market they decide to trade. In other words, in ideal theoretical market conditions, the price of the IBM stock in London should always be the same as the price of IBM in New York, after adjusting for foreign exchange.

When prices of the same financial instrument in different markets diverge for whatever reason, high-frequency latency arbitrageurs jump in and trade away the price discrepancies. For example, HF latency traders sell IBM in the market where the stock is temporarily overpriced, while simultaneously buying it where the stock trades too cheaply. In the process, the demand and supply produced by the high-frequency traders serves to equilibrate the market prices in previously divergent markets. The high-frequency trader then quickly reverses his position to capture the gain, and investors of all frequencies can be assured that prices on traded financial instruments are consistent across the globe, upholding the Law of One Price.

Latency arbitrage is an example of a trading strategy that is based on taking advantage of high speeds. A question commonly asked by market participants and regulators alike is how much speed is enough? When does the race end? Should there be a limit on how much speed is acceptable in the markets? From the economic point of view, the race for speed will end as soon as there is equilibrium between increasing technological capacity and trading profitability: when an additional dollar spent on technology no longer generates extra return. Until that time, competition among high-frequency traders will continue to foster innovation in the area of trading.

■ Spread Scalping

High-frequency *spread scalping* often refers to an automated market-making activity that some market participants think is simple: a continuous two-sided provision of liquidity that generates or "scalps" the spread value for the account of the HFT. As discussed in Chapter 10, such activity is subject to extensive inventory and adverse selection risks and can hardly be profitable in its simplest incarnation. Even in a nearly stagnant market, market making is subject to inventory risk, whereby the market maker's accumulated positions rise and fall with variations in the markets. In the absence of opposing market orders, the market maker may not be able to profitably liquidate his positions. Significant analysis of market conditions, presented in Chapters 10 and 11, is necessary to ensure profitability of seemingly naïve spread-capturing strategies.

As discussed in Chapter 11, even in their normal state, markets are fraught with informational asymmetries, whereby some traders know more than the market maker. Better-informed traders may have superior information about industry fundamentals or just superior forecasting skills. In such situations, better-informed traders are bound to leave the market maker on the losing end of trades, erasing all other spread-scalping profits the market maker may have accumulated.

For a specific example, consider a news announcement. Suppose an allegedly spread-scalping HFT has positions on both sides of the market, ahead of the impending announcement on the jobs figures—information on how many jobs were added or lost during the preceding month. A better-informed trader, whether of the low- or high-frequency variety, may have forecasted with reasonable accuracy that the jobs number is likely to have increased. Suppose the better-informed trader next decides to bet on his forecast, sending a large market buy order to the market. The presumed spread-scalping market maker then takes the opposite side of the informed-trader's order, selling large quantities in the market that is just about to rise considerably on the news announcement. In a matter of seconds, and due to activity of lower-frequency traders, our high-frequency market maker may end up with a considerable loss in his portfolio.

In summary, spread scalping may seem like a predatory strategy to some market participants, yet it is hardly profitable in its most naïve incarnation. Spread scalping enhanced with inventory and informational considerations is what most market participants call market making, a legitimate activity that is the integral part of market functionality. Without limit orders sitting on either side of the spread, traders desiring immediacy would not be capable of executing their market orders. Compensation of a spread is a tiny profit comparable to the amount of work required to be able to provide the limit orders on both sides of the market on the daily basis.

■ Rebate Capture

Another strategy often put forth as an example of the dangers of HFT is the *rebate capture*. Under this strategy, high-frequency traders are presumed to generate profit simply by arbitraging the costs and benefits of limit and market orders on various exchanges. The strategy is thought to be an empty exercise with no economic value, and a frequent example of what is wrong with market fragmentation. In reality, as this section illustrates, rebates help improve the profitability of trading strategies, but cannot deliver profitability without other forecasting methodologies, such as the ones presented in Chapters 8 through 11.

To be profitable, a high-frequency trader needs to execute an order and hold a position long enough to realize a gain. As outlined in Chapter 3, rebates for limit and market orders presently exist only in equities, where a myriad of exchanges seek to differentiate them from the rest of the pack. The minimum gain per trade in most U.S. equity markets is currently $0.01. In normal rebate markets, the exchanges pay rebates to traders posting limit orders, and providing liquidity by doing so. The New York Stock Exchange (NYSE), for example, pays $0.13 to $0.30 for every 100 shares to traders posting limit orders. Consider a trader who estimates ahead of each trade the directional probability of a stock going up 1 tick or $0.01 is p_{up}. In the current NYSE environment, a rational high-frequency trader will post a limit buy order only when the marginal cumulative rebate value exceeds the trader's expected return:

$$\$0.01\, p_{up} - \$0.01(1 - p_{up}) - \$(transaction\ costs) \geq - \$rebate \qquad (1)$$

where $rebate is the value of the rebate per share, and $(transaction costs) represents the costs the trader needs to pay per share to execute his trades. Transaction costs in equities may include a clearing fee, a transaction fee, a FINRA pass-through fee, and a NYSE pass-through fee, in addition to broker-dealer commissions.

Equation (1) is equivalent to

$$P_{up} \geq \frac{\$ transaction\ costs-\$ rebate}{\$0.02} + 50\% \qquad (2)$$

As the inequality (2) shows, in the absence of rebates, a limit order–posting trader has to predict direction of the price correctly with probability greater than 50 percent. A broker-dealer advertises that transaction costs for selling 30 million shares without considering NYSE rebates run about $50,000, or $0.0016 per share. When executed as a market order, the 30 million shares incur the additional NYSE fee, a negative rebate, for removing liquidity of about $70,000 or another $0.0023 per share. To be profitable under such cost structure, a rational high-frequency trader needs to have forecasting that reliably predicts probability of market movement, P_{up}, to be at least 70 percent:

$$P_{up} \geq \frac{\$0.0016-(-\$0.0023)}{\$0.02} + 50\% = 70\% \qquad (3)$$

When posting the same 30 million shares as limit orders, the trader receives $60,000 in rebates or $0.0020 per share, offsetting the nonrebate transaction costs and generating about $10,000 or $0.0003 in profit per trade. This rebate-driven profitability allows the high-frequency trader to lower his required probability of correct directional forecasting, but just to 48 percent:

$$P_{up} \geq \frac{\$0.0016-(-\$0.0020)}{\$0.02} + 50\% = 48\% \qquad (4)$$

In other words, while rebates decrease the required accuracy of high-frequency forecasts, and the respective probability of forecast correctness, the rebates do not allow random trading strategies to be profitable. As with the spread-scalping strategy, a successful rebate capture is a complex market-making operation, with rebates serving as a minor improvement of performance, and not as a primary source of profitability.

Quote Matching

In a so-called quote-matching strategy, a high-frequency trader is thought to mimic the limit orders of another trader. A high-frequency trader is then thought to ride the market impact the original orders generate. If feasible, such a strategy could negatively impact block trades of a large investor by amplifying the market impact and worsening the pricing the investor obtains on subsequent child trades. The strategy assumes that the high-frequency trader is capable of identifying which limit orders always move the markets in the certain direction in the short term, allowing the high-frequency trader to quickly take advantage of the move, reversing positions and capturing the profit. Specifically, the success of the strategy is predicated on the high-frequency trader's ability to foresee which limit orders generate positive or negative market impact.

The key assumption of the strategy is the primary reason for its infeasibility. Most of today's exchanges are anonymous: They protect the identity of traders, disallowing the HFTs the ability to tag and follow orders of a specific entity. Furthermore, as discussed in Chapter 5, while many buy orders are followed by a positive price movement in the short term, the movement is by no means guaranteed. In the case of limit orders, while the market impact following a limit buy order is positive on average, it is very small even for top-of-the-book orders, and can be mostly negative or not statistically persistent for orders behind the market price. As a result, a quote matching strategy solely relying on copying other trader's limit orders is likely to be a disappointment.

■ Layering

In *layering,* a high-frequency trader enters limit orders at different price levels away from the market price, often to cancel the orders in the near future, and then to resubmit the orders again. The objectives of layering often confound casual observers, who in turn suspect wrongdoing.

Some layering may indeed be manipulative. The manipulative layering is one-sided: a market participant "layers" either buy or sell side of the order book with limit orders and then promptly cancels the orders with the intent of changing other traders' inferences about available supply and demand, The Securities and Exchange Commission (SEC) penalized such layering in highly publicized cases in September 2012.

Much of layering, however, is a legitimate strategy, practiced by many executing brokers as well as market makers in limit order books with price-time priority, described in Chapter 3. In most layering, a broker or a market maker leaves "placeholder" limit orders at different price points with the intent of securing a time priority in a given price queue of a limit order book. When the market price reaches a broker's order, the broker may pursue one of two paths:

- The broker may use his priority to execute a slice of an order, securing a preferential price for his customer.
- In the absence of customer orders, the broker may simply cancel the placeholder order.

Similarly, a market maker may decide to execute on the order or cancel it, depending on his estimates of inventory and information risks.

As such, most incarnations of the layering strategy are not manipulative but do create unwanted noise in the markets by clogging the networks and the matching engine with order cancellations. A successful solution implemented by the Chicago Mercantile Exchange (CME), for example, changes the execution of the matching engine from the price-time priority to a pro-rata schedule. As described in Chapter 3, under the pro-rata schedule, all limit orders posted at a given price level are executed at the same when the price level becomes the best bid or the best ask. Each limit order in the given price queue is matched partially, proportional to the size of each limit order. Such strategy eliminates the need to secure the time priority in the given queue, and, as a result, entirely removes the need for layering as means of securing priority of execution.

Ignition

In an *ignition* strategy, a high-frequency trader is thought to detect the location of long-term investors' stop-loss orders and match against them, or "ignite" them. Next, the strategy assumes that large stop-loss positions will have a substantial impact on the market, allowing the high-frequency trader to ride the market impact wave, swiftly closing out his positions, all the while capturing small gains at the expense of long-term investors' losses.

In today's exchanges and other "lit" trading venues, such a strategy may work only as a result of market manipulation, such as pump-and-dump. To match against someone's orders placed well away from the market price, one needs to move the market price substantially in the direction of said stop loss orders. Market manipulation has always been illegal and can be screened using methodology described later in the chapter.

While a manipulation-free ignition strategy is not feasible in lit trading venues, such as all regulated exchanges, it can be deployed in dark pools. The dark pools, however, have been created for sophisticated institutional investors, explicitly without regulatory protection, and operate under the "buyer beware" principle.

Pinging/Sniping/Sniffing/Phishing

Pinging, sniping, sniffing, and *phishing* monikers typically refer to the same general type of strategy. The pinging strategy, much like the ignition strategy, identifies hidden pools of limit orders and matches against those orders, creating and riding temporary market impact for small gains. Much like the ignition strategy, such a strategy is often observed in dark pools. Some dark pools, for example, Citibank's Automated Trading Desk, have designed ways to screen for pingers and charge them for pinging behavior. Such charges render pinging unprofitable and discourage pingers with market mechanisms.

While pinging is feasible in dark pools, it is not generally possible in lit markets, such as exchanges, unless it is accompanied by illegal market manipulation. Just as in the case of ignition strategies, in lit markets traders cannot selectively execute at random price levels away from the present market price, unless they expressly move the price away from the market first. Such price movements construe market manipulation.

As discussed later in this chapter, some market conditions are more conducive to market manipulation than others. Avoiding conditions favorable to market manipulation may help traders to eliminate risks associated with ignition and other variants of pinging strategies.

Quote Stuffing

Quote stuffing refers to a purported high-frequency strategy whereby a trader intentionally clogs the networks and the matching engine with a large number of limit orders and order cancellations. Unlike layering, where the high-frequency trader is seeking to ensure execution priority in the order book queues, quote-stuffing traders are thought to send in rapid orders and cancellations with the expressed purpose of slowing down other traders, and thus manipulating markets. Quote-stuffing traders are further thought to do so to delay other traders, ensure quote stuffers' priority access to the matching engine and the quote stream, and then effectively front-run other traders.

The idea of the quote-stuffing strategy contains one critical flaw: as any network engineer will confirm, an individual network account cannot selectively slow down network communication for some participants, while still receiving high-speed access to the trading venue. When a matching engine gets clogged with orders and cancellations, it is equally clogged for all market participants, irrespective of who caused the problem. Obviously, such network-clogging exercises do little for traders equipped with fast technology; if anything, network clogging only voids the benefits of fast technology. However, the network-clogging maneuver may be advantageous for low-frequency traders, those who indeed desire to slow down matching capabilities. If anyone can be suspected of intentionally clogging up the lines (a market manipulation), the natural trail leads to low-frequency culprits unequipped with fast technology, for whom such manipulation may indeed result in increased profitability.

■ Spoofing

The *spoofing* strategy is similar to layering but executed with a radically different intent. In spoofing, the trader intentionally distorts the order book without execution; in the process, the trader changing other traders' inferences about available supply and demand, and resulting prices. In principle, spoofing can be screened for and detected in most lit markets: while layering calls for fairly balanced entry of limit orders across all price ranges, spoofing would show one-sided peaks of limit orders in selected trading accounts. Spoofing has been made expressly illegal in the United States under the Dodd-Frank Act, and has been actively prosecuted. In 2011, for example, the U.S. CFTC fined Bunge Global Markets $550,000 for spoofing at the market's open.

In summary, most strategies considered to be illicit HFT activity and reasoned to be the cause for which HFTs should be banned do not exist or are a direct consequence of already illegal activity, such as market manipulation. Identification of market manipulation activity and the market conditions conducive to market manipulation are discussed in the following section.

■ Pump-and-Dump

Pump-and-dump is a truly adverse activity, whether implemented at high or low frequencies. The low-frequency pump-and-dump was well portrayed in the film *Boiler Room,* where unscrupulous brokers "pumped" or raised the value of a particular financial instrument just to dump it at the first opportunity, realizing a profit at the expense of other investors. The flip side of the pump-and-dump is the *bear raid,* whereby the trader artificially depresses the price of a financial instrument, only to close his position at a profit at the first available opportunity, all while leaving other investors in the dust.

In the high-frequency pump-and-dump, computer-assisted traders are thought to momentarily drive up or down the prices of securities, only to promptly

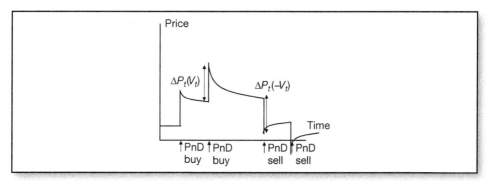

FIGURE 12.1 Market Impact that Rules Out High-Frequency Pump-and-Dump Manipulation

reverse their positions and capitalize on false momentum at the expense of other traders. Huberman and Stanzl (2004) and Gatheral (2010) have developed necessary conditions for the absence of high-frequency pump-and-dump opportunities: the posttrade permanent market impact function should be symmetric in size for buyer-initiated and seller-initiated trades. When the posttrade permanent market impact for buyer-initiated trades exceed that for seller-initiated trades, for example, a high-frequency trader could "pump" the security price through repeated purchases to a new high level and then "dump" the security, closing out his positions at a profit. The gain would originate solely from the asymmetric market impact: the absolute value of market impact following buy trades would differ from that following sell trades. On the other hand, when pump-and-dump is *not* feasible, the price change following a sell-initiated trade of size V is equal to the negative of the price change following a buy-initiated trade of size V, as shown in Figure 12.1. A pump-and-dump arbitrage opportunity exists when the "no-pump-no-dump" condition is violated.

Aldridge (2012e) formally describes pump-and-dump strategies using a measure of permanent market impact $f(V_t)$ of a trade of size V_t processed at time t, where $V_t > 0$ indicates a buyer-initiated trade and $V_t < 0$ describes a seller-initiated trade. If $f(V) > -f(-V)$, a trader could artificially pump and then dump by first buying and then selling at the same trade size V. Conversely, if $f(V) < -f(-V)$, the trader could manipulate the markets by first selling and then buying the securities back.

To examine the evolution of market impact over time, we consider market impact within different event windows, where the length of the window is determined by a number of trade ticks before and after the market order event, as shown in Figure 12.2.

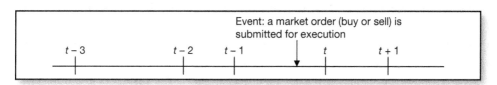

FIGURE 12.2 Sequence of Events Used in Market Impact Computation

Denoting market impact function f, we obtain the following specification:

$$f_{t+1} = \ln[P_{t+1}] - \ln[P_{t-1}]$$

$$\vdots$$

$$f_{t+\tau} = \ln[P_{t+\tau}] - \ln[P_{t-1}]$$

To evaluate the feasibility of the pump and dump, we use a linear specification for the market impact as a function of trading volume, V, consistent with Breen, Hodrick, and Korajczyk (2002); Kissell and Glantz (2002); and Lillo, Farmer, and Mantegna (2003), following Huberman and Stanzl (2004) and Gatheral (2010):

$$f_{t+\tau}(V_t) = \alpha_\tau + \beta_\tau V_t + \varepsilon_{t+\tau} \tag{5}$$

where V_t is the size of trade executed at time t, β_τ is the trade size–dependent market impact, and α_τ is the trade size–independent impact of each trade recorded at time t. If the high-frequency pump-and-dump is feasible, β_τ for buyer-initiated trades will be different from $-\beta_\tau$ estimated for seller-initiated trades. The null hypothesis, that pump-and-dump exists in trading activity of a financial instrument, can then be specified as follows:

$$H_0 : \beta_\tau \big|_{buyer-initiated\ trades} \neq -\beta_\tau \big|_{seller-initiated\ trades} \tag{6}$$

And the alternative hypothesis ruling out pump and dump can be specified as:

$$H - A. :\ ,,\beta - \tau .\big| - buyer - initiated\ trades = -,, \beta - \tau.\big| - seller - initiated\ trades \tag{7}$$

The framework above allows for straightforward screening for market manipulative activity in various financial instruments.

What does pump-and-dump detect? The example in Figure 12.3 illustrates the analysis on a sequence of Eurex Eurobund futures (symbol FGBL) trades, recorded sequentially and time-stamped with millisecond granularity. In addition to the time-stamp, the data includes the trade price and trade size. The data is the "official" copy of the Eurex trading tape, and is commercially distributed to traders. The data does not contain best bid/offer information or identification of whether the trades were initiated by the buyer or seller. To identify whether the trade was initiated by a market buy or a market sell, a tick rule discussed in Chapter 3 is used.

In computing market impact (MI), overnight returns are treated as missing observations, ensuring that the MI on a specific day is a function of data recorded on that day only.

Table 12.1 reports estimates of equation (5) for trades of all sizes by month of 2009–2010 period. Figure 12.3 graphically illustrates the relationship of volume coefficients for buy and sell trades. Figure 12.4 shows the results of the difference tests of volume coefficients observed for buy and sell trades.

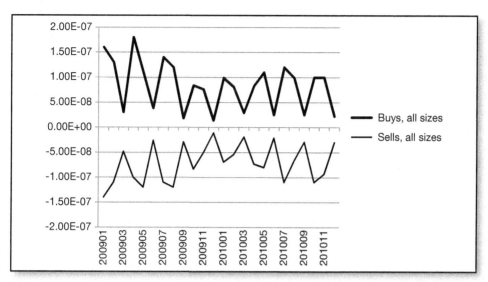

FIGURE 12.3 Volume Coefficients of Market Impact of Buy-and-Sell Trades, FGBL Futures, 2009–2010

| TABLE 12.1 | Estimation of Size-Dependent Market Impact for Large and Small Trades in Eurobund Futures, by Month |

	Buys, All Trade Sizes					Sells, All Trade Sizes				
	# obs	α_s	t-stat	β_s	t-stat	# obs	α_s	t-stat	β_s	t-stat
200901	373631	1.6E-5	50.7	1.6E-7	24.1	367857	−2E-5	−50.5	−1.4E-7	−18.6
200902	332584	1.4E-5	37.4	1.3E-7	20.0	334078	−1.7E-5	−46.0	−1.1E-7	−17.6
200903	400829	1.5E-5	54.8	3E-8	11.8	402137	−1.6E-5	−55.5	−4.8E-8	−17.4
200904	319454	1.0E-5	39.5	1.8E-7	37.3	318556	−1.4E-5	−46.2	−1E-7	−21.8
200905	298859	1.2E-5	37.1	1.1E-7	23.3	300020	−1.4E-5	−41.4	−1.2E-7	−23.4
200906	348640	1.2E-5	32.4	3.8E-8	11.9	341341	−1.5E-5	−38.5	−2.6E-8	−7.7
200907	310745	7.5E-6	20.8	1.4E-7	22.8	303278	−1.2E-5	−29.3	−1.1E-7	−17.1
200908	284896	8.6E-6	23.1	1.2E-7	20.1	285690	−1.3E-5	−30.3	−1.2E-7	−17.0
200909	331673	9.5E-6	43.5	1.8E-8	12.4	325211	−1.1E-5	−42.5	−2.9E-8	−15.0
200910	337226	7.2E-6	35.6	8.4E-8	32.4	330927	−8.1E-6	−38.2	−8.3E-8	−28.9
200911	283547	7.5E-6	35.1	7.6E-8	29.6	281327	−9.6E-6	−39.2	−5E-8	−18.6
200912	249533	8.6E-6	23.2	1.4E-8	6.4	248061	−1.3E-5	−36.1	−1.1E-8	−5.1
201001	247741	5.7E-6	14.9	9.9E-8	21.0	247258	−1.1E-5	−22.7	−6.9E-8	−12.1
201002	298294	6.5E-6	16.9	8.1E-8	19.8	295019	−1.1E-5	−29.5	−5.4E-8	−14.1
201003	295452	6.6E-6	26.4	2.9E-8	16.4	297502	−9.5E-6	−34.8	−1.9E-8	−11.9
201004	297115	6.4E-6	23.1	8.3E-8	26.2	298106	−8.3E-6	−31.7	−7.3E-8	−24.6
201005	413507	1.1E-5	33.5	1.1E-7	22.9	409226	−1.3E-5	−45.1	−8E-8	−20.3
201006	393351	1.1E-5	41.1	2.5E-8	11.8	387231	−1.4E-5	−45.8	−2.1E-8	−9.0
201007	314054	6.3E-6	18.5	1.2E-7	23.9	307322	−1.1E-5	−29.4	−1.1E-7	−20.4
201008	299741	7.1E-6	17.4	9.9E-8	18.6	296117	−1.2E-5	−26.9	−6.6E-8	−12.4
201009	422772	1.3E-5	61.0	2.5E-8	15.5	419480	−1.4E-5	−55.0	−2.9E-8	−17.0
201010	345432	8.7E-6	41.6	1.0E-7	35.5	328033	−9.6E-6	−42.2	−1.1E-7	−35.2
201011	447795	1.1E-5	55.6	1.0E-7	33.8	426999	−1.3E-5	−52.9	−9.3E-8	−27.8
201012	305279	1.4E-5	45.2	2.2E-8	8.8	302936	−1.8E-5	−49.3	−3E-8	−9.3

Note: Coefficients for the entire sample, large trades and small trades, were estimated using the following linear regressions: $MI_{t+\tau}(V)=\alpha_\tau +\beta_\tau V_t+\varepsilon_{t+\tau}$, where the observations were separated into buys and sells.

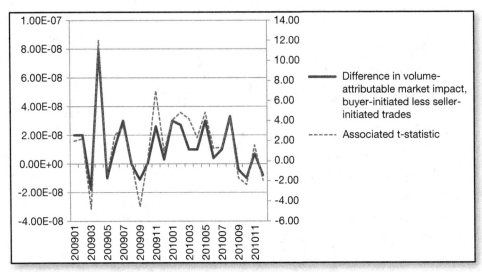

FIGURE 12.4   Difference in Volume-Attributable Market Impact, of Buyer-Initiated Trades Less That of Seller Initiated Trades

The observed differences in buyer-initiated and seller-initiated market impact change from month to month and lack statistical significance. Based on the results, the FGBL futures data does not support the possibility of high-frequency pump-and-dump.

The results presented in Table 12.1 indicate another interesting phenomenon: trade-size-related MI does not begin to register until the trade size rises to about 100 contracts. The unexplained variation, intercept α, in the market impact equation is large (on the order of 10^{-5}), and the trade-related MI is on the order of 10^{-7}, a single trade of up to 100 contracts may incur as much impact as a trade of 1 contract. This is great news for institutions and other large fund managers who are concerned about the impact of their trades—in the FGBL futures market, a single trade of a size considerably larger than the median trading size on average leaves no trace. Unlike the equities markets, the Eurex FGBL market is resilient to a much larger capacity.

To check whether the results are robust, several auxiliary explanatory variables can be added to the analysis: volatility, spread, and intertrade duration. Other studies found such additional explanatory variables for temporary market impact.

For example, in futures, Burghardt, Hanweck, and Lei (2006) show that posttrade MI is also dependent on liquidity characteristics, such as the market depth. Other studies have focused on equities. Breen, Hodrick, and Korajchyk (2002); Lillo, Farmer, and Mantegna (2003); and Almgren, Thum, Hauptmann, and Li (2005) showed that the permanent MI function in equities is dependent on stock-specific liquidity characteristics. Dufour and Engle (2000) find that longer intertrade duration leads to lower MI, and vice versa. Ferraris (2008) reports that several commercial models for equity MI use volatility and bid-ask spread prevailing at the time of the trade as predictive inputs to forecasts of MI of the trade. In the current study, we find that volatility, spread, and intertrade duration help explain market impact in futures as well. None of the auxiliary variables, however, change the symmetry between the volume-dependent MI coefficient created by buyer-initiated and seller-initiated trades. The auxiliary variables also do not alter the value or the statistical significance of the trade size–independent component, the intercept, leaving the dominant size-independent market impact unexplained.

■ Machine Learning

Machine learning is often cited as one of the most worrisome event accompanying HFT. A CNBC commentator, Doug Kass, for example, in the conversation about HFT proposed that investors should shut down machines before machines attack investors. The belief that machines are capable of independent reasoning and intelligence similar to Arnold Schwarzenegger's *Terminator* film character resonates among some traditional market participants with little exposure to the fundamentals of technology. Machine learning is then cited as evidence of such machine intelligence.

In reality, machine learning originates in control theory and is often a series of nested analyses. Each analysis can be parametric, as basic as a simple linear regression, or nonparametric, a set free-form functional estimators. Independent of the type of the analysis used, the nature of machine learning remains the same: uncover patterns in data. As a result, machine learning is less threatening intelligence, and more basic data mining.

Machine learning can be broken down into two major categories: supervised learning and unsupervised learning. Supervised learning is the iterative estimation of data relationships, whereby each subsequent iteration seeks to minimize the deviations from the previous analysis. Models used to fit data in supervised learning models may range from regression to neural networks to boosting algorithms discussed below. Unsupervised learning seeks to identify patterns in so-called unstructured data, devoid of any relationships. Techniques used to distill information under an unsupervised learning umbrella include identification of important signals by observing clustering of data points.

A supervised boosting algorithm, for example, works as follows: a dependent variable Y, for instance, a time series of returns on a particular financial instrument, is fitted with a function G, expressing dependence of Y on returns of another financial instrument, X, and parameters θ:

$$Y_t = G(X_t, \theta) + \varepsilon_t \tag{8}$$

Next, the boosting error term is computed as follows:

$$E = \sum W_t I_{st<>0} \tag{9}$$

where $I_{st<>0}$ is the indicator function taking on value of 0 when $G(X_t, \theta)$ matches Y_t precisely, and 1 when ε_t is not equal to 0. The time series w_t represents boosting weights assigned to each observation time, with all weights in the first iteration set to 1, and weights in later iterations recomputed according to the following calculation:

$$w_t' = w_t \exp(\alpha_t I_{st<>0}) \tag{10}$$

where
$$\alpha = \log\left(\frac{1-s_t}{s_t}\right)$$
(11)

This machine learning methodology ultimately produces a function $G(X_t, \theta)$ that closely fits Y_t. Human researchers running the machine learning simulation select the parameters such window sizes for training and testing, additional predictors, etc.

Machine learning algorithms may suffer from a critical flaw: data mining devoid of economic underpinnings may produce relationships that may have been stable in the past, but are not stable in the long term. Such accidental relationships are known as *spurious* inferences, and are not reliable predictors for future behavior of dependent variables. At the time this book was written, no machine learning algorithm was capable of intelligence beyond its immediate trading application and was certainly not threatening to humans.

Summary

This chapter discusses algorithms often presented as evidence of adverse outcomes from HFT. As the chapter illustrates most of the fears surrounding HFT strategies are unwarranted. Some strategies, however, are a direct consequence of high-frequency market manipulation, yet even those strategies can be screened for, greatly reducing the risks to all market participants.

End-of-Chapter Questions

1. What is latency arbitrage?
2. Suppose a stock of IBM is simultaneously trading at 125.03 on the NYSE and at 125.07 in Tokyo. Does latency arbitrage deliver positive or negative impact on the price of IBM from the market efficiency point of view?
3. What is spread scalping? What is rebate capture?
4. What kind of layering is manipulative? What kind of layering is benign?
5. How can one detect pump-and-dump high-frequency manipulation?
6. What is machine learning?

CHAPTER 13

Regulation

A t the time this book was written, high-frequency trading (HFT) was already a heavily regulated market activity, tracked at the broker-dealer level. Current regulation of HFT follows much the same rules as other forms of trading in a given financial instrument. Indeed, as this book shows, HFT is little more than automation of traditional trading processes and should be regulated as such. Proponents of HFT regulation, however, call for stricter monitoring of machines, citing examples of market failures such as the flash crash of May 6, 2010; the botched initial public offering (IPO) of electronic ATS BATS (Best Alternative Trading System) on March 23, 2012; and the spectacular $10-million-per-minute loss of Knight Capital Group on August 1, 2012. This chapter discusses modern legislation relevant to HFT, traditional and current approaches, and likely imminent directions.

■ Key Initiatives of Regulators Worldwide

Currently, main issues on the regulatory table include:

- Jurisdiction
- Stability of systems
- Investor protection
- Efficient trade matching
- Market structure

This section considers each of the issues in detail.

Jurisdiction

The long shadow cast by market regulators covers HFT as part of their mandate to provide legal oversight to markets at large. Roles and objectives of market regulators have evolved on a regional basis due to philosophies and histories of individual jurisdictions.

Most of U.S. regulation represents a rule-based approach, in which regulators prescribe specific remedies as well as punishments for certain behaviors observed in the markets. By contrast, regulators of the European Union have established a principle-based regulatory system, whereby each regulatory case is evaluated in its conformance with the general principles of desired market systems. The differences between the U.S. and EU regulatory models can be traced to the philosophical differences that exist between regulatory systems in the two regions. In the United States, the objective of regulation has been to level the playing field, allowing equal access to the markets for large investors and for "widows and orphans" alike. Behaviors blocking fair access are considered to go against the grain of the U.S. markets. Such behaviors are actively identified, documented, and dealt with. In the European Union, however, the main tenet of regulation can be distilled to fairness of gains—an action that is deemed unfair to a contingent of traders may run afoul of European regulators.

Other countries have developed their own regulatory styles. The key objective of Australian regulators, for example, tends to be market integrity. The U.K. government has taken more of a forward-looking approach to regulation, working to anticipate future developments and then assessing the resulting impact. Canadian regulators seek to conform to the international standards of financial regulation, and, specifically those promulgated by the International Organization of Securities Commissions (IOSCO).

Jurisdictional issues arise within each country, as well. In the United States, for example, regulatory rules for various markets are developed and adopted by several agencies. The Securities and Exchange Commission (SEC) oversees trading in equities and related products, like equity options, exchange-traded funds, and so on. The Commodity Futures Trading Commission (CFTC) deals with futures contracts and related markets, such as options on futures. Swaps and futures on fixed income and foreign exchange also fall under the jurisdiction of the CFTC, even though foreign exchange itself is not regulated outside of basic common investor frameworks. In addition to the SEC and CFTC, the U.S. regulatory system includes industry self-regulatory organizations (SROs). Financial Industry Regulatory Authority (FINRA) navigates the world of equities. In this role, FINRA administers industry licensing examinations and maintains first-level supervision of market abuses. Potential cases of market manipulation detected by FINRA are next sent over to the SEC for further examination. The Futures Industry Association (FIA) is the futures equivalent to FINRA and promotes best practices among futures traders.

Regulatory approaches can vary dramatically from one asset regulator to the next. The U.S. equities, for example, have been subject to three groundbreaking regulations in the past 15 years. The 1997 Order Display Rule required exchanges to display limit orders of all customers, no matter how small. The rule for the first time allowed all sorts of trading entities, including individuals, to make markets. Previously, such privileges were bestowed only on members of the exchange and selected broker-dealers paying dearly for such ability. Regulation Automated Trading Systems (Reg ATS), that went into force in 1998, further mandated electronization of exchanges and has led to the ability to receive, process and store quotes electronically, bringing in great transparency of prices at tick levels. Regulation National Market Systems (Reg NMS), enacted in 2005, further enhanced an investor's ability to track a broker-dealer's execution. In the 1980s, a client executing a market order had only the daily open, high, low, and close quotes, printed in the next day's newspaper, as a reference for the price given by the broker. Under Reg NMS, all investors can be assured of validity of their execution prices within a minute from trade prints recorded in the centralized ticker-data tape, Securities Information Processor (SIP). The one-minute window for submitting quotes into SIP under Reg NMS may seem too large by now. After all, most broker-dealers in the United States can guarantee the execution of a market order in as little as one-hundredth of a second (10 milliseconds) or faster, while selected U.S. exchanges can receive a market order, match it, and send back the acknowledgment in as little as a quarter of a one-thousandth of a second (250 microseconds). Still, even with a 1-minute window Reg NMS delivers investors and end traders much needed execution benchmark prices.

Reg NMS has introduced another structure peculiar to equities: the National Best Bid and Offer rule (NBBO). Under NBBO, all equity exchanges may only execute at the price distributed in SIP or better. If a given exchange does not have enough limit orders on hand to execute an incoming market order at the NBBO, the exchange must route the market order to another exchange.

The order-forwarding rule of the Reg NMS created a new line of differentiation for exchanges: flash orders. When a U.S. exchange does not possess limit orders satisfying the NBBO, the exchange may choose to broadcast or "flash" the incoming and instantly departing market orders to the subscribers of the exchange data. At present, most exchanges have voluntarily banned flash orders, yet some exchanges, such as DirectEdge, persist in flash order executions. The flashing is really a negotiation tactic for traders choosing to place their orders on the DirectEdge exchange: when DirectEdge does not have NBBO, the traders flash their intent to execute, and invite matching limit orders with potential price improvements over contemporary NBBO to the table. Most orders from DirectEdge are typically forwarded to Boston OMX, where flash order observers at DirectEdge can immediately direct their orders, should they be inclined to take on the orders flashing on DirectEdge. While the flash order system as a whole is not set up for investors with slow communication, the system is fair as it is based on voluntary participation: only the traders desiring to flash or be flashed trade at DirectEdge, rendering DirectEdge a special negotiation venue and separating the exchange from the pack. A study by Brodsky (2011), for example, confirms that flash orders result in price improvements, yet disincentivize liquidity provision on flashing exchanges, reducing the traded volume.

The U.S. SEC has also taken steps to ban *naked access,* also known as *sponsored access* and *direct market access* (DMA). Under DMA, broker-dealers would lend traders their identification information and allow traders to use the information to access exchanges directly, without any risk checks. DMA makes complete sense to sophisticated traders, who can develop their own execution systems (discussed in Chapter 15 of this book) and avoid paying fees to broker-dealers. At present, however, most exchanges use broker-dealer identification to stamp the trades. When many traders use the same broker-dealer's ID without a broker-dealer's checks and records under

DMA, the exchanges or the ID-lending broker-dealers are unable to discern which trader caused which type of market reaction, complicating existing surveillance. The legal entity identifier (LEI), discussed in the following section, is likely to resolve this issue by granting the exchanges the ability to track and measure risks of end traders numbered with individual LEIs. Once implemented, the LEI initiative may lead to reinstatement of DMA privileges, this time with even smaller involvement by broker-dealers.

The U.S. CFTC has also taken on co-location and proximity services. As discussed in Chapter 2, co-location implies that the location of a trader's machine in the same facility as the exchange's servers. Proximity hosting, however, leaves traders' machines in a building in the proximity of the exchange, but not in the same exact facility. To ensure transparent pricing and fair access, in June 2010 the CFTC recommended that all co-location and proximity hosting facilities implement uniform fees to all their customers, and to disclose their longest, shortest, and average latencies to all current and prospective clients.[1]

Following the flash crash, the SEC and CFTC introduced clear rules under which erroneous trades can be corrected or "busted." The new rules were successfully applied in the Knight Capital fiasco of August 2012.

European regulators have generally followed the U.S. model; they have voted against naked access, flash orders, and quote stuffing, discussed in Chapter 12. They have also called for risk and error controls for algorithmic systems, minimum quote life, and equal access to co-location services. Overall, however, the Europeans have treaded lightly on the HFT. In light of European financial woes, HFT has been viewed by some as the source of free money for all. A transaction taxation proposal, introduced by Greek parliamentarians and recently ratified by the broader EU Parliament, calls for a small tax on all trading activity. The proposal finds substantial riches in the European financial markets and considers that the trading activity will shrink little in response to the tax.

Given today's mobility of international capital, however, such a tax is likely to backfire. Most of today's trading systems communicate using Financial Information eXchange (FIX), a computer mark-up language discussed in detail in Chapter 6. Changing from trading in one country to trading in another takes as little as changing a few lines in FIX code; after such a minute change, the trader can execute in a jurisdiction free of transaction taxes. Even if all the countries around the world agree

---

[1] At the time this book was finalized, the U.S. Senate Committee on Banking was weighing in on disallowing co-location altogether, with the idea that co-location offers unfair data advantage to technologically savvy market participants. The Senate hearings tend to focus only on the negative aspects of co-location and ignore most positives. As detailed in Chapter 2, however, co-location provides an enormous benefit to all market participants: security of trading communications. In co-located operations, the trader's machine has a dedicated private line to the exchange's computer. Most of the trading traffic in today's markets is sent in plain text; sending it over co-located networks ensures secrecy of communications. Without co-location, one can imagine an outright attack on financial markets: a computer bandit may intercept trading communication, redirecting funds to his personal accounts and outright annihilating trading venues, broker-dealers, and traders in the process. A ban on co-location, therefore, would create a tremendous gap in market security and stability of financial systems worldwide.

to impose an identical transaction tax, the measure would likely fail as the temptation and the instantaneous benefits from breaking the agreement would be just too high—the first jurisdiction to defect the agreement would collect all the global trading activity that can move quickly, generating great trading and settlement premia.

The U.K. regulators have taken a most proactive approach, that of creating rules for envisioned future of computer trading. The U.K. government has identified the following four dimensions of instability potentially caused by computer trading:

1. Nonlinear sensitivities to change, whereby small perturbations in code of trading systems or matching engines have large system-wide impact.
2. Incomplete information, where some market participants are able to assemble a more accurate picture of the markets than others.
3. Normalization of variance, where unexpected and risky events can be seen increasingly as normal.
4. Internal risks amplified by system-wide feedback loops that include risk-management systems, changes in market volatility, market news, and a delay in obtaining reference data, as illustrated in Figure 13.1.

Stability of Systems: Detecting Error-Prone Algorithms

The stability of systems refers to the ideal operational scenario of markets: trading free of inadvertent algorithmic errors. Nothing in recent memory illustrates the host of issues surrounding erroneous algorithms better than the recent "incident"

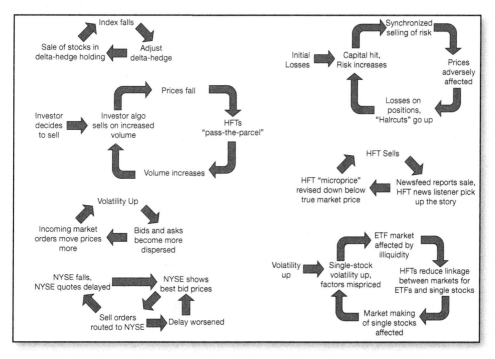

FIGURE 13.1 Key Findings of the U.K. Foresight Initiative on Computerized Trading: Problem-Amplifying Feedback Loops
Source: Zigrand, Cliff, Hendershott (2011)

of Knight Capital Group, when a poorly tested and ill-operated algorithm wreaked havoc in the markets. A whopping 45 minutes after the start of trading, employees at the New York Stock Exchange noticed that Knight Capital's system was losing on average US$10 million every minute. (Employees at Knight Capital still appeared to be oblivious to the fact at that moment.)

In the case of Knight Capital, it was the portfolio of Knight Capital itself that bore the brunt of the incident. However, it is easy to imagine how a similar scenario could have affected other market participants. To limit or eliminate the occurrences of such rampant algo issues, regulators are naturally mulling ways to police markets with the goal of ensuring stability, much like the highway patrol polices roads for errant drivers who may present dangers to themselves and others.

The surveillance for erroneous algos is best performed in real time. As the example of Knight Capital shows, even a 45-minute delay before pinpointing Knight's problem cost Knight's shareholders US$440 million. Modern regulators, however, are ill equipped for such a task. In the United States, both FINRA and CFTC currently collect volumes of tick data from every executed transaction the following business day, or "on the T+1 basis."[2] While the T+1 data is perfectly suitable for identification of market manipulation or other activity requiring multiday recurrence, as discussed in the next subsection, next-day data cannot detect algorithmic problems in real time.

Instead of implementing complex data screening systems for real-time surveillance at their offices, however, regulators may be much more productive in the field. At the level of clearing firms, for example, regulators can observe all the counterparties and their trades. Yet, most clearing happens at the end of the trading day, and such surveillance would be tardy for many fast-moving markets. Surveillance at the executing firm level, that is, broker-dealers, is also feasible, yet can be complicated, as many traders utilize services of multiple brokers, and aggregating trades across brokers in real time can be a challenge. Surveillance at the matching level may prove to be the best solution, with exchanges best positioned to observe and detect market irregularities across multiple accounts in real time. After all, in the case of the Knight Capital Group debacle, it was the exchange, NYSE, that was first to sound an alarm about unusual behavior of Knight's trading. While it took the NYSE 45 minutes to establish erroneous trading patterns on the exchange, modern technology can detect patterns in much shorter time frames.

Still, unresolved issues surrounding exchange-level surveillance persist: for example, how to aggregate data among exchanges to track cross-asset trading strategies. Some proposed synchronizing timestamps of exchanges using equipment used in global positioning systems (GPSs). The opponents of time synchronization, however, cite market participants' reluctance to forfeit freedom to deploy technology of choice. In addition, the opponents point to the latency inherent in GPS-based

---

[2] The SEC does not obtain tick data and is commonly cited as lacking funds to do so. Part of the reason behind the SEC's reluctance to build the data capability is the agency's implicit agreement with FINRA. At present, FINRA detects potential instances of market manipulation and forwards them to the SEC. The SEC on average prosecutes every eighth case forwarded by FINRA.

synchronization: depending on the location of the exchange, even GPS-wound clocks may differ by several microseconds—an issue in today's fast-paced markets.

Currently Deployed Measures for System Stability

At present, most exchanges have already enabled some forms of real-time surveillance. All exchanges today, for example, are required to implement circuit breakers that halt trading in a selected financial instrument for several minutes following an intraday price drop of several percentage points. Futures exchanges like the CME and the Intercontinental Commodity Exchange (ICE) have also introduced the following measures described in detail next:

- Interval price limits
- No-cancel range
- Protection points
- Cancel orders on system disconnect
- Message throttle limits
- Maximum quantity limits
- Real-time position validation
- Price reasonability

Interval Price Limits *Interval price limits* (IPLs) are circuit breakers that are triggered by extreme short-term moves. The IPL-based halts work as follows. For each traded financial instrument, the exchange computes a moving average price level and a "normal" variation determined on the highs and lows evidenced in the moving data window used in computation. The moving average price plus and minus the variation parameter define the upper and lower IPLs, illustrated in Figure 13.2. As shown in Figure 13.2, when the price falls below the lower IPL, the trading is halted until one of the two following situations occur:

- The price reverts to a higher level above the lower IPL.
- The IPL computational period shifts and the new IPL is lower than the previous limit, allowing trading.

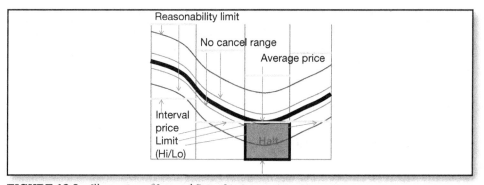

FIGURE 13.2 Illustration of Interval Price Limits
Source: ICE

The width of the window used for computing the price bands is determined by the trading frequency of the financial instrument: the price bands for a frequently traded instrument will be recomputed more often than those for the instrument with little activity.

No-Cancel Range   *No-cancel range* refers to the depth of quotes in the limit order book, where the limit orders cannot be cancelled for a predetermined period of time. When the no-cancel range comprises only the best bid and the best ask, the measure is also known as the minimum quote life (MQL). At the foreign exchange interdealer broker EBS, for example, limit orders placed at the best bid and the best ask cannot be canceled for 250 milliseconds (ms) from the time the order was placed. As a result, within the quarter of a second, the best bid and best ask quotes may change only when the limit orders are matched with an incoming market order. The ICE has also instituted a measure whereby limit orders falling in the no-cancel range may not be canceled altogether. In the case of both EBS and ICE, the limit orders can be canceled as soon as they fall out of the no-cancel range due to natural price movements.

Introduction of MQL appears to be of little consequence to the markets. A study by Chaboud (2012), for example, showed that the markets were much more impacted by overhaul in the EBS matching algorithm than the introduction of MQL. The no-cancel range may gain popularity with other exchanges or be mandated in the near future.

Protection Points   *Protection points* stipulate the maximum number of price levels or ticks a large incoming market order can sweep through in the limit order book. When a market buy order sweeps through the maximum number of price levels and is still not filled in its entirety, the unfilled remainder of the order is automatically converted into a limit buy order. Protection points are currently in use on the CME. Protection points were created in response to a previously common occurrence in the futures markets—large market orders that could sweep as many as 100 ticks of the order book at once. The sweeps disadvantaged the traders and the markets alike: traders received poor average prices on their large orders, and markets were left bare, with little or no liquidity, as a result of the sweeps. Today, protection points are welcomed by the trading community.

Cancel Orders on System Disconnect   Exchanges and broker-dealers alike continuously monitor "heartbeat" messages from their clients, as described in Chapter 16. When a client fails to check in with the regular heartbeat, and then misses further scheduled "pings," the client connection is assumed to have been terminated. Exchanges such as CME take cancel limit orders of disconnected clients as a protective measure. The cancellation of limit orders is performed to ensure that the clients do not execute orders when they are unable to monitor their positions, reducing the incidence of unwanted trade executions.

Message Throttle Limits   The *message throttle limits,* also known as *minimum fill ratios,* dictate the maximum ratio of order cancellations to order executions. For example, a trader may be required to execute at least 1 order for every 10 canceled orders. At the ICE, the message throttle limits are determined on a case-by-case basis in consultation with each trader. Appropriate message throttle limits ensure that the limits detect algorithmic problems without impacting properly operating trading strategies.

Maximum Quantity Limits *Maximum quantity limits* help prevent human and algorithmic "fat finger" errors by enforcing the maximum order sizes and trading positions. Maximum quantities are often determined in consultation with algorithm designers, in order to take into account optimal operation of the trading system.

Real-Time Position Validation At present, futures markets are uniquely positioned to withstand blow-ups of clients' trading systems, like the one incurred by Knight Capital. The secret to stable futures markets is the continuous real-time check of position market values vis-à-vis credit worthiness of trading account. When the market value in a given account exceeds the critical margin limit, the client's trading algorithm is prohibited from entering into new positions. In extreme situations, some of the account holdings may be liquidated to satisfy margin requirements. In most equity markets, similar checks are performed only at the end of each trading day.

Price Reasonability Under *price reasonability,* exchanges allow orders only at price levels within a predetermined range away from the market price. On most U.S. exchanges, traders may not place limit orders higher or lower than 10 percent away from the prevailing market price. The rule was instituted after the flash crash to prevent market orders in crisis from executing at unreasonably low prices, known as *stub quotes.*

Overall, many existing exchange measures are robust in catching errant algorithms. Wider proliferation of measures, as well as additional near-term measures, described next, will ensure that the markets identify and deter errant algorithms before problems occur.

Near-Term Surveillance Measures Both regulators and exchanges are seeking to further improve market surveillance and stability with the following measures, expected to be rolled out in the near future:

- Kill switches
- Legal entity identifiers

Kill Switches Kill switches are designed to automatically block and unblock order entry at the following levels:

- Execution firm
- Account
- Asset class
- Side of market
- Product
- Exchange

At the execution firm's level, a kill switch allows termination of all flow from a broker-dealer whose algorithms are determined to be corrupt. In the Knight Capital case, an execution-firm-level kill switch would have stopped all Knight's trading upon detection of irregularities. An account-level kill switch disables trading by a specific account, while the asset-class kill switch disallows trading in a specific type of financial instrument, for instance, options, potentially allowing trading in other markets. The side-of-market kill switch turns off buying or selling capability. The product kill switch bars trading in one particular financial instrument, while the exchange kill switch takes away ability to trade on a given execution venue.

Kill switches may be operated by exchanges following some specific risk guidelines. In addition, API-based kill switches may be programmed directly into a client's algorithm, shutting down trading ability whenever the algorithm's particular risk tolerance conditions are exceeded. Various risk-tolerance metrics are described in Chapter 14.

Legal Entity Identifiers Real-time regulatory surveillance at the exchange level is further likely to be aided by one of the key new regulatory initiatives: legal entity identifiers (LEIs). An LEI is a unique identifier assigned to all market participants:

- Financial intermediaries
- Banks
- Finance companies
- All listed companies
- Hedge funds
- Proprietary trading organizations
- Pension funds
- Mutual funds
- Private equity funds
- Other entities

There are expected to be no thresholds (capitalization or other) required to obtain an LEI. Such configuration will extend the LEI-based surveillance to all trading entities, except for natural persons.

Presently proposed LEIs are composed of 20 alphanumeric characters, with special sequencing of digits that can be validated using a check character system. Each LEI will be associated with the official name of the legal entity or with the fund manager for pooled investments, the address of the headquarters, the country of incorporation, the date of the first LEI assignment, the date of last update of LEI information, and the date of expiry, if any.

The LEI system will be administered by the International Organization for Standardization (ISO). The ISO will take on validation of LEI applications, assignment of LEIs, maintenance of LEI registry, as well as the annual review of LEI records. The LEI system is expected to operate on an international level; in addition to the U.S. regulators, authorities in Canada, Hong Kong, and Australia have already expressed intention to apply the LEI system in their respective jurisdictions.

The LEIs are expected to phase in by asset class, beginning with over-the-counter (OTC) derivatives, like credit default swaps, and later extending to all asset classes. The U.S. CFTC already requires the use of LEIs for all dealers executing OTC derivative transactions.

Investor Protection

Investor protection is one of the explicit goals of several regulators, like the U.S. SEC. The SEC and most other regulators seek to safeguard traders and investors by minimizing the following activities in the markets:

- Market manipulation
- Front-running
- Market crashes

This section considers each of these issues.

Detecting Intentional Market Manipulation   Whole classes of strategies attributed to high-frequency market distortions often prove ill thought through, as discussed in Chapter 12. Having said that, HFT market manipulation is as feasible in principle as is the screening and detection of such manipulation.

From the regulatory perspective, establishing credible market manipulation requires two principles:

1. The activity should be recurrent.
2. The activity was performed with the intent of manipulating markets.

In other words, to credibly detect market-manipulating activity, regulators need to establish a pattern of intentional market manipulation. To do so, after observing an instance of potentially harmful activity, regulators need to consider previous and subsequent market activity by the same entity and detect a sequence of actions along the same trajectory.

Manipulation can be detected following the blueprints discussed in Chapter 12. As shown in the previous section on stability of systems, the extent of market manipulation can be measured by the symmetry of a market impact following buy-and-sell market orders of equal size. Investors and regulators alike can successfully monitor markets for high-frequency manipulation by screening markets in real-time for asymmetric market impact. Account-level trading in asymmetric markets can next be examined for high-frequency manipulation.

Front-Running   Naturally, unscrupulous brokers possessing order-flow data may choose to front-run their own clients whenever they detect a large impending price move. The regulation has tried to deal with this problem. Under the Volcker rule, for example, banks were forced to dispose of their proprietary trading operations, with the intent of minimizing incentives for using client order-flow information, to ensure stability of the banking sector. In some banks, however, the proprietary trading operations of high-frequency nature were not shut down. Instead, the HFT was moved directly into the execution area with a new moniker of *prehedging* function, where the same HFT strategies are now executed with clients' money on the banks' behalf. The Dodd-Frank rule further complicates the problem by proposing to exempt brokers from their obligation to execute in customer interests first, essentially creating a front-running bonanza at any broker-dealer's execution desk. To prevent front-running, clients can take matters into their own hands and diversify brokers, effectively limiting the information each broker has about the client's order flow. Small traders are at a disadvantage, however, as few have enough capital to establish positions with various brokers.

The Australian regulators have placed the goal of market integrity above all other issues. One of the key initiatives on the table of the Australian regulators is the requirement for pretrade transparency, designed to stem front-running. The Australian Securities and Investment Commission (ASIC) has specifically concerned itself with detecting shifts in liquidity in response to orders, moving market prices before traders obtained execution but after they placed their orders.

Predicting Market Crashes   Following the flash crash of May 6, 2010, a considerable body of research focused on advanced prediction of such events going forward. Two main streams of crash predictability have emerged:

1. Based on asymmetry of liquidity in the limit order books.
2. Based on abnormal trading patterns.

Crash Prediction Based on Asymmetry of Liquidity in the Limit Order Books   The first stream of research first developed by Easley, Lopez de Prado, and O'Hara (2011) takes root in the observation that the May 6, 2010, crash was a direct result of asymmetric liquidity in the markets: the limit orders on the bid side of E-minis, for example, were "eaten up" by incoming market sell orders a few hours before the market activity precipitated into a full-blown crash.

To estimate the incidence of a crash, the authors develop a volume-based probability of informed trading, or VPIN metric:

$$VPIN \approx \frac{\sum_{\tau=1}^{n} \left| V_\tau^S - V_\tau^B \right|}{nV} \tag{1}$$

where V_τ^S and V_τ^B are volumes initiated by sell and buy market orders, respectively, computed within each volume-based clock unit. Easley, Lopez de Prado, and O'Hara (2011) consider volume clocks where each "time" unit corresponds to 50 E-mini contracts: within each volume-clock unit τ, then, $V_\tau^S + V_\tau^B = 50$ contracts. The authors show that extreme asymmetry in trading volume as measured by VPIN is capable of predicting extreme crashes a few hours ahead of crash time. Tudor Investment Corporation has applied for a patent in *VPIN*, and may require fees for utilization of the methodology.

Crash Prediction Based on Abnormal Trading Patterns   A separate stream of literature considers "normal" patterns in trading and uses deviations from those normalities as the predictors of crashes. Normal market movements are calibrated to fit the Mandelbrot-like growth parameter, known as the *Hurst exponent*. A Hurst exponent of returns of 0.5 describes the market where the returns evolve in a completely random manner. A lower Hurst coefficient indicates a mean-reverting market, while a higher Hurst value points to a trending market. Florescu et al. (2012) shows that in most normal real-life markets, the Hurst exponent value has been shown to be about 0.6. A heightened value of Hurst exponent is likely to precede a crash. For example, Florescu et al. (2012) shows that ahead of financial services mini-crash of March 2008, Hurst exponent values in financial services stocks reached 0.85. Aldridge 2012f develops a separate crash-predicting methodology that can be shown to identify onset of market crashes hours and sometimes days ahead of the events.

Efficient Trade Matching

Regulators are actively encouraging internalization, seeking to minimize the situations where broker-dealers execute trades against their own orders. Such incidents are known as *wash trades*. An example of a wash trade may consist of a broker-dealer's placing an order for one customer at the best bid of the exchange, only to match it with a market sell order for another customer. Wash trades have been deemed feasible for money laundering and are closely monitored and discouraged.

Market Structure

Regulatory dimensions surrounding market structure presently span two main areas: new markets, such as swap execution facilities, and "lit" versus "dark" pools. This section briefly considers the issues on the table.

Swap Execution Facilities Following the Dodd-Frank regulation, swaps are a new asset class to be traded electronically in the United States The newly established computerized swap trading falls under the jurisdiction of the CFTC, and will trade in specialized swap-execution facilities (SEFs) that will have a new market structure, are bound to attract high-frequency traders due to their electronic nature, and will require new regulatory rules.

"Lit" and "Dark" Pools Regulation Alternative Trading Systems (Reg ATS) introduced by the SEC in 1998 streamlined definitions and applicability of lit and dark pools. The term *pool* refers to a trading venue attracting or "pooling" trading capital for matching less formal than a regulator-supervised exchange. The terms *lit pool* and, more often, *lit market* usually refer to a traditional exchange-like trading venue, where the limit order book is observable by all engaged market participants. While the transparency of the lit order book may induce confidence in some investors, it may disadvantage others, particularly those desiring to trade large volumes and seeking to avoid order-related market impact and other information leakage. As discussed in Chapter 11, lit order books contain information about impending directions of the market price and order flow, items many market participants prefer to retain in secret.

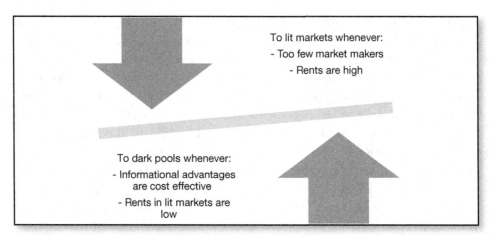

FIGURE 13.3 Market-Making Equilibrium between Dark and Lit Trading Venues

Dark pools are largely unregulated trading venues that do not disclose their limit order books. By keeping their order books "in the dark," dark pools create advantages to large investors and market makers. Large investors are enticed by limited information signaling associated with their orders. The orders are revealed only when executed—trade prints are disseminated to all participants of a given market.

Large investors are not the only group benefiting from dark pools. Market makers also tend to earn more in dark pools than in lit markets. According to the research of Boulatov and George (2011), for instance, market makers are able to hide informational revisions to their quotes, discussed in Chapter 11, trading longer on their information. Examples of dark pools include Citigroup's Automated Trading Desk (ATD) and Liquidnet's offerings.

Even though dark pools tend to offer higher profitability to market participants than do lit venues, an equilibrium controls proportion of market makers engaged in dark pools versus lit trading operations. Once the majority of market makers' moves to the dark pools, lit venues become less competitive and market makers in these lit venues earn higher rents. When the value of the market makers' rents in the lit markets exceeds the informational advantages in the dark markets, more market-makers moves from dark to lit venues, until an equilibrium is reached. Figure 13.3 illustrates the mechanism by which the equilibrium between the dark and lit markets is achieved.

Canadian regulators have singled out dark pools as trading venues suitable only to large investors trading amounts greater than a cut-off "Dark Order Size Threshold." In the United States, the NYSE went the opposite direction and created a segregated dark pool for small investors, the success of which is yet to be determined.

■ Summary

Regulators worldwide are proactively tackling issues relating to HFT. New ideas have emerged to monitor markets in real time and screen for issues such as market manipulation and market crashes. Expanding monitoring activity at the exchange level will likely deliver most substantial improvements of current enforcement; the legal entity identifier initiative is bound to be helpful in the process.

■ End-of-Chapter Questions

1. What are the latest key regulatory developments in the United States? In the United Kingdom? In Canada? In Australia?
2. What kind of HFT protection mechanisms are already deployed in selected U.S. markets?
3. What is the interval price limit? How does it work?
4. What is the message throttle limit? How is it determined?
5. What is a legal entity identifier?

Risk Management of HFT

Media coverage of risks accompanying high-frequency trading (HFT) tends to focus on and overstate the risks of market manipulation, as detailed in Chapter 12. However, little or no attention is paid to the real risks inherent in many HFT strategies and the ways to mitigate or minimize said risks. These risks include those incurred by high-frequency traders themselves and their trading venues and clearing parties. Chapters 14 through 16 describe the nature of such risks and existing strategy for dealing with them. Chapter 14 covers the risks facing high-frequency traders. Chapter 15 discusses mitigation of risks associated with market impact (MI) that can be used by both HFTs and other market participants, such as institutional investors. Chapter 16 covers best practices in development of HFT with specific consideration placed on minimizing risks embedded in technology implementation. Chapter 16 also discusses minimization of operational risks, and suggests best practices for execution of HFT.

■ Measuring HFT Risk

As recent problems on Nasdaq and the Best Alternative Trading Systems (BATS) illustrate, the risks from poorly executed HFT systems alone may result in multimillion-dollar losses, incurred almost instantaneously. Understanding and management of risks embedded in HFT therefore is critical to ensuring operational success of HFT enterprises.

The following sections detail the quantification and management of risk exposure for different types of risk. Chapter 16 documents best practices for ongoing oversight of risk exposure. The methodology for measuring risk depends on the type of risk under consideration. All risk can be broken down into the following categories:

- Regulatory and legal risk
- Credit and counterparty risk

- Market risk
- Liquidity risk
- Operational risk

Regulatory and legal risk, credit and counterparty risk, market risk, and liquidity risks are discussed in the sections below. Chapter 15 describes mitigation of market impact. Chapter 16 focuses on operational risk.

Regulatory and Legal Risk

Regulatory and legal risk comprises the demands of new legislations that may affect the operation of HFT systems. As discussed in Chapter 13, recent regulatory reforms strengthened risk controls surrounding HFT, and are therefore beneficial to both the markets and the HFTs themselves. As the latest U.S. Senate hearings indicate, however, the risks of adverse to HFT regulatory reform, such as the ill-thought-through idea of banning co-location, still exist. (As discussed in footnote 1 in Chapter 13, co-location is imperative for computer security and therefore stability of market systems.)

Credit and Counterparty Risk

Credit risk specifies potential issues in a high-frequency trader's ability to secure leverage. Leverage refers to the trader's ability to borrow capital for his trading needs. HFTs generally have leverage abilities comparable to those of other traders. In equities, for example, HFTs can generally borrow and trade three or more times as much capital as the amount of cash available in their account, on a three-to-one or greater margin, at the discretion of the margin-advancing broker-dealer. Because most HFTs do not need to hold positions overnight, their leverage is considerably cheaper than that of long-term investors. From the broker-dealers' perspective, it is the typically unsupervised overnight changes in market value of long-term investors that are subject to blow-ups and defaults on broker's leverage. The intraday margin of HFTs is tightly monitored along with HFT positions by the responsible HFT oversight employee, at least in the best practices configurations. In futures markets, margin positions are automatically monitored and enforced by the exchanges in real time.

Counterparty risk reflects the probability of financial loss should the high-frequency trader's partners in the trading equation not live up to their obligations. An example of losses due to a counterparty failure is a situation in which a fund's money is custodied with a broker-dealer, and the broker-dealer goes bankrupt. The collapse of Lehman Brothers in October 2008 was the most spectacular counterparty failure in recent memory. According to Reuters, close to $300 billion was frozen in bankruptcy proceedings as a result of the bank's collapse, pushing many prominent hedge funds to the brink of insolvency. The high-frequency traders may prevent similar conditions by tracking the creditworthiness of their brokers, as well as diversifying their exposure among different brokers and trading venues.

Market Risk

Market risk is the risk of loss of capital due to an adverse price movement of the traded financial instrument. A long position in E-mini futures following a buy order at 1446.02 begins incurring market risk as soon as the order is executed. Even before any market movement takes place, instantaneous liquidation of the position will cost the trader money: to immediately close down the position, the trader or the trading system will need to pay the bid-ask spread.

The proliferation of automated trading has not changed the nature of market risk carried by market makers and other intraday trading strategies. However, on the per-trade basis and due to their ability to read every tick of market data and react in the matter of nanoseconds, high-frequency traders face considerably lower market risks than do their human counterparts.

The bulk of high-frequency market risk management focuses on the following four key aspects:

1. First order: Stop losses
2. Second order: Volatility cutouts
3. Third and fourth order: Short-term value-at-risk (VaR)
4. Higher order: Hedging with other instruments

The order of the risk management methodologies previously noted refers to the methodology relationship with the price of the traded financial instrument. Stop losses are linear in price, and are therefore "first-order" functions of price. Volatility is computed from squared price deviations and is referred to as a "second-order" metric. VaR takes into account skewness and kurtosis of the trading returns, the third- and fourth-order distributional parameters. Finally, hedging may be related to any functional shape of price, and is therefore "higher-order."

Each order of risk management is discussed in detail next.

First-Order Risk Management: Stop Losses   Stop losses denote hard loss limits for each position and can be fixed or variable, absolute or trailing. Fixed stop losses outline the absolute maximum each position can potentially lose and are same for each trade within a given trading strategy. Variable stop losses can be determined for each trade within a strategy and can be a strategy-specific function of market volatility and other related variables. Absolute stop losses specify the hard amount a strategy can afford to lose relative to the price level at which the position was opened. The trailing stop loss, however, stipulates the hard price an amount a strategy can lose relative to the price at which the strategy has achieved the highest gain after the position was opened. Figure 14.1 illustrates the difference between fixed and trailing stop losses.

Determining Stop-Loss Parameters   The optimal stop-loss parameter should satisfy the following three requirements:

1. The stop loss should limit losing trades without affecting the winning trades.
2. A stop loss should not be triggered due to natural market volatility alone.
3. Stop losses should be executed immediately.

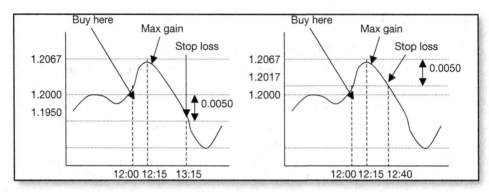

FIGURE 14.1 Difference between Simple (Fixed) and Trailing Stop-Loss Thresholds

The preceding requirements translate into the following mathematical conditions for stop losses:

$$E[Profit] > 0$$

where $E[Profit]$

$$= E(Gain) * Pr(Gain) + E(Loss \mid Loss > StopLoss)$$
$$* Pr(Loss \mid Loss > StopLoss)$$
$$+ E(Loss \mid Loss \leq StopLoss)$$
$$* Pr(StopLoss \mid Loss \leq StopLoss)$$

Probability of gain, $Pr(Gain)$, as well as the cumulative probability of loss, $Pr(Loss \mid Loss > StopLoss) + Pr(StopLoss \mid Loss \leq StopLoss)$, can be estimated from the simulation, as can be the average gain, $E(Gain)$, and average losses above and below the stop loss values, $E(Loss \mid Loss > StopLoss)$ and $E(Loss \mid Loss \leq StopLoss)$.

During periods of high volatility, natural oscillations of the market price may trigger "false" stop losses, adversely affecting performance of trading strategies. The simplest way to account for variable volatility is via the following analysis:

- In the in-sample back-test, estimate the volatility parameter over a rolling window. Within each time window, the volatility parameter can be estimated as a simple standard deviation, or (better) weighted toward later observations using a triangular or exponential weighting function. The duration of the window can match the average position holding time of the strategy.

- Distribution of the volatility parameters obtained in the previous step can be used to create a multiplier for the stop-loss parameter: higher volatility should result in larger absolute value of the stop loss.

- An out-of-sample back-test should confirm higher profitability of the stop-loss-enabled strategy.

Second-Order Risk Management: Volatility Cutouts *Volatility cutouts* refer to rules surrounding market conditions during which the HFT systems are halted. Some HFT strategies work better in high-volatility conditions, while others work best in low volatility. To optimize capital performance, volatility cutouts "pass through" orders of some strategies when one set of conditions takes place and allow orders of other strategies when a different state of the world is realized. Volatility "states of the world" can be determined empirically by computing a rolling volatility estimate, such as the standard deviation of short-term returns of the underlying asset or a market index over a certain past window of data. Such backward-looking volatility estimates are risky, as they are assuming that the past volatility conditions will persist into the future (volatility tends to "cluster" or persist for long periods of time, so the assumption is plausible if not bulletproof). Alternatively, volatility cutouts can be tied to a variable measuring forward-looking volatility, such as the volatility index (VIX) or an implied volatility derived from the options on the traded security. Since volatility cutouts are tied to the squared changes in the value of the traded security, volatility cutouts can be considered a "second-order" risk metric.

Determining Volatility Cutouts   Many trading strategies perform better in certain volatility conditions independent of the stop-loss parameters. To enhance performance of a strategy, it may be desirable to limit execution of such strategies in adverse volatility conditions. To determine the volatility conditions optimal for strategy execution, one may use the following technique:

1. In the in-sample back-test, estimate the volatility parameter over a rolling window. Within each time window, the volatility parameter can be estimated as a simple standard deviation, or (better) weighted toward later observations using triangular or exponential weighting function. The duration of the window can match the average position holding time of the strategy.
2. Regress strategy gains on the obtained volatility estimates using the following equation:

$$R_t = \alpha + \beta \hat{\sigma}_t + \varepsilon_t$$

where R_t represents the gain of the last completed round-trip trade realized at time t, and $\hat{\sigma}_t$ is the moving volatility estimate obtained in the previous step. Instead of realized strategy returns, the R_t on the left-hand side of the regression can be mark-to-market strategy gain sampled at regular time intervals.
3. If the estimate of β is positive (negative) and statistically significant, the strategy performs better in high (low) volatility conditions. A median of volatility estimates obtained in step 1 above can be used as a turn-on/turn-off volatility switch for the strategy.

A successful risk management process should establish the risk budget that the operation is willing to take in the event that the operation ends up on the losing side of the equation. The risks should be quantified as worst-case scenario losses tolerable per day, week, month, and year and should include operational costs, such as overhead and personnel costs. Examples of the worst-case losses to be tolerated may be 10 percent of organizational equity per month or a hard dollar amount—for example, $15 million per fiscal year.

Determining Volatility Cutouts Ex-Ante   Forecasting volatility is important in many trading applications. In addition to option-based strategies that directly arbitrage volatility, some spot and futures strategies may work better in some volatility conditions than in others. Many risk management models also call for volatility-dependent treatment of the strategies: stop losses may be "tighter" in low-volatility conditions and "looser" in high-volatility ones.

Forecasting volatility can be simple in principle. Volatility has been shown to "cluster" in time: volatility "builds up" into peaks and reverses into valleys gradually, resulting in clusters of high-volatility observations. As a result, volatility is straightforward to predict: high-volatility observations are usually followed by more or less high observations, while low-volatility cases are surrounded by similarly low volatility figures.

Popular tools for measuring volatility are quite simple: a standard deviation of returns (a simple average of square deviations from the mean) presents the most basic metric of volatility calculations. Since most recent observations can be more relevant than observations in the past, some researchers weigh later observations by computing a weighted average of square deviations from the mean. The weights can be either linear or exponential. Another popular metric of volatility is the average of squared intraperiod returns; it has been shown to be superior to standard deviation–based computations.

Given the tendency of volatility to cluster, it is reasonable to assume that the next period's volatility will be the same as the last period's volatility. Alternatively, one may calculate if the latest volatility observations form a trend, and then extrapolate the trend into the future. A popular trending volatility forecasting tool is called the generalized autoregressive conditional heteroskedasticity (GARCH) estimator and is built into many software packages.

Yet, when the key research question is whether the volatility is high or low, another technique, known as *Markov state dependency,* developed by Aldridge (2011), may work best. The Markov technique divides historical observations into high and low volatility states, and then assesses probabilities of transition from high to low probability and vice versa. Specifically, the technique can be used as follows:

1. Run a linear regression of price changes on past price changes.
2. Examine the distribution of error terms; separate them into two groups: low and high errors, based on the arbitrary yet appropriate cutoff point.
3. Estimate historical "transition probabilities" based on the sequential changes from low to high states and vice versa:
   a. For each sequential error observation, determine whether the error was a change from low to high, a change from high to low, a stay in the low state, or a stay in the high-volatility state.
   b. Count the totals and express them in a percentage probability form.
4. During run-time, assess whether the current volatility level is high or low. Given the probabilities of transition determined in step 3, assess the likelihood of a volatility change in the next period. Adjust the trading accordingly.

Markov switching models can be very fast and effective in HFT applications and many other models.

Third- and Fourth-Order Risk Management: Value-at-Risk Value-at-risk (VaR) is a probabilistic metric of potential loss that takes into consideration distributional properties of returns of the HFT. Intraday VaR is typically used in HFT applications to set the ceiling for the intraday market exposure and the floor for the intraday mark-to-market loss. If the strategy hits the intraday VaR threshold, the strategy is moved into paper trading for review of its stability until further notice. VaR considers the entire historical distribution of the traded security, including skewness and kurtosis of the security returns, the third and fourth moments of returns. As a result, VaR represents a "fourth-order" risk measure.

The concept of VaR has by now emerged as the dominant metric in market risk management estimation. The VaR framework spans two principal measures—VaR itself and the expected shortfall (ES). VaR is the value of loss in case a negative scenario with the specified probability should occur. The probability of the scenario is determined as a percentile of the distribution of historical scenarios that can be strategy or portfolio returns. For example, if the scenarios are returns from a particular strategy and all the returns are arranged by their realized value in ascending order from the worst to the best, then the 95 percent VaR corresponds to the cutoff return at the lowest fifth percentile. In other words, if 100 sample observations are arranged from the lowest to the highest, then VaR corresponds to the value of the fifth lowest observation

The ES measure determines the average worst-case scenario among all scenarios at or below the prespecified threshold. For example, a 95 percent ES is the average return among all returns at the 5 percent or lower percentile. If 100 sample observations are arranged from the lowest to the highest, the ES is the average of observations 1 through 5. Figure 14.2 illustrates the concepts of VaR and ES.

To compute VaR, the trader or risk manager may use the following steps:

1. Compute daily net (after transaction costs) historical returns of the strategy either live or simulated (back-tested) returns.
2. Determine the cut-off corresponding to the worst 5 percent of strategy returns.

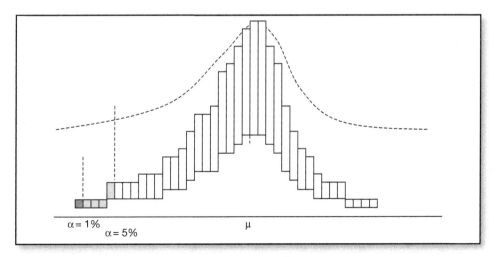

$\alpha = 1\%$

$\alpha = 5\%$

μ

FIGURE 14.2 The 99 Percent VaR ($\alpha = 1$ Percent) and 95 Percent VaR ($\alpha = 5$ Percent) Computed on the Sample Return Population

3. Set the shutdown threshold equivalent to the lowest 5 percentile of strategy returns, place the strategy "on probation" in paper trading until the cause of the low return is ascertained and the strategy is adjusted.

An analytical approximation to true VaR can be found by parameterizing the sample distribution. The parametric VaR assumes that the observations are distributed in a normal fashion. Specifically, the parametric VaR assumes that the 5 percent in the left tail of the observations fall at $\mu-1.65\sigma$ of the distribution, where m and s represent the mean and standard deviation of the observations, respectively. The 95 percent parametric VaR is then computed as $\mu-1.65\sigma$, while the 95 percent parametric ES is computed as the average of all distribution values from $-\infty$ to $\mu-1.65\sigma$. The average can be computed as an integral of the distribution function. Similarly, the 99 percent parametric VaR is computed as $\mu-2.33\sigma$, while the 99 percent parametric ES is computed as the average of all distribution values from $-\infty$ to $\mu-2.33\sigma$. The parametric VaR is an approximation of the true VaR; the applicability of the parametric VaR depends on how close the sample distribution resembles the normal distribution. Figure 14.3 illustrates this idea.

While the VaR and ES metrics summarize the location and the average of many worst-case scenarios, neither measure indicates the absolute worst scenario that can destroy entire trading operations, banks, and markets. Most financial return distributions have fat tails, meaning that the very extreme events lie beyond normal distribution bounds and can be truly catastrophic.

The limitations of VaR methodology have hardly been a secret. In a *New York Times* article published on January 2, 2009, David Einhorn, the founder of the hedge fund Greenlight Capital, stated that VaR was "relatively useless as a risk-management tool and potentially catastrophic when its use creates a false sense of security among senior managers and watchdogs. This is like an air bag that works all the time, except when you have a car accident." The article also quoted Nassim Nicholas Taleb, the best-selling author of *The Black Swan*, as calling VaR metrics "a fraud." Jorion (2000) points out that the VaR approach both presents a faulty measure of risk and actively pushes strategists to bet on extreme events. Despite all the criticism, VaR and ES have been mainstays of corporate risk management for years Most recently, daily VaR has made forays into risk management of active trading, quickly becoming a tool of choice on many trading floors.

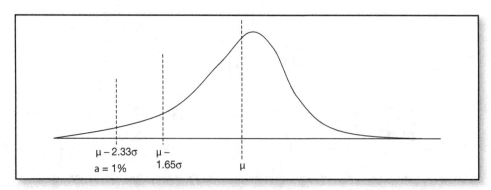

FIGURE 14.3   The 95 Percent Parametric VaR Corresponds to $\mu-1.65\sigma$ of the Distribution, While the 99 Percent Parametric VaR Corresponds to $\mu-2.33\sigma$ of the Distribution

To alleviate the shortcomings of the VaR, many quantitative outfits began to parameterize extreme tail distributions to develop fuller pictures of extreme losses. Once the tail is parameterized based on the available data, the worst-case extreme events can be determined analytically from distributional functions, even though no extreme events of comparable severity were ever observed in the sample data.

The parameterization of the tails is performed using the extreme value theory (EVT). *EVT* is an umbrella term spanning a range of tail modeling functions. Dacorogna et al. (2001) note that all fat-tailed distributions belong to the family of Pareto distributions. A Pareto distribution family is described as follows:

$$G(x) = \begin{cases} 0 & x \leq 0 \\ \exp(-x^{-\alpha}) & x > 0, \, \alpha > 0 \end{cases} \tag{1}$$

where the tail index α is the parameter that needs to be estimated from the return data. For raw security returns, the tail index varies from financial security to financial security. Even for raw returns of the same financial security, the tail index can vary from one quoting institution to another, especially for really high-frequency estimations.

When the tail index a is determined, we can estimate the magnitude and probability of all the extreme events that may occur, given the extreme events that did occur in the sample. Figure 14.4 illustrates the process of using tail parameterization:

1. Sample return observations obtained from either a back-test or live results are arranged in ascending order.
2. The tail index value is estimated on the bottom 5 percentile of the sample return distribution.
3. Using the distribution function obtained with the tail index, the probabilities of observing the extreme events are estimated. According to the tail index distribution function, a −7 percent return would occur with a probability of 0.5 percent while a return of −11 percent would register with a probability of 0.001 percent.

The tail index approach allows us to deduce the unobserved return distributions from the sample distributions of observed returns. Although the tail index approach

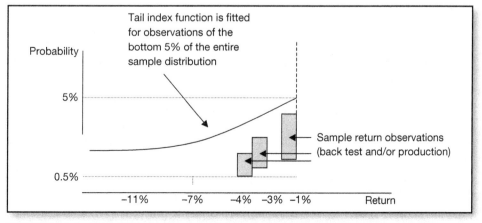

FIGURE 14.4   Using Tail Index Parameterization to Predict Extreme Events

is useful, it has its limitations. For one, the tail index approach "fills in" the data for the observed returns with theoretical observations; if the sample tail distribution is sparse (and it usually is), the tail index distribution function may not be representative of the actual extreme returns. In such cases, a procedure known as *parametric bootstrapping* may be applicable.

Parametric bootstrap simulates observations based on the properties of the sample distribution. The technique "fills in" unobserved returns based on observed sample returns. The parametric bootstrap process works as follows:

The sample distribution of observed returns delivered by the manager is decomposed into three components using a basic market model:

1. The manager's skill, or alpha.
2. The manager's return due to the manager's portfolio correlation with the benchmark.
3. The manager's idiosyncratic error.

The decomposition is performed using the standard market model regression:

$$R_{i,t} = \alpha_i + \beta_{i,x} R_{x,t} + \varepsilon_t \tag{2}$$

where $R_{i,t}$ is the manager's raw return in period t, $R_{x,t}$ is the raw return on the chosen benchmark in period t, α_i is the measure of the manager's money management skill or alpha, and $\beta_{i,x}$ is a measure of the dependency of the manager's raw returns on the benchmark returns.

4. Once parameters $\hat{\alpha}_i$ and $\hat{\beta}_{i,x}$ are estimated using equation (2), three pools of data are generated: one for $\hat{\alpha}_i$ (constant for given manager, benchmark, and return sample), $\hat{\beta}_{i,x} R_{x,t}$, and $\varepsilon_{i,t}$.[1] For example, if $\hat{\alpha}_i$ and $\hat{\beta}_{i,x}$ were estimated to be 0.002 and –0.05, respectively, then the component pools for a sample of raw returns and benchmarked returns may look as shown in Table 14.1.

5. Next, the data is resampled as follows:
    a. A value $\varepsilon^S_{i,t}$ is drawn at random from the pool of idiosyncratic errors, $\{\varepsilon_{i,t}\}$.
    b. Similarly, a value $\hat{\beta}_{i,x} R^S_{x,t}$ is drawn at random from the pool of $\{\beta_{i,x} R_{x,t}\}$
    c. A new sample value is created as follows:

$$\hat{R}^S_{i,t} = \hat{\alpha}_i + \hat{\beta}_{i,x} R^S_{x,t} + \varepsilon^S_t \tag{3}$$

The sampled variables $\varepsilon^S_{i,t}$ and $\hat{\beta}_{i,x} R^S_{x,t}$ are returned to their pools (not eliminated from the sample).

TABLE 14.1 **Examples of Generated Bootstrap Components**

Observation No.	$R_{i,t}$	$R_{x,t}$	$\hat{\alpha}_i$	$\hat{\beta}_{i,x} R_{x,t}$	$\varepsilon_{i,t}$
1	0.015	–0.001	0.002	0.00005	0.01295
2	0.0062	0.0034	0.002	–0.00017	0.00403

---

[1] The "hat" notation on variables, as in $\hat{\alpha}_i$ and $\hat{\beta}_{i,x}$, denotes that the parameters were estimated from a sample distribution, as opposed to comprising the true distribution values.

RISK MANAGEMENT OF HFT

The resampling process outlined in steps a–c is then repeated a large number of times deemed sufficient to gain a better perspective on the distribution of tails. As a rule of thumb, the resampling process should be repeated at least as many times as there were observations in the original sample. It is not uncommon for the bootstrap process to be repeated thousands of times. The resampled values $\hat{R}_{i,t}^{S}$ can differ from the observed sample distribution, thus expanding the sample data set with extra observations conforming to the properties of the original sample.

6. The new distribution values obtained through the parametric process are now treated as were other sample values and are incorporated into the tail index, VaR, and other risk management calculations.

The parametric bootstrap relies on the assumption that the raw returns' dependence on a benchmark as well as the manager's alpha remain constant through time. This does not have to be the case. Managers with dynamic strategies spanning different asset classes are likely to have time-varying dependencies on several benchmarks. Despite this shortcoming, the parametric bootstrap allows risk managers to glean a fuller notion of the true distribution of returns given the distribution of returns observed in the sample.

To incorporate portfolio managers' benchmarks into the VaR framework, Suleiman, Shapiro, and Tepla (2005) propose analyzing the "tracking error" of the manager's return in excess of his benchmark. Suleiman et al. (2005) define tracking error as a contemporaneous difference between the manager's return and the return on the manager's benchmark index:

$$TE_t = \ln(R_{i,t}) - \ln(R_{X,t}) \tag{4}$$

where $R_{i,t}$ is the manager's return at time t and $R_{x,t}$ is return on the manager's benchmark, also at time t. The VaR parameters are then estimated on the tracking error observations.

In addition to VaR, statistical models may include Monte Carlo simulation–based methods to estimate future market values of capital at risk. The Monte Carlo simulations are often used in determining derivatives exposure. Scenario analyses and causal models can be used to estimate market risk as well. These auxiliary types of market risk estimation, however, rely excessively on qualitative assessment and can, as a result, be misleading in comparison with VaR estimates, which are based on realized historical performance.

Higher-Order Risk Management: Hedging   The objective of hedging is to create a portfolio that maximizes returns while minimizing risk—downside risk in particular. Hedging can also be thought of as a successful payoff matching: the negative payoffs of one security "neutralized" by positive payoffs of another.

Hedging can be passive or dynamic. Passive risk hedging is most akin to insurance. The manager enters into a position in a financial security with the risk characteristics that offset the long-term negative returns of the operation. For example, a manager whose main trading strategy involves finding fortuitous times for being long in USD/CAD may want to go short the USD/CAD futures contract to offset his exposure to USD/CAD. As always, detailed analysis of the risk characteristics of the two securities is required to make such a decision.

Dynamic hedging is most often done through a series of short-term, potentially overlapping, insurance-like contracts. The objective of the short-term insurance contracts is to manage the short-term characteristics of trading returns. In the case of market risk hedging, dynamic hedging may be developed for a particular set of recurring market conditions, when behaviors of the trading systems may repeat themselves. It may be possible to find a set of financial instruments or trading strategies the returns of which would offset the downside of the primary trading strategy during these particular market conditions. For example, during a U.S. Fed announcement about the level of interest rates, the USD/CAD exchange rate is likely to rise following a rise in the U.S. interest rates, while U.S. bond prices are likely to fall following the same announcement. Depending upon return distributions for USD/CAD and U.S. bonds, it may make sense to trade the two together during the U.S. interest rate announcements in order to offset the negative tail risk in either. Mapping out extensive distributions of returns as described previously in this chapter would help in determining the details of such a dynamic hedging operation.

High-frequency portfolio management can be applied to manage market risks of instruments used in HFT strategies as well as to extend capacity of strategies by carrying it over to other instruments.

Hedging can be further broken down into the following categories:

- Delta hedging
- Portfolio hedging

Delta Hedging In delta hedging HFT in a particular financial instrument, the portfolio system enters and closes positions in a liquid related instrument. The related instrument for a single stock or a spot commodity can be a near-term futures contract written on that stock or commodity. Delta hedging instruments related to stocks, commodities or futures may be a liquid option. Most liquid options tend to be with near expiration dates and "at-the-money," with strike prices close to the present price of the underlying instrument.

In delta hedging, for every unit of the HF-traded instrument, the system purchases a specific quantity of the hedging instrument. This hedging quantity is determined by the average relative changes in the prices of the HF-traded instrument and the hedging instrument:

$$Q_{hedging,t} = \frac{\Delta P_{HFT,t}}{\Delta P_{hedging,t}} \tag{5}$$

where $\Delta P_{HFT,t}$ is the average return on the HF-traded instrument computed per chosen unit of time, and $\Delta P_{hedging,t}$ represents the return on the selected hedging instrument computed over the same unit of time. To standardize the units of HF-traded and hedging instruments, both returns need to be time-based; the volume and tick clocks are inappropriate for the hedging application. In dynamic hedging, the quantity of the hedging instrument, $Q_{hedging,t}$, needs to be recalculated continuously in the moving-window specification to ensure the average price changes are accurately captured.

In dynamic hedging, after the latest quantity of the hedging instrument, $Q_{hedging,t}$, is estimated, a new challenge arises: executing the trades in the primary and the hedging instruments. The situation becomes particularly demanding in cases when the high-frequency trading strategy relies on limit orders, as the risk of non-execution in either instrument may compromise hedging activity altogether. A possible solution involves always trading the hedging instrument using market orders, and only after the trades in the principal instrument were completely executed. Care should be taken to ensure that such solution does not destroy profitability of the HFT strategy.

Portfolio Hedging The main challenge of dynamic hedging of high-frequency strategies is speed: computation of risk-minimizing allocations takes time, during which the markets move and render the just-computed allocations stale. The hedging problem becomes a moving target in fast-paced markets, as illustrated in Figure 14.5.

To overcome the challenge described in Figure 14.5, trading systems can deploy fast portfolio optimization algorithms discussed in detail below.

A classic portfolio hedging strategy, developed by Markowitz (1952), solves the following optimization problem:

$$\max x E[R] - Ax'Vx$$

$$s.t. \sum x_i = 1 \tag{6}$$

where x_i is the portfolio weight of security i, $i \in [1,\ldots,I]$, $E[R]$ is a vector of expected returns of I securities, V is an $I \times I$ variance-covariance matrix of returns, and A is the

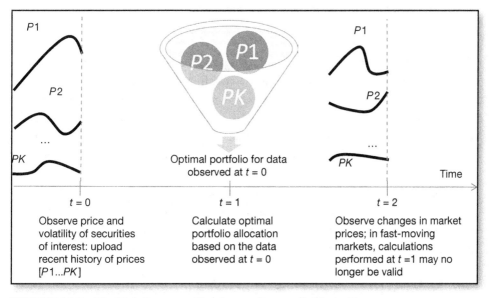

FIGURE 14.5 The High-Frequency Hedging as a Perpetually Moving Target

coefficient reflecting the risk aversion of the trading operation. A is commonly assumed to be 0.5 to simplify the solution. A dynamic state-dependent hedging would repeat the process outlined in equation (6), but only for returns pertaining to a specific market state.

The solution to equation (6) calls for an inversion of the variance-covariance matrix V, a computationally demanding operation the execution time of which has been shown to grow as a square of number of financial instruments considered.

Several classes of algorithms have been proposed to simplify and speed up setting the optimal portfolio weights:

- Simultaneous equations
- Nonlinear programming
- Critical-line optimizing algorithms
- Discrete pairwise (DPW) optimization
- Genetic algorithms

The following sections describe each of the algorithms in detail.

Simultaneous Equations   The *simultaneous equations* framework is the algorithm that directly follows the Markowitz (1952) specification. It has been shown to be inefficient for optimization if the portfolio exceeds 10 strategies, and it may produce highly erroneous forecasts when 20 or more assets are involved. The forecast errors are due to the estimation errors that occur when the average returns and variances are computed. The Bayesian error-correction framework, discussed later in this chapter, can be used to alleviate some of the input estimation errors. Still, in addition to the issues of forecast errors, the estimation time of this algorithm grows exponentially with the number of trading strategies involved, making this method hardly suitable for high-frequency trading of many assets. Tsagaris, Jasra, and Adams (2010) show that computational speed improvement can be improved by updating portfolio weights using eigenvalue decomposition, instead of recalculating portfolio weights afresh with each new tick of data.

Nonlinear Programming   *Nonlinear programming* is a class of optimizers popular in commercial software. The nonlinear algorithms employ a variety of techniques with the objective of maximizing or minimizing the target portfolio optimization function given specified parameters such as portfolio allocation weights. Some of these algorithms employ a gradient technique whereby they analyze the slope of the objective function at any given point and select the fastest increasing or decreasing path to the target maximum or minimum, respectively. The nonlinear programming algorithms are equally sensitive to the estimation errors of the input means and variances of the returns. Most often, the algorithms are too computationally complex to be feasible in the high-frequency environments. A recent example of a nonlinear optimizer is provided by Steuer, Qi, and Hirschberger (2006).

The Critical Line–Optimizing Algorithm   The *critical line–optimizing algorithm* was developed by Markowitz (1959) to facilitate the computation of his own portfolio theory. The algorithm is fast and comparatively easy to implement. Instead of providing point weights for each individual security considered in the portfolio allocation, the critical line optimizer delivers a set of portfolios on the efficient frontier, a drawback that has precluded many commercial companies from adapting this method. A recent algorithm by Markowitz and Todd (2000) addresses some of the issues. According to Niedermayer and Niedermayer (2007), the Markowitz and Todd (2000) algorithm outperforms the algorithm designed by Steuer, Qi, and Hirschberger (2006) by a factor of 10,000 when at least 2,000 assets considered simultaneously.

Discrete Pairwise (DPW) Optimization   The existing algorithms, whatever the complexity and accuracy of their portfolio allocation outputs, may not be perfectly suited to the high-frequency trading environment. First, in environments where a delay of one microsecond can result in a million-dollar loss, the optimization algorithms in their current form still consume too much time and system power. Second, these algorithms ignore the liquidity considerations pertinent to the contemporary trading settings; most of the transactions occur in blocks or "clips" of a prespecified size. Trades of larger-than-normal sizes as well as trades of smaller blocks incur higher transaction costs that in the high-frequency environment can put a serious strain on the system's profitability.

A simple high-frequency alternative to the complex optimization solutions is a discrete pairwise (DPW) optimization developed by Aldridge (2010). The DPW algorithm is a fast compromise between the equally weighted portfolio setting and a full-fledged optimization machine that outputs portfolio weights in discrete clips of the prespecified sizes. No fractional weights are allowed. The algorithm works as follows:

1. Candidates for selection into the overall portfolio are ranked using Sharpe ratios and sorted from the highest Sharpe ratio to the lowest. This step of the estimation utilizes the fact that the Sharpe ratio itself is a measure of where each individual strategy lies on the efficient frontier.
2. An even number of strategies with the highest Sharpe ratios are selected for inclusion into the portfolio. Half of the selected strategies should have historically positive correlations with the market, and half should have historically negative correlations with the market.
3. After the universe of financial instruments is selected on the basis of the Sharpe ratio characteristics, all selected strategies are ranked according to their current liquidity. The current liquidity can be measured as the number of quotes or trades that have been recorded over the past fixed number of seconds or even minutes of trading activity.
4. After all the strategies have been ranked on the basis of their liquidity, the pairs are formed through the following process: the two strategies within each pair have opposite historical correlation with the market. Thus, strategies historically positively correlated with the market are matched with strategies historically negatively correlated with the market. Furthermore, the matching should occur according to the strategy liquidity rank. The most

liquid strategy positively correlated with the market should be matched with the most liquid strategy negatively correlated with the market, and so on until the least liquid strategy positively correlated with the market is matched with the least liquid strategy negatively correlated with the market. The liquidity-based matching ensures that the high-frequency dynamic captured by correlation is due to idiosyncratic movements of the strategy rather than the illiquidity conditions of one strategy.

5. Next, for each pair of strategies, the high-frequency volatility of a portfolio of just the two strategies is computed for discrete position sizes in either strategy. For example, in foreign exchange, where a common transactional clip is $1 million, the discrete position sizes considered for the pairwise optimization may be −$3 million, −$2 million, −$1 million, 0, $1 million, $2 million, and $3 million, where the minus sign indicates the short position. Once the volatility for the various portfolio combinations is selected within each pair of strategies, the positions with the lowest portfolio volatility are selected.

6. The resulting pair portfolios are subsequently executed given the maximum allowable allocation constraints for each strategy. The maximum long and short allocation is predetermined and constrained as follows: the cumulative gross position in each strategy cannot exceed a certain size, and the cumulative net position cannot exceed another, separately set, limit that is smaller than the aggregate of the gross limits for all strategies. The smaller net position clause ensures a degree of market neutrality.

The DWP algorithm is particularly well suited to high-frequency environments because it has the following properties:

- The DPW algorithm avoids the brunt of the impact of input estimation errors by reducing the number of strategies in each portfolio allocation decision.

- The negative historical correlation of input securities ensures that within each pair of matched strategies, the minimum variance will result in long positions in both strategies most of the time. Long positions in the strategies are shown to historically produce the highest returns per unit of risk, as is determined during the Sharpe ratio ranking phase. The times that the system results in short positions for one or more strategy are likely due to idiosyncratic market events.

- The algorithm is very fast in comparison with other portfolio optimization algorithms. The speed of the algorithm comes from the following "savings" in computational time:

  - If the total number of strategies selected in the Sharpe ratio ranking phase is $2K$, the DPW algorithm computes only K correlations. Most other portfolio optimization algorithms compute correlation among every pair of strategies among the $2K$ securities, requiring $2K(K-1)$ correlation computations instead.

  - The grid search employed in seeking the optimal portfolio size for each strategy within each portfolio pair optimizes only between two strategies, or in two dimensions. A standard algorithm requires a $2K$-dimensional optimization.

- Finally, the grid search allows only a few discrete portfolio weight values. In the main example presented here, there are seven allowable portfolio weights: −$3 MM, −$2 MM, −$1 MM, 0, $1 MM, $2 MM, and $3 MM. This limits the number of iterations and resulting computations from, potentially, infinity, to $7^2 = 49$.

Alexander (1999) notes that correlation and volatility are not sufficient to ensure long-term portfolio stability; both correlation and volatility are typically computed using short-term returns, which only partially reflect dynamics in prices and necessitate frequent portfolio rebalancing. Instead, Alexander (1999) suggests that in portfolio optimization more attention should be paid to cointegration of constituent strategies. Auxiliary securities, such as options and futures, can be added into the portfolio mix based on cointegration analysis to further strengthen the risk-return characteristics of the trading operation. The cointegration-enhanced portfolios can work particularly well in trading operations that are tasked with outperforming specific financial benchmarks.

Genetic Algorithms   *Genetic algorithms* "learn" from past forecasts via the so-called Bayesian approach. Specifically, the Bayesian self-correction model compares the realized performance of portfolio with forecasted values, and adjusts future forecasts on the basis of errors retrieved from the comparison. Bayesian methodology continuously recalculates the trajectory of prices of portfolio instruments and updates the optimal portfolio weights. In many cases, genetic algorithms adjust, but do not fully recalculate portfolio weights, saving considerable computational time.

In the Bayesian approach, the average return estimate of a particular security is considered to be a random variable and is viewed probabilistically in the context of previously obtained information, or priors. All expectations are subsequently developed with respect to the distribution obtained for the estimate. Multiple priors, potentially representing multiple investors or analysts, increase the accuracy of the distribution for the estimate.

Under the Bayesian specification, all mean and variance-covariance estimates are associated with a confidence interval that measures the accuracy of the forecast. An accurate forecast has a tight confidence interval, while the inaccurate forecast has a wide confidence interval. After the accuracy of the previous forecast has been determined, the portfolio weight of a security is scaled depending on the width of the confidence intervals of these securities. The wider the confidence intervals for parameter estimates, the smaller is the portfolio weight for that security. When the confidence intervals approach zero, the weights are similar to those of the classic mean-variance optimization.

The traditional Bayesian approach, applied to mean-variance optimization by Jorion (1986), works as follows: both mean and variance estimates of a portfolio computed on a contemporary data sample are adjusted by lessons gleaned from historical (prior) observations.

The dispersion of the distributions of the true mean and variance of the distributions shrinks as more observations are collected and analyzed with time. If $R_{p,t}$ is the portfolio return following the mean-variance optimization of equation (7) from time $t-1$ to time t, and $\hat{E}[R_{i,t}]$ is the average return estimate for security i,

$\hat{E}[R_{i,t}]=\dfrac{1}{t}\sum_{\tau=1}^{t}R_{i,\tau}$, the "Bayes-Stein shrinkage estimators" for expected return and variance of an individual security i to be used in the mean-variance optimization for the next period $t+1$, are computed as follows:

$$E[R_{i,t+1}]_{BS}=(1-\phi_{i,BS})\hat{E}[R_{i,t}]+\phi_{i,BS}R_{p,t}$$

$$V[R_{i,t+1}]_{BS}=V[R_{i,t}]\left[1+\dfrac{1}{t+v}\right]+\dfrac{v}{t(t+1+v)}V[R_{i,t}]$$

where v is the precision of the mean estimates: $v=\dfrac{(N-2)}{t}\dfrac{V[R_{i,t}]}{(R_{p,t}-\hat{E}[R_{i,t}])^{2}}$,

N is the number of observations in the sample at time t, and ϕ_{BS} is the shrinkage factor for the mean: $\phi_{BS}=\dfrac{v}{t+v}$. The case of zero precision ($v=0$) corresponds to completely diffuse estimates.

Despite the computational complexities of high-frequency hedging, HFT hedging can be very effective due to the following feature of high-frequency data: low correlations between any two financial instruments. Figure 14.6 illustrates the point with empirical correlations observed on the S&P 500 ETF and iShares MSCI Index (EFA). Trade correlations are particularly low, just 3 percent when the data is sampled every 45 seconds, and decrease to zero as data sampling frequency increases to 200 ms. Quote correlations are much higher, around 30 percent when sampled every 45 seconds. The quote correlations also decrease dramatically with sampling frequency, to about 7 percent with 200-ms sampling. Relatively higher correlations of quote data may illuminate relative informativeness of tick data: quote data likely reflects market makers' information unavailable in trade data. The daily close

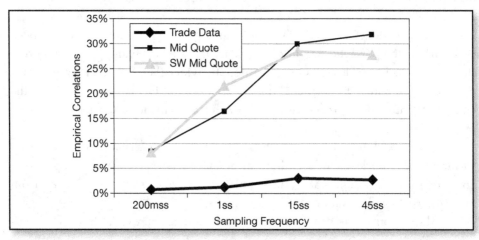

FIGURE 14.6 Correlations in High-Frequency Data.
Source: Aldridge (2010).

correlation of the Standard & Poor's (S&P) 500 ETF and iShares MSCI Index (EFA) often reaches 65 percent.

Liquidity Risk

Liquidity risk may affect high-frequency traders during the normal intraday trading or during the end-of-day liquidation. Liquidity risk measures the firm's potential inability to unwind or hedge positions in a timely manner at current market prices. The inability to close out positions is normally due to low levels of market liquidity relative to the position size. The lower the market liquidity available for a specific instrument, the higher the liquidity risk associated with that instrument. Levels of liquidity vary from instrument to instrument and depend on the number of market participants willing to transact in the instrument under consideration. Bervas (2006) further suggests the distinction between the trading liquidity risk and the balance sheet liquidity risk, the latter being the inability to finance the shortfall in the balance sheet either through liquidation or borrowing.

In mild cases, liquidity risk can result in minor price slippages due to the delay in trade execution and can cause collapses of market systems in its extreme. For example, the collapse of Long-Term Capital Management (LTCM) in 1998 can be attributed to the firm's inability to promptly offload its holdings.

To properly assess the liquidity risk exposure of a portfolio, it is necessary to take into account all potential portfolio liquidation costs, including the opportunity costs associated with any delays in execution. While liquidation costs are stable and are easy to estimate during periods with little volatility, the liquidation costs can vary wildly during high-volatility regimes. Bangia et al. (1999), for example, document that liquidity risk accounted for 17 percent of the market risk in long USD/THB positions in May 1997, and Le Saout (2002) estimates that liquidity risk can reach over 50 percent of total risk on selected securities in CAC40 stocks.

Bervas (2006) proposes the following measure of liquidity risk:

$$VaR^l = VaR + Liquidity\ Adjustment = VaR - (\mu^S + z_\alpha \sigma^S) \qquad (7)$$

where VaR is the market risk value-at-risk discussed previously in this chapter, μ^S is the mean expected bid-ask spread, σ^S is the standard deviation of the bid-ask spread, and z_α is the confidence coefficient corresponding to the desired α–percent of the VaR estimation. Both μ^S and σ^S can be estimated either from raw spread data or from the Roll (1984) model.

Using Kyle's λ measure, the VaR liquidity adjustment can be similarly computed through estimation of the mean and standard deviation of the trade volume:

$$VaR^l = VaR + Liquidity\ Adjustment = VaR - (\hat{\alpha} + \hat{\lambda}(\mu^{NVOL} + z_\alpha \sigma^{NVOL})) \qquad (8)$$

where $\hat{\alpha}$ and $\hat{\lambda}$ are estimated using OLS regression following Kyle (1985):

$$\Delta P_t = \alpha + \lambda NVOL_t + \varepsilon_t \qquad (9)$$

ΔP_t is the change in market price due to market impact of orders, and $NVOL_t$ is the difference between the buy and sell market depths in period t.

Hasbrouck (2005) finds that the Amihud (2002) illiquidity measure best indicates the impact of volume on prices. Similar to Kyle's λ adjustment to VaR, the Amihud (2002) adjustment can be applied as follows:

$$VaR^l = VaR + Liquidity\ Adjustment = VaR - (\mu^\gamma + z_\alpha \sigma^\gamma) \quad (10)$$

where μ^γ and σ^γ are the mean and standard deviation of the Amihud (2002) illiquidity measure γ, $\gamma_t = \dfrac{1}{D_t} \sum_{d=1}^{D_t} \dfrac{|r_{d,t}|}{v_{d,t}}$, D_t is the number of trades executed during time period t, $r_{d,t}$ is the relative price change following trade d during trade period t, and $v_{d,t}$ is the trade quantity executed within trade d.

The liquidity risk also applies in multiasset HFT upon entering positions. When the strategy calls for simultaneous acquisition of multiple instruments via limit orders, the less liquid instruments may compromise the strategy as they may be difficult to acquire. In such cases, the limit orders for the illiquid instruments are sent first; if executed, orders for the liquid instruments are placed.

■ Summary

Competent risk management protects deployed capital, reduces risk and often enhances overall performance of high-frequency strategies. The risk management framework of HFT should take into account all aspects of HFT operation, including HFT suppliers and the government.

■ End-of-Chapter Questions

1. What are the key types of risk faced by a high-frequency trading operation?
2. How to measure and mitigate market risk?
3. What is the credit and counterparty risk from a high-frequency trading perspective?
4. What are the key problems in high-frequency portfolio optimization?
5. What is liquidity risk? How to measure it?

CHAPTER 15

Minimizing Market Impact

Algorithmic execution, also known as *algo execution* or *smart order routing*, refers to a set of programmatic computer methodologies used to determine the optimal way to parcel and execute an order. An ideal execution algo would consistently execute the customer's buy order at the lowest price available during a given period of time and transmit the sell when the price is at its peak, delivering "best execution." Given the difficulties of precisely pinpointing the price lows and the highs within a period of time, a good algo produces a certain price improvement according to prespecified optimality conditions. The optimality conditions may be based on the trader's risk aversion, concurrent market state, the benchmark chosen by the trader, and a range of other features, discussed in detail for the remainder of this part of the book. The execution algorithms can be built "in-house" by a buy-side trader, purchased "off-the-shelf" from the algorithm provider, or licensed on a one-off execution basis from the trader's broker. The brokers may provide algos for a commission or in exchange for a portion of the cost savings delivered by the algorithm relative to some executional benchmark.

Algo execution evolved naturally from human-driven best execution practice. For decades, brokers competed for client order flow by promising unique ability to pinpoint market highs and lows, and to negotiate preferred terms for the clients. Algorithmic execution builds on the human broker practice in developing an automated human-free approach.

From the point of view of classical finance and the quantitative portfolio management, best execution algorithms exist to smooth out natural market imperfections.

■ Why Execution Algorithms?

Execution algorithms have become essential for all investors, as execution algos help traders accumulate or liquidate large positions by breaking up orders into pieces, and reducing market impact and visibility of orders. To avoid being "picked off" in

245

the markets, algos deploying limit orders cancel many of the orders when the orders fail to execute. The orders are then resubmitted almost immediately, often at a price closer to the market.

Different algorithms have been shown to substantially lower execution costs, in different ways. Execution costs comprise exchange and broker-dealer fees, bid-ask spread, opportunity cost associated with nonexecution of a limit order, and market impact (MI), to name a few. According to Engle, Russell, and Ferstenberg (2007), for example, the costs delivered by an algorithm depend on the level of order aggressiveness the algo produces: passive orders "save" investor capital by avoiding the spread, yet may aggravate costs whenever passive orders fail to execute. Other design aspects of the algo, such as the timing of the order parcels and size of each parcel relative to the market depth, also impact the obtained execution costs.

In addition to net execution costs, traders may consider the costs associated with the risk of the algorithms. The risk of nonexecution can be the largest risk component in algorithmic execution, but can be minimized with market orders at the expense of higher execution costs, resulting from crossing the spread, higher MI, transaction costs, and so on. Other risk metrics used in algo execution may include variability of the execution price of order slices, and value-at-risk (VaR) measure designed to contain execution costs below certain maximum limit.

To compare the performance of several algorithms, Almgren and Chriss (2000) proposed the concept of an efficient trading frontier. Like the efficient markets frontier developed in the framework of the capital asset pricing model (CAPM), the efficient trading frontier provides a convenient graphical representation of performance of various execution algorithms per unit of risk incurred by each algorithm. A sample efficient trading frontier is shown in Figure 15.1. Analytically, it can be described as in equation (1):

$$\min \; Cost(\alpha) + \lambda Risk(\alpha) \qquad (1)$$

where

- α is a measure of order aggressiveness, for example, counting the number of ticks away from the market each child order is placed.

- $Cost(\alpha)$ is the aggregate expected execution cost, including expected market impact, for all child orders of the strategy executed at the aggressiveness level α.

- $Risk(\alpha)$ is the cumulative risk associated with all the child orders placed at aggressiveness level α.

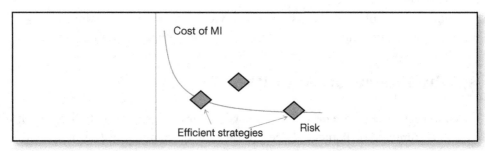

FIGURE 15.1 Illustration of the Efficient Trading Frontier

- λ is the degree of risk aversion, specific to the trader. A risk aversion level $\lambda=0$ indicates a trader who does not care about the execution risk. A risk aversion level $\lambda=0.5$ indicates a fairly risk-averse trader.

Order-Routing Algorithms

Order-routing algorithms are designed to seamlessly navigate various issues differences between securities markets and deliver investors a cost-effective execution schedule that would fit the investors' risk profile. As such, the order-routing algorithms target the following objectives:

- Minimize execution costs

- Obtain best price

- Maximize execution speed

- Maximize trading size

- Minimize trade footprint

To minimize costs, algorithms select appropriate venues and market conditions. Venue selection can reduce the fee structure, and picking the right time to execute a trade can pick periods of low bid-ask spreads, and help reduce or eliminate slippage and subsequent market impact (more on these later). To obtain best price, sophisticated algorithms perform short-term forecasting to ensure the sell orders are processed during times with higher market prices and vice versa. To maximize the execution speed for clients desiring to capture present market conditions, the algos seek venues with appropriate market participation and minimal trade impact. To maximize trading size and minimize trade footprint, the algos slice the order into a series of smaller parcels or "child orders," all according to the latest scientific advances and investor's preferences. Large trading size can be particularly important to funds with large positions or strategy capacity. Minimal footprint of the trade ensures minimal detection of the order by outside parties, and helps thwart traders attempting to infer the informational content of orders.

Performance of execution algorithms is typically measured relative to some benchmarks. A benchmark may be the closing price observed at the end of the trading day, an average of the daily open, high, low, and close prices, the daily open, or other, more complex metrics, such as several commonly used execution algorithms.

Algorithmic benchmarks and the daily close are most common algo benchmarks. The daily close is an easy reference for any investor building his forecasting models on daily data, as is often the case with low-frequency quantitative modelers. Daily data analysis is nearly always performed on daily closing prices, and the developed forecasts usually predict future daily closes, too. As a result, algos that consistently outperform the daily close are in high demand by traders of daily close–based models, who are willing to pay a portion of their execution algo-induced gains to the algorithm provider.

Yet the betterment of the closing price is notoriously difficult to achieve. Unlike other benchmarks, closing prices are not at all known in advance, and the only way to approximate them ahead of time is to deploy short-term price-forecasting models. Short-term forecasting utilizes the high-frequency trading models discussed in Chapters 8-11, and requires thorough understanding of the complexities of HFT modeling. is difficult As a consequence, traders often deploy other common algorithms as suitable algo performance benchmarks.

The following sections discuss each of the objectives of algo execution in detail.

Minimize Execution Costs

Trading costs comprise several major components:

■ Broker commissions, both fixed and variable

■ Exchange fees

■ Taxes

■ Bid-ask spread

■ Slippage

■ Opportunity cost

■ Market impact

Obtain Best Price

The core principle of the best price trading is "buy low, sell high." Due to the natural price moves, the direction of the price can be difficult to predict, and advanced short-term forecasting models are required for the purpose.

The best price execution is further complicated by additional factors. Consider the following example. It is 9:30 a.m., and a client wants to buy 10,000 shares of IBM at most at the closing price recorded at 4:00 p.m. later that day. The naturally arising issues create the following questions:

■ Given the market uncertainty, what will the execution price be at 4:00 p.m. that day?

■ The client's desired execution size is considerably bigger than normal trading size. Should the order be broken into smaller parcels? If so, how should the order be split?

■ If the client's 10,000-share order is broken into smaller child orders, how frequently are the child orders executed?

■ Each buy trade (sell trade) will deplete some of the liquidity on the offer side (bid side). The resulting liquidity gaps will lead to adverse prices for subsequent child orders. Can this effect, known as market impact, be eliminated or minimized?

■ Other market participants may observe trading footprint of the client, and decide to trade in the same direction, further moving the price in an adverse direction. Can the trading footprint be minimized?

Maximize Execution Speed

Fast execution helps capture current market conditions. Market orders can be executed most rapidly in the most liquid markets. To maximize the speed of execution of market orders, therefore, investors may poll various exchanges for their available liquidity, and send their orders to the exchange with the most liquidity first. Limit orders, however, are executed most rapidly in the least liquid conditions. As a result, limit orders are best executed on the markets with the fewest limit orders available. Figure 15.2 illustrates a sample process of polling multiple exchanges for their liquidity levels and selecting the proper exchange for a given order or order slice.

In the example shown in Figure 15.2, there are three exchanges: Exchange 1 has available bid-side liquidity of 2,000 trading units (shares, contracts, and so on, available at the best bid); Exchange 2 has liquidity of 3,000 units; and Exchange 3 has available liquidity off 500 units only. To minimize his trading footprint, a trader placing market sell orders would first go to Exchange 2 and place an order for 3,000 or fewer units there. Placing an order equal to or smaller than the top-of-the book matching liquidity available at the exchange ensures that the market order does not move or only slightly moves the market, leaving little or no footprint.

After exhausting the top-of-the-book liquidity on Exchange 2, the market order trader would turn to the next most liquid exchange: in our example, this is Exchange 1, with the top-of-the-book bid-side liquidity equal to 2,000 units. The trader would then place his order on Exchange 1 for 2,000 units or less, and then proceed to Exchange 3 and trade against the available liquidity there.

A trader desiring to execute limit buy orders, however, would first place a limit order with Exchange 3, as that exchange has the lowest aggregate size of buy limit orders available at the best bid. The trader next would place a limit buy order at Exchange 1, the exchange with the next lowest number of aggregate limit buy orders available at the top of the book. At this point, the limit order trader may or may not proceed to place a buy limit order at Exchange 2, currently the most competitive exchange for buy limit orders.

The underlying rationale for selection of the exchange is this: place limit orders wherever the limit orders are fewest, and place market orders wherever the limit

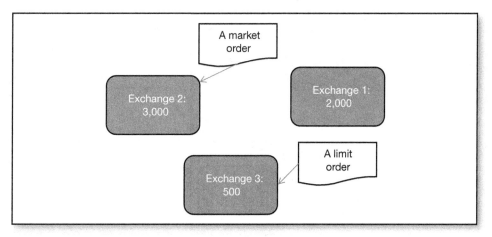

FIGURE 15.2   Maximizing Execution Speed

orders are most numerous. Such process ensures that the orders have the highest probability of fast execution. The process is known as the minimal impact algorithm.

Minimize Footprint

In addition to maximizing execution speed, the MI algorithm can be used to minimize trading footprint, or the disturbance registered in the markets following an order. The exact causes of the disturbance are discussed in Chapter 5. The intuition behind the disturbance can be explained as follows: every order is a credible signal as it reveals the trader's true beliefs committed to trader's capital. As a result, every order carries information about the current views of the trader. Other market participants may desire to trade on these views as well, without necessarily knowing the information content beyond the observed action of placing an order. In such situations, placing child orders of sizes comparable to the sizes available at the best bid or offer at different exchanges minimizes the resulting change in market quotes, and reveals the least information associated with each order slice.

Maximize Trading Size

The ability to process large trading volume is critical to investors deploying sizable capital in their strategies. For example, a large pension fund needs to be able to buy and sell large quantities of securities without incurring much additional cost in order to successfully reallocate pension fund's positions. To maximize the trading size, the large trader may use a combination of market and limit orders in processing each individual order. To do so, a trader seeking to execute a large buy order may first exhaust the top-of-the-book ask liquidity on all accessible markets by sequentially polling for the best ask size available, and placing the market buy orders matching or smaller than the best ask liquidity at each exchange, beginning with the most liquid one. Subsequently, the trader may switch to limit orders and increase the bid-side

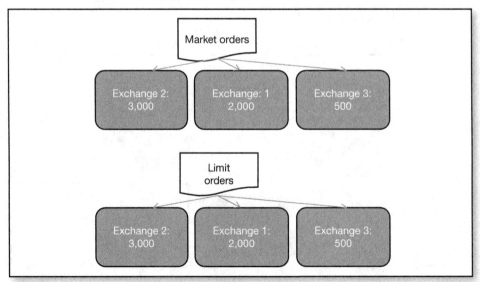

FIGURE 15.3   Maximizing Trading Size Implementation of Execution Algorithms

liquidity by placing the best top-of-the-book buy orders at all the exchanges, beginning with the least liquid and rotating among the exchanges in the direction of increasing bid-liquidity. Figure 15.3 illustrates such strategy.

Most researchers develop execution algorithms in the following sequence:

1. Researchers explore published and not-yet-published academic research in the area of optimal execution algorithm design and implementation. Some traders may be skeptical of using publicly available research, fearing that all known research has been arbitraged in the markets. In reality, a change in parameterization of the algorithm may result in an algo with an entirely different, yet still valuable, output.
2. The researchers model the algorithm in econometric languages such as MatLab or R and, as a result, transition their code to faster programming languages like C++ or optimized Java.
3. The algorithm is tested on historical tick data utilizing assumptions and predictions about price movement generated by the algorithms, own orders.
4. If the previous step results in a satisfactory execution schedule and price, cost, and risk outcome, the algorithm is moved into production, where it is enabled to communicate in real time using quote-receiving and -sending languages such as FIX, ITCH, OUCH, FAST, and the like.

Slicing large orders is imperative: research of Chan and Lakonishok (1995), for example, shows that if a typical institutional trade size were executed all at once, it would account for about 60 percent of the daily trading volume, making simultaneous execution of the order expensive and difficult, if not impossible. The smaller "child" orders are then executed one slice at a time over a certain time period.

According to Gatheral, Schied, and Slynko (2012), algorithmic execution can be broken down into three distinct layers, as shown in Figure 15.4. The first layer, called the *macro trader,* allows us to answer the following questions:

- How to slice the order: What is the general rule behind the algo's order slicing mechanism?

- When the algo should trade: How frequently and at what time of the day should be algo initiate its child trades?

- In what size the algo should trade: How large should each child order be?

- For how long the algo should trade: What is the horizon of the algo? When does the algo stop?

The second layer, which can be described as the *micro trader,* defines additional properties for each child order. In particular, the micro trader is responsible for deciding whether to execute the child order as a limit or market order, and, for limit orders, what price to set.

Finally, the *smart order router* decides to which venues to send the child orders.

Over the past two years, significant progress has been made in developing mathematical solutions for best execution. The decisions of the macro trader, the micro

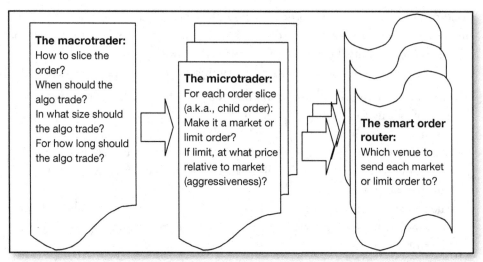

FIGURE 15.4 Layers of Algorithmic Execution
Source: Gatheral, Schied and Slynko (2012)

trader, and the smart order router can all be tailored with great precision to the given market conditions. Optimal execution solutions can be classified into static and dynamic strategy groups. A static strategy is completely determined ahead of trading: it is based on past market conditions. A volume-weighted average price (VWAP) is an example of a static strategy. In contrast, a dynamic strategy is determined and refined during the course of execution. As such, dynamic strategies depend on contemporary market conditions. A simple delta hedge is an example of a dynamic strategy. At first glance, dynamic strategies may seem to always outperform static strategies, since dynamic strategies respond to current market conditions and static strategies do not. In reality, certain static strategies perform well, but only under specific market assumptions.

The performance of both static and dynamic strategies is often compared using benchmarks, for example, the following simple metrics:

- Average realized price compares the actual prices per unit traded received under different algos:

$$\bar{P} = \frac{1}{\sum_j V_j} \sum_j V_j P_j \ \forall \ j \in J \tag{2}$$

  where P_j is the realized price for slice or child order j, and V_j is the size of child order j.
- Pretrade price P_0 is the market price prevailing at the time the order j was placed.
- Posttrade price $P_{j,post}$ is the price of the security after the temporary liquidity effects, induced by trading stream, have disappeared. To identify $P_{j,post}$, Almgren et al. (2005) regress ΔP_t on Δt, and pinpoint the time Δt_{post} when dependency of ΔP_t on Δt ceases to be statistically significant. Then, the price P recorded at t_{post} is the $P_{j,post}$.

- Total trade size $V=\Sigma V_j$ allows comparison of algorithms used to process large trading volumes relative to available liquidity. In such conditions, some algorithms may perform better than others.

- Similarly, volume-adjusted trade size V/V_{Daily}, where V_{Daily} is the total trading volume on a particular day, allows comparison of algorithms' ability to take advantage of available liquidity.

In addition, common benchmarks for evaluating performance of execution algos include other common execution algos, such as time-weighted average price (TWAP), percentage of volume (POV), MI, VWAP, implementations shortfall, and various intraday price benchmarks, discussed in subsequent sections of this chapter.

According to Kissell and Glantz (2005), order execution benchmarks can be grouped into three broad categories: pretrade, intratrade, and posttrade. Table 15.1 summarizes this classification. The pretrade category includes benchmarks known ahead of execution, such as:

- Trading decision price, the price at which the trader or portfolio manager decided was advantageous for trading.

- Previous day's close price, which can be used as a benchmark for traders working with daily.

- Daily open price.

- Arrival price, the price that was prevalent when the executing broker received the order.

The intratrade category includes the following benchmarks:

- VWAP, determined using intraday prices.

- TWAP, also determined on the basis of prices throughout the day.

- The average of daily open, high, low, and close prices (OHLC)

The posttrade category includes the future close, the price not known in advance.

TWAP

TWAP attempts to conceal the order flow by breaking a large order into equally sized parcels, which are then sent out at equally spaced time intervals. Mathematically, TWAP executes a fixed portion $1/T$ of the order every predetermined unit of

TABLE 15.1 Order Execution Benchmarks		
Pretrade	Intratrade	Posttrade
Decision price	VWAP	Future close
Previous close	TWAP	
Opening price	OHLC	
Arrival price		

Source: Kissel and Glantz (2005)

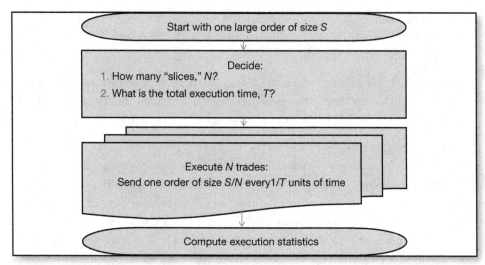

FIGURE 15.5 TWAP Process

time. The resulting TWAP price is the arithmetic average of prices sampled at the regular unit time intervals:

$$TWAP = \frac{1}{T} \sum_{1}^{T} Pt \qquad (3)$$

The TWAP algorithm is illustrated in Figure 15.5. When a trader chooses to execute a large order of size S using TWAP, the trader also needs to decide on the total number N of child orders or slices to execute, and the total execution time T. Next, an order slice of size S/N is sent to the market every T/N seconds, until the entire order of size S is processed. The total number of slices N and the execution time T are best determined using characteristics specific to the traded security. These characteristics may include historical variation in volume throughout the trading day, market depth at the beginning of execution, and a host of other variables. The overarching objective is to select slices small enough so that each child order does not significantly move the market, yet large or frequent enough so that the entire large order can be executed within a reasonable time T. The resulting TWAP order flow can be represented as in Figure 15.6, with each child order drawn as an arrow.

VWAP

The VWAP algorithm is currently one of the most popular execution methodologies. The principle of VWAP is straightforward: break up a large order in such a way that

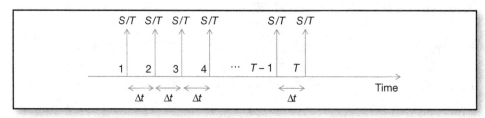

FIGURE 15.6 Diagram of Resulting TWAP Order Flow

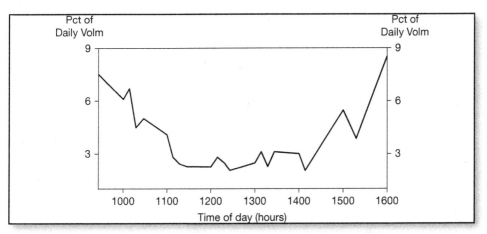

FIGURE 15.7 Map of Historical Volume Averages for Futures
Source: Almgren and Chriss (2000)

VWAP child orders are larger when the trading volume is higher, and child orders are smaller when trading volume is lower. Higher trading volume is likely to provide larger pool of matching orders and result in faster and more cost-effective execution.

To determine the execution schedule, the VWAP algorithm uses a map of historical averages of intraday volume variations, such as the one shown for equities in Figure 15.7. The map is often computed using preceding month of trading data: for every 15-minute (or other duration) interval of the trading day, the VWAP map shows the average volume over the past trading month. With the VWAP map in hand, the sizes of the child orders are determined as follows: for every trading period throughout the day, the total order size S is scaled by the VWAP proportion of volume historically observed during that time period, as shown in equation (3). Figure 15.8 diagrams the VWAP algorithm.

$$s_t = S \frac{\overline{V}_t}{\sum_{\tau \in T} \overline{V}_\tau} \qquad (4)$$

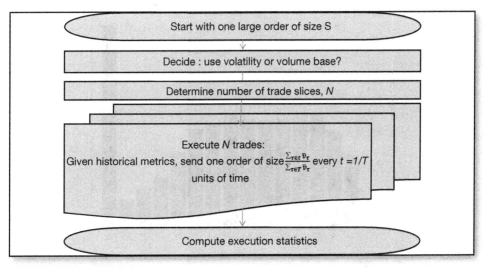

FIGURE 15.8 VWAP Process

The resulting benchmark VWAP price can be determined as follows:

$$VWAP = \frac{\sum_{\tau \in T} \overline{V}_\tau P_\tau}{\sum_{\tau \in T} \overline{V}_\tau} \tag{5}$$

The VWAP map is based solely on historical data and does not accurately reflect concurrent market conditions. Even so, on average, a VWAP algorithm can deliver an allocation of child orders that efficiently utilizes the intraday liquidity. Such relative success of VWAP is based on persistence of the intraday volume patterns: specific markets possess their own intraday volume variations that change little from one month to the next. For example, Figure 15.9 illustrates the hourly VWAP map for Eurobund futures, computed using data for April 2009 and April 2010. While the average hourly trading volumes in the Eurobund futures have grown from 2009 to

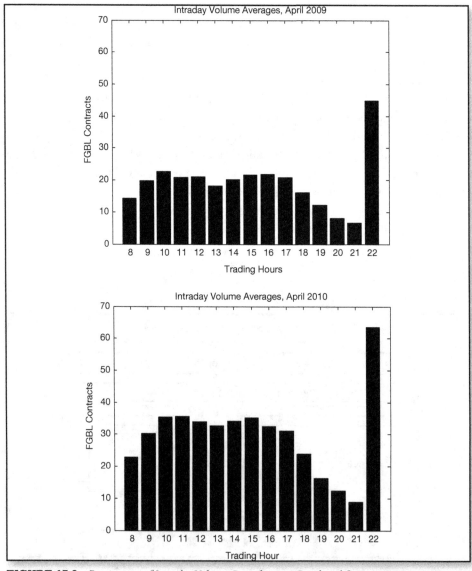

FIGURE 15.9   Persistence of Intraday Volume Distribution, Eurobund futures (FGBL) POV

2010, the shape of the VWAP map remained largely the same: an uptick in volume at the open of the European and the U.S. trading sessions, followed by a lull post–U.S. lunchtime, followed by a spike of activity at the market close.

According to the joint U.S. Commodity Futures Trading Commission (CFTC) and Securities and Exchange Commission (SEC) report on the causes of the flash crash (2010), it was the POV algorithm that created the mayhem in the markets on May 6, 2010. The examination discovered that the significant volatility in market prices first started to occur when "a large fundamental trader" initiated a trade of $4.1 billion of E-minis with POV set at 9 percent of volume over the previous minute.

Figure 15.10 illustrates the algorithm behind the POV. Like TWAP and VWAP, the POV algorithm sends child orders at regular time intervals. Unlike TWAP and VWAP, the size of each POV child order is determined dynamically and set to a fixed percentage of the trading volume recorded during a previous predefined period of time, for example, 10 minutes. The execution next continues until the entire large order is processed. The previous period's trading volume used in calculation of POV child order should exclude the volume generated by the POV trader himself:

$$S_{POV,t} = (V_{t-1} - S_{POV,t-1})(POV) \tag{6}$$

While the joint SEC and CFTC report did not mention whether the POV algorithm used by the large fundamental trader accounted for the volume generated by the trader himself, failure to account for his own volume would generate exponentially increasing child orders, and could have caused the crisis of flash crash proportions.

When properly programmed, POV has one distinct advantage over TWAP and VWAP: POV dynamically adjusts to present market conditions, instantaneously responding to such events as shifts in liquidity.

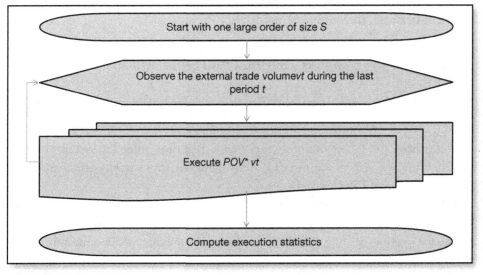

FIGURE 15.10 POV Process

Issues with Basic Models

TWAP, VWAP, and POV execution models discussed in the previous sections were developed in the 1990s and are still widely popular, but suffer from serious shortcomings:

1. These models can be shown to be optimal only in specific, not-very-common market conditions.
2. The models are easy to spot with advanced mathematical tools.

Optimality Conditions for Earlier Models

Under limited assumptions about market dynamics, like martingale pricing or arithmetic Brownian motion (ABM), TWAP, and VWAP can be shown to be optimal. Both martingales and ABM, however, assume that the market does not trend, a hardly realistic condition. One can also show that VWAP is optimal in rapidly trending markets, where the trend completely dominates short-term noise-induced volatility.

In most market conditions where both the trend and the volatility are sizable, however, these models lose their optimality. The later sections of this chapter describe the latest advanced execution models applicable to most market conditions.

Security of Earlier Models

Popular models like TWAP, VWAP, and POV also lack security. The models' primary mission is to break up and hide the order flow in general markets. Due to the regular nature of the child orders these strategies send, their child orders can be surprisingly easy to spot with simple tools like autocorrelation and advanced tools like Fourier analysis.

TWAP, for example, does little to hide the order flow from anyone familiar with the basics of digital signal processing, a core study of electrical engineering that is often deployed to remedy scratched CDs. As shown in Figure 15.6, TWAP comprises the regularly spaced orders of identical size. To detect market TWAP orders in the stream of tick data, therefore, one needs to:

1. Tag all recent market trade tick data as either buys and sells as discussed in Chapter 4.
2. Separate all buy trade ticks into virtual "buckets" by trade size; do the same for sell ticks.
3. Within each bucket, identify trades that occurred at identical time intervals from one another.

This process can be continuously repeated in real time, allowing systems to predict the time and size of the next TWAP installment, and thereby eliminating the original purpose of TWAP orders.

VWAP may seem more secure as the trades are not uniform in size; instead, the VWAP trades are scaled by the time-specific trade volume or volatility observed during the previous trading day or averaged over the previous week or month. While such scaling may appear to prevent reverse-engineering of VWAP order flow, in reality, VWAP flow can be just as transparent as TWAP.

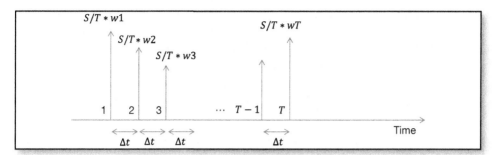

FIGURE 15.11 Sample VWAP Order Flow in Equities

To see the limitations of security VWAP, consider an equity VWAP process as shown in Figure 15.11. Descaling all the trade ticks observed by the same scaling volume or volatility function as the one used in the VWAP-generating process of Figure 15.8 transforms VWAP into TWAP, and subsequently enables TWAP-like identification of the order flow.

VWAP scaling functions used by different traders may differ by the number of days used in averaging either volume or volatility, as well as by the width of time bars over which the intraday averages are computed. Even so, repeating the descaling analysis over the complete order flow several times using different precomputed scaling functions will identify orders sent in with a given scaling function.

The order flow sent via POV algorithms can be similarly identified. Regular spacing of orders, coupled with predictable functional form of order sizes, gives away the order flow. In the case of POV, the functional form of order flow is dependent on the volume executed during the time elapsed since the previous POV order.

In response to such security issues, some market participants and broker-dealers randomize sizes and timing of orders to reduce transparency of the basic algos. While the randomization may restrict other market participants' ability to observe the order flow with the basic methodology described earlier, the orders will still be traceable with advanced digital signal processing techniques, such as Fourier analysis.

Fourier analysis is often used to identify repetitive signals "buried" in the noise. Digital Fourier analysis models are routinely used to restore scratched music CDs or to "correct" the slightly off-key voice of pop singers. Likewise, Fourier analysis can be used to detect slightly randomized order flow of basic algorithms.

The key concept in Fourier analysis is Fourier transform, a mathematical construct connecting time and frequency domains. Continuous (as opposed to digital) forms of the Fourier transform are specified as follows:

$$f(x) = \int_{-\infty}^{\infty} F(k)e^{2\pi i k x}\,dk \tag{7}$$

$$F(k) = \int_{-\infty}^{\infty} f(x)e^{-2\pi i k x}\,dx \tag{8}$$

where x represents a time-based variable, and $F(k)$ is a frequency-domain function. Figures 15.12 through 15.15 illustrate the capabilities of Fourier analysis.

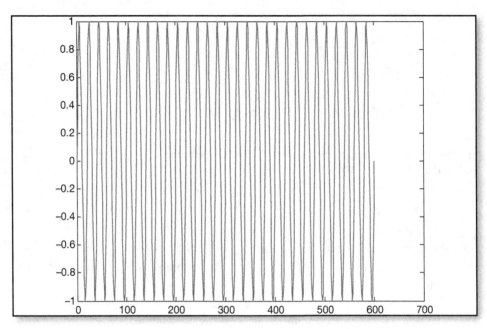

FIGURE 15.12   Sample Recurrent Process

Figure 15.12 shows a simple continuous cyclical process that can be generated by a time-dependent sinusoid function with frequency of 50 Hz (hertz, or repetition of 50 cycles per second). Figure 15.13 shows the same process transformed with Fourier analysis. The perfectly repeating cycles in time domain become a single clear spike in frequency domain. Furthermore, the spike falls directly onto the frequency of the cycles: 50 Hz.

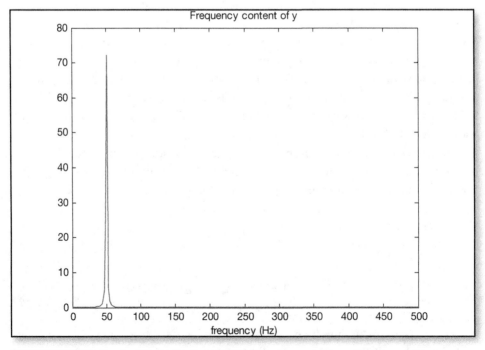

FIGURE 15.13   Fourier Representation of the Process Shown in Figure 15.12

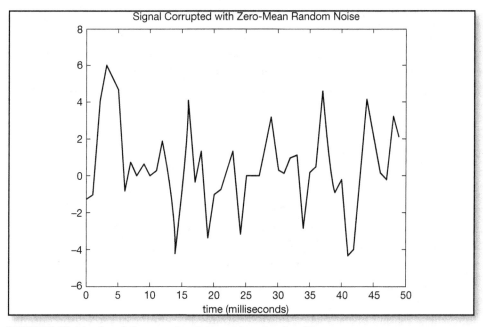

FIGURE 15.14 Signal Corrupted with Zero-Mean Random Noise

Figure 15.14 shows a different time-based function: two sinusoids generated at 50 Hz and 120 Hz corrupted by noise. The noise may represent a random stream of data, such as other traders' orders mixed in with the TWAP or VWAP. The cycles in Figure 15.14 are hard to identify just by eyeballing the chart. However, a pass through the Fourier transform delivers a clear representation of the periodicity,

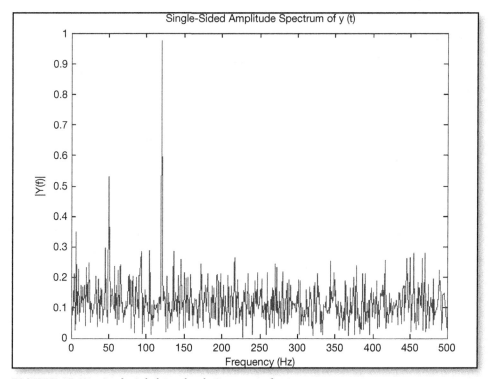

FIGURE 15.15 Single-Sided Amplitude Spectrum of $y(t)$

shown in Figure 15.15: clear peaks at 50 Hz and 120 Hz dominate the frequency domain of this example. Similar ideas extend to identification of periodic order flow in the sea of "noise" orders, placing the usefulness of TWAP and VWAP into question.

Over the past few years, advanced models have been developed to overcome issues embedded in TWAP, VWAP, and POV algorithms. The latest algorithms are discussed in the next section.

■ Advanced Models

To use realistic market assumptions and to avoid transparency of order flow induced by the basic TWAP, VWAP, and POV algorithms, researchers have developed advanced models that work under normal market conditions with a mixture of trend and volatility. Under these conditions, it can be shown that the optimal trading strategy is the one that induces a constant rate of order book replenishment.

The order book replenishment refers to the process of repopulation of the book following a market order. Figure 15.16 illustrates an example of replenishment in a limit order book.

Stylized replenishment function assumes that the order book possesses a "shadow" form, a structure to which the book reverts after some liquidity has been taken away. The shadow order book is assumed to exist independent of the current price level—the shadow book slides up and down the price axis with the movement of the price. The reversion of liquidity in the order book to the book's shadow form is referred to as *resilience* of the book.

The order book's resilience, $h(E_s)$, is a function of the trading process and is specified as follows:

$$E_t = X_t - \int_0^t h(E_s)ds$$

(9)

where E_t is the aggregate size of limit orders available at p ticks away from prevailing market price P at time t, X_t is the aggregate order flow, $E_0 = 0$, and $\Delta X_t = \Delta E_t$ for $0 \leq t \leq T$. The function $h(E_s)$ measures how fast the order book p ticks away from the market recovers following an order of size ΔX_t, and satisfies the following properties:

■ The function is strictly increasing in X, and

■ The function is a locally Lipschitz function on $[0,\infty)$: $|h(x)-h(y)| \leq C|x-y|$ for all x and y, where C is a constant independent of x and y, and the function has a bounded first derivative $\frac{dh}{dX} < \infty$. The trader's execution strategy X measures the amount of the total order still left to be processed in the market. As such, $x_0 = X$ and $x_T = 0$. The trader's rate of trading is defined as

$$v_t = -\frac{\partial x_t}{\partial t}$$

(10)

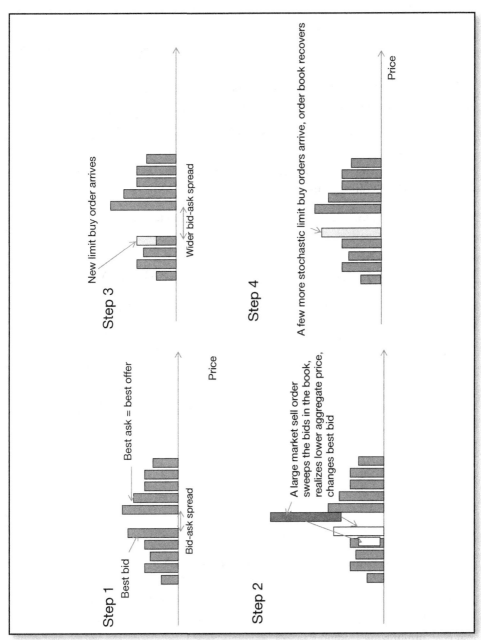

FIGURE 15.16 Replenishment in a Limit Order Book

Price process of the traded instrument, S_t, can be assumed to follow any continuous process. Independent of the shape of the price process S_t, the expected impact inflicted by strategy X on price S can always be measured as cost C:

$$C = \int_0^T S_t dx_t \qquad (11)$$

The expected value of MI cost can be expressed via integration by parts as follows:

$$\mathbb{E}[C] = \mathbb{E}\left[\int_0^T S_t dx_t \right] = \mathbb{E}\left[S_T x_T - S_0 x_0 - \int_0^T x_t dS_t \right] \qquad (12)$$

The most recent stream of research on best execution has focused on developing optimal execution algorithms under the following rigorous assumptions:

1. Geometric Brownian motion, the specification most commonly used in modern asset pricing.
2. Generalized price functions that can be used to describe any empirically observed price evolutions in an MI framework.

This section reviews the latest models developed under the two price evolution models.

When Price Follows Geometric Brownian Motion

Most security pricing models assume that prices follow geometric Brownian motion with price increments dS_t exhibiting dependency on the contemporary price level S_t, as well as incurring drift μ:

$$dS_t = \mu S_t dt + \sigma S_t dZ_t \qquad (13)$$

The vanilla execution cost function, not incorporating any risk optimization measures, can then be specified as follows (see Forsyth et al., 2011):

$$C = \eta \int_0^T v_t^2 dt + \lambda \sigma \int_0^T S_t^2 x_t^2 dt \qquad (14)$$

where, as before, the optimal rate of execution is $v_t = -\dfrac{\partial x_t}{\partial t}$. Under the assumption of geometric Brownian motion, the costs and the resulting optimal solution of the cost minimization problem are dependent on the price of the price path. However, as Forsyth et al. (2011) show, many strategies lead to the almost identical outcome.

Euler-Lagrange equations produce the following closed-form solution for optimal cost-minimizing trading strategy:

$$x_t^* = \frac{T-t}{T}\left[X - \frac{\lambda T}{4} \int_0^t S_u du \right] \qquad (15)$$

The resulting expected minimal cost, $\mathbb{E}[C_{min}(x^*)] = \mathbb{E}[\int_0^T ((v_t^*)^2 + \lambda x_t^* S_t) dt]$ becomes

$$\mathbb{E}\left[C_{min}(x^*)\right] = \frac{X^2}{T} + \frac{\lambda TXS_0}{2} - \frac{\lambda^2}{8\sigma^6} S_0^2 \left(e^{\sigma^2 T} - 1 - \sigma^2 T - \frac{\sigma^4 T^2}{4} \right) \qquad (16)$$

See Forsyth et al. (2011) for derivation.

When Price Follows a Generalized Market Impact–Based Function

While most now-traditional asset-pricing models, such as Black-Scholes, assume Geometric Brownian motion as the model accurately describing evolution of security prices, a new breed of models proposes to model short-term price changes closer to their empirical roots. In such models, the price level at time t is expected to evolve as follows (see Gatheral, 2011):

$$S_t = S_0 + \text{impact of prior trading} + \text{risk (noise)} \qquad (17)$$

where the risk or noise component is the price-level independent $\int_0^t \sigma dZ_s$. The impact of prior trading is quantified using the execution strategy X trading rate dynamics $u_t \equiv -\dfrac{dx}{dt}$ and the function measuring resiliency of the order book $h(E_t)$. The expected execution cost can next be expressed as

$$\mathbb{E}[C] = \frac{1}{2} \int_0^T \int_0^t h(E_s) dX_s dX_t \qquad (18)$$

To minimize expected cost $\mathbb{E}[C]$, one is required to solve the following equation:

$$\frac{\partial}{\partial t} \frac{\partial \mathbb{E}[C]}{\partial u_t} = 0 \qquad (19)$$

which can be interpreted as follows: the optimal value of cost requires cost invariance with trading rate. Since the cost is directly dependent on volume impact E_t, the optimality condition requires that volume impact stays constant:

$$E_t = \text{const} \qquad (20)$$

See Obizaeva and Wang (2005), Alfonsi and Schied (2010), and Gatheral (2011) for details.

Case 1: Exponential Market Resiliency

When the market resiliency can be assumed to follow exponential form, $h(E_t) = e^{-\rho t}$, the equation (20) then can be rewritten as:

$$S_t = S_0 + \eta \int_0^t u_s e^{-\rho(t-s)} ds + \int_0^t \sigma dZ_s \qquad (21)$$

from where the expected execution cost of a trading strategy X can be expressed as

$$\mathbb{E}[C] = \eta \int_0^T u_t \int_0^t e^{-\rho(t-s)} ds\, dt \qquad (22)$$

To derive suitable conditions for E_t, Obizhaeva and Wang (2005) note that E_t can be expressed as

$$E_t = \int_0^t E_{0+} e^{-\rho(t-s)} ds \qquad (23)$$

where E_0 measures the residual impact of trading prior to the chosen time 0. Integration by parts then yields:

$$E_t = E_0 e^{-\rho t} + \rho \int_0^t e^{-\rho(t-s)} ds \qquad (24)$$

Normalizing E_0 by $E_0 = 1$, the optimality condition with constant volume impact becomes

$$E_t = E_0 = 1 \qquad (25)$$

Equation (25) then translates into

$$e^{-\rho t} + \rho \int_0^t e^{-\rho(t-s)} ds = 1 \qquad (26)$$

The original optimality condition for the execution cost [equation (21)] can then be expanded

$$\frac{\partial \mathbb{E}[C]}{\partial u_t} = \eta \int_0^t u_s e^{-\rho(t-s)} ds + \eta \int_t^T u_s e^{-\rho(t-s)} ds = \eta \int_0^T u_s e^{-\rho|t-s|} ds = const \qquad (27)$$

Substituting the volume impact component $\int_0^T u_s e^{-\rho|t-s|} ds$ from equation (27) into equation (26) produces the following result:

$$e^{-\rho t} + \rho \int_0^t e^{-\rho(t-s)} ds = \int_0^T u_s e^{-\rho|t-s|} ds \qquad (28)$$

The optimal trading rate u_t can then be determined as

$$u_t^* = \delta(t) + \rho + \delta(t-T) \qquad (29)$$

Equation (29) can be interpreted as follows: when the market resiliency function can be assumed to be exponential, the optimal execution strategy is composed of:

- A large block trade of size δ at the beginning of execution process.

- A large block trade of size δ at the end of execution horizon, T.

- A continuum of TWAP-like small orders placed at trading rate ρ, where ρ is the parameter in the exponential market resiliency function, $h(E_t) = e^{-\rho t}$.

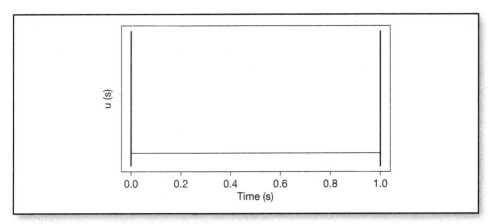

FIGURE 15.17 Optimal Execution in a Market with Linear Permanent Market Impact and Exponential Decay of Temporary Impact
Source: Gatheral, Shied and Slynko (2011)

The resulting optimal execution strategy for $T=1$ and exponential market resiliency with $\rho = 0.1$ is illustrated in Figure 15.17. Figure 15.18 illustrates optimal execution strategies for different trading frequencies.

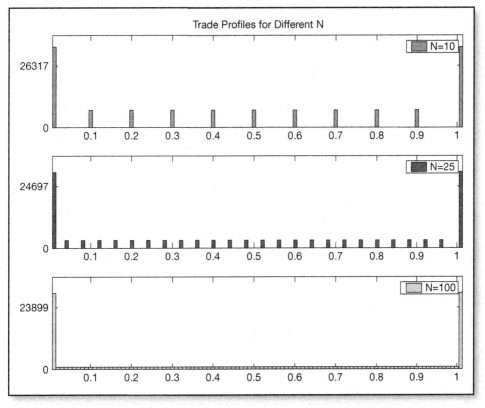

FIGURE 15.18 Optimal Execution with Exponential Resiliency for Different Trading Frequencies
Source: Obizhaeva and Wang (2005)

Case 2: Power-Law Market Resiliency

When the market resiliency can be assumed to fit the power-law function, $h(E_t)=t^{-\gamma}$, the optimal strategy can once again be derived via the constant volume impact requirement, equation (30):

$$E_t = \int_0^T u(s)\,|t-s|^{-\gamma}\,ds = const \tag{30}$$

The optimal trading rate is then

$$u_t{}^* = \delta[t(T-t)]^{-(1-\gamma)/2} \tag{31}$$

with γ representing a parameterized constant from $h(E_t)=t^{-\gamma}$, and δ analytically determined from equation (32):

$$X = \int_0^T u(t)\,dt = \delta\sqrt{\pi}\left(\frac{T}{2}\right)^{\gamma}\frac{\Gamma\left(\dfrac{1+\gamma}{2}\right)}{\Gamma\left(1+\dfrac{\gamma}{2}\right)} \tag{32}$$

where gamma function is defined as $\Gamma(n)=(n-1)!$ for discrete n, and $\Gamma(z)=\int_0^{\infty} e^{-t}t^{z-1}\,dt$ for continuous z. The resulting optimal strategy is continuous with large singular block trades at the beginning and the end of execution times 0 and T. The optimal execution schedule is illustrated in Figure 15.19.

Case 3: Linear Market Resiliency

When the market resiliency fits a straight line until the markets are restored, the market resiliency function is described as $h(E_t)=(1-\rho t)^+$, and the optimal strategy can yet again be deduced via the constant volume impact requirement, equation (33):

$$E_t = \int_0^T u(s)(1-\rho|t-s|)^+\,ds = const \tag{33}$$

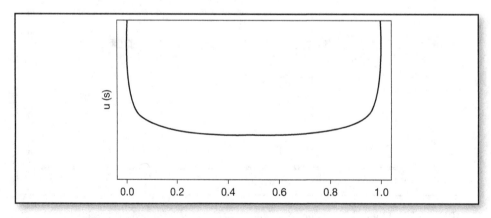

FIGURE 15.19 Optimal Execution in a Market with Linear Permanent Market Impact and Power-Law Decay of Temporary Impact
Source: Gatheral, Shied and Slynko (2011)

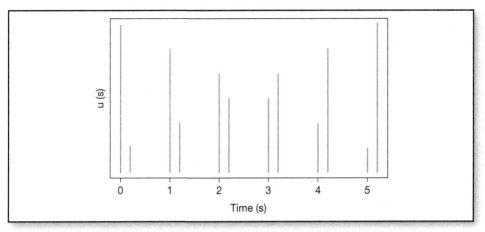

FIGURE 15.20 Optimal Execution in a Market with Linear Permanent Market Impact and Linear Decay of Temporary Impact

Source: Gatheral, Shied and Slynko (2011)

The optimal trading strategy comprises harmonic block trades with no-trading intervals between the blocks, as shown in Figure 15.20.

The aggregate execution schedule is broken down into $2N$ trades each of the size $\delta\left(1-\dfrac{i}{N+1}\right)$, so that the total trading size X satisfies

$$X = \int_0^T u(t)\,dt = \delta \sum_{i=0}^{N} 2\left(1 - \frac{i}{N+1}\right) \tag{34}$$

■ Practical Implementation of Optimal Execution Strategies

To determine the optimal order slices per the framework presented in the previous section, the execution trader can go through the following steps:

1. Estimate the empirical MI function.
2. Fit distributions of temporary and permanent MI of the traded security.
3. Derive optimal allocation on the basis of step 1.
4. Back test the execution strategy.
5. Put the strategy to use in real-life production environment.
   The resulting strategies perform well in chosen market conditions.

■ Summary

Algorithmic order execution is inseparable from today's markets. It is a necessary function that delivers considerable value to all investors, large and small. With plummeting technology costs, most investors today can afford to build and use advanced order routing and best execution algos, previously available only to a select few market participants. Services such as co-location provide added benefits of security and speed.

■ End-of-Chapter Questions

1. The best offer on exchange A contains 300 units of instrument X, the best offer on exchange B contains 500 units, and the best offer on exchange C contains just 100 units. Your customer wants you to buy 550 units on his behalf. How would you break up the customer's order and send them to exchanges under the minimal impact algorithm?
2. What is TWAP? VWAP? POV? Explain.
3. What are the main shortcomings of TWAP, VWAP, and POV?
4. How can the disadvantages of TWAP, VWAP, and POV be remedied?
5. What is resilience of the order book?

CHAPTER 16

Implementation of HFT Systems

High-frequency trading (HFT) systems tend to be "mission-critical applications," comparable with software piloting NASA shuttle launches and having little room for error. This chapter describes best practices of implementing accurate and reliable HFT systems.

Model Development Life Cycle

HFT systems, by their nature, require rapid hesitation-free decision making and execution. Properly programmed computer systems typically outperform human traders in these "mission-critical" trading tasks, particularly under treacherous market conditions—see Aldridge (2009b), for example. As a result, computer trading systems are rapidly replacing traditional human traders on trading desks around the world.

The development of a fully automated trading system follows a path similar to that of the standard software development process. The typical life cycle of a development process is illustrated in Figure 16.1.

A sound development process normally consists of the following five phases:

1. Planning
2. Analysis
3. Design
4. Implementation
5. Maintenance

The circular nature of the process illustrates the continuous quality of system development. When a version of the system appears to be complete, new issues demand advanced modifications and enhancements that lead to a new development cycle.

The purpose of the planning phase is to determine the goals of the project as well as to generate a high-level view of what the completed project may look like. The

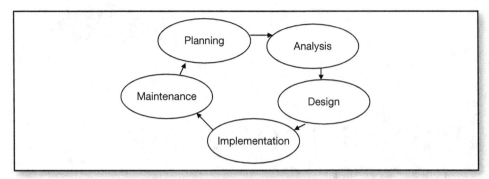

FIGURE 16.1 Typical Development Cycle of a Trading System

planning is accompanied by a feasibility study that evaluates the project in terms of its economics, operating model, and technical requirements. The economical considerations explore whether the project has a sufficient profit-and-loss (P&L) potential, whereas operational and technical issues address the feasibility of the project from the compliance, human resources, and other day-to-day points of view. The outputs of the planning phase include concrete goals and targets set for the project, established schedules, and estimated budgets for the entire system.

During the analysis stage of the process, the team aggregates requirements for system functionality, determines the scope of the project (which features are in and which features are out of the current release), and solicits initial feedback from users and management. The analysis stage is arguably the most critical stage in the development process, because it is here that stakeholders have the ultimate ability to shape the functionality of the system given the allocated budget.

The design phase incorporates detailed specifications of functionality, including process diagrams, business rules, and screenshots, along with other output formats such as those of daily reports and other documents. An objective of the design stage is to separate the whole project into discrete components subsequently assigned to teams of software developers; the discrete components will have well-specified interfaces that can lock in seamlessly with other components designed by different teams of software developers. Such early specification of software packaging of internal computer modules streamlines future communication among different software development teams and enables smooth operation of the project going forward. The design phase also outlines test cases—that is, the functionality paths that are later used as blueprints to verify the correctness of the completed code.

The implementation phase, finally, involves actual programming; the software teams or individual programmers develop software modules according to the specifications defined in the design stage. The individual modules are then tested by the development teams themselves against the predefined test cases. When the project management is satisfied that the individual modules have been developed according to the specifications, the project integration work begins. Integration, as its name implies, refers to putting together the individual modules to create a functional system.

While successfully planned projects encounter little variance or problems in the integration stage, some work still remains. Scripts may have to be written to ensure proper communication among various system components, installation wrappers may have to be developed, and, most important, the system has to be comprehensively tested to ensure proper operation. The test process usually involves dedicated personnel other than the people who developed the code. The test staff diligently monitors the execution of each functionality according to testing procedures defined in the design stage. The test personnel then documents any "bugs"—that is, discrepancies between the prespecified test case performance and observed performance. The bugs are then sent back over to the development team for resolution and are subsequently returned to the testing teams.

Successful implementation is followed by the deployment and subsequent maintenance phase of the system. The maintenance phase addresses system-wide deviations from planned performance, such as troubleshooting newly discovered bugs.

■ System Implementation

Key Steps in Implementation of High-Frequency Systems

Most systematic trading platforms are organized as shown in Figure 16.2. This section discusses each component of the process in detail.

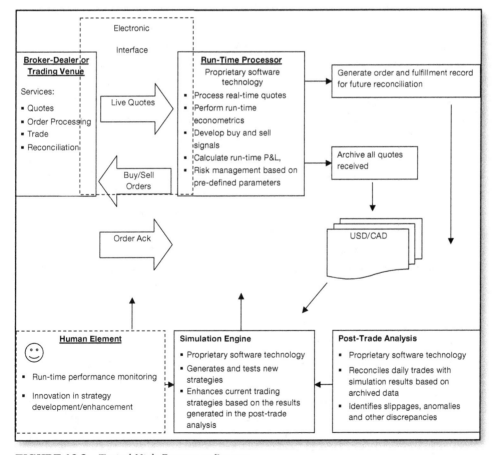

FIGURE 16.2 Typical High-Frequency Process

Step 1: The Core Engine   The core engine is composed of one or several run-time processors that contain the core logic of the trading mechanism and perform the following functions:

- Receive, evaluate, and archive incoming quotes.

- Perform run-time econometric analysis.

- Implement run-time portfolio management.

- Initiate and transmit buy and sell trading signals.

- Listen for and receive confirmation of execution.

- Calculate run-time P&L.

- Dynamically manage risk based on current portfolio allocations and market conditions.

Most of the high-frequency production-bound systems are written in C++, although some high-frequency trading firms are known to use Java and Q, a commercial hybrid of language syntax and database organization distributed by Kx Systems. The matching engine of Nasdaq OMX, for example, is said to be written in Java, yet the code disables "garbage collection," a core functionality of Java that distinguishes it from C++, but also slows down the systems. C++ is often considered to be "lighter" and "faster" than Java, meaning that C++ programs do not have the processing power overhead required by Java; as a result, C++ systems often work faster than Java-based systems.

The core engine and the portfolio management framework then initiate and transmit orders to the broker-dealer. Upon receiving and executing an order, the broker-dealer sends back the order status and order-filling price and size to the client. The system then calculates the P&L and assesses risk management parameters that feed back into the portfolio management piece.

The design and implementation of run-time portfolio management reflects the core econometric engine. In addition to the raw quote inputs, the portfolio management framework incorporates inputs from the econometric model, current position sizes, and other information relevant to portfolio diversification and maximization of portfolio returns, while minimizing portfolio risk.

Incoming quotes, along with outgoing orders and any other communication between a broker-dealer and a client or an exchange, are most often transmitted via the Financial Information eXchange (FIX) protocol specifically designed for transmission of real-time financial information. Other protocols, like FAST and Nasdaq's proprietary ITCH and OUCH, are also used.

According to the FIX industry web site (www.fixprotocol.org), FIX emerged in 1992 as a bilateral communications framework for equity trading between Fidelity Investments and Salomon Brothers. It has since become the dominant communication method among various broker-dealers, exchanges, and transacting customers. In fact, according to a survey conducted by fixprotocol.org, FIX was used for systematic trading by 75 percent of buy-side firms, 80 percent of sell-side firms, and over 75 percent of exchanges in 2006.

FIX is best described as a programming language that is overseen by a global steering committee, consisting of representatives from banks, broker-dealers, exchanges, industry utilities and associations, institutional investors, and information technology providers from around the world. Its standard is open and free. Implementation of a communication process via FIX, however, requires careful planning and dedicated resources and may demand significant expense, much like any other system development process.

A typical FIX message is composed of a header, a body, and a trailer. The header always contains the following three fields: a string identifying the beginning of a message (FIX field # 8), the number of characters in the body of the message to follow the message header (FIX field # 9), and the type of the message (FIX field # 35). Among many message types are quotation and order execution directives and acknowledgments as well as housekeeping messages designed to ensure that the system remains up and running.

For example, MsgType = 0 is the "Heartbeat" message—a message is sent to the other communication party to ensure that the communication connection remains operational and has not been lost as a result of any unforeseen technical problems. The heartbeat message is typically sent after a prespecified number of seconds of inactivity. If either communication party has not received a heartbeat message from the other party, it sends a TestRequest message (MsgType = 1) to "poll" the other communication party. If no heartbeat message is received following a TestRequest message, the connection is considered lost and steps are taken to restart it.

MsgType = 6 is known as "Indication of Interest." Exchanges and broker-dealers use Indication of Interest messages to transmit their interest in either buying or selling in either a proprietary or an agency capacity. MsgType = R indicates a "Quote Request" message with which a client of a broker-dealer requests a quote stream. Under normal circumstances, the broker-dealer responds to the Quote Request message with a continuous stream of Quote messages (MsgType = S) that carry actual quote information, such as bid or ask prices.

Other message types include orders such as single-name orders, list orders, day limit orders, multiday orders, various cancellation requests, and acknowledgments. All fields in the body are included in the following format:

[Field #] = [data]

For example, to communicate that the message carries the status of an order, the following sequence is used:

35 = 8 |

All field sequences are terminated with a special character that has a computer value of 0x01. The character looks like " | " when seen on-screen.

The body of the message contains the details of the message, whether it is a quote request, a quote itself, or order and trade information. The message body further specifies the exchange of interest, a timestamp that includes milliseconds, a security symbol, and other necessary transaction data. Like the header, all fields in the body are included in the following format:

[Field #] = [data]

and each field sequence is terminated by a special computer character 0x01.

Finally, at the end of the body of every message is the "checksum"—a sum of digital values of all the characters in the message included as a verification of whether the message has arrived in full. An example of a FIX message is shown in Chapter 2 of this book.

The risk management functionality can include the following components: tracking the basic components of the system performance and generating warning messages should the performance limits be breached. Appropriate risk management parameters may include message count limits per unit time, P&L parameters, and other variables discussed in detail later in this chapter.

Step 2: Quote Archival   Most quotes are accepted and archived using proprietary FIX engines that are tested with various message scenarios. The quotes are next archived for reconciliation and simulation purposes.

As discussed in Chapter 2, quote delivery over the public networks can be unreliable: the User Datagram Protocol (UDP) over which some quotes are broadcast does not guarantee point-to-point delivery. As a result, an HFT without co-location may lose quotes. Furthermore, variations in quote-receiving technology from one entity to the next do not guarantee that each entity's recorded datastream will be identical to that of the next entity. In some cases, purchased tick data may not be completely representative of the quote process archived by the data buyer from his own quote interface. While purchased historical data fills an important informational void when a researcher has no data, best practices suggest that each trading entity will benefit most from the internally archived data as such data will be most representative of the data received by the system during production.

Most firms with serious HFT needs archive all received and sent messages in text or binary file formats. The text file, known as a *flat file* in the industry, is the simplest form of storage. The flat file is readable by humans without special translation. The fields in the file can be comma or tab separated, and can be easily loaded into Excel or opened with Notepad on PCs or plain text editors on LINUX. Binary files, commonly referred to as *Large Binary OBjects*, or *BLOBs*, are recorded in hexadecimal (Hex) characters readable by machines. At the expense of readability, BLOBs are faster and much more compact than flat files. Interdealer broker ICAP's foreign exchange matching engine, for example, records all ticks in a continuous weekly BLOB. Along with foreign exchange markets, each ICAP's BLOB begins on Sunday night and ends on Friday night, New York time. Each such BLOB can occupy as much as a terabyte of storage space. Such storage requirements could have been prohibitively expensive just 10 years ago, yet today such storage is very reasonable. Various incarnations of Storage Area Networks (SANs) allow seamless access to stored data.

Many databases have attempted to crack the market for archiving real-time high-frequency data, and replace flat files with their products. Most databases are unsuitable to HFT because in HFT the most time-sensitive functionality is data archival. Slow input/output operation delays execution of the trading engine, compromising performance of the HFT system. Retrieval of tick data occurs only at the simulation level where execution time is not a critical parameter. Most databases, however, are optimized to efficiently retrieve data, and not to enter it into the system. KDB, distributed by Kx Systems, however, has been shown to be a promising tool, adopted by several firms.

Step 3: Posttrade Analytics   The best HFT systems do not stop there. A posttrade analysis engine reconciles production results with simulation results run with the same code on the same data and updates distributions of returns, trading costs, and risk management parameters to be fed back into the main processing engine, portfolio optimization, and risk management components.

Step 4: Simulation   *Simulation* refers to a make-belief execution of a trading strategy. Simulation is important for one key reason: it allows researchers to test a strategy within a short time span, without risking actual capital. A strategy that works well in simulation has a chance on actual money, in "production." Conversely, a strategy that fails in simulation will be hard-pressed to deliver positive results in a real trading environment.

The simulation engine is an independent module that tests new trading ideas on past and run-time data without actually executing the trades. Unlike ideas that are still in the early stages of development that are often coded in MatLab or even Excel, ideas tested in the simulation engine are typically coded in the production language (C++ or Java).

Simulation produces an approximation of real-life trading, and only if the execution part of simulation is programmed correctly. Specifically, execution of market and limit orders requires different treatment. A market order submitted in simulation can be assumed to be executed at the prevailing quote at the time the market order is submitted. Thus, a market buy order can be assumed to be filled at the best ask, providing that the size of the market order is smaller than the size of the best ask queue. Similarly, a small market sell order can be assumed to be executed at the best bid.

The best-quote assumptions about execution of market orders, however, will most of the time overstate performance of the trading system. In live trading, market orders will incur MI or slippage, resulting in worse prices than predicted by the best bid and best offer (for more details on market impact, please see Chapter 5). To better approximate the live trading results, the HFT researcher can estimate the average MI per unit trade size, and then adjust the best quotes by the estimated values of the MI. The market buy orders will then be considered executed at the prevailing ask plus the expected size-dependent MI, closer reflecting real-market conditions and applying a great degree of conservatism to simulation. Similarly, the market sell orders will be expected to execute at the best bid less MI estimation.

Simulation of execution of limit orders is also complex. A limit order can be considered to be executed only when the market price "crosses" the order price, as shown in Figure 10.1. When the market price equals the limit order price, the limit order may or may not to be executed in live trading. As a result, simulations of limit order trading generally consider a limit order to be executed when the market price drops below the price of the buy limit order, or when the market price rises above the price of the limit sell order, and the limit order execution is guaranteed.

Simulation of strategies can be performed in-sample and out-of-sample. In-sample simulation runs the strategy on the same sample of data on which the strategy was first developed. Natural issues dog the in-sample process: the data can be overfitted, and the results may not hold up in normal market conditions.

To make sure that the strategy has a chance in real-life trading, the strategy needs to be tested out-of-sample. Out-of-sample testing involves running the strategy on a copious amount of previously unused data. The out-of-sample testing is usually performed in the following order:

1. Back-test
2. Paper trading
3. Production

Back-Test A strategy run on historical data is called a *back-test*. The back-test typically utilizes at least two years of most recent tick data. The two-year minimum for the test is likely an overhang from low-frequency monthly performance evaluation days: 24 months provides a number of monthly observations nearly sufficient for making statistically significant inferences under the central limit theorem in statistics.

In theory, the minimum number of days sufficient to prove the performance of a strategy is determined by the Sharpe ratio it is thought to produce, as discussed in Chapter 6. In practice, however, a larger number of observations is preferred to the smaller set because the larger the number of observations, the more opportunities to evaluate the strategy performance, and the more confidence in the strategy results.

A large reserve of historical data (at least two years of continuous tick data) also ensures that the model minimizes the data-snooping bias, a condition that occurs when the model overfits to a nonrecurring aberration in the data. Running the back-test on a fresh set of historical data unused in the model development is known as making *out-of-sample inferences*.

A back-test is also useful in estimation of risk of a given trading system. The preferred distributions of returns used as inputs into HFT risk quantification models are obtained from running the system on live capital. Still, a back-test distribution of trade returns obtained from running the model over at least two years of tick data can also be used in risk management applications, even though the back-test distribution may generate misleading results: back-tests may fail to account for all the extreme returns and hidden costs that occur when the system is trading live.

To mitigate the unexpected and low probability extreme returns, known as *black swans* (Taleb, 2007), the HFT researcher may consider running the HFT code through historical or simulated data representing made-up "stress-test scenarios." The data surrounding the flash crash of May 6, 2010, represents a historical example of a stress event. However, data corresponding to some hypothetical simultaneous failure of global financial markets can be simulated.

The out-of-sample back-test results need to be evaluated. At a minimum, the evaluation process should compute basic statistical parameters of the trading idea's performance: cumulative and average returns, Sharpe ratio, and maximum drawdown, as explained in Chapter 6.

Once a strategy is determined to perform satisfactorily in the back-test, the strategy is moved into paper trading, discussed next.

Paper Trading A strategy run in real time on live data, but without placing the actual trades, is known as paper trading. The *paper-trading* stage records all orders in a text file. The orders and trades records at a minimum should include:

- A granular timestamp of the order, with a minimum of 1 ms or finer precision.

- A code of the traded financial instrument.

- Last observed best bid price, best bid size, best ask price, and best ask size, for end-of-day reconciliation of orders and data.

- Order quantity.

- Assumed execution price.

The main difference between the live trading model and the back-test model should be the origin of the quote data; the back-test system includes a historical quote-streaming module that reads historical tick data from archives and feeds it sequentially to the module that has the main functionality. In the paper trading system, a different quote module receives real-time tick data from trading venues and broker-dealers.

Except for differences in receiving quotes, paper-trading and back-test systems should be identical; they can be built simultaneously and use the same code for core functionality. This chapter reviews the systems implementation process under the assumption that both back-testing and paper-trading engines are built and tested in parallel. The following sections summarize key steps in the process of developing high-frequency systems, detail the system development process, including common pitfalls, as well as discuss the best practices for testing developed trading systems.

Production A strategy running in real time on live capital is usually referred to live trading or as *production*. Production orders are sent to live trading venues via FIX or other messaging protocols. An HFT system running in production will still need to locally archive all orders, as for the paper trading discussed above. The paper trading records and the live trading records will help generate order fulfillment and reconciliation analysis, as well as assess executional performance of the strategy.

The difference in performance of the live strategy and paper trading is formally known as *implementation shortfall*. Implementation shortfall provides the most reliable measures of slippage and other latent costs by allowing direct observation of prices obtained in real markets and their simulated counterparts.

Step 5: Human Supervision Continuous human supervision of the system is required to ensure that the system does not fall victim to some malicious activity such as a computer virus or a market event unaccounted for in the model itself. The role of the human trader, however, should normally be limited to making sure that the performance of the system falls within specific bounds. Once the bounds are breached, the human trader should have the authority to shut down trading for the day or until the conditions causing the breach have been resolved.

Common Pitfalls in Systems Implementation

Message Acknowledgment Loops   A market order communication process includes the following steps:

- The client sends a market order to the broker or a trading venue.
- The venue receives the order/the broker forwards the order to the exchange.
- The trading venue sends out an order acknowledgment.
- The client receives the order acknowledgment.
- The order is executed.
- The trading venue sends out the execution acknowledgment.
- The client receives the execution acknowledgment.

Time elapses from the instance the client sends an order to the moment the client receives an order execution acknowledgment. In the United States, the round-trip execution speed of a market order is 10 ms or less; in Europe, this number may grow to 50 to 100 ms, and in Asia the round-trip time may still take a whole minute or two. Regardless of the speed of the execution process, the finite time that elapses between the order origination and confirmation of execution is sufficient to produce wildly runaway algos.

A frequent rookie cause for the runaway condition is an ill-programmed position counter. Consider the following logic: a trading algorithm sends out orders in response to specific market conditions and until the total portfolio reaches a certain position limit. When the position counter is adjusted only upon receiving execution acknowledgments, the system keeps spewing out orders during the time the order is being executed, potentially resulting in an extreme quantity of executions, well above the set position limit. The mistake is common and is easy to fix. One solution involves keeping two position counters: one for sent-in orders, and the other for executed positions. The idea, however, does not occur easily to someone lacking HFT experience.

Time Distortion   The simulation runs in its own time using quotes collected and stored during a run time of another process. The frequency of the quotes recorded by the process that collected the data that is now historical data can vary greatly, mostly because of the following two factors:

1. The number of financial instruments for which the original process collected quotes.
2. The speed of the computer system on which the original process ran.

Their impact is due to the nature of the quote process and its realization in most trading systems. Most systems comprise a client (the quote collecting and/or trading application) that is geared to receive quotes and the server (a broker-dealer application supplying the quotes). The client is most often a "local" application that runs "locally": on computer hardware over which the trader has full control. The broker-dealer server is almost always a remote application, meaning that the client has to communicate with the server over a remote connection, such as the Internet. To receive quotes, the client application usually has to perform the following communication with the server process:

1. The client sends the server a message or a series of messages with the following information:
   a. Client identification (given to the client by the broker-dealer that houses the server).
   b. Names of financial securities for which the quotes are requested.
2. The server will respond, acknowledging the client's message. The server's response will also indicate whether the client is not allowed to receive any of the quotes requested for any reason.
3. The server will begin to stream the quotes to the client. The quotes are typically streamed in an "asynchronous" manner—that is, the server will send a quote to the client as soon as a new quote becomes available. Some securities have higher-frequency quotes than others. For example, during high-volatility times surrounding economic announcements, it is not unusual for the EUR/USD exchange rate to be accompanied by as many as 300 quotes per second. At the same time, some obscure option may generate only one quote per trading day. It is important to keep in mind the expected frequency of quotes while designing the quote-receiving part of the application.
4. Quote distortion often happens next. It is the responsibility of the client to collect and process all the quotes as soon as they arrive at the client's computer. Here, several issues can occur. On the client's machine, all incoming quotes are placed into a queue in the order of their arrival, with the earliest quotes located closest to the processor. This queue can be thought of as a line for airport check-in. Unlike the airport line, however, the queue often has a finite length or capacity; therefore, any quote arrivals that find the queue full are discarded, hence the first issue: quote time series may vary from client to client if the client systems have queues of varying lengths, all other system characteristics being equal.

   Once the quotes are in the queue, the system picks the earliest quote arrival from the queue for processing; then all the quotes in the queue are shifted closer to the processing engine. As noted previously, the quotes may arrive faster than the client is able to process them, filling up the queue and leading the system to discard new quote arrivals until the older quotes are processed. Even a seemingly simple operation such as copying a quote to a file or a database stored on the computer system takes computer time. While the quote-storing time may be a tiny fraction of a second and thus negligible by human time standards, the time can be significant by computer clock and slow down the processing of incoming quotes.

   A client system may assign the quote an arrival time on taking the quote from its arrival queue. The timestamp may therefore differ from the timestamp given to the quote by the server. Depending on the number of securities for which the quotes are collected and the market's volatility at any given time of day, the timestamp distortion may differ significantly as a result of the quote-processing delay alone. If the quotes are further mathematically manipulated to generate trading signals, the distortions in timestamps may be even more considerable.

5. Naturally, systems running on computers with slower processing power will encounter more timestamp distortion than systems running on faster machines. Faster machines are quicker at processing sequential quotes and drop fewer quotes as a result. Even the slightest differences in system power can result in different quote streams that in turn may produce different trading signals.

The reliability of quote delivery can be improved in the following four ways:

1. Time-stamping quotes immediately when each quote arrives before putting the quote into the queue.
2. Increasing the size of the quote queue.
3. Increasing system memory to the largest size feasible given a cost/benefit analysis.
4. Reducing the number of securities for which the quotes are collected on any given client.

These four steps toward establishing greater quote reliability are fairly easy to implement when the client application is designed and built from scratch, and in particular when using the FIX protocol for quote delivery. However, many off-the shelf clients, including those distributed by executing brokers, may be difficult or impossible to customize. For firms planning to use an off-the-shelf client, it may be prudent to ask the software manufacturer how the preceding issues can be addressed in the client.

Speed of Execution   Duration of execution can make or break HFT models. Most strategies for arbitraging temporary market mispricings, for example, depend on the ability to get the orders posted with lightning speed. Whoever detects the mispricing and gets his order posted on the exchange first is likely to generate the most profit.

Speed of execution is controlled by the following components of trading platforms:

- The speed of applications generating trading signals.

- The proximity of applications generating trading signals to the executing broker.

- The speed of the executing broker's platform in routing execution requests.

- The proximity of the executing broker to the exchange.

- The speed of the exchange in processing the execution orders.

Figure 16.3 illustrates the time-dependent flow of execution process.

To enhance message security and to alleviate delays due to the physical transmission of trading signals between clients and the broker or the exchange, clients dependent on the speed of execution often choose to co-locate or house their servers in proximity centers. Co-location and proximity hosting services typically employ systems administration staff that are capable of providing recovery services in case of systems or power failure, making sure that the client applications work at least 99.999 percent of the time. Co-location and proximity hosting are discussed in detail in Chapter 2 of the book.

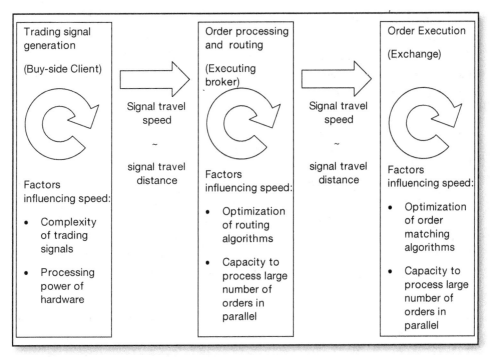

FIGURE 16.3 Execution Process

■ Testing Trading Systems

The costs of rolling out a system that contains programmatic errors, or bugs, can be substantial. Thorough testing of the system, therefore, is essential prior to wide roll-out of the model. Testing has the following stages:

- Data set testing

- Unit testing

- System testing

- Integration testing

- Regression testing

- Automation testing

Data Set Testing

Data set testing refers to testing the validity of the data, whether historical data used in a back-test or real-time data obtained from a streaming data provider. The objective of data testing is to ascertain that the system minimizes undesirable influences and distortions in the data and to ensure that the run-time analysis and trading signal generation work smoothly.

Data set testing is built on the premise that all data received for a particular security should fall into a statistical distribution that is consistent throughout time. The data should also exhibit consistent distributional properties when sampled at different frequencies: one-minute data for USD/CAD, for example, should be consistent with historical one-minute data distribution for USD/CAD observed for the past year. Naturally, data set testing should allow for distributions to change with time, but the observed changes should not be drastic, unless they are caused by a large-scale market disruption.

A popular procedure for testing data is based on testing for consistency of autocorrelations. It is implemented as follows:

1. A data set is sampled at a given frequency—say, 10-second intervals.
2. Autocorrelations are estimated for a moving window of 30 to 1,000 observations.
3. The obtained autocorrelations are then mapped into a distribution; outliers are identified, and their origin is examined. The distributional properties can be analyzed further to answer the following questions:

   ▪ Have the properties of the distribution changed during the past month, quarter, or year?

   ▪ Are these changes due to the version of the code or to the addition or removal of programs on the production box?

The testing should be repeated at different sampling frequencies to ensure that no systemic deviations occur.

Unit Testing

Unit testing verifies that each individual software component of the system works properly. A unit is a testable part of an application; the definition of a unit can range from the code for the lowest function or method to the functionality of a medium-level component—for example, a latency measurement component of the posttrade analysis engine. Testing code in small blocks from the ground up ensures that any errors are caught early in the integration process, avoiding expensive system disruptions at later stages.

Integration Testing

Integration testing follows unit testing. As its name implies, integration testing is a test of the interoperability of code components; the test is administered to increasingly larger aggregates of code as the system is being built up from modular pieces to its completed state. Testing modular interoperability once again ensures any that code defects are caught and fixed early.

System Testing

System testing is a postintegration test of the system as a whole. The system testing incorporates several testing processes described as follows.

Graphical user interface (GUI) software testing ensures that the human interface of the system enables the user (e.g., the person responsible for monitoring trading activity) to perform her tasks. GUI testing typically ensures that all the buttons and displays that appear on screen are connected with the proper functionality according to the specifications developed during the design phase of the development process.

Usability and performance testing is similar in nature to GUI testing but is not limited to GUIs and may include such concerns as the speed of a particular functionality. For example, how long does the system take to process a "system shutdown" request? Is the timing acceptable from a risk management perspective?

Stress testing is a critical component of the testing of high-frequency trading systems. A stress-testing process attempts to document and, subsequently, quantify the impact of extreme hypothetical scenarios on the system's performance. For example, how does the system react if the price of a particular security drops 10 percent within a very short time? What if an act of God occurs that shuts down the exchange, leaving the system holding its positions? What other worst-case scenarios are there, and how will they affect the performance of the system and the subsequent P&L?

Security testing is another indispensable component of the testing process that is often overlooked by organizations. Security testing is designed to identify possible security breaches and to either provide a software solution for overcoming the breaches or create a breach-detection mechanism and a contingency plan in the event a breach occurs. HFT systems can be vulnerable to security threats coming from the Internet, where unscrupulous users may attempt to hijack account numbers, passwords, and other confidential information in an attempt to steal trading capital. However, intraorganizational threats should not be underestimated; employees with malicious intent or disgruntled workers having improper access to the trading system can wreak considerable and costly havoc. All such possibilities must be tested and taken into account.

Scalability testing refers to testing the capacity of the system. How many securities can the system profitably process at the same time without incurring significant performance impact? The answer to this question may appear trivial, but the matter is anything but trivial in reality. Every incremental security measure added to the system requires an allocation of computer power and Internet bandwidth. A large number of securities processed simultaneously on the same machine may considerably slow down system performance, distorting quotes, trading signals, and the P&L as a result. A determination of the maximum permissible number of securities will be based on the characteristics of each trading platform, including available computing power.

Reliability testing determines the probable rate of failure of the system. Reliability testing seeks to answer the following questions: What are the conditions under which the system fails? How often can we expect these conditions to occur? The failure conditions may include unexpected system crashes, shutdowns due to insufficient memory space, and anything else that leads the system to stop operating. The failure rate for any well-designed high-frequency trading system should not exceed 0.01 percent (i.e., the system should be guaranteed to remain operational 99.99 percent of time).

Recovery testing refers to verification that in an adverse event, whether an act of God or a system crash, the documented recovery process ensures that the system's integrity is restored and it is operational within a prespecified time. The recovery testing also ensures that data integrity is maintained through unexpected terminations of the system. Recovery testing should include the following scenarios: When the application is running and the computer system is suddenly restarted, the application should have valid data upon restart. Similarly, the application should continue operating normally if the network cable should be unexpectedly unplugged and then plugged back in.

Use-Case Testing

The term *use-case testing* refers to the process of testing the system according to the system performance guidelines defined during the design stage of the system development. In use-case testing, a dedicated tester follows the steps of using the system and documents any discrepancies between the observed behavior and the behavior that is supposed to occur. Use-case testing ensures that the system is operating within its parameters.

Use-case testing is typically performed by professional software testers, not the programmers who coded the system. The deployment of testers is important for several reasons:

- Testers are trained to document discrepancies between a given scenario and actual performance of the system module.

- Testers are not emotionally involved in code development and are impartial to found errors.

- Testers' labor is considerably less expensive than that of programmers, resulting in savings for the organization.

Discrepancies or "bugs" reported by testers usually span three levels: critical, moderate, and inconsequential. Critical bugs significantly impair intended system performance and need to be addressed with the highest priority. Moderate bugs are considerable issues and need to be addressed following the bugs in the critical functionality. Inconsequential bugs are more of a cosmetic variety and may not need to be addressed until a downtime occurs within the ranks of coders.

■ Summary

Implementation of high-frequency systems is a time-consuming process, in which mistakes can be very costly. Outsourcing noncritical components of the system may be a prudent strategy. Testing, however, is the paramount activity that has to be conducted according to best practices established for software development.

End-of-Chapter Questions

1. What are the stages in development of high-frequency trading systems? What are the stages in HFT implementation?
2. What is a back-test? What are the peculiarities of back-testing?
3. Suppose the back-testing system is placing a limit buy order at 125.13 when the market price is 125.14. At what market price level can the researcher assume that the limit order was executed?
4. Suppose a system produces a Sharpe ratio of 12 in the back-test. How much paper-trading testing does this system need to ascertain its performance?
5. What methodologies can be deployed in data testing?
6. What is use-case testing? Why is it valuable?

IRENE ALDRIDGE is an investment consultant, portfolio manager, a recognized expert on the subjects of quantitative investing and high-frequency trading, and a seasoned educator. Aldridge is currently Industry Professor at New York University, Department of Finance and Risk Engineering, Polytechnic Institute, as well as Managing Partner and Quantitative Portfolio Manager at ABLE Alpha Trading, LTD, an investment consulting firm and a proprietary trading vehicle specializing in quantitative and high-frequency trading strategies. At ABLE Alpha, Aldridge designs, implements, and deploys proprietary trading strategies. As part of her duties, Aldridge also advises broker-dealers, large hedge funds, government entities and trading venues (including exchanges and dark pools) on high-frequency research and optimal high-frequency strategy design, implementation of trading systems, risk management and regulation of both high- and low-frequency operations. Aldridge is also a founder of AbleMarkets.com, an online resource making the latest high-frequency research for institutional investors and broker-dealers. Finally, Aldridge runs an HFT training program for institutional market participants; the first-of-it-kind program was developed and is continuously updated by Aldridge and has been well-received by hundreds of industry professionals. The upcoming schedule of training sessions worldwide is available at HFTtraining.com.

Prior to ABLE Alpha, Aldridge worked for various institutions on Wall Street and in Toronto, including Goldman Sachs and CIBC. Over the years, Aldridge has been called to contribute to numerous government regulatory panels, including the U.K. Government Foresight Committee for Future of Computer Trading and the U.S. Commodity Futures Trading Commission's Subcommittee on High-Frequency Trading.

Aldridge holds an MBA from INSEAD, an MS in financial engineering from Columbia University, and a BE in electric engineering from the Cooper Union in New York, and is presently in the process of completing her PhD at New York University. Aldridge is a frequent speaker at top industry events and a contributor to academic, practitioner and mainstream media publications, including the *Journal of*

Trading, Futures Magazine, Reuters HedgeWorld, Advanced Trading, FX Week, FINalternatives, Dealing with Technology, and *Huffington Post*.

Aldridge often appears on major television networks, including BBC, CNBC, FOX Business, CBC, BNN, German ZDF, and has been invited to discuss current economic issues on National Public Radio (NPR) and Bloomberg radio. In addition, Aldridge has been quoted by the *New York Times*, the *Wall Street Journal,* Associated Press, Financial Times, Thomson/Reuters, Bloomberg LP, *Forbes, The Daily Show with Jon Stuart,* and other major business news outlets.

Aldridge strongly believes into giving back to the community, and she presently serves as treasurer at Carnegie Hill Neighbors, a not-for-profit organization charged with continuous improvement of the jewel-like area in New York City.

This book is accompanied by a web site, www.hftradingbook.com. The web site supplements the materials in the book with teaching materials like PowerPoint presentations, in-class project ideas, and related materials. The web site requires a valid e-mail address to register. Once registered, subscribers also receive updates on the latest activity in the HFT space.

To receive these free benefits, visit the book's web site at www.hftradingbook .com. When prompted for a password, please enter "high-frequency."

REFERENCES

Agarwal, V. and N. Y. Naik, 2004. "Risk and Portfolio Decisions Involving Hedge Funds." *Review of Financial Studies* 17 (1), 63–98.

Aggarwal, R. and D. C. Schirm, 1992. "Balance of Trade Announcements and Asset Prices: Influence on Equity Prices, Exchange Rates, and Interest Rates." *Journal of International Money and Finance* 11, 80–95.

Ahn, H., K. Bae and K. Chan, 2001. "Limit Orders, Depth and Volatility: Evidence from the Stock Exchange of Hong Kong." *Journal of Finance* 56, 767–788.

Ajayi, R. A. and S. M. Mehdian, 1995. "Global Reactions of Security Prices to Major US-Induced Surprises: An Empirical Investigation." *Applied Financial Economics* 5, 203–218.

Aldridge, I. E., 2009a. "Discrete Pair-Wise Portfolio Management in High-Frequency Trading." Working paper.

Aldridge, I. E., 2009b. "Systematic Funds Outperform." Working paper.

Aldridge, I. E., 2010. "Working with High-Frequency Data." In H. Markowitz and F. Fabozzi, eds., *Equity Valuation and Portfolio Management*, Wiley & Sons, Hoboken, NJ.

Aldridge, I. E., 2011, "Estimating volatility cut-outs using Markov switching models." Working paper.

Aldridge, I. E., 2012a. "Determining Percent of HFT Participation in Financial Markets." U.S. Patent and Trademarks Office, Patent Pending.

Aldridge, I. E., 2012b. "The Consequences of Transaction Tax." Working paper.

Aldridge, I. E., 2012c. "Estimating Market Impact," U.S. Patent and Trademarks Office, Patent Pending.

Aldridge, I. E., 2012d. "Predicting Liquidity," working paper.

Aldridge, I. E., 2012e. "Can High-Frequency Traders Game Futures?" *Journal of Trading*, 7, 75–82.

Aldridge, I. E., 2012f. "Estimating Probability of a Market Crash." U.S. Patent and Trademarks Office, Patent Pending.

Alexander, C., 1999. "Optimal Hedging Using Cointegration." *Philosophical Transactions of the Royal Society*, Vol. 357, No. 1758, 2039–2058.

Alfonsi, A. and A. Schied, 2010. "Optimal Trade Execution and Absence of Price Manipulations in Limit Order Book Models." Working paper.

Almeida, Alvaro, Charles Goodhart and Richard Payne, 1998. "The Effect of Macroeconomic 'News' on High Frequency Exchange Rate Behaviour." *Journal of Financial and Quantitative Analysis* 33, 1–47.

Almgren, R. and N. Chriss, 2000. "Optimal Execution of Portfolio Transactions." *Journal of Risk*, 12, 61–63.

Almgren, R. C. Thum, E. Hauptmann and H. Li, 2005. "Equity Market Impact." *Risk* 18, 57–62.

Amihud, Y., 2002. "Illiquidity and stock returns: Cross-section and time-series effects." *Journal of Financial Markets* 5, 31–56.

Amihud, Y. and H. Mendelson, 1986. "Asset pricing and the bid-ask spread." *Journal of Financial Economics* 17, 223–249.

Amihud, Y. and H. Mendelson, 1989. "The Effects of Beta, Bid-Ask Spread, Residual Risk and Size on Stock Returns." *Journal of Finance* 44, 479–486.

Anand, A., S. Chakravarty and T. Martell, 2005. "Empirical Evidence on the Evolution of Liquidity: Choice Of Market versus Limit Orders by Informed and Uninformed Traders." *Journal of Financial Markets* 8, 289–309.

Andersen, T. G., T. Bollerslev, F. X. Diebold and C. Vega, 2003. "Micro Effects of Macro Announcements: Real-Time Price Discovery in Foreign Exchange." *American Economic Review* 93, 38–62.

Andersen, T. G., T. Bollerslev and N. Meddahi, 2005. "Correcting the Errors: Volatility Forecast Evaluation Using High-Frequency Data and Realized Volatilities." *Econometrica* 73, 279–296.

Andritzky, J. R., G. J. Bannister and N. T. Tamirisa, 2007. "The Impact of Macroeconomic Announcements on Emerging Market Bonds." *Emerging Markets Review* 8, 20–37.

Angel, J., 1992. "Limit versus Market Orders." Working paper, Georgetown University.

Arnuk, S. and J. Saluzzi, 2012. *Broken Markets*. FT Press, Upper Saddle River, NJ.

Artzner, P., F. Delbaen, J. M. Eber, and D. Heath, 1999. "Coherent Measures of Risk." *Mathematical Finance* 9, 203–228.

Asquith, P., R. Oman and C. Safaya, 2008. "Short Sales and Trade Classification Algorithms." NBER Working Paper No. w14158.

Atiase, R. K. 1985. "Predisclosure information, firm capitalization, and security price behavior around earnings announcements." *Journal of Accounting Research* (Spring), 21–36.

Avellaneda, Marco and Sasha Stoikov, 2008. "High-Frequency Trading in a Limit Order Book." *Quantitative Finance*, Vol. 8, No. 3., 217–224.

Bagehot, Walter (pseudonym). "The Only Game in Town." *Financial Analysts Journal*, (Mar/April 1971), 12-14, 22.

Bailey, W., 1990. "US Money Supply Announcements and Pacific Rim Stock Markets: Evidence and Implications." *Journal of International Money and Finance* 9, 344–356.

Balduzzi, P., E. J. Elton and T. C. Green, 2001. "Economic News and Bond Prices: Evidence From the U.S. Treasury Market." *Journal of Financial and Quantitative Analysis* 36, 523–543.

Ball, R. and P. Brown, 1968. "An Empirical Evaluation of Accounting Income Numbers." *Journal of Accounting Research* 6, 159–178.

Bangia, A., F. X. Diebold, T. Schuermann and J. D. Stroughair, 1999. "Liquidity Risk, with Implications for Traditional Market Risk Measurement and Management." Wharton School, Working Paper 99–06.

Barany, E., M. P. Varela, I. Florescu and I. Sengupta, 2012. "Detecting Market Crashes by Analysing Long-Memory Effects Using High-Frequency Data." *Quantitative Finance* 12, 623–634.

Becker, Kent G., Joseph E. Finnerty and Kenneth J. Kopecky, 1996. "Macroeconomic News and the Efficiency of International Bond Futures Markets." *Journal of Futures Markets* 16, 131–145.

Berber, A. and C. Caglio, 2004. "Order Submission Strategies and Information: Empirical Evidence from the NYSE." Working paper, University of Lausanne.

Bernanke, Ben S. and Kenneth N. Kuttner, 2005. "What Explains the Stock Market's Reaction to Federal Reserve Policy?" *Journal of Finance* 60, 1221–1257.

Bervas, Arnaud, 2006. "Market Liquidity and Its Incorporation into Risk Management." *Financial Stability Review* 8, 63–79.

Biais, B., P. Hillion, and C. Spatt, 1995. "An empirical analysis of the limit order book and the order flow in the Paris Bourse." Journal of Finance 50, 1655–1689.

Black, Fisher, 1972. "Capital Market Equilibrium with Restricted Borrowing." *Journal of Business* 45, 444–455.

Boscaljon, B., 2005. "Regulatory Changes in the Pharmaceutical Industry." *International Journal of Business* 10, 151–164.

Boulatov, A., and T. J. George, 2008. "Securities trading when liquidity providers are informed." Working paper.

Boulatov, A. and T. J. George, 2011. "Hidden and Displayed Liquidity in Securities Markets with Informed Liquidity Providers." Working paper.

Boyd, John H., Jian Hu and Ravi Jagannathan, 2005. "The Stock Market's Reaction to Unemployment News: Why Bad News Is Usually Good for Stocks." *Journal of Finance* 60, 649–672.

Bredin, Don, Gerard O'Reilly and Simon Stevenson, 2007. "Monetary Shocks and REIT Returns." *The Journal of Real Estate Finance and Economics* 35, 315–331.

Breen, W. J., L. S. Hodrick, and R. A. Korajczyk, 2002. "Predicting equity liquidity." *Management Science* 48, 470–483.

Brennan, M. J., T. Chordia and A. Subrahmanyam, 1998. "Alternative Factor Specifications, Security Characteristics, and the Cross-Section of Expected Stock Returns." *Journal of Financial Economics* 49, 345–373.

Brennan, M. J. and A. Subrahmanyam, 1996. "Market Microstructure and Asset Pricing: On the Compensation for Illiquidity in Stock Returns." *Journal of Financial Economics* 41, 441–464.

Brodsky, E., 2011. "The spatial density of foreshocks." *Geophysical Research Letters* 38, L10305

Brooks, C. and H. M. Kat, 2002. "The Statistical Properties of Hedge Fund Index Returns and Their Implications for Investors." *Journal of Alternative Investments*, 5 (Fall), 26–44.

Burgardt, G., J. Hanweck Jr., and L. Lei, 2006. "Measuring Market Impact and Liquidity." Journal of Trading 1, 70–84.

Burke, G., 1994. "A Sharper Sharpe Ratio." *Futures* 23, 56.

Cao, C., O. Hansch and X. Wang, 2004. "The Informational Content of an Open Limit Order Book." Working paper, Pennsylvania State University.

Chaboud, A., E. Hjalmarsson, C. Vega and B. Chiquoine, 2011. "Rise of the Machines: Algorithmic Trading in the Foreign Exchange Market." FRB International Finance Discussion Paper No. 980.

Chaboud, Alain P. and Jonathan H. Wright, 2005. "Uncovered Interest Parity: It Works, but Not for Long." *Journal of International Economics* 66, 349–362.

Challe, Edouard, 2003. "Sunspots and Predictable Asset Returns." *Journal of Economic Theory* 115, 182–190.

Chan, L. K. C., J. Karceski and J. Lakonishok, 1998. "The Risk and Return from Factors." *Journal of Financial and Quantitative Analysis* 33, 159–188.

Chan, L. and J. Lakonishok, 1995. "The Behavior of Stock Price around Institutional Trades." *Journal of Finance* 50, 1147–1174.

Cohen, K., S. Maier, R. Schwartz and D. Whitcomb, 1981. "Transaction Costs, Order Placement Strategy, and Existence of the Bid-Ask Spread." *Journal of Political Economy* 89, 287–305.

Connolly, Robert A. and Chris Stivers, 2005. "Macroeconomic News, Stock Turnover, and Volatility Clustering in Daily Stock Returns." *Journal of Financial Research* 28, 235–259.

Cont, R., A. Kukanov, and S. Stoikov, 2011, "The price impact of order book events." Working paper.

Copeland, T., and D. Galai, 1983. "Information effects on the bid-ask spread." *Journal of Finance* 38, 1457–1469.

Corsi, Fulvio, Gilles Zumbach, Ulrich Müller and Michel Dacorogna, 2001. "Consistent High-Precision Volatility from High-Frequency Data." *Economics Notes* 30, No. 2, 183–204.

Cutler, David M., James M. Poterba and Lawrence H. Summers, 1989. "What Moves Stock Prices?" *Journal of Portfolio Management* 15, 4–12.

Dacorogna, M. M., R. Gencay, U. A. Muller, R. Olsen and O. V. Pictet, 2001. *An Introduction to High-Frequency Finance*. Academic Press: San Diego, CA.

Datar, Vinay T., Narayan Y. Naik and Robert Radcliffe, 1998. "Liquidity and Asset Returns: An Alternative Test." *Journal of Financial Markets* 1, 203–219.

Demsetz, H., 1968. "The Cost of Transacting." The Quarterly Journal of Economics, 82, 1, 33-53.

Dennis, P. J. and J. P. Weston, 2001. "Who's Informed? An Analysis of Stock Owner-ship and Informed Trading." Working paper.

Diamond, D. W. and R. E. Verrecciha, 1987. "Constraints on Short-Selling and As-set Price Adjustment to Private Information." *Journal of Financial Economics* 18, 277–311.

Ding, X., B. Liu and P. S. Yu. 2008. "A Holistic Lexicon-Based Approach to Opinion Mining." Proceedings of WSDM 2008.

Dowd, K., 2000. "Adjusting for Risk: An Improved Sharpe Ratio." *International Re-view of Economics and Finance* 9 (3), 209–222.

Dufour, A. and R. F. Engle, 2000. "Time and the Price Impact of a Trade." *Journal of Finance* 55, 2467–2498.

Easley, David, Nicholas M. Kiefer, Maureen O'Hara and Joseph B. Paperman, 1996. "Liquidity, Information, and Infrequently Traded Stocks." *Journal of Finance* 51, 1405–1436.

Easley, David, Lopez de Prado, Marcos and O'Hara, Maureen, 2012. "Flow Toxicity and Liquidity in a High Frequency World." *Review of Financial Studies* 25, 1457–1493.

Easley, David, and Maureen O'Hara, 1987. "Price, trade size, and information in securities markets." *Journal of Financial Economics* 19, 69–90.

Easley, David, and Maureen O'Hara, 1992. "Time and the process of security price adjustment." *Journal of Finance* 47, 577–606.

Ederington, Louis H. and Jae Ha Lee, 1993. "How Markets Process Information: News Releases and Volatility." *Journal of Finance* 48, 1161–1191.

Edison, Hali J., 1996. "The Reaction of Exchange Rates and Interest Rates to News Releases." Board of Governors of the Federal Reserve System, International Finance Discussion Paper No. 570 (October).

Edwards, Sebastian, 1982. "Exchange Rates, Market Efficiency and New Informa-tion." *Economics Letters* 9, 377–382.

Eichenbaum, Martin and Charles Evans, 1993. "Some Empirical Evidence on the Effects of Monetary Policy Shocks on Exchange Rates", NBER Working Paper No. 4271.

Eisler, Z., J. Bouchaud, and J. Kockelkoren, 2009. "The Price Impact of Order Book Events: Market Orders, Limit Orders and Cancellations." Working Paper.

Eleswarapu, V. R., 1997. "Cost of Transacting and Expected Returns in the Nasdaq Market." *Journal of Finance* 52, 2113–2127.

Eling, M. and F. Schuhmacher, 2007. "Does the Choice of Performance Measure Influence the Evaluation of Hedge Funds?" *Journal of Banking and Finance* 31, 2632–2647.

Ellis, K., R. Michaely and M. O'Hara, "The Accuracy of Trade Classification Rules: Evidence from Nasdaq." *Journal of Financial and Quantitative Analysis* 35, 529–551

Ellul, A., C. Holden, P. Jain and R. Jennings, 2007. "Determinants of Order Choice on the New York Stock Exchange." Working paper, Indiana University.

Engle, R. and R. Ferstenberg, 2007. "Execution Risk." *Journal of Portfolio Management* 33, 34–45.

Errunza, V. and K. Hogan, 1998. "Macroeconomic Determinants of European Stock Market Volatility." *European Financial Management* 4, 361–377.

Evans, M. and R. K. Lyons, 2002. "Order Flow and Exchange Rate Dynamics." *Journal of Political Economy* 110, 170–180.

F. Fabozzi, ed., 2012. *Encyclopedia of Financial Models*. Hoboken, NJ: John Wiley & Sons.

Fama, Eugene, 1970. "Efficient Capital Markets: A Review of Theory and Empirical Work." *Journal of Finance* 25: 383–417.

Fama, E. F., L. Fisher, M. C. Jensen, and R. Roll, 1969. "The Adjustment of Stock Prices to New Information." *International Economic Review* 10, 1–21.

Fan-fah, C., S. Mohd and A. Nasir, 2008. "Earnings Announcements: The Impact of Firm Size on Share Prices." *Journal of Money, Investment and Banking*, 36–46.

Farmer, J. D., A. Gerig, F. Lillo and H. Waelbroeck, 2011. "How Efficiency Shapes Market Impact." Working paper.

Favre, L. and J.-A. Galeano, 2002. "Mean-Modified Value-at-Risk Optimization with Hedge Funds." *Journal of Alternative Investments*.

Ferraris, A. 2008. "Equity Market Impact Models." Working paper, Deutsche Bank AG.

Flannery, M. J. and A. A. Protopapadakis, 2002. "Macroeconomic Factors Do Influence Aggregate Stock Returns." *Review of Financial Studies* 15, 751–782.

Fleming, Michael J. and Eli M. Remolona, 1997. "What Moves the Bond Market?" Federal Reserve Bank of New York Economic Policy Review 3, 31–50.

Fleming, Michael J. and Eli M. Remolona, 1999a. "Price Formation and Liquidity in the U.S. Treasury Market: The Response to Public Information." *Journal of Finance* 54, 1901–1915.

Fleming, Michael J. and Eli M. Remolona, 1999b. "The Term Structure Of Announcement Effects." BIS Working paper No. 71.

Forsyth, P. A., J. S. Kennedy, S. T. Tse and H. Windcliff, 2011. "Optimal Trade Execution: A Mean-Quadratic-Variation Approach." Working paper, University of Waterloo.

Foster, F. and S. Viswanathan, 1996. "Strategic Trading When Agents Forecast the Forecasts of Others." *Journal of Finance* 51, 1437–1478.

Foucault, T., O. Kadan and E. Kandel, 2005. "Limit Order Book As a Market for Liquidity." *Review of Financial Studies* 18, 1171–1217.

Thierry Foucault & Sophie Moinas & Erik Theissen, 2007. "Does Anonymity Matter in Electronic Limit Order Markets?" *Review of Financial Studies* 20, 1707–1747.

Freeman, C. 1987. *Technology Policy and Economic Performance: Lessons from Japan*. London, Frances Pinter.

Frenkel, Jacob, 1981. "Flexible Exchange Rates, Prices and the Role of 'News': Lessons from the 1970s." *Journal of Political Economy* 89, 665–705.

Fung, W. and D. A. Hiseh, 1997. "Empirical Characteristics of Dynamic Trading Strategies: The Case of Hedge Funds." *Review of Financial Studies* 10, 275–302.

Garman, Mark, 1976. "Market Microstructure." *Journal of Financial Economics* 3, 257–275.

Garman, M. B. and M. J. Klass, 1980. "On the Estimation of Security Price Volatilities from Historical Data." *Journal of Business* 53: 67–78.

Gatev, E., W. N. Goetzmann, & K. G. Rouwenhorst, 2006. "Pairs Trading: Performance of a Relative-Value Arbitrage Rule," *Review of Financial Studies*, 797–827.

Gatheral, J., 2010. "No-Dynamic Arbitrage and Market Impact." *Quantitative Finance* 10, 749–759.

Gatheral, J. and A. Schied, 2011. "Optimal trade execution under geometric Brownian motion in the Almgren and Chriss framework." *International Journal of Theoretical and Applied Finance* 14, 353–368.

Gatheral, J., A. Schied, and A. Slynko, 2012. "Transient linear price impact and Fredholm integral equations." *Mathematical Finance* 22, 445–474.

George, T. J., G. Kaul, and M. Nimalendran, 1991. "Estimation of the Bid-Ask Spread and its Components: A New Approach." *Review of Financial Studies* 4, 623–656.

Getmansky, M., A. Lo, and I. Makarov. 2004. "An econometric model of serial correlation and illiquidity in hedge fund returns." *Journal of Financial Economics* 74, 529–610.

Glosten, L. R, 1987. "Components of the bid-ask spread and the statistical properties of transaction prices." *Journal of Finance.*

Glosten, L., 1994. "Is the Electronic Open Limit Order Book Inevitable?" *Journal of Finance* 49, 1127–1161.

Glosten, L. R. and L. E. Harris, 1988. "Estimating the Components of the Bid-Ask Spread." *Journal of Financial Economics* 21, 123–142.

Gomber, P., B. Arndt, M. Lutat, and T. E. Uhle, 2011. "High-Frequency Trading." Working paper.

Goodhart, C. A. E. and M. O'Hara, 1997. "High Frequency Data in Financial Markets: Issues and Applications." *Journal of Empirical Finance* 4, 73–114.

Gorton, G. B. and K. G. Rouwenhorst, 2006. "Facts and Fantasies about Commodity Futures." *Financial Analysts Journal* 62, 47–68.

Gregoriou, G. N. and Gueyie, J.-P., 2003. "Risk-Adjusted Performance of Funds of Hedge Funds Using a Modified Sharpe Ratio." *Journal of Alternative Investments* 6, 77–83.

Griffiths, M., B. Smith, A. Turnbull and R. White, 2000. "The Costs and Determinants of Order Aggressiveness." *Journal of Financial Economics* 56, 65–88.

Grilli, V. and N. Roubini, 1993. "Liquidity and Exchange Rates: Puzzling Evidence from the G-7 Countries." Mimeo, Birkbeck College.

Handa, P., R. Schwartz, and A. Tiwari, 2003. "Quote Setting and Price Formation in an Order Driven Market." *Journal of Financial Markets* 6, 461–489.

Hardouvelis, G. A., 1987. "Macroeconomic Information and Stock Prices." *Journal of Economics and Business* 39, 131–140.

Harris, R., 1997. "Stock Markets and Development: A Re-assessment." *European Economic Review* 41, 139–46.

Harris, L., 1998. "Optimal Dynamic Order Submission Strategies in Some Stylized Trading Problems." *Financial Markets, Institutions & Instruments* 7, 1–76.

Hasbrouck, Joel, 1991. "Measuring the Information Content of Stock Trades." *Journal of Finance* 46, 179–207.

Hasbrouck, J., 2005. "Trading Costs and Returns for US Equities: The Evidence from Daily Data." Working paper.

Hasbrouck, J., 2007. *Empirical Market Microstructure: The institutions, Economics, and Econometrics of Securities Trading.* Oxford University Press.

Hasbrouck, J. and G. Saar, 2002. "Limit Orders and Volatility in a Hybrid Market: The Island ECN." Working paper, New York University.

Hasbrouck, J. and G. Saar, 2011. "Low-Latency Trading." Working paper, New York University.

Hautsch, N. & R. Huang, 2011. "Limit Order Flow, Market Impact and Optimal Order Sizes: Evidence from NASDAQ TotalView-ITCH Data," SFB 649 Discussion Papers, SFB649DP2011-056, Sonderforschungsbereich 649, Humboldt University, Berlin, Germany.

Hedvall, K., J. Niemeyer and G. Rosenqvist, 1997. "Do Buyers and Sellers Behave Similarly in A Limit Order Book? A High-Frequency Data Examination of the Finnish Stock Exchange." *Journal of Empirical Finance* 4, 279–293.

Hollifield, B., R. Miller and P. Sandas, 2004. "Empirical Analysis of Limit Order Markets." *Review of Economic Studies* 71, 1027–1063.

Horner, M. R., 1988. "The Value of the Corporate Voting Right: Evidence from Switzerland," *Journal of Banking and Finance* 12, 69–84.

Huang, R., and H. Stoll, 1997. "The Components of the Bid-Ask Spread: A General Approach." *Review of Financial Studies* 10, 995–1034.

Huberman, G. and W. Stanzl, 2004. "Price Manipulation and Quasi-Arbitrage." *Econometrica* 72, 1247–1275.

Hvidkjaer, Soeren, 2006. "A Trade-Based Analysis of Momentum." *Review of Financial Studies* 19, 457–491.

ITG Global Trading Cost Review, 2010. Investment Technology Group.

Jegadeesh, N. and S. Titman, 2001. "Profitability of momentum strategies: An evaluation of alternative explanations." *Journal of Finance*, 56, 699–720.

Jobson, J. D. and B. M. Korkie, 1981. "Performance hypothesis testing with the Sharpe and Treynor measures." *Journal of Finance* 36, 889–908.

Jones, C., G. Kaul and M. Lipson, 1994. "Transactions, Volume and Volatility." *Review of Financial Studies* 7, 631–651.

Jones, C. M., O. Lamont and R. L. Lumsdaine, 1998. "Macroeconomic News and Bond Market Volatility." *Journal of Financial Economics* 47, 315–337.

Jorion, Philippe, 1986. "Bayes-Stein Estimation for Portfolio Analysis." *Journal of Financial and Quantitative Analysis* 21, 279–292.

Jorion, Philippe, 2000. "Risk Management Lessons from Long-Term Capital Management." *European Financial Management*, Vol. 6, Issue 3, 277–300.

Kandir, Serkan Yilmaz, 2008. "Macroeconomic Variables, Firm Characteristics and Stock Returns: Evidence from Turkey." *International Research Journal of Finance and Economics* 16, 35–45.

Kaniel, R. and H. Liu, 2006. "What Orders Do Informed Traders Use?" *Journal of Business* 79, 1867–1913.

Kaplan, P. D. and J. A. Knowles, 2004. "Kappa: A Generalized Downside Risk-Adjusted Performance Measure." *Journal of Performance Measurement* 8, 42–54.

Kavajecz, K. and E. Odders-White, 2004. "Technical Analysis and Liquidity Provision." *Review of Financial Studies* 17, 1043–1071.

Kawaller, I. G, P. D. Koch and T. W. Koch, 1993. "Intraday Market Behavior and the Extent of Feedback Between S&P 500 Futures Prices and the S&P 500 Index." *Journal of Financial Research* 16, 107–121.

Kestner, L. N., 1996. "Getting a Handle on True Performance." *Futures* 25, 44–46.

Kirilenko, A. A., A. S. Kyle, M. Samadi, and T. Tuzun, 2011. "The Flash Crash: The Impact of High Frequency Trading on an Electronic Market." Working paper.

Kissell, Robert and Morton Glantz, 2003. *Optimal Trading Strategies*. AMACOM, New York.

Kissell, R. and R. Malamut, 2005. "Understanding the Profit and Loss Distribution of Trading Algorithms." *Institutional Investor*, Guide to Algorithmic Trading, Spring 2005.

Krueger, Anne B., 1996. "Do Markets Respond More to Reliable Labor Market Data? A Test of Market Rationality." NBER working paper 5769.

Kyle, A., 1985. "Continuous Auctions and Insider Trading," *Econometrica* 53, 1315–1335.

Le Saout, E., 2002. "Intégration du Risque de Liquidité dans les Modéles de Valeur en Risqué." Banque et Marchés, No. 61, November–December.

Lee, C. and M. Ready, 1991. "Inferring Trade Direction from Intraday Data." *Journal of Finance* 46, 733–747.

Lhabitant, F.-S., 2004. "The future is bright, the future is hedge funds." *Thunderbird International Business Review* 46, 1–11.

Li, Li and Zuliu F. Hu, 1998. "Responses of the Stock Market to Macroeconomic Announcements across Economic States." IMF Working Paper 98/79.

Lillo F., J. Farmer and R. Mantegna, 2003. "Master curve for price-impact function." *Nature* 421, 129–130.

Lintner, John, 1965. "The Valuation of Risk Assets and the Selection of Risky Investments in Stock Portfolios and Capital Budgets." *Review of Economics and Statistics* 47, 13–37.

Lo, Andrew W. and A. Craig MacKinlay, 1990. "When Are Contrarian Profits Due to Stock Market Overreaction?" *Review of Financial Studies* 3, 175–208.

Löflund, A. and K. Nummelin, 1997. "On Stocks, Bonds and Business Conditions." *Applied Financial Economics* 7, 137–146.

Love, R. and R. Payne, 2008. "The Adjustment of Exchange Rates to Macroeconomic Information: The Role of Order Flow." *Journal of Financial and Quantitative Analysis* 43, 467–488.

Lyons, Richard K., 1995. "Tests of Microstructural Hypotheses in the Foreign Exchange Market." *Journal of Financial Economics* 39, 321–351.

Lyons, Richard K., 2001. *The Microstructure Approach to Exchange Rates*. MIT Press.

Mahdavi, M., 2004. "Risk-Adjusted Return When Returns Are Not Normally Distributed: Adjusted Sharpe Ratio." *Journal of Alternative Investments* 6 (Spring), 47–57.

Markowitz, Harry M., 1952. "Portfolio Selection," *Journal of Finance*, 7 (1), 77–91.

Markowitz, Harry, 1959. *Portfolio Selection: Efficient Diversification of Investments*. John Wiley, New York. Second Edition, 1991, Basil Blackwell, Cambridge, MA.

Markowitz, H. M. and P. Todd, 2000. *Mean-Variance Analysis in Portfolio Choice and Capital Markets*. Frank J. Fabozzi Associates, New Hope, Pennsylvania.

McQueen, Grant and V. Vance Roley, 1993. "Stock Prices, News, and Business Conditions." *Review of Financial Studies* 6, 683–707.

Muth, J. F., 1961. "Rational Expectations and the Theory of Price Movements." Econometrica, 29, 315-335.

Navissi, F., R. Bowman, and D. Emanuel, 1999. "The Effect of Price Control Regulation on Firms' Equity Values." Journal of Economics and Business 51, 33–47.

Nenova, Tatiana, 2003. "The Value of Corporate Voting Rights and Control: A Cross-Country Analysis." *Journal of Financial Economics*, 68, 325–351.

Niedermayer, Andras and Daniel Niedermayer, 2007. "Applying Markowitz's Critical Line Algorithm." Working paper, University of Bern.

Nikkinen, J., M. Omran, P. Sahlström and J. Äijö, 2006. "Global Stock Market Reactions to Scheduled US Macroeconomic News Announcements." *Global Finance Journal* 17, 92–104.

Obizhaeva, A. and J. Wang, 2005. "Optimal Trading Strategy and Supply/Demand Dynamics." Working paper, MIT.

Odders-White, H. R. and K. J. Ready, 2006. "Credit Ratings and Stock Liquidity." *Review of Financial Studies* 19, 119–157.

Orphanides, Athanasios, 1992. "When Good News Is Bad News: Macroeconomic News and the Stock Market." Board of Governors of the Federal Reserve System.

Parlour, C. and D. Seppi, 2008. "Limit Order Markets: A Survey." In A. W. A. Boot and A. V. Thakor, eds, *Handbook of Financial Intermediation & Banking*, North-Holland, Amsterdam.

Pástor L. and R. Stambaugh, 2003. "Liquidity risk and expected stock returns." *Journal of Political Economy*, 113, 642–685.

Pearce, D. K. and V. Vance Roley, 1985. "Stock Prices and Economic News." *Journal of Business* 58, 49–67.

Perraudin, W. and P. Vitale, 1996. "Interdealer Trade and Information Flows in the Foreign Exchange Market." In J. Frankel, G. Galli, and A. Giovannini, eds., *The Microstructure of Foreign Exchange Markets*. University of Chicago Press.

Pragma Securities, 2011. "Inverted-Price Destinations and Smart Order Routing." Research Note Series.

Ranaldo, A., 2004. "Order Aggressiveness in Limit Order Book Markets." *Journal of Financial Markets* 7, 53–74.

Rock, Kevin, 1996. "The Specialist's Order Book and Price Anomalies." Working paper, Harvard.

Roll, R., 1984. "A Simple Implicit Measure of the Effective Bid-Ask Spread in an Efficient Market", *Journal of Finance*, 39, 1127–1139.

Ross, S. A., 1977. "Return, Risk and Arbitage." in I. Friend and J.I. Bicksler eds., *Risk and Return in Finance*, Massachusetts: Ballinger, 189–218.

Rosu, I., 2005. "A Dynamic Model of the Limit Order Book." Working paper, University of Chicago.

Rosu, I., 2010. "Liquidity and Information in Order Driven Markets." Working paper.

Sadeghi, M., 1992. "Stock Market Response to Unexpected Macroeconomic News: The Australian Evidence." International Monetary Fund Working Paper. 92/61.

Sandas, P., 2001. "Adverse Selection and Competitive Market Making: Empirical Evidence from a Limit Order Market." *Review of Financial Studies* 14, 705–734.

Savor, P. and M. Wilson, 2008. "Asset Returns and Scheduled Macroeconomic News Announcements." Working paper, The Wharton School, University of Pennsylvania.

Schwert, G. W., 1989. " Why Does Stock Market Volatility Change over Time?," *Journal of Finance*, 44, 1115-53.

Seppi, D., 1997. "Liquidity Provision with Limit Orders and a Strategic Specialist." *Review of Financial Studies* 10, 103–150.

Shadwick, W. F. and Keating, C., 2002. "A Universal Performance Measure." *Journal of Performance Measurement* 6 (3), 59–84.

Sharma, M., 2004. "A.I.R.A.P.—Alternative RAPMs for Alternative Investments." *Journal of Investment Management* 2 (4), 106–129.

Sharpe, William F., 1964. "Capital Asset Prices: A Theory of Market Equilibrium under Conditions of Risk." *Journal of Finance* 19, 425–442.

Sharpe, William F., 1966. "Mutual Fund Performance." *Journal of Business* 39, 119–138.

Sharpe, William F., 1992. "Asset Allocation: Management Style and Performance Measurement." *Journal of Portfolio Management*, Winter 1992, 7–19.

Simpson, Marc W. and Sanjay Ramchander, 2004. "An Examination of the Impact of Macroeconomic News on the Spot and Futures Treasury Markets." *Journal of Futures Markets* 24, 453–478.

Simpson, Marc W., Sanjay Ramchander and James R. Webb, 2007. "An Asymmetric Response of Equity REIT Returns to Inflation." *Journal of Real Estate Finance and Economics* 34, 513–529.

Smith, Brian F. and Ben Amoako-Adu, 1995. "Relative Prices of Dual Class Shares." *Journal of Financial and Quantitative Analysis* 30, 223–239.

Sortino, F. A. and R. van derMeer, 1991. "Downside Risk." *Journal of Portfolio Management*, 17 (Spring), 27–31.

Sortino F. A., R. van der Meer and A. Plantinga, 1999. "The Dutch Triangle." Journal of Portfolio Management 18, 50–59.

Sotiropoulos, M. G., 2012. "Order Execution Using Trading Signals," working paper, Algorithmic Trading Quantitative Research, Bank of America Merrill Lynch.

Steuer, R. E., Y. Qi and M. Hirschberger, 2006. "Portfolio Optimization: New Capabilities and Future Methods." *Zeitschrift für BWL*, 2.

Stoikov, S. and W. Rolf, 2012. "Optimal Asset Liquidation Using Limit Order Book Information." Working Paper.

Stoll, H. R., 1989. "Inferring the Components of the Bid-Ask Spread: Theory and Empirical Tests." *Journal of Finance,* 44, 115-134.

Stoll, H. R. and R. E. Whaley, 1990. "The Dynamics of Stock Index and Stock Index Futures Returns." *Journal of Financial and Quantitative Analysis* 25, 441–468.

Suleiman, B., A. Shapiro and L. Tepla, 2005. "Risk Management with Benchmarking." LBS Working Paper.

Taleb, Nassim, 2007. *The Black Swan: The Impact of Highly Improbable.* Random House.

Thomas, D. B., Howes, L., and W. Luk, 2009. "A Comparison of CPUs, GPUs, FPGAs, and Massively Parallel Processor Arrays for Random Number Generation," *FPGA '09: Proc. ACM / SIGDA Int'l Symp. Field Programmable Gate Arrays,* 63–72.

Theodoros Tsagaris & Ajay Jasra & Niall Adams, 2010. "Robust and Adaptive Algorithms for Online Portfolio Selection." Working paper.

Vega, C., 2007. "Informed and Strategic Order Flow in the Bond Markets," *Review of Financial Studies,* 20, 1975–2019.

Veronesi, P., 1999. "Stock Market Overreaction to Bad News in Good Times: A Rational Expectations Equilibrium Model." *Review of Financial Studies* 12, 975–1007.

Valeri Voev & Asger Lunde, 2007. "Integrated Covariance Estimation using High-frequency Data in the Presence of Noise." *Journal of Financial Econometrics* 5, 68–104.

Wasserfallen, W., 1989. "Macroeconomic News and the Stock Market: Evidence from Europe." *Journal of Banking and Finance.* 13, 613–626.

Wongbanpo, P. and S. C. Sharma, 2002. "Stock Market and Macroeconomic Fundamental Dynamic Interactions: ASEAN-5 Countries." *Journal of Asian Economics* 13, 27–51.

Young, T. W., 1991. "Calmar Ratio: A Smoother Tool." *Futures* 20 (1), 40.

Zigrand, Jean-Pierre, Dave Cliff and Terrence Hendershott, 2011. "Financial stability and computer based trading." Working paper, UK Government's Foresight Project on The Future of Computer Trading in Financial Markets.

INDEX

Printed in the United States
By Bookmasters